INTRO

ALL ABOUT

MW00745490

1994

HARRY SHAY, EDITOR

This is the first edition of this unique Ohio book, which is the second state in a series started with the Michigan book in 1989 (and since updated).

User-friendly, it is completely indexed (starting on the next page), to provide instant answers to a multitude of questions. It is useful to everyone, from the student to the senior citizen, from alert residents to informed leaders. And it is indeed a "pathfinder" for new arrivals to the state.

A delight to the trivia buff too, a browse through its pages is both entertaining and informative. The multitude of statistics and facts are arranged to focus on the significant aspects. Brief commentary brings much of the information to "life".

Your comments and suggestions are sincerely welcome. We want it to be the reference resource that you want.

Instant Information Company
P.O. Box 202
Hartland, MI 48353

Available at leading bookstores $14.95, or by mail to the above address. To order by mail, please send $14.95, plus $1.90 shipping/handling and state sales tax.

Associate Editors & Specialists:
Susan Shay (M.L.S.), Donna Carlstrom, Teresa Dryer, Kathryn Guzowski, Lee Hickey, Kathleen Imre, Jodie Kleymeer & Barbara Loggins.

ISBN 1-883351-01-4

Printed in the United States of America

INDEX

DETAILED

INDEX

OVERVIEW OF

OHIO   & RANK IN U.S.

Unless otherwise noted, all data is for year 1990 and all quantities are in thousands.

Ohio, based on population, is ranked 7th largest state. For comparative purposes, this rank form is used here. Compiled by the Almanac from multiple sources, including the U.S. Stat. Abst.

SUBJECT	OHIO	US
PEOPLE		
Population	10,847	248,710
Rank (among 50 states)	7	
Density, per Sq. mile	264	70
Rank	8	
White	9,522	199,686
Rank	6	
Black	1,155	29,986
Rank	12	
American Indian	20	1,878
Rank	21	
Asian	91	7,274
Rank	14	
Hispanic	140	22,354
Rank	16	
Age (1991)		
Under 5 years	796	19,222
5 - 17 years	2,023	45,923
18 - 24 years	1,129	26,385
25 - 34 years	1,768	42,876
35 - 44 years	1,690	39,273
45 - 44 years	1,130	25,739
55 - 64 years	969	21,005
65 - 74 years	837	18,280
75 - 84 years	454	10,314
85 and older	141	3,160
16 and older	8,421	193,754
% 65 and older	13.1	12.6%
Total (1991)	10,939	252,177
Urban	8,039	187,053
Rank	4	
%	74.1%	75.2%

Rural	2,808	61,656
Rank	3	
%	25.9%	24.8%
Metro Areas	8,567	192,726
Percent	29%	77.5%
Rank	6	
Net change (1980-1990)	+47	20,047
% Total	+0.5%	11.6%
Non Metro	2,280	55,984
Percent	21%	
Rank	3	
Net change (1980-1990)	3	2,120
% Total	+0.1%	22.5%
Households	4,088	91,947
% change (1980 - 1990)	+6.6%	+14.4%
Families	2,895	64,518
Persons per household	2.59	2.63
Married couple	2,294	50,708
Married w/children	1,099	24,552
One parent w/children	374	8,551
Non-family	1,192	27,429
One person	1,020	22,580
Non Households		
Correctional Institutions	41	1,115
Nursing homes	93	1,772
College dormitories	88	1,953
Shelters, homeless	4	190
Religious, Adherents		
Christian (1980)	5,306	111,736
Jewish	131	5,981
Muslim		8,000
Others		
<u>**Vital Statistics**</u>		
Births		
Rate	15.1	16.7
% low birth weight [1]	6.8%	7.0%
% teenage mothers [2]	13.5%	12.5%
% unmarried mothers [1]	28%	27.1%
Abortions [2]	53	1,591
Rate	21	27.3
ratio to 1,000 live births [2]	324	401
Deaths	99	2,162
Rate per 1,000 pop.	9.0	8.6
Infant mortality, per		
1,000 live births [2]	9.7	10.0
white	8.6	8.5
black	15.9	17.6
Marriages	95.8	2,248
Rate per 1,000 pop.	8.7	9.8
Divorces	51	1,175
Rate per 1,000 pop.	47	4.7

HEALTH

Physicians		532,638
Rate per 100,000 pop.		216
Dentists		145,500
Rate, per 100,000 pop		59
Nurses		1,666
Rate, per 100,000 pop.		676
Hospitals	224	6,649
Hospital Beds	52	1,210
Rate per 100,000 pop.		206
Occupancy rate		69.7
Average cost,		
per patient		
Community hospitals		
Daily	$720	$687
Rank	13	
Per stay	$4,801	$4,947
Rank	17	
Patients, millions	18	368
Patients, average daily	35	843
Occupancy rate per	67.4	69.7
100 beds		
Outpatient visits,	18	368
millions		
Personnel	190	4,063
Medicare		
Enrollment	1,543	34,203
Pymt., $ millions	$4,844	$108,707
Medicaid		
Recipients	1,221	25,255
Pymt., $millions	$3,132	$64,859

*Tied with one or more
states
1 = 1989
2 = 1988
3 = 1987
*Largest nationality is Asian
Indian,21,000

EDUCATION

Public school students		
K-8th grade, 1992	1,268	30,663
Rank	7	
9 - 12 grade, 1992	519	11,587
Rank	5	
Teachers, 1991		2,400
Rank		
Salary, ave. 1991		$33
Rank		
Revenue, Publ. School,		
in $ millions 1991	$9,950	$232,985
Rank	7	
Expenditures, Public		
schools $ millions, 1991	$9,338	$225,693
Rank	7	
Per capita, dollars	$861	$907
Rank	31	

Public High School		
Graduates, 1993	107.1	2,215
Rank	4	
Colleges		
Numbers, actual	154	3,559
Rank		
Students	555	13,710
Rank		
CRIME		
Rate per 100,000 people		
Total	4,843	5,820
Rank	34	
Violent	506	732
Rank	28	
Murder	6.1	9.4
Rank	27	
Rape, Forcible	47	41
Rank	16	
Robbery	189	257
Rank	35	
Property Crime	4,337	5,088
Rank	32	
Larceny-theft	2,864	3,195
Rank	33	
Theft-motor vehicle	491	658
Rank	23	
Police, full-time, actual[2]	24,947	671,654
Rank	8	
Per 10,000 population	23	273
Rank	36	
Per Capita, $ actual	$196	$230
Rank	23	
Correction employees		
full-time, actual	13,485	435,237
Rank	10	
Per 10,000 population	12.4	17.7
Rank	35	
Correction, $ millions	729	18,963
Rank	6	
Lawyers[2]	28,290	723,187
Rank	8	
Population per lawyer	384	340
Rank	6	
Adults under		
correctional		
supervision	124	4,053.9
Rank	10	
GOVERNMENT		
Black Elected Officials		
1/1/91, actual	214	7,445
Rank	13	
Hispanic Public Officials	8	4,202
1991, actual		
Women Public Officials		
1992, actual	1,175	17,760
Registered Voters	5,834	121,273
Rank	7	
% of voting		
age population	72%	67%
Rank		

Votes cast % of registered voters	60%	55%
Rank	6	
Federal aid to state & local government, $ millions	$5,388	$134,457
Rank	5	
Per Capita, $ actual	$497	$533
Rank	31	
Federal Aid for education of the disadvantaged, millions	$144	$4,437
Rank	8	
Federal Aid for waste treat-ment facilities, $ millions	$108	$2,294
Rank	5	
Federal Aid for family support, including ADC, incentives, refugees assistance, etc., $ millions	$607	$15,140
Rank	5	
Federal Aid for Medicaid	$1,957	$40,857
Rank	3	
Federal Aid for low income housing, $ millions	$322	$7,372
Rank	7	
Federal Aid for community development, $ millions	$140	$2,818
Rank	6	
Federal Aid for job training, $ millions	$250	$5,735
Rank	6	
Federal Aid for job training, $ millions	$250	$5,735
Rank		
Revenue State Government $ millions	$11,209	$318,237
Rank	7	
Per capita, $ actual	$1,033	$1,283
Rank	29	
Taxes, State $ millions	$11,436	$300,489
Rank	7	
Expenditures, State $ millions	$25,237	$571,909
Rank	3	
Education, $ millions	$7,720	$184,529
Rank	5	
Public Welfare, $ millions	$5,058	$104,971
Rank	4	
Highways, $ millions	$1,700	$44,249
Rank	7	
Health & Hospitals $ millions	41,585	$42,662
Rank	8	

Natural Resources		
$ millions	$237	$9,900
Rank	13	
Tax Collections, State		
$ millions	$11,436	$300,499
Rank	8	
Sales & gross receipts		
$ millions	$11,436	$300,499
Rank	8	
Sales & Gross receipts		
$ millions	$5,752	$147,069
Rank	8	
Income Tax, $ millions	$4,125	
Rank	5	
Corporation net income tax, $ millions	$643	
Per capital, $ actual	$1,626	$1,827
Rank	24	
Paid Fed Civilian employees	91	2,906
Rank	10	
% Defense	37.8%	31.4
Rank	14	

VETERANS, 1991

Wartime total	933	20,280
Rank	5	
World War I	3	
Rank	7	
World War II	389	8,443
Rank	6	
Korean Conflict	201	4,693
Rank	6	
Vietnam Era	363	8,269
Rank	6	
Persian Gulf War	14	263
Rank	6	

SOCIAL SERVICES

Social Security		
Number of beneficiaries	1,803	38,889
Rank	6	
Annual pymts.		
$ millions	$11,616	$244,020
Rank	7	
Ave. monthly benefit		
$ actual	$618	$606
Rank	10	
Food stamp recipients		
Persons	1,114	20,472
Rank	3	
Expenditures, $ millions	$861	$14,205
Rank	4	
School lunch program		
Persons	919	24,589
Rank	7	

Aid to families with dependent children (AFDC)		
Recipients	657	12,160
Rank	5	
Expenditure, $ millions	$896	$19,067
Rank	4	
Avg. monthly pymt. per family, $ actual	$323	$362
Rank	29	
Supplemental Security Income (SSI)		
Recipients	156	4,817
Rank	8	
Expenditure, $ millions	$483	$16,133
Rank	8	
Grants to state & local government, $ millions	$5,388	$130,861
Rank	5	
Salaries & wages, $ millions	$3,922	$145,165
Rank	11	
Public aid recipients as % of population (AFDC and FSSI)	7.3%	6.5%
Rank	9	
LABOR		
State Unemployment		
Insurance $ millions	$665	$18,057
Rank	8	
Average weekly $ actual	$155	$162
Rank	23	
Workers Compensation $ millions[1]	$1,816	$34,316
Rank	4	
Civilian Labor Force 1991		
Total	5,440	125,303
Rank	7	
Female	2,474	58,893
Rank	7	
Employees, non farm		
Total, 1991	4,811	108,981
Rank	7	
Construction	176	4,696
Rank	7	
Manufacturing	1,068	18,426
Rank	2	
Transportation & Public Utilities	211	5,824
Rank	8	
Finance, Insurance & real estate	257	6,708
Rank	6	
Services	1,201	28,799
Rank	7	

Government	727	18,423
Rank	6	
Average Annual Pay, All		
$ actual	$22,843	$23,602
Rank	16	
Union membership manufacturing [1]	438.8	4,603.1
Rank	4	
% of employed, mfg. [1]	39.6%	23.8%
Rank	4	

GROSS STATE PRODUCT

Current dollars, $ billions	$212	$5,165
Rank	7	
By Industry, $ billions		
Farms, forestry & fisheries, $ billions	$3	$113
Rank (tied)	8*	
Construction, $ billions	$8	$248
Rank	10	
State Aid to Local Government		
$ millions	$8,214	$153,320
Rank	3	
Local Government Units		
actual, 1987	3,393	81,186
Rank	7	
Employees, State & Local		
Education		
State	67.2	1,418.5
Rank	3	
Local	200.1	5,067.5
Rank	7	
Health & Hospitals		
State	23.1	695
Rank	9	
Local	28.5	695
Rank	6	
Highways		
State	8.7	256.7
Rank	10	
Local	13.1	293.3
Rate	5	
Police & Fire		
State	2.2	88.1
Rank	12	
Local	35.7	864.5
Rank	6	
Public Welfare		
State	2.1	212.9
Rank	32	
Local	22.7	252.1
Rank	2	

Full-time equiv. employees		
State	2.1	212.9
Rank	5	
Local	316	9,239
Rank	8	
Per 10,000 population		
State	155	154
Rank	38	
Local	340	371
Rank	34	
Federal Funds		
Distribution $ millions		
State	$37,920	$993,418
Rank	6	
Per Capita	$3,496	$3,994
Rank	37	
Direct to individuals		
$ millions	$21,785	$494,011
Rank	7	
Federal Individual Income Tax		
Number of returns	5,017	113,242
Rank	7	
Income Tax $ millions	$17,740	$453,494
Rank	7	
Manufacturing, $ billions	$58	$966
Rank	3	
Transportation & Public Utilities, $ billions	$19	$461
Rank	8	
Wholesale trade, $ billions	$13	$339
Rank	8	
Retail Trade, $ billions	$20	$486
Rank	6	
Finance, insurance & real estate $ billions	$34	$897
Rank	9*	
INCOME		
Disposable personal income per capita		
1991, $ current	$15,396	$16,318
Rank	23	
Personal Income		
1991, $ billions	$196	$4,812
Rank	8	
Personal Income per capita, 1991		
$ current	$17,961	$19,082
Rank	23	
Median Income household, actual $	$30,013	$29,943
Rank	23	
% of persons below poverty level	11.5%	13.5%
Rank	30	

BANKING, FINANCE & INSURANCE

Banks

Number	288	12,327
Rank	17	
Assets, $ billions	$113.1	$3,388.9
Rank	6	
Deposits, $ billions	$89.7	$2,650
Rank	7	
Banks closed or assisted	1	

Life insurance in force

Policies	18,048	389,186
Rank	6	
Value, $ billions	$409	$9,393
Rank	7	
Avg. per household		
$ actual	$95,900	$98,400
Rank	28*	

BUSINESS

Women owned firms		
1987	154.1	4,114.8
Rank	7	
% of total		307.
Rank (tied)		
Sales & receipts, $ millions	$8,872	$278,138
Rank	10	
% of total		14%
Rank (tied)		
Black owned, 1987, actual[3]	15,983	424,165
Rank	10	
Sales & receipts $ millions	$626	$19,763
Rank	13	
Hispanics owned, actual[3]	1,989	422,373
Rank	18	
Sales & receipts, $ millions	$192	$24,732
Rank	11	
American Indian owned actual[3]	152	21,380
Rank	23	
Sales & receipts, $ millions	N/A	$911
Asian owned, actual[3]	3,859	355,331
Rank	14	
Sales & receipts $ millions	N/A	$33,124
New corporations, 1991, actual	17,895	628,580
Rank	10	
Failures, actual	2,254	60,432
Rank	5	

Bankruptcy, petitions	42.8	880.4
1991		
Rank	5	
Patents, total	2,727	52,855
Rank	7	

COMMUNICATIONS
Newspapers

Daily, number, actual	87	1,611
Rank	4	
Circulation, paid	2,745	62,328
Rank	6	
Per capita	0.25	.025
Rank	12*	
Sunday, number, actual	34	863
Rank	7	
Circulation, paid	2,893	62,634
Rank	6	
Radio stations, act.		
Television stations		

ENERGY
Gas Utility

Customers, total	2,991	54,293
Rank	5	
Residential	2,755	49,830
Rank	5	
Revenues, $ millions	$2,362	
Total		$45,174
Rank	4	
Residential	$1,622	$25,014
Rank	4	

Electric Energy Sales

Total, billions of kilowatt hours		2,705
Residential		921

Nuclear Power Plants

Units	2	111
Rank	18*	
Net generation, billion kilowatts	10,664	576,784
Rank	21	

Energy Consumption*

Total, trillions of BTU	3,863	81,342
Rank	3	
Per capita, millions BTU	354	327
	18	
Residential, trillions BTU	864	16,630
Rank	4	
Commercial, trillions of BTU	585	12,867
Rank	5	
Industrial, trillions of BTU	1,585	29,463
Rank	4	
Transportation, trillions of BTU	828	22,382

Source, Primary		
Petroleum	31%	42%
Natural gas	22%	24%
Coal	38%	23%
Hydroelectric		4%
Nuclear		7%
Expenditures, End use [1]		
Total, $ millions	$20,599	$436,643
Rank	4	
Per capita, $ actual	$1,889	$1,759
Rank	14	
% change (1988-89)	+7.6%	+7.1%
Rank	24	
Residential, $ millions	$5,420	$109,171
Rank	6	
Commercial, $ millions	$3,408	$75,605
Rank	6	
Industrial, $ millions	$5,362	$94,891
Rank	3	
Trans. ,$ millions	$6,409	$156,977
Rank	5	

RESEARCH & DEVELOPMENT

Total, $ millions	$5,465	$140,486
Rank	8	
Federal Government	$1,056	$15,121
Rank	4	
Industry	$3,946	$101,599
Rank	9	
Universities & College	$417	$19,716
Rank	10*	

TRANSPORTATION

Federal Funds, $ millions		
Highways, $ millions		$13,557
Rank		
Per capita, $ actual		$54.5
Rank		
Urban Mass Transit		
$ millions		$3,731
Rank		
Per capita, $ actual		$15
Rank		
State Gasoline Tax, per gallon, 1991		14.1¢
Rank (tied)		
Motor Vehicle Registrations		188,655
Rank		
Miles traveled, billions		2,147
Rank		
Drivers licenses		167,015
Rank		
Motor Vehicle Deaths		
actual	1,550	46,300
Rank	8	
Per million vehicle miles, actual	1.9	2.2
Rank (tied)	31	

STATE LAW, ROAD SAFETY

Alcohol, 21 years	yes	all
Open containers prohibited	yes	24
% blood alcohol	1%	all (.08-.12)
seat belt, mandatory		38

AGRICULTURE

Farms, 1991	80	2,105
Rank	9	
Acreage, millions	16	983
Rank (tied)	19*	
Acreage per farm	196	467
Rank	37*	
Farms with sales of $10,000+ [3]	40	1,060
Rank	10	
Value of land & bldgs., 1991 $ millions	$19,107	$672,235
Rank	11	
Average value, land & bldgs.per acre, 1991		
$ actual	$1,217	$682
Rank	15	
Farm assets, $ million	$29,229	$997,935
Rank	10	
Farm Debt, $ millions	$3,367	$145,067
Rank	15	
Farm Debt/Asset Ratio	11.5%	14.6%
Rank (tied)	36*	
Farm Gross Income $ millions	$4,783	$195,123
Rank	14	
Farm Net Income, $ millions	$1,173	$50,832
Rank	10	
Farm Mrkt. $ millions		
Total	$4,172	$169,987
Rank	14	
Crops, $ millions	$2,335	$80,364
Rank	10	
Livestock & products $ millions	$1,836	$89,623
Rank	20	
Government pymts. $ millions	$197	$9,298
Rank	17	
Principal Commodities	1.Corn	Cattle
	2. Soybeans	Dairy Prod
	3.Dairy Prod.	Corn
	4.Hogs	Hogs
Crops, Acres harvested, 1991	9,972	304,308
Rank	11	
Farm value, $ millions, 1991	$2,237	$79,858
Rank	11	
Livestock, 1991		
Cattle & calves, number	1,580	99,436
Rank	17	

Commercial slaughter $ millions	$262	$37,758
Rank	13	
Hogs & pigs, number	2,000	54,362
Rank	8	
Commercial slaughter $ millions	$642	$21,230
Rank	9	

MINING & MINERALS
Value of nonfuel mineral production

$ millions	$729	$33,319
Rank	14	
Minerals in order of value	stone sand & gravel salt	

CRUDE PETROLEUM
Millions of barrels	8	2,685
Rank	18	
Value, $ millions	$196	$53,772
Rank	18	
Natural gas		
Billions of cubic feet	155	18,562
Rank	13	
Value, $ millions	$393	$31,658
Rank	12	

CONSTRUCTION & HOUSING
Total Value, construction, contracts

1991, millions	$9,460	$226,760
Rank	6	
Residential, 1991	$4,064	$97,416
Rank	5	
Existing Home Sales		
1991	149.8	3,220
Rank	5	
Housing Units, total	4,372	102,264
Rank	5	
% change, 1980-90	6.4%	+15.7%
1 unit, detached	2,897	60,383
Rank	5	
Mobil homes-trailers	206	7,400
Rank	10	
2 - 10 + units	1,081	27,981
Owner occupied	2,241	44,918
Rank	6	
Median value $ actual	$63,500	$79,100
Rank	29	
Renter occupied	1,231	30,490
Rank	6	
Median rent,$ actual	$296	$375
Rank	31	

MANUFACTURERS
Employees, total	1,085	18,840
Rank	3	

Payroll, total, $ millions	$33,318	$532,317
Rank	3	
Payroll per employee		
$ actual	$30,705	$28,254
Rank	11	
Production workers, number	711	12,129
Rank	2	
Value added, mfg. $ millions	$80,377	$1,326,362
Rank	4	
Value of shipments $ millions	$177,787	$2,873,502
Rank	3	
Avg. hourly earnings, mfg. production workers	$12.64	$10.83
Rank	2	
Export [3]		
Mfg., shipment value $ billions	$25.8	$378.8
Rank	3	
% of total mfg. value	16.3%	15.3%
Rank	12*	
Employment, export related	176.8	2,770
Rank	3	
Retail Trade		
Establishments [3]	96,973	2,419,641
Rank	7	
Sales, $ millions [3]	$64,705	$1,540,263
Rank	7	
Annual payroll, $ millions [3]	$7,434	$177,548
Rank	7	
Employees [3]	804	17,780
Rank	7	
Sales, by type		
Food Stores, $ millions	$14,304	$362,667
Rank	7	
General Merchandise, $ millions	$9,808	$211,806
Automobile dealers, $ millions	$15,950	$381,799
Rank	7	
Eating & drinking places, $ millions	$7,184	$182,107
Rank		
Gasoline service stations, $ millions	$6,596	$131,381
Rank		
Building materials and hardware dealers, $ millions	$3,889	$92,730
Rank		

Apparel & accessory stores, $ million	$3,018	$94,645
Rank	9	
Furniture & appliance stores, $ millions	$3,499	$92,595
Rank	9	
Shopping Centers, 1991 Number, actual	1,465	38,000
Rank	4	
Retail sales, $ billions	$29.7	$717
Rank	5	
Wholesale Trade Establishments, actual [3]	18,577	466,680
Rank	7	
Sales, $ billions	104	2,523
Rank	7	
Employees	247.5	5,580
Rank	7	

Foreign investment in U.S., book value of property, plant & equipment, $ millions	$17,315	$461,3131
Rank	5	
% of all business [1]	5%	4.8%
Rank	14*	
% of all manufacturing[1] employment's	10.2	9.3%
Rank	14*	
Total employment [1]	207.6	4,406
Rank	6	
U.S. Exports, 1991 $ millions	$14,855	$421,851
Rank	7	

*Tied with one or more states
[1] = **1989**
[2] = **1988**
[3] = **1987**
* **Largest nationality is Asian Indian, 21,000**

Source - Ohio Chamber of Commerce

OHIO FIRSTS

Automotive Firsts

America's first gasoline-powered automobile was made in 1891 by John W. Lambert of Ohio City.

First automobile sold in the United States by Alexander Winton, Cleveland, March 24, 1898.

First automobile advertisement by Alexander Winton, Cleveland, in an American Science magazine, July 30, 1898.

First full-time, fully equipped auto repair garage initiated by a bicycle repairman, Frank E. Avery, Columbus, 1899.

First automobile police patrol wagon, operated in Akron, 1899.

First automobile mail truck, constructed in Cleveland, 1899.

First Packard automobile was manufactured at Warren by Ward Packard, 1899.

First automobile ignition system, Charles F. Kettering, Dayton, 1908.

First practical auto electric generator, T. A. Willard, Cleveland and Norwalk.

First practical electric storage battery, T. A. Willard, Cleveland and Norwalk.

First to drive an automobile a mile a minute, Barney Oldfield, Wauseon, 1910.

First cord tire, Akron, 1910.

First automobile self-starter, Charles F. Kettering, Dayton, 1911.

First non-skid tire, Akron, 1914.

First automobile filling station dealing exclusively in the sale of gasoline and petroleum products was located in Columbus by the Standard Oil Company of Ohio, 1917.

First balloon tire introduced in Akron, April 5, 1923.

First synthetic rubber tire, marketed from Akron, 1940.

Tetraethyl for automobile gasoline invented by Thomas Midgley, Franklin County.

Aviation Firsts

Orville and Wilbur Wright conducted the pioneer experiments in their bicycle shop in Dayton which enabled them to make the world's first successful flight in a powered airplane at Kitty Hawk, North Carolina, December 17, 1903.

First American Ace of Aces (World War I), Eddie Rickenbacker, Columbus.

First air express shipment, from Dayton to Columbus, November 7, 1910.

First live free-type parachute jump, Dayton, April 28, 1919.

First government-sponsored air research facilities, Dayton, McCook Field.

First American-designed bomber airplane, by Glenn Martin, Cleveland.

First airmail flight, Cleveland to Chicago, May 15, 1919.

Continued on next page

First shock-absorbing landing gear (pneumatic) invented by E. W. Cleveland, 1926.

First controllable pitch propeller for aircraft invented by Harold Smith, Cleveland, about 1928.

First airport radio landing traffic control system, by Major Jack Berry and Claude King, Cleveland, 1934.

First airway traffic control for inflight airliners, Berry and King, Cleveland, 1934.

First airplane race of importance in which both men and women were contestants, National Air Races, 1931, Los Angeles to Cleveland.

First American to orbit the earth and first man to fly across the U. S. at supersonic speed, Lieutenant Colonel John H. Glenn, Jr., of Cambridge and New Concord, February 20, 1962.

First woman to fly solo around the world and first woman to fly a single engine airplane, west to east, across the Pacific Ocean, Jerrie Mock, Columbus, March 19—April 17, 1964.

First man on the moon, Neil Armstrong, July 20, 1969.

Baseball Firsts

The first major league professional baseball team was the Cincinnati Reds, organized in 1866.

First World Series unassisted triple play, Cleveland, 1920, by Bill Wambsganss (Wamby) of the Indians.

First night baseball game played May 24, 1935, at Cincinnati.

First major league player to pitch two successive no-hit no-run games, June 10 and 15, 1938, Cincinnati, Johnny Vander Meer.

The Cincinnati Reds pioneered air travel as a means of transporting players to games, 1938.

Communication Firsts

The first colored comic strip, "The Yellow Kid," was created by Richard F. Outcalt, Lancaster.

The first syndicated newspaper column was written by O. O. McIntyre, Gallipolis.

The first abolitionist newspaper in the United States, "The Philanthropist," was published at Mount Pleasant, 1817.

The first labor newspaper in the United States was published in Cincinnati in 1831.

The first radio license in the United States was issued in 1911 to a resident of Cincinnati.

The first photo-telegraph system was devised by Noah S. Amstutz, Wayne County.

The first license for an FM radio station owned and operated by a Board of Education was issued to WBOE, Cleveland.

The ship-to-shore method of communications was developed at Lorain and first placed in operation on the ship William C. Atwater, on the Great Lakes in 1934.

Continued on next page

Continued from preceeding page

Education Firsts

The three "R's" (Readin', 'Ritin', and 'Rithmetic) were developed for American school children by Ohioans. Reading—McGuffey's Reader, William Holmes McGuffey, Oxford. Writing—Spencerian Penmanship, Platt Rogers Spencer, Geneva and Cleveland. Arithmetic—Mathematical Calculations, Joseph Ray, Cincinnati.

The first school boy safety patrol in America originated in Columbus.

The first night school classes in the nation were authorized by Ohio legislators in 1829.

The Ohio State School for the Blind was opened in Columbus in 1837, the first of its kind in the United States.

The Phi Beta Kappa Chapter at Western Reserve Academy, Hudson, was the first in the United States to designate scholarship as a basis for Phi Beta Kappa membership.

The first college music department in the United States was established in 1865 at Oberlin College, Oberlin.

Mount Union College, Alliance, has the distinction of founding the first summer session in the United States, 1870. The college also provided the team that played the first basketball game west of the Allegheny Mountains in 1897.

The University of Cincinnati was the nation's first city university.

The first public county library in the United States, the Brumback Library, was dedicated at Van Wert in 1901.

WCET, UHF Channel 48 in Cleveland, was the first noncommercial educational television station in the United States.

The world's first teaching machine (that rewarded students with candy for correct answers) was built in 1925 by Dr. Sidney L. Pressey, Ohio State University, Columbus.

Football Firsts

Canton is the birthplace of professional football, where a league was formed in 1920. An early powerhouse was the Canton Bulldogs, and the Professional Football Hall of Fame is located in that city.

Health Firsts

The first dental school in the world was started at Bainbridge, Ross County, February 21, 1828, by John M. Harris, M. D.

The first successful blood transfusion was performed by Dr. George Crile, internationally known surgeon-scientist of Cleveland, 1905.

First free dental care in the nation for all school children, by Dr. William G. Ebersole, Cleveland, 1908-1909.

The international Crippled Children's movement was founded in Elyria by Edgar "Daddy" Allen.

The first private industrial mobile unit on the peaceful applications of atomic energy, AccuRay Corp., Columbus.

The original chapter of the National Polio Foundation was chartered in Coshocton in 1938.

The first operation using X-ray was performed by John E. Gilman, Marietta.

Continued on next page

The first health museum in the United States was opened in Cleveland in 1940.

The first birth defect study center in the world originated in Columbus.

Industrial Firsts

The first roller bearing was designed and manufactured by Henry Timken of Canton.

The first tubular metal chair was manufactured by the Shott Furniture Division of Balcrank, Inc., Cincinnati.

The world's first cash register, "Ritty's Incorruptible Cashier," was patented by James Ritty, November 4, 1879, Dayton.

The nation's first computing scale company was incorporated in Dayton, 1891.

The first book matches were made at Barberton, 1896.

The first paint spraying device in the nation was employed in 1909 by A. DeVilbiss, Toledo.

Charles Martin Hall discovered the electrolytic process of freeing aluminum from its ore.

The first motion picture projector was invented by an Ohioan, Charles F. Jenkins.

The first manufacturer of vacuum cleaners was the Hoover Company, North Canton.

The Cummins' Canning Company, Conneaut, was the first to pack pumpkin in tin cans.

The first daylight factory buildings in America were built by the National Cash Register Company, Dayton. The walls of the plant were 80 percent glass panels supported by columns of brick-veneered steel.

Charles F. Kettering, Dayton, designed the first main line diesel passenger locomotive. General Motors built it in 1935 and it continued in service until 1956.

The first mechanical refrigerator was originated in Dayton by Frigidaire.

Armco Steel Corporation, Middletown, invented and developed the continuous process of rolling steel — a procedure now universally used.

Light Firsts

The world was given electric light by Thomas A. Edison, Milan, when he invented the incandescent bulb, 1879.

The world's first electric arc lights, invented by Ohioan Charles F. Bush, were installed on Cleveland streets in 1879.

The world's first and largest lighting research laboratory was established at Nela Park, Cleveland, in 1910 by General Electric.

First inside frosted bulb, patented by M. Pipkin, Nela Park, 1928.

The first city to introduce complete Mazda tungsten street lighting, Warren.

Continued on next page

Continued from preceeding page

Various Firsts

Laws Protecting Women—In 1852 Ohio became the first state to enact laws protecting the working woman.

Mail Delivery—Joseph W. Briggs, Cleveland, is credited with conceiving and carrying into effect free home delivery of mail, 1863. He also designed the first mail carrier uniform.

Soldiers' Home—The first national soldiers' home was authorized in Dayton, March 21, 1866.

Chewing Gum—The first chewing gum patent was issued to W. F. Semple of Mount Vernon, 1869.

Flavored Chewing Gum—First flavored chewing gum in America was produced by Dr. Edwin E. Beeman, Wakeman, who added pepsin to gum as an aid to digestion.

Fish Bait—The first artificial fish bait was invented by Ernest Pflueger, Akron, in 1880.

Labor Union—The American Federation of Labor was founded in Columbus in 1886.

Weather Service—The first public weather service in America was established at Cincinnati in 1869.

Hot Dog—Ohio gave America its first hot dog. Harry M. Stevens of Niles was the first person to think of wrapping up a frankfurter in a piece of bread — later a roll. He capitalized on the name ''hot dog'' after seeing a caricature of a frankfurter made to look like a Dachshund in the New York Daily Times, 1900.

4-H Club—A. B. Graham started the first club in Springfield, 1902.

Water Works—The world's first combined purification and softening water works plant was opened in Columbus in 1908.

Conservancy District—The first conservancy district in the United States was the Miami Conservancy District, Dayton, followed by the Muskingum Conservancy District, New Philadelphia. These played an important part in passage of the National Conservancy Act.

Explorer of Grand Canyon—First explorer of the Grand Canyon of Arizona was Major John Wesley Powell, Jackson.

Boy Scouts—Daniel Beard, Cincinnati, organized a boys' group called the Sons of Dan'l Boone, from which grew the Boy Scouts.

Billionaire—America's first billionaire was John D. Rockefeller, Cleveland.

Coal Pipeline—The country's first coal pipeline is the 108-mile line in eastern Ohio, built to carry coal from mines near Cadiz to a Cleveland electric-generating plant.

Shopping Center—America's first shopping center, Town and Country, is in Columbus.

Ice Cream Cones, Hamburgers and Crackerjacks—All these items were creations of Charles E. Menches, Akron.

Atomic Power Plant—The Atomic Energy Commission built the nation's first commercial organic-cooled atomic power plant at Piqua. The plant provides light for Piqua homes and electrical power for business and industry.

Continued on next page

Symbols of the State of Ohio

Source - Ohio Secretary of State

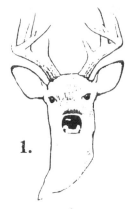

1. The State Animal

The Ohio legislature adopted the white-tailed deer, the state's largest game animal, as the state animal in May 1988. The white-tailed deer can be found in all of Ohio's 88 counties, although about 80 percent of the herd lives in hilly eastern Ohio.

2. The State Insect

In June 1975, the Ohio legislature declared the common ladybug, officially named the Ladybird Beetle as the state insect. The ladybug was chosen for its attractive markings and helpful eating habits.

3. The State Bird

Ohio adopted the cardinal as its official bird in 1933. A permanent resident of Ohio, the cardinal is known for its clear, strong song and brilliant plummage.

4. The State Fossil

Ohio's state fossil is the isotelus, commonly known as the trilobite. This now extinct sea creature existed in Ohio 440 million years ago when salt water covered the state. It resembles the modern horseshoe crab and is about 14 inches long.

Continued from preceeding page

5.

5. The State Flag

Ohio's state flag was adopted in 1902. The Ohio burgee, as the swallowtail design is properly called, was designed by John Eisemann. The large blue triangle represents Ohio's hills and valleys, and the stripes represent roads and waterways. The thirteen stars grouped about the circle represent the original states of the union; the four stars added to the peak of the triangle symbolize that Ohio was the 17th state admitted to the union. The white circle with its red center not only represents the "O" in Ohio, but also suggests Ohio's famous nickname, "The Buckeye State."

6.

7.

6. The State Seal

The current design of the Great Seal of the State of Ohio was officially adopted in 1967. In the foreground, a sheaf of wheat represents Ohio's agricultural strength. A bundle of 17 arrows on the left and the 17 rays around the sun symbolize Ohio's status as the 17th state admitted to the union. The background contains a portrayal of Mount Logan, with a three-quarter full sun rising behind it -- symbolizing that Ohio was the first state west of the Allegheny Mountains. The Scioto River flows between the mountain and the cultivated fields in the foreground.

7. The State Motto

In 1959, the Ohio legislature adopted the state's motto, "With God all things are possible" (Matthew 19:26). An earlier motto, "Imperium in Imperio" (An Empire within an Empire) was adopted in 1865 but repealed two years later because Ohioans thought it too pretentious.

8.

8. The State Flower

The red carnation was adopted as Ohio's state flower in 1904 in memory of President William McKinley, who always wore a red carnation in his lapel.

Continued on next page

Continued from preceeding page

9. The State Tree

The nickname for Ohio and its inhabitants -- Buckeye -- became official in 1953 when the legislature named the American Horsechestnut (or the Ohio Buckeye) the state tree. The buckeye tree derives the name from its large brown seeds, which resemble the eyes of the eastern white-tailed deer.

10. The State Beverage

Tomato juice was adopted as the state beverage in 1965. Ohio leads the country in the production of tomato juice and is second only to California in tomato growing.

11. The State Gemstone

Flint, the state gemstone since 1965, is a smooth hard rock of sedimentary origin. The Indians used flint to make knives, spear points and arrowheads. Later, Ohio settlers used it for flint-lock guns and millstones.

The State Song

Beautiful Ohio became the state song in 1969. The music was composed by Mary Earl, and the original lyrics were written by Ballard McDonald. In 1989, the Ohio legislature adopted an amendment to section 5.09 of the Ohio Revised Code that changed the words of the state song. The new lyrics are the work of Youngstown attorney Wilbert McBride.

The State Rock Song

Hang On Sloopy, a favorite of the Ohio State University Marching Band, became the state rock song in 1985. Composed by Celina-born guitarist Rick Derringer, it was first recorded by The McCoys, a rock band from Dayton, in 1965.

Source - Ohio's Business Fact Book 1993

LEADING PUBLIC COMPANIES
AT-A-GLANCE

Earnings (in millions)

1.	Procter & Gamble Co.	$1,773.0
2.	Federated Department Stores Inc.	836.4
3.	American Electric Power	497.9
4.	Limited Inc.	403.3
5.	Borden Inc.	294.9
6.	Ohio Edison Co.	264.8
7.	Centerior Energy Corp.	237.2
8.	Cincinnati Gas & Electric Co.	207.0
9.	Rubbermaid Inc.	162.7
10.	Chiquita Brands International Inc.	128.5

Return on assets

1.	Premier Industrial Corp.	22.3%
2.	Rubbermaid Inc.	13.8
3.	The J.M. Smucker Co.	12.9
4.	Bob Evans Farms Inc.	12.8
5.	Limited Inc.	12.8
6.	A. Schulman Inc.	12.6
7.	Cooper Tire & Rubber Inc.	12.3
8.	Nordson Corp.	11.9
9.	Cleveland-Cliffs Inc.	11.0
10.	The Lubrizol Corp.	10.8

Market value (in millions)

1.	Procter & Gamble Co.	$33,618.6
2.	Limited Inc.	7,646.3
3.	American Electric Power Inc.	5,951.3
4.	The Goodyear Tire & Rubber Co.	4,707.4
5.	Rubbermaid Inc.	4,445.4
6.	Borden Inc.	4,375.6
7.	TRW Inc.	3,411.1
8.	Ohio Edison Co.	3,070.5
9.	Eaton Corp.	2,783.0
10.	Roadway Services Inc.	2,773.6

Return on sales

1.	Cleveland-Cliffs Inc.	14.8%
2.	Cincinnati Gas & Electric Co.	13.6
3.	Borden Chemicals & Plastics	12.6
4.	Federated Department Stores Inc.	12.1
5.	Premier Industrial Corp.	11.7
6.	DPL Inc.	11.5
7.	Ohio Edison Co.	11.2
8.	American Electric Power Inc.	9.9
9.	Rubbermaid Inc.	9.8
10.	Centerior Energy Corp.	9.3

Return on equity

1.	Reliance Electric Co.	54.8%
2.	Value City Department Stores	29.5
3.	Premier Industrial Corp.	27.5
4.	Scotts Co.	27.3
5.	Riser Foods Inc.	26.3
6.	Nordson Corp.	23.9
7.	Limited Inc.	23.5
8.	Procter & Gamble Co.	23.2
9.	Rubbermaid Inc.	19.7
10.	Cooper Tire & Rubber Co.	19.6

PUBLIC COMPANIES

Continued on next page

Miscellany

If states were corporations, Gov. George Voinovich would be CEO of the 25th-largest corporation in the United States, according to a Fortune 500/State 50 ranking of 1991 revenues. In terms of sales (general revenues for states), General Motors Corp. tops the list with $126 billion, ahead of Exxon Corp. and Ford Motor Co. California leads all states in revenue with $69 billion and ranks fourth on the combined list, ahead of IBM and General Electric Co. Ohio is the seventh-largest state in terms of revenues, with $19.9 billion, just ahead of Michigan's $19.7 billion. Its corporate neighbors on the list include PepsiCo and Eastman-Kodak.

Employment
(as of June 1992)

Total civilian work force: 5,426,500
Employment by selected sectors:
Manufacturing: 1,050,000
Retail: 879,000
Government: 731,000
Health services 420,000
Wholesale: 261,000
Finance/insurance/real estate: 253,600
Transportation/public utilities: 202,200
Construction: 143,900
Unemployed: 433,800 (8.0%)
Average statewide hourly earnings: $13.22
Average statewide weekly earnings: $549.95

Vital Statistics

1990 population (1990 census): 10,847,115 (No. 6 in the U.S.)
Estimated 1991 population: 10,938,801
Projected 2000 population: 11,436,000
Population growth ('80-'90): 0.5% (No. 42 in the U.S.)
Population density: 264.9 people/square mile (No. 9 in the U.S.)
Population living in metropolitan areas: 79.0% (No. 17 in the U.S.)
Birth rate (1991): 15.4/1,000
Death rate (1991): 9.1/1,000
Five most densely populated counties:

Cuyahoga (Cleveland): 3,080.3/square mile
Hamilton (Cincinnati): 2,126.2/square mile
Franklin (Columbus): 1,780.4/square mile
Lucas (Toledo): 1,358.3/square mile
Summit (Akron): 1,247.6/square mile
Montgomery (Dayton): 1,242.8/square mile

Continued on next page

Ohio has:

9,158,862 licensed drivers
7,228,023 registered cars
1,156,112 registered trucks
380,412 registered boats
53,305 liquor permits
23,700 other liquor locations
20,000 licensed security guards
17,911 eating and drinking establishments
1,500 licensed bingo halls
1,074 hotels and motels
600 licensed private investigators
434 bowling centers
259 public golf courses
210 state liquor stores
147 colleges and universities
132 museums and art galleries
65 taxicab companies
36 libraries or library systems
30 amusement parks

Sources: U.S. Bureau of the Census, State of Ohio

Geography

Total area: 44,828 square miles
Land area: 40,952 square miles
Water area: 3,875 square miles
Counties: 88
Highest point: Cambell Hill (1,549 ft. above sea level) in Logan County, 40 miles NW of Columbus
Lowest point: Ohio River (455 ft. above sea level)
National Forest: 833,000 acres
State Park recreation areas: 208,000 acres
Highways (1988): 113,340 miles
Interstate highways (1988): 1,565 miles

Government
(Oct. 1, 1992)

Governor: George V. Voinovich
Legislature: House of Representatives
61 Democrats
38 Republicans
Speaker: Vern Riffe
Senate: 12 Democrats
21 Republicans
President: Stanley Aronoff
Registered voters: (March 31, 1992):
Democrat: 1,808,941
Republican: 1,243,813
Other: 2,773,824
Total: 5,826,601

Fastest growing industries,
by employment growth ('89-'92):

1. Social services - 19%
2. Educational services - 18%
3. Membership organizations - 12%
4. Health services - 9%
5. Education, local government (tie) - 7%

Fastest shrinking industries,
by decline in employment ('89-'92):

1. Coal mining - (33%)
2. Heavy construction - (23%)
3. Amusements - (23%)
4. Special trade contractors - (15%)
5. Apparel and textile products - (14%)

Weather

CINCINNATI WEATHER STATION

	JAN.	FEB.	MARCH	APRIL	MAY	JUNE	JULY	AUG.	SEPT.	OCT.	NOV.	DEC.	ANNUAL
Normal Daily Mean Temp.	28.1	31.8	43.0	53.2	62.9	71.0	75.1	73.5	67.3	55.1	44.3	33.5	53.2
Normal Daily High Temp.	36.6	40.8	53.0	64.2	74.0	82.0	85.5	84.1	77.9	66.0	53.3	41.5	63.2
Normal Daily Low Temp.	19.5	22.7	33.1	42.2	51.8	60.0	64.8	62.9	56.6	44.2	35.3	25.3	43.2
Highest Temp. of Rec.	29	69	73	84	89	93	103	102	98	88	81	75	103
Lowest Temp. of Rec	29	-25	-11	-11	17	27	39	47	43	16	1	-20	-25
Normal Percipitation "	2.59	2.69	4.24	3.75	4.28	3.84	3.35	2.88	2.86	2.86	3.46	3.15	41.33
Average No. of Days With Precipitation .01 Plus	12	11	13	12	11	11	10	9	8	8	11	12	129
Snow and Ice Pellets "	7.0	5.4	4.3	0.5	-	-	-	-	-	0.2	2.1	4.0	23.5
Average Percentage of Possible Sunshine Length of Record, 7 years													52
Average Wind Speed, MPH Length of Record, 43 years	10.7						7.1						9.1
Average Relative Humidity% Morning	59						67						28
Afternoon Length of Record, 28 years	78						85						81

Source: U.S. National Oceanic and Atmospheric Administration

OHIO WEATHER

CLEVELAND WEATHER STATION

Weather

	JAN.	FEB.	MARCH	APRIL	MAY	JUNE	JULY	AUG.	SEPT.	OCT.	NOV.	DEC.	ANNUAL
Normal Daily Mean Temp.	24.8	27.2	37.3	47.6	59.0	67.6	71.9	70.4	63.9	52.8	42.6	30.9	49.6
Normal Daily High Temp.	31.9	35.0	46.3	57.9	68.6	78.3	82.4	80.5	73.6	62.1	50.0	37.4	58.7
Normal Daily Low Temp.	17.6	19.3	28.2	37.3	47.3	56.8	61.4	60.3	54.2	43.5	35.0	24.5	40.5
Highest Temp. of Rec.	73	69	83	83	92	104	103	102	101	90	82	77	104
Lowest Temp. of Rec.	-19	-15	-5	10	25	31	41	38	32	19	3	-15	-19
Normal Percipitation	2.04	2.19	2.91	3.14	3.49	3.70	3.52	3.40	3.44	2.54	3.17	3.09	36.63
Average No. of Days With Precipitation,.01	16	14	15	14	13	11	10	10	10	11	14	16	156
Snow and Ice Pellets	12.3	11.7	10.3	2.4	0.1	-	-	-	T	0.6	5.0	11.9	54.3
Average Percentage of Possible Sunshine, Length of Record, 47 years													
Average Wind Speed, MPH Length of Record, 49 years	12.3						8.6						10.6
Average Relative Humidity% Morning	77						81						79
Afternoon	69						57						62
Length of Record, 30 years													

ALL ABOUT OHIO ALMANAC - 1994

35

Weather

Source: U.S. National Oceanic and Atmospheric Administration.

COLUMBUS WEATHER STATION

	JAN.	FEB.	MARCH	APRIL	MAY	JUNE	JULY	AUG.	SEPT.	OCT.	NOV.	DEC.	ANNUAL
Normal Daily Mean Temp.	26.4	29.6	40.9	51.0	61.2	69.2	73.2	71.5	65.5	53.7	42.9	31.9	51.4
Normal Daily High Temp.	34.1	38.0	50.5	62.0	72.3	80.4	83.7	82.1	76.2	64.5	51.4	39.2	61.2
Normal Daily Low Temp.	18.5	21.2	31.2	40.0	50.1	58.0	62.7	60.8	54.8	42.9	34.3	39.2	61.2
Highest Temp. of Rec.	74	73	85	89	94	102	100	101	100	90	80	76	102
Lowest Temp. of Rec.	-19	-13	-6	14	25	35	43	39	31	20	5	-17	-19
Normal Percipitation	2.18	2.24	3.27	3.21	3.93	4.04	4.31	3.72	2.96	2.15	3.22	1.86	38.09
Average No. of Days With Precipitation,.01	13	12	14	13	13	11	11	9	8	9	11	13	137
Snow and Ice Pellets	8.3	6.2	4.5	1	-	T	-	-	T	-	2.3	5.7	28.0
Average Percentage of Possible Sunshine, Length of Record, 39 years													
Average Wind Speed, MPH, Length of Record, 41 years	10.1						6.6						8.5
Average Relative Humidity% Morning	76						84						80
Afternoon, Length of Record, 31 years	67						56						59

METROPOLITAN AREAS OF OHIO

Ohio has 14 Metropolitan areas. They are defined by the U.S. office of Management and Budget as one or more large central cities with a high degree of economic and social integration with the surrounding communities.

A "Consolidated Metropolitan Area" is created when two or more metro areas are somewhat integrated. Ohio has two such considerations, Cleveland Akron-Lorain and Cincinnati-Hamilton.

Thirty six of the state's 88 counties are in metro areas. Two of them (Lawrence and Belmont) are classified in Kentucky and West Virginia metro areas, while six counties of Indiana, Kentucky and West Virginia are classified in Ohio metro areas.

This "non-metropolitan" area covers the remaining 52 countries and includes such larege cities as Findlay, Marion, Portsmouth, Sandusky and Zanesville.

METRO

COUNTIES (in shadow)

1. Metro Canton

Counties
  Carroll
  Stark
Cities
  Canton
  Massilion

2. Metro Cincinati - Hamilton
Metro Cincinnati
Counties
  Clermont
  Hamilton
    (Dearborn, IN)
    (Boone, KY)
    (Campbell, KY)
    (Kenton, KY)
Cities
  Cincinnati
  Delhi Hills
  Norwood
    (Covington, KY)
Metro Hamilton-Middletown
  Counties
    Butler
  Cities
    Fairfield
    Hamilton
    Middletown

3. Metro Cleveland-Akron
  Metro Akron
  Counties
    Portage
    Summit
  Cities
    Akron
    Cuyahoga Falls
    Kent
    Stow
  Metro Cleveland- Lorain-Elyria
    Counties
      Cuyahoga
      Geauga

Metro Cleveland,

County Cont'd.
Lorain
Lake
Medina

Cities
Brook Park
Brunswick
Cleveland
Cleveland Hts.
E. Cleveland
Elyria
Euclid
Garfield Hts.
Lakewood
Lorain
Maple Hts.
Mentor
N. Oldstead
Parma
Shaker Hts.
S. Euclid
Strongsville

4. Metro Columbus

Counties
Delaware
Fairfield
Franklin
Licking
Madison
Pickaway
Union

Cities
Columbus
Lancaster
Newark
Upper Arlington

5. Metro Dayton-Springfield

Counties
Clark
Greene
Miami
Montgomery

Metro Dayton-Springfield , Cont'd

Cities
Beavercreek
Dayton
Fairborn
Huber Hts.
Kettering
Springfield

6. Metro Lima

Counties
Allen
Auglaize

Cities
Lima

7. Metro Mansfield

County
Richland

City
Mansfield

8. Metro Parkersburg-Marietta

Counties
Washington
(Wood, W.V.)

Cities
Marietta
(Parkersburg, W.V.)

9. Metro Steubenville-Weirton

Counties
Jefferson
(Brooke, W.V.)
(Hancock, W.V.)

Cities
Steubenville
(Weirton, W.V.)

10. Metro Toledo

Counties
Fulton
Lucas
Wood

Metro Toledo, Cont'd.
   Cities
     Bowling Green
     Toledo

11. Metro Youngstown -
   Warren
    Counties
     Mahoning
     Trumbull
    Cities
     Austintown
     Boardman
     Youngstown
     Warren

PERSONAL INCOME - PER CAPITA - BY METRO AREA

Source - U.S. Bureau of Economic Analysis

	1988	1989	1990	1991
OHIO	$15,576	$16,532	$17,422	$17,767
CONSOLIDATED METRO AREAS:				
CINCINNATI-HAMILTON	$16,376	$17,338	$18,445	$18,937
CLEVELAND-AKRON	17,102	18,248	19,312	19,889
METRO AREAS:				
AKRON	15,960	17,025	17,992	18,234
CANTON-MASSILLON	14,730	15,569	16,550	16,778
CINCINNATI	16,612	17,603	18,766	19,273
CLEVELAND-LORAIN-ELYRIA	17,440	18,611	19,706	19,995
COLUMBUS	16,267	17,345	18,161	18,680
DAYTON-SPRINGFIELD	16,115	17,011	17,808	18,302
HAMILTON-MIDDLETOWN	15,125	15,939	16,768	17,200
HUNTINGTON-ASHLAND	12,354	13,164	14,070	14,622
LIMA	14,684	15,416	16,004	16,369
MANSFIELD	14,103	14,740	15,236	15,348
PARKERSBURG-MARIETTA	13,508	14,128	15,080	15,671
STEUBENVILLE-WEIRTON	12,725	13,732	14,781	15,115
TOLEDO	16,054	16,861	17,416	17,713
WHEELING, WV-OH	13,112	14,083	14,996	15,396
YOUNGSTOWN-WARREN	13,746	14,640	15,375	15,739

Continued on next page

PERSONAL INCOME - PER CAPITA - BY COUNTY

Source - U.S. Bureau of Economic Analysis

OHIO COUNTIES	1988	1989	1990	1991
OHIO (METRO PORTION)	$16,160	$17,158	$18,088	$18,464
OHIO (NON-METRO PORT)	13,027	13,803	14,514	14,726
ADAMS	8,794	9,410	10,060	10,297
ALLEN	14,871	15,547	16,139	16,609
ASHLAND	13,260	14,067	14,721	14,934
ASHTABULA	12,224	12,842	13,486	13,764
ATHENS	10,215	10,897	11,506	11,958
AUGLAIZE	14,220	15,092	15,672	15,793
BELMONT	12,389	13,163	13,978	14,312
BROWN	11,950	12,584	13,063	13,590
BUTLER	15,125	15,939	16,768	17,200
CARROLL	11,420	12,179	12,961	13,008
CHAMPAIGN	12,810	13,573	14,437	14,710
CLARK	14,915	15,721	16,487	17,019
CLERMONT	14,477	15,338	16,042	16,499
CLINTON	13,664	14,780	15,780	16,155
COLUMBIANA	11,214	11,951	12,483	12,795
COSHOCTON	12,361	13,004	13,468	13,631
CRAWFORD	12,667	13,224	13,615	13,788
CUYAHOGA	18,412	19,706	20,901	21,203
DARKE	13,816	14,898	15,397	15,603
DEFIANCE	13,759	14,504	15,324	15,546
DELAWARE	16,865	18,302	19,110	19,400
ERIE	15,343	16,290	16,745	17,141
FAIRFIELD	14,410	15,406	16,543	16,883
FAYETTE	11,794	12,897	13,783	13,777
FRANKLIN	17,008	18,091	18,890	19,417
FULTON	15,034	16,061	16,789	16,798
GALLIA	11,378	12,163	12,692	13,252
GEAUGA	18,554	19,648	20,762	20,924
GREENE	16,062	17,195	18,159	18,663
GUERNSEY	11,677	12,077	12,661	13,204
HAMILTON	18,272	19,354	20,799	21,369
HANCOCK	17,021	17,827	18,704	18,992
HARDIN	11,345	11,982	12,463	12,388
HARRISON	9,724	10,477	10,893	11,184
HENRY	11,940	15,160	15,929	15,873
HIGHLAND	11,046	12,834	13,073	13,284
HOCKING	9,191	11,721	12,170	12,557
HOLMES	14,490	9,905	10,470	10,449
HURON	10,091	15,359	15,810	15,903
JACKSON	12,456	10,710	11,356	11,730
JEFFERSON	12,688	13,403	14,463	14,809
KNOX	17,125	13,508	14,611	14,985
LAKE	10,272	18,397	19,406	19,706
LAWRENCE	14,400	10,921	11,643	12,077
LICKING	14,490	15,447	16,295	16,665
LOGAN	13,038	13,829	15,195	15,877
LORAIN	14,417	15,224	16,062	16,392
LUCAS	16,233	16974	17,524	17,885
MADISON	13,253	14,200	14,805	15,047

Continued on next page

	1988	1989	1990	1991
MAHONING	14,269	15,210	16,032	16,480
MARION	11,972	12,628	13,238	13,586
MEDINA	16,924	17,845	18,902	19,094
MEIGS	10,178	10,978	11,610	11,928
MERCER	13,782	14,863	15,730	15,386
MIAMI	15,232	16,179	17,031	17,316
MONROE	11,545	12,019	12,825	13,063
MONTGOMERY	16,580	17,435	18,810	18,705
MORGAN	11,770	12,345	12,965	13,050
MORROW	11,465	12,015	12,502	12,766
MUSKINGUM	13,009	13,936	14,600	14,967
NOBLE	10,600	11,541	11,977	12,179
OTTAWA	16,686	17,359	18,040	18,113
PAULING	12,862	13,476	13,945	14,122
PERRY	10,632	11,188	11,695	12,130
PICKAWAY	12,022	12,811	13,306	13,585
PIKE	10,452	11,138	11,906	12,335
PORTAGE	14,235	15,096	15,702	15,881
PREBLE	13,394	14,146	15,260	15,366
PUTNAM	13,999	14,968	15,646	15,487
RICHLAND	14,650	15,316	15,850	15,938
ROSS	12,022	12,561	13,210	13,469
SANDUSKY	15,324	16,038	16,800	16,837
SCIOTO	10,999	11,667	12,566	12,853
SENECA	12,991	13,901	14,728	14,934
SHELBY	14,796	15,993	17,301	17,825
STARK	14,968	15,813	16,810	17,053
SUMMIT	16,434	17,558	18,627	18,889
TRUMBULL	14,336	15,253	15,988	16,287
TUSCARAWAS	13,370	13,967	14,834	14,805
UNION	15,911	17,355	18,362	18,207
VAN WERT	13,782	14,148	14,631	14,548
VINTON	9,842	10,474	11,122	11,359
WARREN	15,162	15,998	16,907	17,298
WASHINGTON	12,992	13,593	14,362	14,867
WAYNE	14,830	15,458	16,090	16,158
WILLIAMS	15,079	15,956	16,442	16,603
WOOD	15,656	16,671	17,189	17,327
WYANDOT	13,650	14,632	15,238	15,154

BLACK POPULATION
COUNTIES BY %

Source - U.S. Bureau of the Census

Blacks numbered 5% or more of the total population of 19 of Ohio's 88 counties (1990 U.S. Census).

RANK	COUNTY	% BLACK
1	Cuyahoga	24.7%
2	Hamilton	20.9
3	Montgomery	17.7
4	Franklin	15.8
5	Mahoning	14.9
6	Lucas	14.8
7	Summit	11.8
8	Allen	11.2
9	Clark	8.8
10	Erie	8.2
11	Richland	7.9
12	Lorain	7.8
13	Madison	7.4
14	Greene	7.0
15	Stark	6.8
16	Trumbull	6.6
17	Ross	6.4
18	Pickaway	6.2
19	Jefferson	5.52

Continued on next page

POPULATION – OHIO & COUNTIES
1970 – 1980 – 1990 – 1991

COUNTY	1970 CENSUS	1980 CENSUS	1990 CENSUS	1991 ESTIMATE	PERCENT CHANGE 1980-90	PERCENT CHANGE 1990-91
Ohio Totals	10,657,423	10,797,604	10,847,115	10,940,999	0.5%	0.9%
Adams	18,957	24,328	25,371	25,979	4.3%	2.4%
Allen	111,144	112,241	109,755	109,447	-2.2%	-0.3%
Ashland	43,303	46,178	47,507	48,111	2.9%	1.3%
Ashtabula	98,237	104,215	99,821	100,405	-4.2%	0.6%
Athens	55,747	56,399	59,549	60,354	5.6%	1.4%
Auglaize	38,602	42,554	44,585	45,426	4.8%	1.9%
Belmont	80,917	82,569	71,074	70,917	-13.9%	-0.2%
Brown	26,635	31,920	34,966	35,583	9.5%	1.8%
Butler	226,207	258,787	291,479	298,770	12.6%	2.5%
Carroll	21,579	25,598	26,521	26,997	3.6%	1.8%
Champaign	30,491	33,649	36,019	36,357	7.0%	0.9%
Clark	157,115	150,236	147,548	147,849	-1.8%	0.2%
Clermont	95,372	128,483	150,187	154,335	16.9%	2.8%
Clinton	31,464	34,603	35,415	36,023	2.3%	1.7%
Columbiana	108,310	113,572	108,276	109,344	-4.7%	1.0%
Coshocton	33,486	36,024	35,427	35,606	-1.7%	0.5%
Crawford	50,364	50,075	47,870	47,750	-4.4%	-0.3%
Cuyahoga	1,720,835	1,498,400	1,412,140	1,414,041	-5.8%	0.1%
Darke	49,141	55,096	53,619	53,703	-2.7%	0.2%
Defiance	36,949	39,987	39,350	39,542	-1.6%	0.5%
Delaware	42,908	53,840	66,929	69,498	24.3%	3.8%
Erie	75,909	79,655	76,779	77,012	-3.6%	0.3%
Fairfield	73,301	93,678	103,461	106,290	10.4%	2.7%
Fayette	25,461	27,467	27,466	27,859	-0.0%	1.4%
Franklin	833,249	869,126	961,437	977,563	10.6%	1.7%
Fulton	33,071	37,751	38,498	38,990	2.0%	1.3%
Gallia	25,239	30,098	30,954	31,288	2.8%	1.1%
Geauga	62,977	74,474	81,129	82,094	8.9%	1.2%
Greene	125,057	129,769	136,731	138,038	5.4%	1.0%
Guernsey	37,665	42,024	39,024	39,337	-7.1%	0.8%
Hamilton	925,944	873,204	866,228	870,492	-0.8%	0.5%
Hancock	61,217	64,581	65,536	66,203	1.5%	1.0%
Hardin	30,813	32,719	31,111	31,218	-4.9%	0.3%
Harrison	17,013	18,152	16,085	16,060	-11.4%	-0.2%
Henry	27,058	28,383	29,108	29,256	2.6%	0.5%
Highland	28,996	33,477	35,728	36,596	6.7%	2.4%
Hocking	20,322	24,304	25,533	25,921	5.1%	1.5%
Holmes	23,024	29,416	32,849	33,333	11.7%	1.5%
Huron	49,587	54,608	56,240	57,204	3.0%	1.7%
Jackson	27,174	30,592	30,230	30,883	-1.2%	2.2%
Jefferson	96,193	91,564	80,298	80,044	-12.3%	-0.3%
Knox	41,795	46,304	47,473	47,865	2.5%	0.8%
Lake	197,200	212,801	215,499	217,942	1.3%	1.1%

Continued on next page

COUNTY	1970 CENSUS	1980 CENSUS	1990 CENSUS	1991 ESTIMATE	PERCENT CHANGE 1980-90	PERCENT CHANGE 1990-91
Lawrence	56,868	63,849	61,834	62,372	-3.2%	0.9%
Licking	107,799	120,981	128,300	130,503	6.0%	1.7%
Logan	35,072	39,155	42,310	43,198	8.1%	2.1%
Lorain	256,843	274,909	271,126	273,436	-1.4%	0.9%
Lucas	483,551	471,741	462,361	461,742	-2.0%	-0.1%
Madison	28,318	33,004	37,068	37,572	12.3%	1.4%
Mahoning	304,545	289,487	264,806	264,922	-8.5%	0.0%
Marion	64,724	67,974	64,274	64,296	-5.4%	0.0%
Medina	82,717	113,150	122,354	125,423	8.1%	2.5%
Meigs	19,799	23,641	22,987	23,202	-2.8%	0.9%
Mercer	35,558	38,334	39,443	39,654	2.9%	0.5%
Miami	84,342	90,381	93,182	94,144	3.1%	1.0%
Monroe	15,739	17,382	15,497	15,370	-10.8%	-0.8%
Montgomery	608,413	571,697	573,809	576,104	0.4%	0.4%
Morgan	12,375	14,241	14,194	14,183	-0.3%	-0.1%
Morrow	21,348	26,480	27,749	28,126	4.8%	1.4%
Muskingum	77,826	83,340	82,068	82,391	-1.5%	0.4%
Noble	10,428	11,310	11,336	11,645	0.2%	2.7%
Ottawa	37,099	40,076	40,029	40,088	-0.1%	0.1%
Paulding	19,329	21,302	20,488	20,316	-3.8%	-0.8%
Perry	27,434	31,032	31,557	31,790	1.7%	0.7%
Pickaway	40,071	43,662	48,255	48,712	10.5%	0.9%
Pike	19,114	22,802	24,249	24,681	6.3%	1.8%
Portage	125,868	135,856	142,585	144,630	5.0%	1.4%
Preble	34,719	38,223	40,113	40,574	4.9%	1.1%
Putnam	31,134	32,991	33,819	34,203	2.5%	1.1%
Richland	129,997	131,205	126,137	126,408	-3.9%	0.2%
Ross	61,211	65,004	69,330	70,360	6.7%	1.5%
Sandusky	60,983	63,267	61,963	62,527	-2.1%	0.9%
Scioto	76,951	84,545	80,327	80,922	-5.0%	0.7%
Seneca	60,696	61,901	59,733	59,671	-3.5%	-0.1%
Shelby	37,748	43,089	44,915	45,573	4.2%	1.5%
Stark	372,210	378,823	367,585	369,961	-3.0%	0.6%
Summit	553,371	524,472	514,990	519,915	-1.8%	1.0%
Trumbull	232,579	241,863	227,813	228,927	-5.8%	0.5%
Tuscarawas	77,211	84,614	84,090	84,970	-0.6%	1.0%
Union	23,786	29,536	31,969	32,676	8.2%	2.2%
Van Wert	29,194	30,458	30,464	30,437	0.0%	-0.1%
Vinton	9,420	11,584	11,098	11,254	-4.2%	1.4%
Warren	85,505	99,276	113,909	116,519	14.7%	2.3%
Washington	57,160	64,266	62,254	62,331	-3.1%	0.1%
Wayne	87,123	97,408	101,461	102,574	4.2%	1.1%
Williams	33,669	36,369	36,956	36,994	1.6%	0.1%
Wood	89,722	107,372	113,269	113,635	5.5%	0.3%
Wyandot	21,826	22,651	22,254	22,340	-1.8%	0.4%

VOTE FOR PRESIDENT
BY COUNTY

Source: Ohio Secretary of State

County	1992			1988	
	Clinton (D)	Bush (R)	Perot (I)	Dukasis (D)	Bush (R)
Adams	3,998	4,722	1,993	3,740	5,916
Allen	13,777	25,322	8,131	13,727	31,021
Ashland	5,985	9,864	4,950	6,072	12,726
Ashtabula	18,843	13,254	10,765	20,536	17,654
Athens	13,423	7,184	5,074	10,795	9,314
Auglaize	4,960	10,455	4,840	4,756	13,562
Belmont	18,527	8,614	6,142	19,515	12,214
Brown	5,540	5,912	3,676	5,047	7,539
Butler	39,682	63,375	27,527	33,770	75,725
Carrol	4,731	4,224	3,434	4,667	6,179
Champaign	5,201	7,004	3,992	4,272	8,995
Clark	26,692	24,011	12,571	23,247	32,729
Clermont	17,558	32,065	14,279	15,352	37,417
Clinton	4,638	7,290	3,402	3,746	8,856
Columbiana	19,765	15,016	12,611	21,581	21,175
Coshocton	6,212	5,705	4,081	6,020	8,282
Crawford	6,351	8,618	5,764	6,018	12,472
Cuyahoga	337,548	187,186	112,352	353,401	242,439
Darke	7,016	11,098	6,217	6,851	14,914
Defiance	5,735	7,195	4,187	5,448	9,566
Delaware	9,263	18,225	9,244	7,590	20,693
Erie	14,531	12,459	8,720	15,097	16,670
Fairfield	14,249	24,125	12,246	12,504	29,208
Fayette	2,976	4,916	2,162	2,623	6,186
Franklin	176,656	186,324	79,049	147,585	226,265
Fulton	5,576	8,358	4,798	5,076	10,230
Gallia	5,350	5,776	2,549	4,834	7,399
Geauga	11,466	18,200	10,577	11,874	22,339
Greene	20,139	27,651	11,459	18,025	34,432
Guernsey	6,428	5,749	4,103	5,926	8,507
Hamilton	18,409	192,447	60,145	140,354	227,004
Hancock	7,944	16,821	7,002	7,435	19,896
Hardin	4,364	5,851	2,867	4,145	7,291
Harrison	3,830	2,289	1,679	3,881	3,298
Henry	3,933	6,196	3,178	3,764	8,618
Highland	4,866	7,020	3,315	4,278	8,776
Hocking	3,935	3,761	2,831	3,706	5,426
Holmes	1,969	5,079	1,945	2,179	5,064
Huron	7,930	9,480	6,751	7,794	12,633
Jackson	5,016	5,422	2,389	4,505	6,671

County	1992 Clinton	Bush	Perot	1988 Dukasis	Bush
Jefferson	20,978	10,764	6,910	22,095	14,141
Knox	7,259	9,044	5,282	6,882	12,180
Lake	37,682	40,766	26,878	39,667	52,963
Lawrence	12,325	10,044	4,536	11,628	12,937
Licking	18,898	26,918	13,806	16,793	34,540
Logan	4,889	9,364	4,472	4,484	11,099
Lorain	50,962	36,803	30,425	55,600	50,410
Lucas	99,989	63,297	38,108	99,755	83,788
Madison	3,998	6,865	3,170	3,421	8,303
Mahoning	64,731	31,191	29,417	75,524	43,722
Marion	9,444	11,675	6,471	9,596	14,864
Medina	18,995	24,090	17,290	19,505	29,962
Meigs	4,226	3,916	2,098	3,699	5,486
Mercer	4,883	8,683	4,913	4,978	11,162
Miami	12,547	19,741	10,544	11,138	24,915
Monroe	4,235	1,823	1,505	4,269	2,557
Montgomery	108,017	104,751	47,854	95,737	131,596
Morgan	2,402	2,719	1,551	2,085	3,713
Morrow	3,907	5,208	3,623	3,515	7,130
Muskingum	11,670	14,168	8,731	11,691	19,736
Noble	2,201	2,223	1,429	2,079	3,155
Ottawa	8,128	6,782	4,832	8,038	10,352
Paulding	3,293	3,652	2,510	3,114	5,381
Perry	4,972	4,712	3,810	5,011	6,602
Pickaway	5,765	8,690	4,319	4,905	10,796
Pike	5,057	4,094	2,192	5,191	5,611
Portage	26,325	18,447	17,065	25,607	26,334
Preble	5,557	8,023	4,460	4,937	10,297
Putnam	3,962	9,338	3,648	4,004	11,183
Richland	19,606	23,532	13,370	19,617	30,047
Ross	10,452	10,825	5,616	9,271	14,563
Sandusky	9,878	10,772	6,682	9,709	14,203
Scioto	14,715	11,931	6,860	14,442	16,029
Seneca	9,280	9,763	6,967	9,504	13,704
Shelby	5,262	8,854	5,835	5,065	12,198
Stark	70,064	61,863	42,413	69,639	87,087
Summit	107,881	77,530	55,151	112,612	101,155
Trumbull	54,591	25,831	26,791	58,674	38,815
Tuscarawas	14,787	13,179	8,785	14,185	17,145
Union	3,465	7,818	3,433	3,130	8,846

County	1992 Clinton	Bush	Perot	1988 Dukasis	Bush
Van Wert	3,822	7,227	3,102	3,848	9,410
Vinton	2,308	1,975	1,050	2,385	2,652
Warren	13,542	27,998	11,115	11,145	31,419
Washington	10,380	12,204	5,415	9,967	14,767
Wayne	13,953	18,350	9,482	13,571	22,320
Williams	4,862	7,614	4,902	4,666	10,782
Wood	20,754	20,579	11,682	18,579	26,013
Wyandot	3,031	4,411	2,929	2,936	6,178
Totals	1,984,942	1,894,310	1,036,426	1,939,629	2,416,549

SUMMARY COUNTY VOTE FOR PRESIDENT

1992		1988
Clinton	Democratic ◉	Dukakis
Bush	Republican ◯	Bush

OHIO VOTE FOR PRESIDENT
1804 - 1992

Candidates listed in the order of their vote in Ohio. Candidate elected by U.S. vote in bold. Included are third party candidates when their vote exceeded the winner's plurality. Source: Ohio Secretary of State.

Year	Candidates	Politics	Vote
1804	**Thomas Jefferson**	**Democractic Republican**	**2,593**
	Charles C. Pinckney	Federalist	364
1808	**James Madison**	**Democratic Republican**	**3,645**
	Charles C. Pinckney	Federalist	1,174
1812	**James Madison**	**Democratic Republican**	**7,420**
	DeWitt Clinton	Clintonian Republican	3,301
1816	**James Monroe**	**Democratic Republican**	**3,326**
	Rufus King	Federalist	593
1820	**James Monroe**	**Democratic Republican**	**7,164**
1824	Henry Clay	Democratic Republican	19,255
	Andrew Jackson	Democratic Republican	18,489
	John Q. Adams	**Democratic Republican**	**12,280**
1828	**Andrew Jackson**	**Democrat**	**67,596**
	John Q. Adams	National Republican	63,456
1832	**Andrew Jackson**	**Democrat**	**81,246**
	Henry Clay	National Republican	76,539
1836	William H. Harrison	Whig	104,958
	Martin Van Buren	**Democrat**	**96,238**
1840	**William H. Harrison**	**Whig**	**148,333**
	Martin Van Buren	Democrat	124,782
1844	Henry Clay	Whig	155,113
	James K. Polk	**Democrat**	**149,061**
	James G. Birney	Liberty	8,808
1848	Lewis Cass	Democrat	154,773
	Zachary Taylor	**Whig**	**138,359**
	Martin Van Buren	Free Soil	35,347
1852	**Franklin Pierce**	**Democrat**	**168,933**
	Winfield Scott	Whig	152,523
	John P. Hale	Free Soil	31,732
1856	John C. Fremont	Republican	187,497
	James Buchanan	**Democrat**	**170,184**
	Milard Filmore	American	28,126
1860	**Abraham Lincoln**	**Republican**	**231,809**
	Stephen A. Douglas	Ind. Democrat	187,421
1864	**Abraham Lincoln**	**Union**	**265,654**
	George B. McClellan	Democrat	205,599
1868	**U.S. Grant**	**Republican**	**243,605**
	Horatio Seymour	Democrat	238,606
1872	**U.S. Grant**	**Republican**	**238,273**
	Horace Greeley	Liberal Republican	244,321
1876	**R. B. Hayes**	**Republican**	**330,698**
	Samuel J. Tilden	Democrat	323,182
1880	**James A. Garfield**	**Republican**	**375,048**
	Winfield S. Hancock	Democrat	340,821
1884	James G. Blaine	Republican	400,082
	Grover Cleveland	**Democrat**	**368,280**
1888	**Benjamin Harrison**	**Republican**	**416,054**
	Grover Cleveland	Democrat	396,455
1892	Benjamin Harrison	Republican	405,187
	Grover Cleveland	**Democrat**	**404,115**
	John Bidwell	Prohibition	26,012
	James B. Weaver	People's	14,850

OHIO VOTE FOR PRESIDENT Cont'd
1804- 1992

Year	Candidates	Politics	Vote
1896	**William McKinley**	**Republican**	**525,991**
	William J. Bryan	Democrat	477,497
1900	**William McKinley**	**Republican**	**543,918**
	William J. Bryan	Democrat	474,882
1904	**Theodore Roosevelt**	**Republican**	**600,095**
	Alton B. Parker	Democrat	344,674
1908	**William H. Taft**	**Republican**	**572,312**
	William J. Bryan	Democrat	502,721
1912	**Woodrow Wilson**	**Democrat**	**424,834**
	William H. Taft	Republican	278,168
	Theodore Roosevelt	Progressive	229,807
1916	**Woodrow Wilson**	**Democrat**	**514,753**
	Charles E. Hughes	Republican	604,161
1920	**Warren G. Harding**	**Republican**	**1,182,022**
	James M. Cox	Democrat	780,037
1924	**Calvin Coolidge**	**Republican**	**1,176,130**
	John W. Davis	Democrat	477,888
1928	**Herbert Hoover**	**Republican**	**1,627,546**
	Alfred E. Smith	Democrat	864,210
1932	**Franklin D. Roosevelt**	**Democrat**	**1,301,695**
	Herbert Hoover	Republican	1,227,319
1936	**Franklin D. Roosevelt**	**Democrat**	**1,747,140**
	Alfred M. Landon	Republican	1,127,855
1940	Franklin D. Roosevelt	Democrat	1,733,139
	Wendell L. Willkie	Republican	1,586,773
1944	Thomas E. Dewey	Republican	1,582,293
	Franklin D. Roosevelt	**Democrat**	**1,570,763**
1948	**Harry S. Truman**	**Democrat**	**1,452,791**
	Thomas E. Dewey	Republican	1,445,684
1952	**Dwight D. Eisenhower**	**Republican**	**2,100,391**
	Adlia E. Stevenson	Democrat	1,600,367
1956	**Dwight E. Eisenhower**	**Republican**	**2,262,610**
	Adlai E. Stevenson	Democrat	1,439,655
1960	Richard M. Nixon	Republican	2,217,611
	John F. Kennedy	**Democrat**	**1,944,248**
1964	**Lyndon B. Johnson**	**Democrat**	**2,498,331**
	Barry M. Goldwater	Republican	1,470,865
1968	**Richard M. Nixon**	**Republican**	**1,791,014**
	Hubert H. Humphrey	Democrat	1,700,586
	George C. Wallace	AM. Independent	467,485
1972	**Richard M. Nixon**	**Republican**	**2,441,827**
	George S. McGovern	Democrat	1,558,889
1976	**Jimmy Carter**	**Democrat**	**2,011,621**
	Gerald R. Ford	Republican	2,000,505
1980	**Ronald Reagan**	**Republican**	**2,206,545**
	Jimmy Carter	Democrat	1,752,414
1984	**Ronald Reagan**	**Republican**	**2,678,560**
	Walter F. Mondale	Democrat	1,825,440
1988	**George Bush**	**Republican**	**2,416,549**
	Michael S. Dukakis	Democrat	1,939,629
1992	**William Clinton**	**Democrat**	**1,984,942**
	George Bush	Republican	1,894,310
	Ross Perot	Independent	1,036,426

Continued on next page

OHIO VOTE FOR GOVERNOR
1803 - 1990
Candidates listed in the order of the votes received. Included are third pary candidates when their vote exceeded the winner's plurality. Source: Ohio Secretary of State.

Year	Candidates	Politics	Vote
1803	Edward Tiffin	Democratic Republican	4,564
1805	Edward Tiffin	Democratic Repubican	4,738
1807	Return J. Meigs, Jr.	Democratic Republican	3,299
	Nathaniel Massie	Democratic Republican	2,317
1808	Samuel Huntington	Democratic Republican	7,293
	Thomas Worthington	Democratic Republican	5,601
	Thomas Kirker	Democratic Republican	3,397
1810	Return J. Meigs, Jr.	Democratic Republican	9,924
	Thomas Worthington	Democratic Republican	7,731
1812	Return J. Meigs, Jr.	Democratic Republican	11,859
	Thomas Scott	Democratic Republican	7,903
1814	Thomas Worthington	Democratic Republican	15,879
	Othniel Looker	Democratic Republican	6,171
1816	Thomas Worthington	Democratic Republican	22,931
	James Dunlap	Democratic Republican	6,295
1818	Ethan A. Brown	Democratic Republican	30,194
	James Dunlap	Democratic Republican	8,075
1820	Ethan A. Brown	Democratic Republican	34,836
	Jeramiah Morrow	Democratic Republican	9,426
	William H. Harrison	Democratic Republican	4,348
1822	Jeremiah Morrow	Democratic Republican	26,059
	Allen Trimble	Democratic Republican	22,899
	William W. Irvian	Democratic Republican	11,050
1824	Jeremiah Morrow	Democratic Republican	39,526
	Allen Trimble	Democratic Republican	37,108
1826	Allen Trimble	Democratic Republican	71,475
	Alex Campbell	Democratic Republican	4,765
1828	Allen Trimble	National Republican	53,970
	John W. Campbell	Democrat	51,951
1830	Duncan McArthur	National Republican	49,668
	Robert Lucas	Democrat	49,186
1832	Robert Lucas	Democrat	71,251
	Darius Lyman	Anti-Mason	63,185
1834	Robert Lucas	Democrat	70,738
	James Findlay	Whig	67,414
1836	Joseph Vance	Whig	92,204
	Eli Baldwin	Democrat	86,158
1838	Wilson Shannon	Democrat	107,884
	Joseph Vance	Whig	102,146
1840	Thomas Corwin	Whig	145,442
	Wilson Shannon	Democrat	129,312
1842	Wilson Shannon	Democrat	119,774
	Thomas Corwin	Whig	117,902
1844	Mordecai Bartley	Whig	146,333
	David Tod	Democrat	145,062
	Leicester King	Liberty	8,808
1846	William Bebb	Whig	118,869
	David Tod	Democrat	116,484
	Samuel Lewis	Liberty	10,797

Continued on next page

OHIO VOTE FOR GOVERNOR
1803 - 1990
Candidates listed in the order of the votes received.
Source: Ohio Secretary of State.

Year	Candidates	Politics	Vote
1848	Seabury Ford	Whig	148,756
	John B. Weller	Democrat	148,445
1850	Reuben Wood	Democrat	133,093
	William Johnston	Whig	121,105
	Edward Smith	Free Soil	13,747
1851	Reuben Wood	Democrat	145,654
	Samuel F. Vinton	Whig	119,548
1853	William Medill	Democrat	147,663
	Nelson Barrere	Whig	85,857
1855	Salmon P. Chase	Republican	146,770
	William Medill	Democrat	131,019
	Allen Trimble	American	24,276
1857	Salmon P. Chase	Republican	160,568
	H.B. Payne	Democrat	159,065
	P. Van Trump	American	10,272
1859	William Dennison	Republican	184,557
	Rufus P. Ranney	Democrat	171,226
1861	David Tod	Republican	206,997
	Hugh J. Jewett	Democrat	151,794
1863	John Brough	Republican	288,374
	C. L. Vallandingham	Democrat	187,492
1865	Jacob D. Cox	Republican	223,633
	George W. Morgan	Democrat	193,797
1867	Rutherford Hayes	Republican	243,605
	A. G. Thurman	Democrat	240,622
1869	Rutherford B. Hayes	Republican	236,082
	G. H. Pendleton	Democrat	228,581
1871	Edward F. Noyes	Republican	238,273
	George W. McCook	Democrat	218,105
1873	William Allen	Democrat	214,654
	Edward F. Noyes	Republican	213,837
	Issac C. Collins	Prohibition	10,278
1875	R. B. Hayes	Republican	297,817
	William Allen	Democrat	292,273
1877	Richard M. Bishop	Democrat	271,625
	William H. West	Republican	311,220
1879	Charles Foster	Republican	274,120
	Thomas Ewing	Democrat	319,132
1881	Charles Foster	Republican	362,021
	John W. Bookwalter	Democrat	288,426
1883	George Hoadley	Democrat	288,426
	Joseph B. Foraker	Republican	347,164
1885	Joseph B. Foraker	Republican	359,281
	George Hoadley	Democrat	341,830
1887	Joseh B. Foraker	Republican	356,534
	Thomas E. Powell	Democrat	333,205
1889	James E. Campbell	Democrat	379,423
	Joseph B. Foraker	Republican	368.551

Continued on next page

Continued from preceeding page

OHIO VOTE FOR GOVERNOR
1803 - 1990
Candidates listed in the order of the votes received.
Source: Ohio Secretary of State.

Year	Candidates	Politics	Vote
1891	William McKinley, Jr.	Republican	386,739
	James E. Campbell	Democrat	365,228
1893	William McKinley	Republican	433,342
	Lawrence T. Neal	Democrat	352,347
1895	Asa S. Bushnell	Republican	427,141
	James E. Campbell	Democrat	334,519
1897	Asa S. Bushnell	Republican	429,915
	Horace L. Chapman	Democrat	401,750
1899	George K. Nash	Republican	417,199
	John R. McLean	Democrat	368,176
1901	George K. Nash	Republican	436,092
	James Kilbourne	Democrat	368,525
1903	Myron T. Herrick	Republican	475,560
	Tom L. Johnson	Democrat	361,748
1905	John M. Pattison	Democrat	473,264
	Myron T. Herrick	Republican	430,617
1908	Judson Harmon	Democrat	552,569
	Andrew L. Harris	Republican	533,312
1910	Judson Harmon	Democrat	477,077
	Warren G. Harding	Republican	376,700
1912	James M. Cox	Democrat	439,323
	Robert B. Brown	Republican	272,500
1914	Frank B. Willis	Republican	523,074
	James M. Cox	Democrat	493,804
1916	James M. Cox	Democrat	568,218
	Frank B. Willis	Republican	561,602
1918	James M. Cox	Democrat	486,403
	Frank B. Willis	Republican	474,459
1920	Harry L. Davis	Republican	1,039,835
	Vic Donahey	Democrat	918,962
1922	Vic Donahey	Democrat	821,948
	Carmi A. Thompson	Republican	803,300
1924	Vic Donahey	Democrat	1,064,981
	Harry L. Davis	Republican	888,139
1926	Vic Donahey	Democrat	702,733
	Myers Y. Cooper	Republican	685,957
1928	Myers Y. Cooper	Republican	1,355,517
	Martin L. Davey	Democrat	1,106,739
1930	George White	Democrat	1,033,168
	Myers Y. Cooper	Republican	923,538
1932	George White	Democrat	1,356,518
	David S. Ingalls	Republican	1,151,933
1934	Martin L. Davey	Democrat	1,118,257
	Clarence J. Brown	Republican	1,052,851
1936	Martin L. Davey	Democrat	1,539,461
	John W. Bricker	Republican	1,412,773
1938	John W. Bricker	Republican	1,265,548
	Charles Sawyer	Democrat	1,147,323
1940	John W. Bricker	Republican	1,824,863
	Martin L. Davey	Democrat	1.460.396

Continued on next page

Continued from preceeding page

OHIO VOTE FOR GOVERNOR
1803 - 1990
Candidates listed in the order of the votes received.
Source: Ohio Secretary of State.

Year	Candidates	Politics	Vote
1942	John W. Bricker	Republican	1,086,937
	John McSweeney	Democrat	709,599
1944	Frank J. Lausche	Democrat	1,603,809
	James G. Stewart	Republican	1,491,450
1946	Thomas J. Herbert	Republican	1,166,550
	Frank J. Lausche	Democrat	1,125,997
1948	Frank J. Lausche	Democrat	1,619,775
	Thomas J. Herbert	Republican	1,398,514
1950	Frank J. Lausche	Democrat	1,522,249
	Don H. Ebright	Republican	1,370,570
1952	Frank J. Lausche	Democrat	2,015,110
	Charles P. Taft	Republican	1,590,058
1954	Frank J. Lausche	Democrat	1,405,262
	James A. Rhodes	Republican	1,192,528
1956	C. William O'Neill	Republican	1,948,988
	Michael V. DiSalle	Democrat	1,557,103
1958	Michael V. DiSalle	Democrat	1,869,260
	C. William O'Neill	Republican	1,414,874
1962	James A. Rhodes	Republican	1,836,432
	Michael V. DiSalle	Democrat	1,280,521
1966	James A. Rhodes	Republican	1,795,277
	Frazier Reams, Jr.	Democrat	1,092,054
1970	John J. Giligan	Democrat	1,725,560
	Roger Cloud	Republican	1,382,659
1974	James A. Rhodes	Republican	1,493,679
	John J. Giligan	Democrat	1,482,191
1978	James A. Rodes	Republican	1,402,167
	Richard F. Celeste	Democrat	1,354,631
1982	Richard F. Celeste	Democrat	1,981,882
	Clarence J. Brown	Republican	1,303,962
1986	Richard F. Celeste	Democrat	1,858,372
	James A. Rhodes	Republican	1,207,264
1990	George V. Voinovich	Republican	1,938,103
	Anthony J. Celebrezze	Democrat	1,539,416

Source: Ohio Secretary of State.   Winner identified in bold.

Year	Candidates	Politics	Vote
1992	John Glenn	Democratic	2,444,000
	Devine	Republican	2,028,000
1988	Howard M. Metzenbaum	Democratic	2,480,000
	George V. Vornovich	Republican	1,872,000
1986	John Glenn	Democratic	1,949,000
	Thomas N. Kindness	Republican	1,171,000
1982	Howard M. Metzenbaum	Democratic	1,923,000
	Paul E. Pfeifer	Republican	1,396,000
1980	John Glenn	Democratic	2,770,000
	James E. Betts	Republican	1,137,000
1976	Howard M. Metzenbaum	Democratic	1,941,000
	Robert Taft Jr.	Republican	1,823,000
1974	John Glenn	Democratic	1,930,000
	Ralph J. Perk	Republican	918,000
1970	Robert Taft Jr.	Republican	1,565,000
	John M. Metzenbaum	Democratic	1,495,000
1968	William B. Saxbe	Republican	1,928,000
	John J. Tilligan	Democratic	1,814,000
1964	Stephen M. Young	Democratic	1,923,000
	Robert Taft Jr.	Republican	1,906,000
1962	Frank J. Lausche	Democratic	1,843,000
	John Marshall Briley	Republican	1,151,000

largest cities

Largest (square miles)

1.	Columbus	190.9
2.	Toledo	80.6
3.	Cincinnati	77.2
4.	Cleveland	77.0
5.	Akron	62.2
6.	Dayton	55.0
7.	Youngstown	33.8
8.	Mansfield	27.9
9.	Mentor	26.8
10.	Beavercreek	25.7

Highest density
(residents per square mile)

1.	Lakewood	10,857.8
2.	East Cleveland	10,676.1
3.	Cleveland Heights	6,673.1
4.	Cleveland	6,566.4
5.	Maple Heights	5,209.4
6.	Euclid	5,128.5
7.	Shaker Heights	4,893.8
8.	Cincinnati	4,715.5
9.	Garfield Heights	4,408.2
10.	Parma	4,393.8

VOTE FOR U.S. HOUSE OF REPRESENTATIVES
NOV. 3, 1993

Candidates are listed in the order of their votes and their political party in parenthesis (). Elected candidates are listed in bold. D = Democratic; R = Republican; I = Independent. "Third party" candidates shown when their vote exceeded the winner's plurality.

Source: Ohio Secretary of State

DIST	CANDIDATE (PARTY)	VOTE
1	**MANN (D)**	120,190
	GROTE (I)	101,498
2	**GRADISON JR (R)**	177,720
	CHANDLER (D)	75,924
3	**HALL (D)**	146,072
	DAVIS (R)	98,733
4	**OXLEY (R)**	147,346
	BALL (D)	92,608
5	**GILLMOR (R)**	187,860
	UNOPPOSED	
6	**STRICKLAND (D)**	122,720
	MCEWEN	119,252
7	**HOBSON (R)**	164,195
	HESKETT (D)	66,237

DIST	CANDIDATE (PARTY)	VOTE
8	**BOEHNER (R)**	176,362
	SENNET (D)	62,033
9	**KAPTUR (D)**	178,879
	BROWN	53,011
10	**HOKE (R)**	136,433
	OAKAR (D)	103,788
11	**STOKES (D)**	154,178
	ROTHSCHILD (R)	43,866
12	**KASICH (R)**	170,297
	FITRAKIS (D)	68,761
13	**BROWN (D)**	134,486
	MUELLER (R)	88,889
14	**SAWYER (D)**	165,335
	MORGAN (R)	78,659
15	**PRYCE (R)**	110,390
	CORDRAY	94,907
	REIDELBACH (I)	44,906
16	**REGULA (R)**	158,489
	MENDENHALL (D)	90,224
17	**TRAFICANT JR (D)**	216,503
	PANSINO (R)	40,743
18	**APPLEGATE (D)**	166,189
	RESS (R)	77,229
19	**FINGERHUT (D)**	138,465
	GARDNER (R)	124,608

VOTE FOR STATE SENATORS - 1992
Source: Ohio Secretary of State

Winner of election Nov. 3, 1992 listed in **bold**. Political party in parenthesis ( ). D = Democratic; R = Republican; I = Independent. "third party" candidates are included when their vote exceeded the winner's plurality.

Source: Ohio Secretary of State

DIST	CANDIDATE (PARTY)	VOTE
2	**MONTGOMERY (R)**	88,521
	HARTMAN (D)	52,989
4	**LEVEY (R)**	95,896
	UNOPPOSED	
6	**HORN (R)**	103,435
	FULLER (D)	47,756
8	**ARONOFF (R)**	102,914
	PORTUNE (D)	40,088
10	**KEARNS (R)**	75,501
	TACKETT (D)	54,598
12	**CUPP (R)**	96,845
	HESS (D)	42,423

DIST	CANDIDATE (PARTY)	VOTE
14	**SNYDER (R)**	82,079
	HERRON (D)	52,617
15	**ESPY (D)**	72,068
	ROSENBAUM (R)	33,006
16	**WATTS (R)**	92,986
	MICHAEL (D)	51,895
18	**BOGGS (D)**	68,023
	PURATY (R)	66,542
20	**NEY (R)**	89,906
	GROFF (D)	49,922
22	**DRAKE (R)**	93,929
	FYNN (D)	55,253
24	**SUHADOLNIK (R)**	93,458
	DUNNING (D)	71,137
26	**GILLMOR (R)**	86,309
	COMBS (D)	50,956
28	**NETTLE (D)**	84,483
	SCHMITZ (R)	39,787
30	**BURCH (D)**	106,986
	UNOPPOSED	
32	**LATELL JR (D)**	69,981
	HENRY (R)	67,300

VOTE FOR OHIO SUPREME COURT
November 3, 1992

Source - Ohio Secretary of State

Winning candidates listed in **bold**

	CANDIDATE (PARTY)	VOTE		CANDIDATE (PARTY)	VOTE
CHIEF JUSTICE	**MOYER (R)**	**1,775,596**	JUSTICE	**SWEENEY (D)**	**2,008,854**
	GORMAN (D)	1,670,248		PAINTER (R)	1,838,307
	HAFFEY (I)	354,944	JUSTICE	**PFEIFER (R)**	**2,015,685**
				PATTON (D)	1,785,215

VOTE FOR STATE REPRESENTATIVES - 1992
Source: Ohio Secretary of State

Winner of election Nov. 3, 1992 listed in **bold**. Political party in parenthesis (). D = Democratic; R = Republican; "Third party" candidates shown when their vote exceeded the winner's plurality.

Source: Ohio Secretary of State

DIST	CANDIDATE (PARTY)	VOTE
1	**THOMPSON (R)**	36,010
	HAMILTON (WI)	52
2	**TERWILLEGER (R)**	29,098
	TURNER (D)	20,467
3	**LOGAN (D)**	29,352
	HORNING (R)	16,809
4	**GARDNER (R)**	34,076
	SINN (D)	15,618
5	**BOGGS JR (D)**	24,078
	SCHULTZ (R)	16,681
6	**MYERS (R)**	27,929
	SHONK JR (D)	16,348
7	**AMSTUTZ (R)**	26,476
	VIMMERSTEDT(D)	13,565
8	**PRENTISS (D)**	27,606
	KING (R)	4,228
9	**BOYD (D)**	30,285
	BYRNE (R)	6,014
10	**JAMES (D)**	20,238
	CARSON (R)	3,098
11	**CAMPBELL (D)**	33,534
	ANDERSON (R)	7,873
12	**WHALEN (D)**	30,847
	GARLAND (R)	5,173
13	**PRINGLE (D)**	18,844
	JOHANEK (I)	7,130
	CLINE (R)	3,798
14	**SUSTER (D)**	32,760
	UNOPPOSED	

DIST	CANDIDATE (PARTY)	VOTE
15	**WISE (R)**	34,102
	MAHNIC JR (D)	26,519
16	**KASPUTIS (R)**	37,080
	SARINGER (D)	21,006
17	**CAIN (D)**	24,555
	POPOVICH (R)	9,516
18	**COLONNA (D)**	29,851
	DIEDEL (R)	22,934
19	**SWEENEY (D)**	36,648
	REEVES (R)	10,111
20	**MOTTL (D)**	36,210
	BARNA (R)	16,232
21	**BEATTY JR (D)**	25,572
	UNOPPOSED	
22	**MILLER (D)**	26,952
	JOHNSTON (R)	8,947
23	**STINZIANO (D)**	23,002
	NEAL JR (R)	11,035
24	**DAVIDSON (R)**	30,801
	PHILLIPS (D)	12,790
25	**MASON (R)**	25,396
	SHULTZ (D)	22,425
26	**TIBERI (R)**	30,347
	RYAN (D)	14,431
27	**THOMAS JR (R)**	27,301
	BRIGGS (D)	23,070
	RYMAN (I)	2,198
28	**MEAD (R)**	32,603
	DICUCCIO (D)	14,398
29	**SCHUCK (R)**	31,237
	SHOEMAKER (D)	17,964
30	**RANKIN (D)**	33,629
	CARNEY (R)	8,822
31	**MALLORY (D)**	21,928
	WALKER (R)	10,114

Continued on next page

Continued from preceeding page

DIST	CANDIDATE (PARTY)	VOTE
32	VAN VYVEN (R)	25,183
	TRANTER (D)	22,309
33	LUEBBERS (D)	20,395
	BEDINGHAUS (R)	18,262
34	WINKLER (R)	38,015
	ANDERSON (D)	15,310
35	BLESSING JR (R)	37,338
	UNOPPOSED	
36	SCHULER (R)	36,120
	STIDHAM (D)	15,600
37	O'BRIEN (R)	38,636
	JOHNSON (D)	15,280
38	McLIN (D)	27,536
	HUSTED (R)	9,552
39	ROBERTS (D)	26,631
	O'NEAL (R)	9,497
40	JACOBSON (R)	26,620
	HART (D)	22,130
41	MOTTLEY (R)	28,796
	BELL (D)	22,448
42	CORBIN (R)	27,693
	SMALLWOOD (D)	19,540
43	NETZLEY (R)	27,575
	BROWN (D)	19,176
44	SYKES (D)	24,808
	DENHOLM (R)	8,903
45	DOTY (D)	29,462
	FINK (R)	26,894
46	JONES (D)	30,585
	WATKINS (R)	25,211
47	WILLIAMS (D)	28,476
	REED (R)	11,664
48	SEESE (D)	28,825
	ROMAN (R)	25,109
49	JONES (D)	25,109
	PACKARD (R)	5,048

DIST	CANDIDATE (PARTY)	VOTE
50	QUILTER (D)	22,511
	LIPINSKI (R)	10,855
51	GREENWOOD (R)	30,567
	SCHWARTZ (D)	15,729
52	PERZ (R)	29,316
	CZARCINSKI (D)	21,506
53	OPFER (D)	30,114
	MYLANDER (R)	19,385
54	HEALY (D)	28.638
	SCHIFFER (R)	14,142
55	JOHNSON (R)	38,191
	MILINI (D)	17,710
56	MAIER (D)	33,284
	MYERS (R)	19,264
57	CARR (D)	26,641
	HOOD (R)	23,224
58	NEIN (R)	29,706
	STOKER (D)	15,710
59	FOX (R)	30,308
	JOHNSTON (R)	15,462
60	KREBS (R)	21,946
	DAY (D)	20,482
61	KOZIURA (D)	33,406
	UNOPPOSED	
62	BENDER (D)	27,291
	BAIRD (R)	22,068
63	WALSH (D)	25,721
	RENCH (R)	24,757
64	HAGAN (D)	34,481
	SUBRAMANIAN(R)	5,557
65	GERBERRY (D)	42,874
	MCCABE (R)	13,,520
66	VERICH (D)	31,876
	SAFFOLD (R)	7,009
67	LUCAS (D)	39,909
	UNOPPOSED	

Continued on next page

DIST	CANDIDATE (PARTY)	VOTE
68	GRENDELL (R)	23,770
	DOLAN (D)	18,710
69	SINES (R)	26,495
	LITTERST (D)	15,692
70	TROY	28,162
	SCHULZ (R)	17,559
71	BATEMAN (R)	31,300
	JACKSON (D)	14,237
72	VESPER (R)	19,728
	SNARR (D)	18,178
	DEAN (I)	5,472
73	HARTLEY (D)	26,585
	FLACK (R)	17,259
74	HAINES (R)	24,301
	SHIRA (D)	19,125
75	JONES (D)	29,840
	MALLCHOK (R)	15,325
76	REID (R)	33,624
	TATONE (D)	8,951
77	GUTHRIE (D)	32,571
	MYERS (R)	19,439
78	ABEL (D)	29,483
	SKINNER (R)	17,350
79	SAWYER (D)	30,984
	JACKSON (R)	15,508
80	LAWRENCE (R)	41,501
	UNOPPOSED	
81	BATCHELDER (R)	31,778
	FALLON (D)	17,638
82	HODGES (R)	29,115
	GRIFFITH (D)	21,295

DIST	CANDIDATE (PARTY)	VOTE
83	WACHTMANN (R)	35,700
	WILLIAMS (D)	15,949
84	BUCHY (R)	36,727
	KOHLHORST (D)	12,674
85	DAVIS (R)	24,107
	HANNA (D)	22,873
86	BRADING (R)	32,681
	RANGE (D)	14,355
87	CORE (R)	28,331
	SCHEIDERER (D)	18,230
88	WHITE (R)	26,666
	RENO (D)	19,174
89	WISE JR (D)	25,129
	DAMSCHRODER(R)	22,829
90	WESTON (D)	28,868
	O'LEARY	17,391
91	SHOEMAKER (D)	30,210
	DETWILER (R)	12,758
92	RIFFE JR (D)	34,513
	MINCH (R)	12,047
93	BYERS (R)	28,298
	WILLIAMS (D)	15,444
94	MALONE (D)	24,794
	CREMEANS (R)	23,081
95	PADGETT (R)	25,727
	MCCULLOUGH (D)	14,619
96	JOHNSON (R)	25,610
	PHILLIPS (D)	19,380
97	DIDONATO (D)	34,725
	WILSON (R)	13,170
98	KRUPINSKI (D)	37,147
	MOORES (R)	11,515
99	CERA (D)	37,848
	DEWEY (R)	14,010

Ohio Statehood

The story of Ohio's statehood dates back to the Ordinance of 1787 and the creation of the Northwest Territory -- a large body of unsettled land that encompassed what is now Ohio, Indiana, Illinois, Michigan, Wisconsin, and part of Minnesota.

The territory was ruled by a governor, a secretary, and three judges, who were all appointed by Congress. These five officials performed the executive, legislative, and judicial functions of government. It wasn't until 1798 -- after the male adult population of the territory reached 5,000 -- that the settlers were given the right to elect a house of representatives. The first meeting of the legislature convened in Cincinnati in 1799. The body elected Edward Tiffin as speaker of the House and William Henry Harrison as the territory's representative to Congress.

Though the territorial government was just getting on its feet in 1799, Ohio settlers were already clamoring for statehood. And just a few years later, in 1802, Congress passed an enabling bill that authorized the formation of a state government in Ohio. Ohio's first constitutional convention convened in Chillicothe in November of that same year. Ohio was admitted to the Union in 1803.

Ohio's capitol building stands on the corner of State and High streets in downtown Columbus. It is listed on the National Register of Historic Places as one of the state's most historically and architecturally significant buildings.

Chillicothe served as the temporary capital for the new state until 1810 when the legislature moved the capital to Zanesville. The capital was shuttled back to Chillicothe in 1812, while the legislature searched for a more centralized locaton. The legislature finally decided to build a new capital on "the high banks of the Scioto River." Columbus became Ohio's permanent capital in 1816.

Source - Ohio Secretary of State

STATE OF OHIO CONSTITUTION
1851 with amendments to 1990

ARTICLE I: BILL OF RIGHTS

Preamble

We, the people of the State of Ohio, grateful to Almighty God for our freedom, to secure its blessings and promote our common welfare, do establish this Constitution.

ARTICLE I: BILL OF RIGHTS

§1 Inalienable Rights. (1851)

All men are, by nature, free and independent, and have certain inalienable rights, among which are those of enjoying and defending life and liberty, acquiring, possessing, and protecting property, and seeking and obtaining happiness and safety.

§2 Right to alter, reform, or abolish government, and repeal special privileges. (1851)

All political power is inherent in the people. Government is instituted for their equal protection and benefit, and they have the right to alter, reform, or abolish the same, whenever they may deem it necessary; and no special privileges or immunities shall ever be granted, that may not be altered, revoked, or repealed by the General Assembly.

§3 [Right to assemble.] (1851)

The people have the right to assemble together, in a peaceable manner, to consult for their common good; to instruct their representatives; and to petition the General Assembly for the redress of grievances.

§4 [Bearing arms; standing armies; military power.] (1851)

The people have the right to bear arms for their defense and security; but standing armies, in time of peace, are dangerous to liberty, and shall not be kept up; and the military shall be in strict subordination to the civil power.

§5 Trial by jury. (1851; amended 1912)

The right of trial by jury shall be inviolate, except that, in civil cases, laws may be passed to authorize the rendering of a verdict by the concurrence of not less than three-fourths of the jury.

§6 [Slavery and involuntary servitude.] (1851)

There shall be no slavery in this state; nor involuntary servitude, unless for the punishment of crime.

§7 [Rights of conscience; education; the necessity of religion and knowledge.] (1851)

All men have a natural and indefeasible right to worship Almighty God according to the dictates of their own conscience. No person shall be compelled to attend, erect, or support any place of worship, or maintain any form of worship, against his consent; and no preference shall be given, by law, to any religious society; nor shall any interference with the rights of conscience be permitted. No religious test shall be required, as a qualification for office, nor shall any person be incompetent to be a witness on account of his religious belief; but nothing herein shall be construed to dispense with oaths and affirmations. Religion, morality, and knowledge, however, being essential to good government, it shall be the duty of the General Assembly to pass suitable laws, to protect every religious denomination in the peaceable enjoyment of its own mode of public worship, and to encourage schools and the means of instruction.

§8 [Writ of habeas corpus.] (1851)

The privilege of the writ of habeas corpus shall not be suspended, unless, in cases of rebellion or invasion, the public safety require it.

§9 Bailable offenses; bail, fine and punishment. (1851)

All persons shall be bailable by sufficient sureties, except for capital offenses where the proof is evident, or the presumption great. Excessive bail shall not be required; nor excessive fines be imposed; nor cruel and unusual punishments inflicted.

Continued on next page

Continued from preceeding page

§10 [Trial for crimes; witness.] (1851; amended 1912)

Except in cases of impeachment, cases arising in the army and navy, or in the militia when in actual service in time of war or public danger, and cases involving offenses for which the penalty provided is less than imprisonment in the penitentiary, no person shall be held to answer for a capital, or otherwise infamous, crime, unless on presentment or indictment of a grand jury; and the number of persons necessary to constitute such grand jury and the number thereof necessary to concur in finding such indictment shall be determined by law. In any trial, in any court, the party accused shall be allowed to appear and defend in person and with counsel; to demand the nature and cause of the accusation against him, and to have a copy thereof; to meet the witnesses face to face, and to have compulsory process to procure the attendance of witnesses in his behalf, and a speedy public trial by an impartial jury of the county in which the offense is alleged to have been committed; but provision may be made by law for the taking of the deposition by the accused or by the state, to be used for or against the accused, of any witness whose attendance can not be had at the trial, always securing to the accused means and the opportunity to be present in person and with counsel at the taking of such deposition, and to examine the witness face to face as fully and in the same manner as if in court. No person shall be compelled, in any criminal case, to be a witness against himself; but his failure to testify may be considered by the court and jury and may be the subject of comment by counsel. No person shall be twice put in jeopardy for the same offense.

§11 [Freedom of speech; of the press; of libels.] (1851)

Every citizen may freely speak, write, and publish his sentiments on all subjects, being responsible for the abuse of the right; and no law shall be passed to restrain or abridge the liberty of speech, or of the press. In all criminal prosecutions for libel, the truth may be given in evidence to the jury, and if it shall appear to the jury, that the matter charged as libelous is true, and was published with good motives, and for justifiable ends, the party shall be acquitted.

§ 12 Transportation, etc. for crime. (1851)

No person shall be transported out of the state, for any offense committed within the same; and no conviction shall work corruption of blood, or forfeiture of estate.

§13 [Quartering troops.] (1851)

No soldier shall, in time of peace, be quartered in any house, without the consent of the owner; nor, in time of war, except in the manner prescribed by law.

§14 Search warrants and general warrants. (1851)

The right of the people to be secure in their persons, houses, papers, and possessions, against unreasonable searches and seizures shall not be violated; and no warrant shall issue, but upon probable cause, supported by oath or affirmation, particularly describing the place to be searched and the person and things to be seized.

§ 15 No imprisonment for debt. (1851)

No person shall be imprisoned for debt in any civil action, on mesne or final process, unless in cases of fraud.

§16 [Redress in courts.] (1851; amended 1912)

All courts shall be open, and every person, for an injury done him in his land, goods, person, or reputation, shall have remedy by due course of law, and shall have justice administered without denial or delay.

Suits may be brought against the state, in such courts and in such manner, as may be provided by law.

§17 Hereditary privileges, etc. (1851)

No hereditary emoluments, honors, or privileges, shall ever be granted or conferred by this State.

§18 Suspension of laws. (1851)

No power of suspending laws shall ever be exercised, except by the General Assembly.

§19 [Inviolability of private property.] (1851)

Private property shall ever be held inviolate, but subservient to the public welfare. When taken in time of war or other public exigency, imperatively requiring its immediate seizure or for the purpose of making or repairing roads, which shall be open to the public, without charge, a compensation shall be made to the owner, in money, and in all other cases, where private property shall be taken for public use, a compensation therefor shall first be made in money, or first secured by a deposit of money; and such compensation shall be assessed by a jury, without deduction for benefits to any property of the owner.

§19a Damages for wrongful death. (1912)

The amount of damages recoverable by civil action in the courts for death caused by the wrongful act, neglect, or default of another, shall not be limited by law.

§20 Powers reserved to the people. (1851)

This enumeration of rights shall not be construed to impair or deny others retained by the people; and all powers, not herein delegated, remain with the people.

STATE OF OHIO ORGANIZATION CHART

Source - Ohio Secretary of State

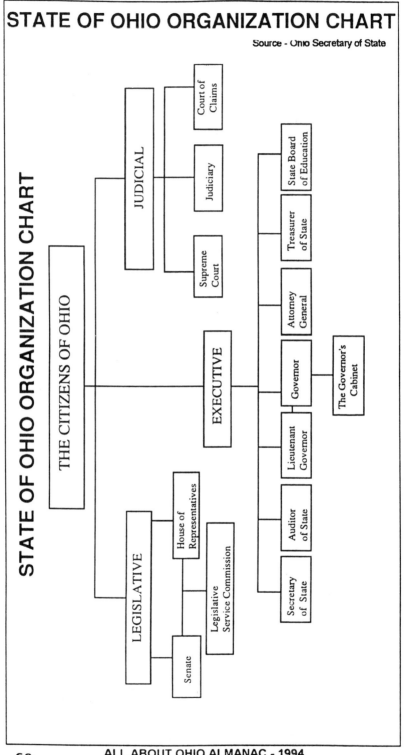

THE GOVERNOR'S CABINET

Source - Office of the Governor

Dept. of the Adjutant General
Maj. Gen. Richard Charles
Alexander, Adj. Gen.
2825 W. Dublin Granville Rd.
Columbus, OH 43235-2789
Phone: 614/889-7070

Dept. of Administrative Services
C. James Conrad, Dir.
30 E. Broad St.
Columbus, OH 43266-0401
Phone: 614/466-6511

Dept. of Aging
Judith Y. Brachman, Dir.
50 W. Broad St.
Columbus, OH 43266-0501
Phone: 614/466-7246

Dept. of Agriculture
Fred Dailey, Dir.
65 S. Front St.
Columbus, OH 43215
Phone: 614/466-2737

Dept. of Alcohol and Drug Addiction Services
Lucille Fleming, Dir.
Two Nationwide Plaza
280 N. High St.
Columbus, OH 43215-2537
Phone: 614/466-3445

Board of Regents
Elaine H. Hairston, Ph.D.
30 E. Broad St.
Columbus, OH 43266-0417
Phone 614/466-0887

Office of Budget and Management
R. Gregory Browning, Dir.
30 E. Broad St.
34th Floor
Columbus, OH 43266-0411
Phone: 614/466-4034

Dept. of Commerce
Nancy Chiles Dix, Dir.
77 S. High St.
Columbus, OH 43266-0550
Phone: 614/466-7047

George V. Voinovich, Governor

GOVERNOR'S OFFICE
Vern Riffe Center
77 S. High Street, 30th Floor
Columbus, OH 43215
General Information: (614) 466-3555
Fax: (614) 466-9354

Dept. of Development
Donald E. Jakeway, Dir.
77 S. High St.
Columbus, OH 43266-0101
Phone: 614/466-9398

Dept. of Education
Ted Sanders, Ph.D., Dir.
65 S. Front St.
Columbus, OH 43266-0308
Phone: 614/466-3304

Bureau of Employment Services
Debra Bowland, Administrator
145 S. Front St.
Columbus, OH 43215
Phone: 614/466-8032

Environmental Protection Agency
Donald R. Schregardus, Dir.
1800 WaterMark Dr.
P.O. Box 1049
Columbus, OH 43266-0149
Phone: 614/644-2782

Continued on next page

Continued from preceeding page

Dept. of Health
Peter Somani, M.D., Dir.
246 N. High St.
P.O. Box 118
Columbus, OH 43266-0188
Phone: 614/466-2253

Dept. of Highway Safety
Charles D. Shipley, Dir.
240 Parsons Ave.
P.O. Box 7167
Columbus, OH 43266-0563
Phone: 614/466-3383

Dept. of Housing & Community Development
Vincent Lombardi, Dir.
77 S. High St.
Columbus, OH 43266-0101
Phone: 614/466-4588

Dept. of Human Services
Arnold P. Tompkins
30 E. Broad St.
Columbus, OH 43266-0142
Phone: 614/466-6282

Industrial Commission
Donald Colasurd
30 W. Spring St.
Columbus, OH 43266-0589
Phone: 614/466-3010

Dept. of Industrial Relations
John P. Stozich, Dir.
2323 W. Fifth Ave.
P.O. Box 825
Columbus, OH 43226-0567
Phone: 614/644-2223

Office of State Inspector General
David D. Sturtz, Insp. Gen.
77 S. High St., 29th Floor
Columbus, OH 43215
Phone: 614/644-9110

Dept. of Insurance
Dir., Hal Duryee
2100 Stella Ct.
Columbus, OH 43266-0566
Phone: 614/644-2651

Dept. of Liquor Control
Michael A. Akrouche, Dir.
2323 W. Fifth Ave.
Columbus, OH 43266-0701
Phone 614/644-2472

Ohio Lottery Commission
Virgil E. Brown, Dir.
Frank J. Lausche Building
615 W. Superior Ave.
Cleveland, OH 44113
Phone: 216/787-3344

Dept. of Mental Health
Dr. Michael Hogan, Dir.
30 E. Broad St.
Columbus, OH 43266-0414
Phone: 614/466-2337

Dept. of Mental Retardation and Developmental Disabilities
Jerome C. Manuel, Dir.
30 E. Broad St.
Columbus, OH 43266-0415
Phone: 614/466-5214

Dept. of Natural Resources
Frances Seiberling Buchholzer, Dir.
1930 Belcher Dr.
Columbus, OH 43224-1387
Phone: 614/265-6875

Public Utilities Commission
Graig Glazer, Dir.
180 E. Broad St.
Columbus, OH 43266-0573
Phone: 614/466-3204

Dept. of Rehabilitation and Correction
Reginald A. Wilkinson, Dir.
1050 Freeway Dr.
Columbus, OH 43229
Phone: 614/721-1164

Dept. of Taxation
Roger W. Tracy, Tax Commissioner
30 E. Broad St., 22nd Floor
Columbus, OH 43215-0030
Phone: 614/466-2166

Dept. of Transportation
Jerry Wray, Dir.
25 S. Front St.
Columbus, OH 43215
Phone: 614/466-2335

Dept. of Youth Services
Geno Nataucci-Persichetti, Dir.
51 N. High St.
Columbus, OH 43266-0582
Phone: 614/466-8783
614/644-5177

U.S. SENATORS FROM OHIO
LOCAL OFFICES, TELEPHONES

Address & Phone
Washington, D.C. & Local

Source - Ohio Chamber of Commerce

John Glenn

Washington, D.C., 20510
503 Hart Office Bldg
Ph (202) 224-3353
Fax (202) 224-7983

Cleveland, 44144
201 Superior Av
Federal Courthouse Bldg, Room 111
Ph (216) 522-7095

Columbus, 43215
200 North High St, Room 600
Ph (614) 469-6697
Fax (614) 469-7733

Cincinnati, 45202
550 Main St
Suite 10407
Federal Bldg
Ph (513)684-3265

Toledo, 43604
234 N Summit St
Room 726
Ph (419) 259-7592

Howard M. Metzenbaum

Washington, D.C. 20510
SR140 Russell Office Bldg
Ph (202)224-2315
Fax (202) 224-6519

Cleveland 44199
1240 E. 9th St.
Room 2915
Ph (216) 522-7272

Columbus 43216
200 North High St.
Ph (614) 469-6774

Cincinnati 45202
10411 Federal Bldg.
Ph (513) 684-3894

Toledo 45202
234 N. Summit St.
Room 722
Ph (419) 259-7536

U.S. REPRESENTATIVES FROM OHIO
LOCAL OFFICES, TELEPHONES

District 1
David S. Mann

Washington, D.C. 20515
503 Cannon House
Office Bldg
Ph (202)225-2216

Cincinnati 45202
2210 Kroger Bldg.
1014 Vine St.
Ph (513) 684-2723
Fax (513) 421-8722

District 2
Rob Portman

Washington, D.C. 20515
238 Cannon House
Office Bldg
Ph (202)225-3164

Cincinnati 45202
550 Main St.
Room 8010
Ph (513) 684-2456
Fax (513) 651-2964

District 3
Tony P. Hall

Washington, D.C. 20515
2264 Rayburn House
Ph (202) 225-6465

Dayton 45202
200 W. 2nd St
Room 501
Ph (513)225-2823
Fax (513) 225-2752

Continued on next page

Continued from preceeding page

District 4
Michael G. Oxley

Washington, D.C. 20515
2233 Rayburn House
Ph (202) 225-2676

Lima 45805
3121 W. Elm Plaza
Ph (419) 999-6455

Findlay 45840
100 E. Main Cross St.
Ph (419) 423-3210

Mansfield 44902
24 W. Third St.
Room 314
Ph (419) 522-5757

District 5
Paul E. Gillmor

Washington, D.C. 20515
1203 Longworth
House Office Bldg.
Ph (202) 225-6405

Port Clinton 43452
120 Jefferson
Ph (414) 734-1999

Perrysburg 43551
148 E. South Boundary
Ph (419) 872-2500

District 6
Ted Strickland

Washington 20515
1429 Longworth
House Office Bldg
Ph (202)225-5705

Portsmouth 45662
1236 Gallia St.
Ph (513) 353-5171

District 7
David L. Hobson

Washington 20515
1507 Longworth
House Office Bldg
Ph (202) 225-4324

Springfield 45501
150 N. Limestone St.
Room 220
Ph (513) 325-0474

Lancaster 43130
212 S. Broad St.
Ph (614) 654-5149

District 8
John A. Boehner

Washington, D.C. 20515
1020 Longworth
Ph (202) 225-6205

Hamilton 45011
5617 Liberty-Fairfield Rd.
Ph (513) 8944-6003
Ph (800) 582-1001
Fax (513) 894-6127

District 9
Marcy Kaptur

Washington, D.C. 20515
2104 Rayburn House
Office Bldg
Ph (202) 225-4146

Toledo 43604
234 Summit St
Room 719
Federal Bldg
Ph (419) 259-7500

District 10
Martin R. Hoke

Washington, D.C. 20515
212 Cannon House
Office Bldg
Ph (202) 225-5871

Fairview Park 44126
21270 Lorain Rd.
Ph (216) 356-2010

District 11
Louis Stokes

Washington, D.C. 20515
2365 Rayburn House
Office Bldg
Ph (202) 225-7032

Cleveland 44199
2947 New Federal Bldg
Ph (216) 522-4900

Continued on next page

District 12
John R. Kasich

Washington, D.C. 20515
1131 Longworth House
Office Bldg
Ph (202) 225-5355

Columbus 43215
200 N. High St
Ph (614) 469-7318

District 13
Sherrod Brown

Washington, D.C. 20515
1407 Longworth House
Office Bldg
Ph (202) 2253401

Lorain 44053
1936 Cooper Foster Park
Ph (216) 282-5100

District 14
Thomas C. Sawyer

Washington, D.C. 20515
1414 Longworth House
Office Bldg
Ph (202) 225-5231

Akron 44311
411 Wolf Ledges Pkwy
Suite 105
Ph (216) 375-5710

District 15
Deborah D. Pryce

Washington, D.C. 20515
128 Cannon House
Office Bldg
Ph (202) 225-2015

Columbus 43216
200 N. High St
Suite 400 Ph (614) 469-5614

District 16
Ralph S. Regula

Washington, D.C. 20515
2309 Rayburn House
Office Bldg
Ph (202) 225-3876

Canton 44178
4150 Beldon Village St NW
Ph (216) 489-4414

District 17
James A. Traficant, Jr.

Washington, D.C. 20515
2446 Rayburn House
Office Bldg
Ph (202) 225-5261

Youngstown 44512
11 Overhill Rd
Ph (216) 788--2414

Niles 44456
555 Youngstown-Warren Rd
Suite 2685
Ph (216) 652-5649

District 18
Douglas Applegate

Washington, D.C. 20515
2183 Rayburn House
Ph (202) 225-6265

St. Clairsville 43950
Scott Complex Suite 2
46060 National Rd W.
Ph (614) 695-4600

Steubenville 43952
500 Market St.
Suite 610
Ph (614) 283-3716

New Philadelphia 44663
1330 4th St. NW
Ph (216) 343-9112

Zanesville 43701
225 Underwood
Ph (614) 452-7023

District 19
Eric D. Fingerhut

Washington, D.C. 20515
431 Cannon House
Office Bldg
Ph (202) 225-5731

Willoughby Hills 44094
2550 Som Center Rd.
Suite 385
Ph (216) 943-1919

STATE LEGISLATIVE DISTRICTS BY COUNTY

Source - General Assembly Staff

SENATE DISTRICT	COUNTY	HOUSE DISTRICT	SENATE DISTRICT	COUNTY	HOUSE DISTRICT
14	Adams	88	31	Licking	77, 78
12	Allen	1	26	Logan	87
19	Ashland	93	13	Lorain	61, 62, 63
18	Ashtabula	5	2, 11	Lucas	49-52, 53
20, 31	Athens	78, 96	10	Madison	74
1, 12	Auglaize	85, 86	33	Mahoning	64, 65, 57
20	Belmont	99	26	Marion	87, 90
14	Brown	72	22	Medina	15, 81
4	Butler	58, 59, 60	17	Meigs	94
33	Carroll	57	12	Mercer	84
12	Champaign	85	5, 12	Miama	43, 84
10	Clark	73, 74	20	Monroe	99
14	Clermont	71, 72	5, 6	Montgomery	38-43
14	Clinton	72	20	Morgan	96
30	Columbiana	3	19	Morrow	80
20	Coshocton	95	20	Muskingum	95, 96
26	Crawford	90	20	Noble	99
21-25	Cuyahoga	8-20	2	Ottawa	53
12	Darke	84	1	Paulding	83
1	Defiance	82	31	Perry	78
19	Delaware	80	16, 17	Pickaway	29, 91
2, 3	Erie	63, 53	14	Pike	88
31	Fairfield	6	28	Portage	48, 75
14	Fayette	88	4	Preble	60
3, 15, 16	Franklin	21-29	1	Putnam	83
1	Fulton	82	19	Richland	79, 80
17	Gallia	94	17	Ross	91
32	Geauga	68	26	Sandusky	89
10	Greene	76, 74	17	Scioto	92
30	Guernsey	97	26	Seneca	89
7-9	Hamilton	30-37	12	Shelby	85
1	Hancock	86	29, 33	Stark	54-56, pt. 57
1	Hardin	86	27, 28	Summit	44-48
30	Harrison	98	32	Trumbull	66, 67, 68
1	Henry	83	30	Tuscarawas	98, 99
14	Highland	88	26	Union	87
31	Hocking	78	1	Van Wert	83
20	Holmes	95	17	Vinton	91
13, 19	Huron	63, 93	7	Warren	2
17	Jackson	94	20	Washington	96. 99
30	Jefferson	98	22	Wayne	7
19	Knox	93	1	Williams	82
18	Lake	69, 70	2	Wood	4
17	Lawrence	92, 94	26	Wyandot	90

STATE SENATE

Address: Senate Bldg., Columbus, Ohio 43266-0604

Note: The 33 State Senators include people with a variety of occupations. The largest group are attorneys (14), identified below by "A," followed by "full time Senator" (11), identified below by an asterisk (*).

Source: Ohio General Assembly Staff

DIST.	NAME	POL.	RESIDENCE	OFFICE PHONE (614)	FULL TIME	FIRST TERM
1	M. Ben Gaeth	R	Defiance	466-8150	*	1974
2	Betty D. Montgomery	R	Columbus	466-8060	A	1990
3	Theodore M. Gray	R	Columbus	466-8064	*	1950
4	Barry Levey	R	Middletown	466-8072	A	1990
5	Neal F. Zimmers, Jr.	D	Dayton	466-6274	A	1974
6	Charles F. Horn	R	Dayton	466-4538	A	1984
7	Richard H. Finan	R	Cincinnati	466-9737	A	1978
8	Stanley J. Aronoff	R	Cincinnati	466-8068	A	1971
9	William F. Bowen	D	Cincinnati	466-5980	*	1970
10	Merle G. Kearns	R	Springfield	466-3780	*	
11	Linda Furney	D	Toledo	466-5204		1986
12	Robert R. Cupp	R	Lima	466-7584	A	
13	Alan J. Zaleski	D	Vermilion	644-7613	*	1982
14	Cooper Snyder	R	Hillsboro	466-8082		
15	Ben E. Espy	D	Columbus	466-5131	A	1992
16	Eugene J. Watts	R	Columbus	466-5981		
17	Jan Micheal Long	D	Circleville	466-8156	A	1986
18	Robert J. Boggs	D	Jefferson	644-7718	*	
19	Richard P. Schafrath	R	Columbus	466-8084		1986
20	Robert W. Ney	R	St. Clairsville	466-8076	*	
21	Jeffrey D. Johnson	D	Cleveland	466-4857	A	1990
22	Grace L. Drake	R	Solon	466-7505	*	
23	Anthony C. Sinagra	R	Lakewood	466-5123	A	1990
24	Gary C. Suhadolnik	R	Parma Hts	466-8056	*	
25	Judy Sheerer	D	Shaker Hts	466-4583	*	
26	Karen L. Gillmor	R	Old Fort	466-8049	*	
27	Roy L. Ray	R	Columbus	466-4823		1986
28	Robert D. Nettle	D	Akron	466-7041	*	
29	W. Scott Oelslager	R	Canton	466-0626	*	1986
30	Robert L. Burch	D	Dover	466-6508	A	
31	Steven O. Williams	R	Lancaster	466-5838	A	1990
32	Anthony A. Latell, Jr.	D	Girard	466-7182	*	
33	Joeph J. Vukovich, III	D	Poland	466-8285	A	1993

STATE HOUSE OF REPRESENTATIVES

Address: Ohio House of Representatives, 77 South High St., Columbus, OH 43266-0603

Note: The 99 State Representatives include people with a variety of occupations. The largest group are "full time legislators" which total 39 (identified below with an asterisk *).

Source - Ohio General Assembly Staff

DIST.	NAME	POL.	RESIDENCE	OFFICE PHONE (614)	FULL TIME	TERMS IN OFFICE
1	William E. Thompson	R	Delphos	466-9624		4
2	George E. Terwilleger	R	Maineville	644-6027	*	1
3	Sean D. Logan	D	Lisbon	466-8022	*	3
4	Randall Gardner	R	Bowling Green	466-8104		5
5	Ross Boggs, Jr.	D	Andover	466-1405	*	5
6	John D. Myers	R	Lancaster	466-8100	*	2
7	Ron Amstutz	R	Wooster	466-1474		7
8	C. J. Prentiss	D	Cleveland	466-7954		2
9	Barbara Boyd	D	Cleveland Hts.	644-5079	*	1
10	Troy Lee James	D	Cleveland	466-1414	*	14
11	Jane Louise Campbell	D	Cleveland	466-5441	*	5
12	Vermel M. Whalan	D	Cleveland	466-1408		5
13	Barbara C. Pringle	D	Cleveland	466-5921	*	7
14	Ronald Suster	D	Euclid	466-8012		7
15	Michael W. Wise	R	Chagrin Falls	644-6041		1
16	Edward F. Kasputis	R	Olmsted	466-0961		2
17	Madeline A. Cain	D	Lakewood	466-3454	*	3
18	Rocco J. Colonna	D	Brook Park	466-4895	*	10
19	Patrick A. Sweeney	D	Cleveland	466-3350	*	14
20	Ronald M. Mottl, Sr.	D	North Royalton	466-3485	*	5
21	Otto Beatty, Jr.	D	Columbus	466-5343		8
22	Ray Miller	D	Columbus	466-8010		7
23	Mike Stinziano	D	Columbus	466-5064		11
24	Jo Ann Davidson	R	Reynoldsburg	466-4847		7
25	James W. Mason	R	Columbus	644-6002		1
26	Patrick J. Tiberi	R	Columbus	644-6030	*	1
27	E. J. Thomas	R	Columbus	466-2473		5
28	Priscilla D. Mead	R	Columbus	644-6005	*	1
29	William B. Schuck	R	Columbus	466-9688		4
30	L. Helen Rankin	D	Cincinnati	466-5130	*	9

Continued on next page

Continued from preceeding page

31 William L. Mallory	D	Cincinnati	466-7197		14
32 Dale N. Van Vyven	R	Sharonville	466-8120		9
33 Jerome F. Luebbers	D	Cincinnati	466-5786		8
34 Cheryl Winkler	R	Cincinnati	466-2715	*	3
35 Louis W. Blessing, Jr.	R	Cincinnati	466-9091	*	6
36 Robert L. Schuler	R	Cincinnati	644-6023		1
37 Jacquelyn O'Brien	R	Anderson	644-6886	*	5
38 Rhine McLin	D	Dayton	466-8038		3
39 Thomas M. Roberts	D	Dayton	466-2960	*	5
40 Jeff Jacobson	R	Dayton	644-8051		2
41 J. Donald Mottley	R	W. Carrollton	644-6008		1
42 Robert L. Corbin	R	Dayton	466-6504		9
43 Robert E. Netzley	R	Laura	466-8114		17
44 Vernon Sykes	D	Akron	466-3100		6
45 Karen M. Doty	D	Akron	644-5085		1
46 Wayne M. Jones	D	Cuyahoga Falls	466-1177		4
47 Betty S. Sutton	D	Barberton	644-6037		1
48 Thomas M. Seese	D	Akron	644-7475	*	5
49 Casey C. Jones	D	Toledo	466-5427		13
50 Barney Quilter	D	Toledo	466-2075		14
51 Tim Greenwood	R	Toledo	644-6070		3
52 Sally A. Perz	R	Toledo	644-6017		1
53 Darrell W. Opfer	D	Oak Harbor	644-6011	*	1
54 William J. Healy	D	Canton	466-8030	*	10
55 Kirk Schuring	R	Canton	752-2435		1
56 Johnnie Maier, Jr.	D	Massillon	466-4491	*	2
57 Judy Carr	D	Alliance	644-5082	*	1
58 Scott R. Nein	R	Middletown	466-8550		2
59 Michael A. Fox	R	Hamilton	644-6721		10
60 Gene Krebs	R	Camden	644-5095		1
61 Joseph F. Koziura	D	Lorain	466-5141		5
62 John R. Bender	D	Elyria	644-5076	*	1
63 Katherine Herald Walsh	D	Vermillon	466-9072		3
64 Robert Francis Hagan	D	Youngstown	466-9435		4
65 Ronald V. Gerberry	D	Austintown Twp	466-6107	*	7
66 Michael G. Verich	D	Warren	466-5358		6
67 June H. Lucas	D	Mineral Ridge	466-3488	*	4
68 Diane V. Grendell	R	Chesterland	644-5088		1
69 Raymond Edward Sines	R	Perry	644-6074		3
70 Daniel P. Troy	D	Willowick	466-7251	*	6
71 Samuel T. Bateman	R	Milford	466-8134		6
72 Rose Vesper	R	New Richmond	644-6034		1
73 David Hartley	D	Springfield	466-3787	*	11
74 Joseph E. Haines	R	Xenia	466-0338		7
75 Paul H. Jones	D	Ravenna	466-8997	*	7
76 Marilyn J. Reid	R	Bevercreek	644-6020		1
77 Marc D. Guthrie	D	Heath	466-4361	*	6
78 Mary Abel	D	Athens	466-2575	*	3
79 Frank S. Sawyer	D	Mansfield	466-5802		6
80 Joan W. Lawrence	R	Galena	644-6711	*	6
81 William G. Batchelder	R	Medina	466-8140		14
82 Richard A. Hodges	R	Metamora	644-5091	*	1
83 Lynn Roger Wachtmann	R	Napoleon	466-3760		5
84 Jim Buchyy	R	Greenville	466-6344		6

Continued on next page

Continued from preceeding page

85	James D. Davis	R	St. Marys	466-8247		5
86	Charles R. Brading	R	Wapakoneta	466-3819		2
87	Edward K. Core	R	Rushsylvania	466-8147		2
88	Doug Whsite	R	Manchester	466-3506		2
89	Dwight Wise	D	Fremont	466-8020	*	6
90	Randy Weston	D	Morral	644-6265		2
91	Michael C. Shoemaker	D	Bourneville	644-7928		6
92	Vern Riffe	D	Wheelersburg	466-3246		18
93	L. Eugene Byers	R	Loudonville	466-9622		4
94	Mark Malone	D	South Point	466-3919	*	6
95	Joy Pudgett	R	Coshocton	644-6014	*	1
96	Tom Johnson	R	New Concord	644-8728	*	9
97	Greg L. DiDonato	D	New Philadelphia	466-5476	*	2
98	Jerry W. Krupinski	D	Steubennville	466-3735	*	4
99	Jack Cera	D	Bellaire	466-8035	*	6

FISHING OHIO RIVERS & LAKES

There are many other **Fishing Rivers** (Ohio Division of Wildlife Fish Management Division (614) 265- 6345) in the state that provide fishermen hours of enjoyment with excellent results. Among the many options, 24 of the best fishing rivers by region include:

Northeast Ohio
(District Three Wildlife Office
(216) 644-2293)
• BlackRiver
• Salt Creek
• VermilionRiver
• Grand River
• Little Beavercreek

Northwest Ohio
(District Two Wildlife Office
(419) 424-5000)
• Maumee River
• Sandusky River
• Huron River
• Vermilion River
• Auglaize River

Central Ohio
(District One Wildlife Office
(614) 481-6300)
• Darby Creek
• Kokosing River
• Olentangy River
• Scioto River
• Deer Creek

Southeast Ohio
(District Four Wildlife Of~Ice
(614) 594-2211)
• Muskingum River
• LittleMuskingumRiver
• Sunfish Creek
• Captina Creek

Southwest Ohio
(District Five Wildlife Office
(513) 426-4961)
• Great Miami River
• Little Miami River
• Stillwater River
• Ohio Brush Creek
• White Oak Creek

Continued on page 76

PROPERTY VALUES IN OHIO & BY COUNTY

CALENDAR YEAR 1992 (COLLECTION 1993)

All real property in Ohio (except real railroad property) is classified by county auditors into one of five categories, depending on the property's highest or best probable use or current use for certain agricultural property. The categories, with their $ taxable value and the percent of the total value is shown on the right for the State, and below for the two principal categories (residential and commercial) for each county.

RESIDENTIAL
$68,970,944,010   67.3 %
COMMERCIAL
$21,916,094,900   21.4 %
INDUSTRIAL
$6,321,948,560   6.2 %
AGRICULTURE
$5,162,416,870   5.0 %
MINERAL
$138,665,430   0.1 %

TOTAL VALUE
$102,510,069,770

COUNTY	RESIDENTIAL	%	COMMERCIAL	%
Total	$68,970,944,010	67.3 %	$21,916,094,900	21.4 %
Adams	66,303,240	38.0	12,482,230	7.2
Allen	574,448,000	67.8	152,458,630	18.0
Ashland	217,453,190	65.1	44,442,990	13.3
Ashtabula	402,835,100	60.0	111,349,200	16.6
Athens	184,780,830	60.6	70,886,470	23.3
Auglaize	231,650,740	65.4	50,100,760	14.1
Belmont	270,224,040	64.6	78,581,900	18.8
Brown	140,626,190	64.7	23,348,950	10.7
Butler	2,115,533,010	72.3	470,535,120	16.1
Carroll	100,732,090	53.8	18,433,670	9.9
Champaign	178,960,280	63.6	28,364,570	10.1
Clark	858,056,230	73.0	201,558,130	17.1
Clermont	971,807,400	69.1	335,056,400	23.8
Clinton	145,535,800	56.0	40,962,350	15.8
Columbiana	477,132,860	70.3	99,746,120	14.7
Coshocton	144,203,350	54.2	33,766,540	12.7
Crawford	188,944,560	61.9	44,736,830	14.7
Cuyahoga	11,353,944,870	67.8	4,307,334,080	25.7
Darke	238,989,980	61.6	42,483,170	10.9
Defiance	181,765,380	63.7	38,879,460	13.6
Delaware	791,876,470	77.9	116,090,380	11.4
Erie	554,895,310	68.4	146,869,690	18.1
Fairfield	725,188,510	73.9	144,778,190	14.8
Fayette	104,217,680	53.9	27,490,310	14.2
Franklin	6,789,002,630	60.2	3,578,939,440	31.8
Fulton	198,107,480	59.3	40,030,160	12.0
Gallia	87,353,850	46.9	62,552,700	33.6
Geauga	852,236,110	76.8	90,230,020	8.1
Greene	1,108,749,560	78.1	210,530,690	14.8
Guernsey	144,066,440	61.8	41,585,630	17.8
Hamilton	6,464,911,300	66.7	2,543,740,690	26.2
Hancock	434,958,620	61.2	119,112,470	16.7

Continued on next page

COUNTY	RESIDENTIAL	%	COMMERCIAL	%
Hardin	$97,686,150	52.6 %	$22,747,170	12.2 %
Harrison	56,565,200	52.5	11,491,480	10.7
Henry	126,299,760	57.6	18,926,850	8.6
Highland	131,725,920	61.4	26,676,520	12.4
Hocking	124,324,490	75.2	15,429,830	9.3
Holmes	114,987,220	43.5	30,051,530	11.4
Huron	274,203,700	65.4	71,176,590	17.0
Jackson	96,032,640	58.4	24,183,940	14.7
Jefferson	280,709,780	63.2	68,228,520	15.4
Knox	230,550,470	64.1	41,345,630	11.5
Lake	1,904,062,250	70.4	547,722,770	20.2
Lawrence	226,465,600	70.3	51,185,220	15.9
Licking	792,187,940	70.5	181,999,600	16.2
Logan	262,380,160	67.3	50,305,750	12.9
Lorain	1,751,435,260	75.9	369,738,530	16.0
Lucas	2,819,699,970	68.6	1,043,604,720	25.4
Madison	174,879,840	64.5	32,058,760	11.8
Mahoning	1,240,069,980	72.1	335,322,480	19.5
Marion	269,903,120	63.2	78,160,570	18.3
Medina	1,078,043,020	75.6	178,695,100	12.5
Meigs	62,965,760	45.5	12,705,280	9.2
Mercer	200,283,890	58.2	42,253,590	12.3
Miami	674,269,170	73.4	118,228,860	12.9
Monroe	45,195,130	42.2	6,951,800	6.5
Montgomery	3,812,714,700	69.6	1,313,811,650	24.0
Morgan	40,729,300	40.2	16,211,900	16.0
Morrow	107,898,600	62.7	13,547,300	7.9
Muskingum	329,213,640	64.0	100,863,260	19.6
Noble	32,406,170	41.2	5,795,420	7.4
Ottawa	389,707,590	67.5	81,184,040	14.1
Paulding	78,291,160	58.2	10,395,700	7.7
Perry	98,731,970	62.1	17,107,950	10.8
Pickaway	209,073,500	63.4	41,273,580	12.5
Pike	70,970,650	61.8	14,006,000	12.2
Portage	826,659,060	73.7	160,572,120	14.3
Preble	182,798,910	64.4	26,592,620	9.4
Putnam	148,532,800	59.5	22,935,370	9.2
Richland	595,505,940	66.8	183,569,680	20.6
Ross	265,400,250	62.6	63,146,200	14.9
Sandusky	313,126,100	65.5	65,378,470	13.7

Continued on next page

COUNTY	RESIDENTIAL	%	COMMERCIAL	%
Scioto	$274,836,900	67.5 %	$78,901,130	19.4 %
Seneca	240,901,900	61.4	53,958,130	13.7
Shelby	230,255,360	60.4	46,902,500	12.3
Stark	2,173,498,460	70.2	609,871,270	19.7
Summit	3,715,187,430	71.7	1,173,443,230	22.7
Trumbull	1,088,531,740	68.0	272,369,570	17.0
Tuscarawas	404,836,600	61.5	113,164,980	17.2
Union	175,204,950	50.2	40,754,220	11.7
Van Wert	132,962,180	57.8	27,455,690	11.9
Vinton	29,307,410	46.1	4,270,370	6.7
Warren	910,582,360	73.2	224,625,100	18.1
Washington	257,807,470	57.1	74,879,760	16.6
Wayne	563,095,630	66.2	117,887,430	13.9
Williams	168,060,830	62.8	32,815,680	12.3
Wood	682,171,450	67.3	185,482,110	18.3
Wyandot	87,525,480	53.2	16,273,440	9.9

Source: Records submitted by county auditors to the Ohio Department of Taxation.

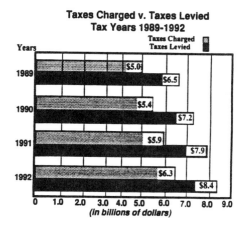

Taxes Charged v. Taxes Levied
Tax Years 1989-1992

Taxes charged on all real estate and public utility tangible property by all local governments in Ohio for calendar year 1992 (1993 collection) were $6,289.9 million on a total assessed value of $117,243.9 million, as reported on abstracts filed by the county auditors. This compares to $8,413.0 million in taxes levied on the same property.

Percentage reductions required by Section 319.301 of the Ohio Revised Code were applied to the gross amount of taxes levied to obtain the net amount of taxes charged.

Planning and
Service Areas or
PSAs for various
aging programs.
★ Denotes area
agency location

CONTINUED FROM PAGE 72
FISHING

Ohio is home to many **Lakes and Reservoirs** that offer an excellent fishing experience. Some of the most popular sites by region and their primary fish populations are included below.

Northeast Ohio (District Three Wildlife Office (216) 644-2293)
- Berlin Reservoir: crappie, smallmouth bass, white bass
- Clendening Reservoir: largemouth bass, saugeye
- Pymatuning Reservoir: walleye, bluegill, smallmouth bass, crappie
- Mosquito Creek Reservoir: walleye, crappie, bluegill
- Leesville Lake: muskellunge
- West Branch Reservoir: muskellunge, striped bass, large mouth bass

Continued on next page

Area Agencies on Aging

PSA 1
Council on Aging of the
Cincinnati Area, Inc.
644 Linn Street
Holiday Office Park/#1100
Cincinnati, Ohio 45203
Phone: 513/721-1025
Fax: 513/721-0090
Bob Logan, Director

PSA 2
Area Agency on Aging,
PSA 2
6 South Patterson Blvd./#200
Dayton, Ohio 45402
Phone: 513/341-3000
Fax: 513/341-3005
Doug McGarry, Director

PSA 3
Area Agency on Aging
311 Building/# 201
311 East Market Street
Lima, Ohio 45801
Phone: 419/222-7723
Fax: 419/222-6212
Harold K. Dahill, Director

PSA 4
Area Office on Aging of
Northwestern Ohio, Inc.
2155 Arlington Avenue
Toledo, Ohio 43609-0624
Phone: 419/382-0624
Fax: 419/382-4560
Billie Johnson, Director

PSA 5
Ohio District 5 Area Agency
on Aging, Inc.
235 Marion Avenue
P.O. Box 1978 (mailing only)
Mansfield, Ohio 44901
Phone: 419/524-4144
Fax: 419/522-9482
Patricia Brammer, Director

PSA 6
Central Ohio Area Agency
on Aging
174 E. Long Street
Columbus, Ohio 43215
Phone: 614/645-7250
Fax: 614/645-3884

PSA 7
Area Agency on Aging
District 7, Inc.
218 N. College
P.O. Box 978 (mail only)
University of Rio Grande
Rio Grande, Ohio 45674
Phone: 614/245-5306
Fax: 614/245-5979
Pamela Matura, Director

PSA 8
Area Agency on Aging
Buckeye Hills-Hocking
Valley Regional
Development District
Route 1/Box 299D
Marietta, Ohio 45750
Phone: 614/374-9436
Fax: 614/374-8038
Cindy Farson, Director

PSA 9
Area Agency on Aging
Region 9
Southgate Office Center
60788 Southgate Road
S. R. 209S
Byesville, Ohio 43723
Phone: 614/439-4478
Fax: 614/432-1060
Shirley Blackledge, Director

PSA 10A
Western Reserve Area
Agency on Aging
1030 Euclid Avenue/#318
Cleveland, Ohio 44115
Phone: 216/621-8010
Fax: 216/621-9262
Ron Hill, Director

PSA 10B
Area Agency on Aging
1550 Corporate Woods
Parkway/#100
Uniontown, Ohio 44685
Phone: 216/896-9172
Fax: 216/896-6644
Toll free: 1/800-421-7277
Joseph Ruby, Director

PSA 11
District XI Area Agency
on Aging
Ohio One Building
25 East Boardman Street
Youngstown, Ohio 44503
Phone: 216/746-2938
Fax: 216/746-6700
Donald J. Medd, Director

CONTINUED FROM PAGE 76 **FISHING**

Northwest Ohio (District Two Wildlife Office (419) 424-5000)
• Findlay Reservoir #1 and #2: walleye, largemouth bass, small
mouth bass, channel catfish and white bass
• Bresler Reservoir: walleye, bluegill, channel catfish, bull
heads
• Ferguson Reservoir: walleye, yellow perch, white bass, small
mouth bass
• Clear Fork Reservoir: muskellunge, crappie
• Lake La Su An Wildlife Area: largemouth bass, bluegill

Continued on page 163

Source - Ohio Dept. of Education.

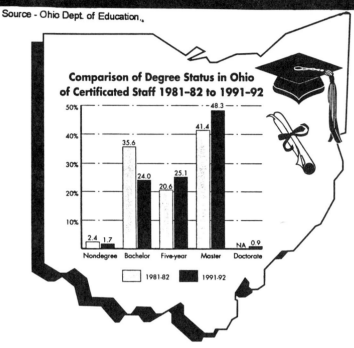

**Comparison of Degree Status in Ohio
of Certificated Staff 1981–82 to 1991–92**

	Nondegree	Bachelor	Five-year	Master	Doctorate
1981-82	2.4	35.6	20.6	41.4	NA
1991-92	1.7	24.0	25.1	48.3	0.9

☐ 1981-82 ■ 1991-92

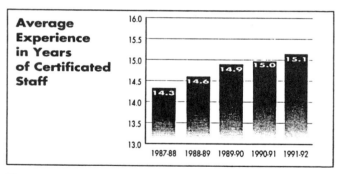

Average Experience in Years of Certificated Staff

1987-88	1988-89	1989-90	1990-91	1991-92
14.3	14.6	14.9	15.0	15.1

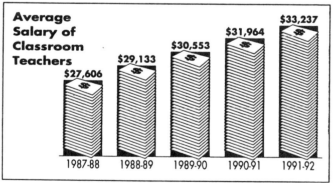

Average Salary of Classroom Teachers

1987-88	1988-89	1989-90	1990-91	1991-92
$27,606	$29,133	$30,553	$31,964	$33,237

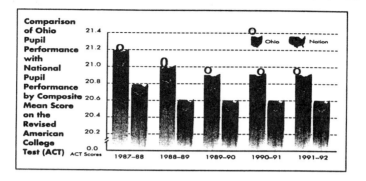

Comparison of Ohio Pupil Performance with National Pupil Performance by Composite Mean Score on the Revised American College Test (ACT)

ACT Scores

| | 1987–88 | 1988–89 | 1989–90 | 1990–91 | 1991–92 |

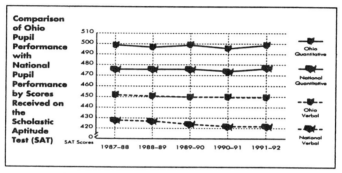

Comparison of Ohio Pupil Performance with National Pupil Performance by Scores Received on the Scholastic Aptitude Test (SAT)

SAT Scores

Ohio Ninth-Grade Proficiency Tests

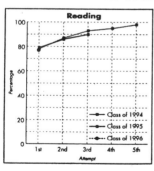

Reading

— Class of 1994
— Class of 1995
—•— Class of 1996

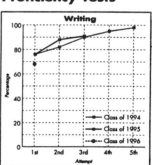

Writing

— Class of 1994
— Class of 1995
—•— Class of 1996

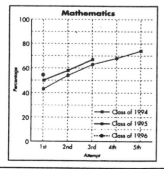

Mathematics

— Class of 1994
— Class of 1995
—•— Class of 1996

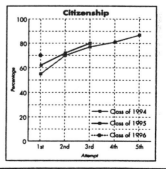

Citizenship

— Class of 1994
— Class of 1995
—•— Class of 1996

ALL ABOUT OHIO ALMANAC - 1994

79

Ohio School Revenue

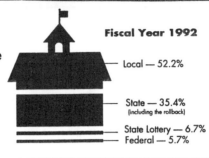

Fiscal Year 1992

Local — 52.2%

State — 35.4%
(including the rollback)

State Lottery — 6.7%
Federal — 5.7%

Ohio and National Average Expenditure Per Pupil

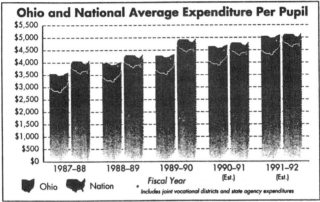

Fiscal Year	1987–88	1988–89	1989–90	1990–91 (Est.)	1991–92 (Est.)

■ Ohio   ■ Nation   • *Includes joint vocational districts and state agency expenditures*

General Revenue Fund Expenditures
(Excluding Federal Aid)
Fiscal Year 1992:
$10,118.2 Million

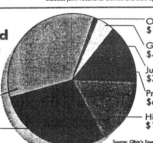

Other Expenditure
$128.0 (1.3%)

General Government
$451.5 (4.5%)

Justice & Corrections
$762.7 (7.5%)

Property Tax Relief
$675.7 (6.7%)

Higher Education
$1,656.8 (16.4%)

Human Services
$3,500.7 (34.5%)

Primary & Secondary
Education
$2,942.8 (29.1%)

Source: Ohio's Taxes – A Brief Summary of Major State
and Local Taxes in Ohio 1993
The Ohio Department of Taxation,
January 1993, p.49.

Schools/Districts

Enrollment by Grades 1991-92	
Grade	Enrollment
1	149,276
2	137,618
3	138,092
4	140,371
5	141,323
6	140,831
7	140,308
8	131,363
Total 1-8	1,119,182
9	146,783
10	126,550
11	119,909
12	113,304
Ungraded	3,283
Total 9-12	506,546
Total 1-12	1,625,728
Preschool	12,425
Kindergarten	142,063
Grand Total	1,783,449

Districts (1991-92)	
City	192
Exempted Village	49
Local	372
TOTAL	613
Joint Vocational	49
County Offices	88

Total Public School Enrollment

Year	State Total
1987-88	1,793,431
1988-89	1,778,397
1989-90	1,764,459
1990-91	1,771,089
1991-92	1,783,499

Nonpublic Schools (1991-92)	
High Schools	136
Middle Schools	6
Elementary Schools	707
Special Needs Schools	1
TOTAL	850

Public Schools (1991-92)	
Senior High Schools	714
Junior High Schools	179
Middle Schools	406
Elementary Schools	2,336
Adult Schools	5
Vocational Schools (Non-Joint Districts)	21
Vocational Schools (Districts)	61
Special Needs Schools	27
TOTAL	3,749

Public School Future Enrollment Trends

	First Grade	State Total
1994-95	144,323	1,792,653
1995-96	152,817	1,806,019
1996-97	152,657	1,819,900
1997-98	153,645	1,830,604
1998-99	154,679	1,838,477
1999-2000	155,704	1,847,016
2000-2001	156,744	1,855,993
2001-2002	157,827	1,867,828

OHIO EDUCATION FACILITIES

—13 public state universities
—23 community and technical colleges
—24 university regional campuses
—48 private liberal arts colleges
—more than 70 specialized colleges
—4,594 public, private and parochial schools

NONPUBLIC SCHOOLS IN OHIO

II. Nonpublic Schools (1991-92)

High Schools	136
Middle Schools	6
Elementary Schools	707
Special Needs Schools	1
TOTAL	850

NOTICE
Recommended College Preparation

To assist students in making a smooth transition from high school to college, the Ohio Department of Education and the Ohio Board of Regents recommend a college preparatory program which includes:

4 years of English, with emphasis on composition,
3 years of mathematics (including algebra I and II, and plane geometry) one of which should be taken in the senior year,
3 years of science,
3 years of social studies, and
2 years of foreign language

Students who pursue this curriculum will have strong preparation for college which, when combined with proper motivation and study habits, should result in academic success. They will also have more flexibility relative to career interests and college plans.

In response to this recommended college preparatory program, most state universities have revised requirements for admission, incorporating coursework appropriate to their particular expectations for entering freshmen. Because requirements vary from university to university, and because changes are still being made, counselors and students are encouraged to check the latest information with each admissions office.

Continued from preceeding page

FOUR-YEAR CAMPUSES

1. University of Akron
2. Allegheny Wesleyan College
3. Antioch University
4. The Art Academy of Cincinnati
5. Ashland University
6. The Athenaeum of Ohio
7. Baldwin-Wallace College
8. Bluffton College
9. Borromeo College of Ohio
10. Bowling Green State University
11. Capital University
12. Case Western Reserve University
13. Cedarville College
14. Central State University
15. Cincinnati Bible College & Seminary
16. Cincinnati Christian College
17. University of Cincinnati
18. Circleville Bible College
19. Cleveland College of Jewish Studies
20. Cleveland Institute of Art
21. Cleveland Institute of Music
22. Cleveland State University
23. Columbus College of Art & Design
24. University of Dayton

25. The Defiance College
26. Denison University
27. Dyke College
28. University of Findlay
29. Franciscan University of Steubenville
30. Franklin University
31. Heidelberg College
32. Hiram College
33. John Carroll University
34. Kent State University
35. Kenyon College
36. Lake Erie College
37. Lourdes College
38. Malone College
39. Marietta College
40. Miami University
41. Mt. Carmel College of Nursing
42. College of Mount St. Joseph
43. Mount Union College
44. Mt. Vernon Nazarene College
45. Muskingum College
46. Northeastern Ohio Universities College of Medicine
47. Notre Dame College of Ohio

48. Oberlin College
49. Ohio Dominican College
50. Ohio Northern University
51. The Ohio State University
52. Ohio University
53. Ohio Wesleyan University
54. Otterbein College
55. Pontifical College Josephinum
56. University of Rio Grande
57. Shawnee State University
58. Temple Baptist College
59. Tiffin University
60. University of Toledo
61. The Union Institute
62. Urbana University
63. Ursuline College
64. Walsh College
65. Wilberforce University
66. Wilmington College
67. Wittenberg University
68. The College of Wooster
69. Wright State University
70. Xavier University
71. Youngstown State University

Continued on next page

COLLEGES & UNIVERSITIES IN OHIO - PUBLIC & PRIVATE
Source: Ohio Department of Education

C   CONTROL   P = Public   PR = Private

T&F   TUITION AND FEES in $1,000, annually. Typically public schools' charges are double the amounts shown for students from out-of-state. Private schools typically charge the same amount for all students from in-state and out-of-state.

TE   TOTAL EXPENSES, in $1,000, annually. Includes tuition & fees, room & board, books and personal travel. Total expenses for out-of-state students at public schools are higher by the amount noted above.

NS   NUMBER OF UNDERGRADUATE STUDENTS, in thousands.

Source - Ohio Dept of Education

MAP	COLLEGE OR UNIVERSITY	C	T&F	TE	S
1	U of Akron, Akron 44325	P	$ 3-	$ 6+	24
2	Allegheny Wesleyan C, Salem 44460	PR	$ 2-	$ 4	0.1-
3	Antioch U, Yellow Springs 45387	PR	$14+	$18+	7
4	Art Acad of Cincinnati, Cincinnati 45202	PR	$ 8	N/A	0.3
5	Ashland U, Ashland 44805	PR	$11	$15	2.3
7	Baldwin-Wallace C, Berea 44017	PR	$10+	$15	4
8	Bluffton C, Bluffton 45817	PR	$ 9-	$12+	0.7
9	Borromeo C of Ohio, Wicklittle 44092	PR	$ 5+	$ 9+	0.1-
10	Bowling Green St U, Bowling Green 43403	P	$ 3+	$ 6	16
11	Capital U, Columbus 43209	PR	$12	$15	2+
12	Case Western Reserve U, Cleveland 44106	PR	$15	$20	3+
13	Cedarville C, Cedarville 45314	PR	$ 6+	$10	2+
14	Central St U, Wilburforce 45384	P	$ 2+	$ 6	3-
15	Cincinnati Bible C & Seminary, Cincinnati 45204	PR	$ 4	$ 7	0.7
16	Cincinnati Christian C, Cincinnati 45229	PR	$ 1+	$ 2+	0.1-
17	U of Cincinnati, Cincinnati 45221	P	$ 3+	$ 7+	14-
18	Circleville Bible C, Circleville 43113	PR	$ 4+	$ 7+	0.2
19	Cleveland C of Jewish Studies, Beachwood 44122	PR	$ 4-	N/A	0.4-
20	Cleveland Inst of Art, Cleveland 44106	PR	$10+	$14+	0.5
21	Cleveland Inst of Music, Cleveland, 44106	PR	$13+	$18	0.2
22	Cleveland St U, Cleveland 44115	P	$ 3-	$ 6+	14-
23	Columbus C of Art & Design, Columbus 43215	PR	$ 9-	$13+	2-
24	U of Dayton, Dayton 45469	PR	$10	$13	6+
25	Defiance C, Defiance 43512	PR	$10-	$14	1
26	Denison U, Grannville 43023	PR	$16	$20	2+
27	Dyke C, Cleveland 44115	PR	$ 5+	N/A	.1+
28	U of Findlay, Findlay 45840	PR	$10	$15	3-
29	Franciscan U of Steubenville, Steubenville 43952	PR	$ 8+	$12+	2-

Continued on next page

MAP	COLLEGE OR UNIVERSITY	C	T&F	TE	S
30	Franklin U, Columbus 43512	PR	$ 4+	N/A	4
31	Heidelberg C, Tiffin 44883	PR	$12+	$17+	1+
32	Hiram C, Hiram 44234	PR	$13	$17	1-
33	John Carroll U, University Hts 44118	PR	$10-	$16	4-
34	Kent State U, Kent 44242	P	$ 3+	$ 7-	20-
35	Kenyon C, Gambler 43022	PR	$18	$22	1+
36	Lake Erie C, Painesville 44077	PR	$ 9-	$13	0.6
37	Lourdes C, Sylvania 43560	PR	$ 6+	N/A	1+
38	Malone C, Canton 44709	PR	$ 8+	$12	2-
39	Marietta C, Marietta 45750	PR	$12+	$16	1+
40	Miami U, Oxford 45056	P	$ 7	$11	14+
41	Mt Carmel C of Nursing, Columbus 43222	PR	$ 8-	$12+	0.1
42	C of Mount St Joseph, Mt St Joseph 45041	PR	$ 9	$13	2+
43	Mount Union C, Alliance 44601	PR	$12	$16	1+
44	Mt Vernon Nazarene C, Mt Vernon 43050	PR	$ 7-	$10	1+
45	Muskingum C, New Concord 43762	PR	$13-	$16	1+
46	NE Ohio U C of Medicine, Rootstown 44272	P	$ 8+	$16+	0.2+
47	Notre Dame C of Ohio, Cleveland 44121	PR	$ 8-	$11	1-
48	Oberlin C, Oberlin 44074	PR	$18	$23	3-
49	Ohio Dominican C, Columbus 43219	PR	$ 7+	$11+	1+
50	Ohio Northern U, Ada 45810	PR	$12+	$16-	2+
51	Ohio State U, Columbus 43210	P	$ 3-	$ 6+	41
52	Ohio U, Athens 45701	P	$ 3+	$ 7	15
53	Ohio Wesleyan U, Delaware 43015	PR	$15	$20+	2+
54	Otterbein C, Westerville 43061	PR	$12-	$16	2+
55	Pontifical C Josephinum, Columbus 43235	PR	$ 5	$ 8+	0.1-
56	U of Rio Grande, Rio Grande 45674	PR	$ 5	$ 8-	0.5
57	Shawnee St U, Portsmouth 45662	P	$ 2+	$ 4	3+
58	Temple Baptist C, Cincinnati 45240	PR	$ 2+	N/A	N/A
59	Tiffin U, Tiffin 44883	PR	$ 7-	$10+	1
60	U of Toledo, Toledo 43606	P	$ 3	$ 6	22
61	Union Inst, Cincinnati 45206	PR	$ 7-	N/A	0.3
62	Urbana U, Urbana 43078	PR	$ 8-	$12	1
63	Ursuline C, Pepper Pike 44124	PR	$ 8-	$12-	1+
64	Walsh C, Canton 44720	PR	$ 7+	$11	1+
65	Wilberforce U, Wilberforce 45364	PR	$ 6+	$10+	1-
66	Wilmington C, Wilmington 45177	PR	$11	$16	1-
67	Wittenberg U, Springfield 45501	PR	$14+	$19	2+
68	C of Wooster, Wooster 44691	PR	$14+	$19	2-
69	Wright St U, Dayton 45435	P	$ 3-	$ 7+	13
70	Xavier U, Cincinnati 45207	PR	$10+	$15+	4+
71	Youngstown St U, Youngstown 44555	P	$ 3-	$ 6+	14+

Continued on next page

Continued from preceeding page

TWO-YEAR CAMPUSES

1. Agricultural Technical Institute -
   The Ohio State University
2. University of Akron - Wayne
3. Belmont Technical College
4. Bowling Green State University - Firelands
5. Central Ohio Technical College
6. Chatfield College
7. Cincinnati College of Mortuary Science
8. Cincinnati Technical College
9. University of Cincinnati - Clermont
10. University of Cincinnati - Raymond Walters
11. Clark State Community College
12. Columbus State Community College
13. Cuyahoga Community College - East
14. Cuyahoga Community College - Metro
15. Cuyahoga Community College - West
16. Edison State Community College
17. Hocking Technical College

18. Jefferson Technical College
19. Kent State University - Ashtabula
20. Kent State University - East Liverpool
21. Kent State University - Geauga
22. Kent State University - Salem
23. Kent State University - Stark
24. Kent State University - Trumbull
25. Kent State University - Tuscarawas
26. Kettering College of Medical Arts
27. Lakeland Community College
28. Lima Technical College
29. Lorain County Community College
30. Marion Technical College
31. Miami University - Hamilton
32. Miami University - Middletown
33. Muskingum Area Technical College
34. North Central Technical College
35. Northwest Technical College

36. The Ohio State University - Lima
37. The Ohio State University - Mansfield
38. The Ohio State University - Marion
39. The Ohio State University - Newark
40. Ohio University - Belmont
41. Ohio University - Chillicothe
42. Ohio University - Ironton
43. Ohio University - Lancaster
44. Ohio University - Zanesville
45. Owens Technical College - Toledo
46. Owens Technical College - Findlay
47. Rio Grande Community College
48. Sinclair Community College
49. Southern State Community College
50. Stark Technical College
51. Terra Technical College
52. Washington Technical College
53. Wright State University - Lake Campus

JR. COLLEGES - OHIO - PUBLIC & PRIVATE
Source: Ohio Department of Education

C   CONTROL   P = Public   PR = Private

T&F   TUITION AND FEES in $1,000, annually. Typically public schools' charges are double the amounts shown for students from out-of-state. Private schools typically charge the same amount for all students from in-state and out-of-state.

TE   TOTAL EXPENSES, in $1,000, annually. Includes tuition & fees, room & board, books and personal travel. Total expenses for out-of-state students at public schools are higher by the amount noted above.

NS   NUMBER OF UNDERGRADUATE STUDENTS, in thousands.

Source - Ohio Dept of Education

MAP	INSTITUTION	C	T&F	TE	S
1	Agricultural Tech Inst-OSU, Wooster 44691	P	$ 2+	$ 7+	0.6
2	U of Akron - Wayne, Orville 44667	P	$ 3-	N/A	1+
3	Belmont Tech C, St Clairsville 43950	P	$ 1	$ 6+	2-
4	Bowling Green St U - Firelands, Huron 44839	P	$ 2+	$ 6+	1+
5	Central Ohio Tech C, Newark 43055	P	$ 2-	$ 5+	2-
6	Chatfield C, St Martin 45118	PR	$ 4-	$ 7-	0.2
7	Cincinnati C of Mortuary Science, Cincinnati 45207	PR	$ 6+	$10	0.1
8	Cincinnati Tech C, Cincinnati 45223	P	$ 2+	$ 6-	5-
9	U of Cincinnati - Clermont, Batavia 45103	P	$ 2-	$ 4+	1+
10	U of Cincinnati - Raymond Walters, Cincinnati 45326	P	$ 3-	$ 4-	4+
11	Clark St Comm C, Springfield 45501	P	$ 2+	$ 5	7+
12	Columbus St Comm C,	P	$ 2-	$ 8+	12
13	Cuyahoga Comm C - East, Warrenville 44122	P	$ 1+	$ 5+	6-
14	Cuyahoga Comm C - Metro, Cleveland 44116	P	$ 1+	$ 5+	5+
15	Cuyahoga Comm C - West, Parma 44130	P	$ 1+	$ 5+	12
16	Edison St Comm C, Piqua 45356	P	$ 1+	$ 2+	4+
17	Hocking Tech C, Nelsonville 45764	P	$ 2-	$ 6+	4+
18	Jefferson Tech C, Steubenville 43952	P	$ 1-	$ 4	1+
19	Kent St U - Ashtabula, Ashtabula 44044	P	$ 2-	$ 6+	1
20	Kent St U - East Liverpool, E. Liverpool 43920	P	$ 2-	$ 6+	0.7
21	Kent St U - Geauga, Burton 44021	P	$ 2-	$ 6-	0.5
22	Kent St U - Salem, Salem 44460	P	$ 2-	$ 6-	1
23	Kent St U - Stark, Canton 44720	P	$ 2-	$ 6+	2-
24	Kent St U - Trumbull, Warren 44483	P	$ 2-	$ 6	1+
25	Kent St U - Tuscarawas, New Philadelphia 44663	P	$ 2-	$ 4+	1-

Continued on next page

MAP	COLLEGE OR UNIVERSITY	C	T&F	TE	S
26	Kettering C of Medical Arts, Kettering 45429	PR	$ 4+	$ 8-	0.6
27	Lakeland Comm C, Mentor 44060	P	$ 1+	$ 5	8+
28	Lima Tech C, Lima 45804	P	$ 2-	$ 4	2+
29	Lorain County Comm C, Elyria 44035	P	$ 1+	$ 4+	6-
30	Marion Tech C, Marion 43302	P	$ 1+	$ 4+	1+
31	Miami U - Hamilton, Hamilton 45011	P	$ 2-	$ 6	2-
32	Miami U - Middletown, Middleton 45042	P	$ 2+	$ 6+	2-
33	Muskingum Area Tech C, Zanesville 43701	P	N/A	N/A	2-
34	North Central Tech C, Mansfield 44901	P	$ 1+	$ 5	2
35	Northwest Tech C, Archbold 43502	P	$ 2+	$ 3-	2+
36	Ohio State U - Lima, Lima 45804	P	$ 2+	$ 8-	1-
37	Ohio State U - Mansfield, Mansfield 44906	P	$ 2+	N/A	1-
38	Ohio State U - Marion, Marion 43302	P	$ 2-	$ 6+	1-
39	Ohio State U - Newark, Newark 43055	P	$ 2-	$ 6+	1+
40	Ohio U - Belmont, St Clairsville 43950	P	$ 2-	N/A	1-
41	Ohio U - Chillicothe, Chillicothe 45601	P	$ 2-	N/A	1+
42	Ohio U - Ironton, Ironton 45638	P	$ 2-	N/A	1+
43	Ohio U - Lancaster, Lancaster 43130	P	$ 2-	$ 4-	1+
44	Ohio U - Zanesville, Zanesville 43701	P	$ 2-	$ 7+	1-
45	Owens Tech C - Toledo, Toledo 43699	P	$ 1+	$ 4+	7-
46	Owens Tech C - Findlay, Findlay 45840	P	$ 1+	$ 4+	1
47	Rio Grande Comm C, Rio Grande 45674	P	$ 2-	$ 5	2
48	Sinclair Comm C, Dayton 45402	P	$ 1+	$ 5	17+
49	Southern St Comm C, Hillsboro 45133	P	$ 2-	$ 6	1+
50	Stark Tech C, Canton 44720	P	$ 2-	$ 6+	3+
51	Terra Tech C, Fremont 43420	P	$ 1+	$ 8+	2+
52	Washington Tech C, Marietta 45750	P	$ 2-	$ 5	1+
53	Wright St U - Lake Campus, Celina 45822	P	$ 2+	$ 5+	1

Continued on next page

DIPLOMA SCHOOLS OF NURSING

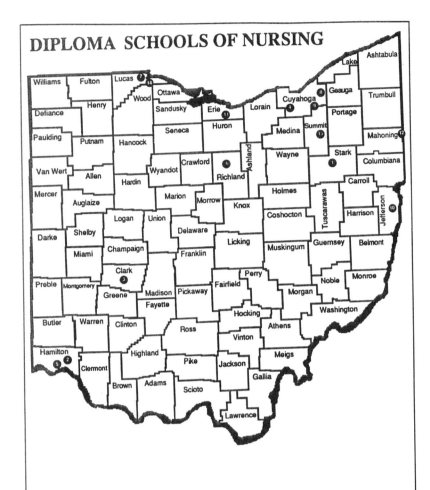

1. Aultman Hospital School of Nursing
2. The Christ Hospital School of Nursing
3. The Community Hospital School of Nursing
4. Fairview General Hospital School of Nursing
5. Good Samaritan Hospital School of Nursing
6. Mansfield General Hospital School of Nursing
7. Mercy School of Nursing
8. Meridia-Huron Road Hospital School of Nursing
9. Metro Health Medical Center School of Nursing
10. The Ohio Valley Hospital School of Nursing
11. Providence Hospital School of Nursing
12. St. Elizabeth Hospital School of Nursing
13. St. Thomas Medical Center School of Nursing
14. St. Vincent Medical Center School of Nursing

DIPLOMA SCHOOLS OF NURSING - OHIO

Source - Dept. Of Education

Schools may vary from two to three year programs.

T & F   TUITION AND FEES, in $1,000

TE   TOTAL EXPENSES, in $1,000

NS   NUMBER OF STUDENTS, actual number

HOS   HOSPITAL

MED   MEDICAL

Source - Ohio Dept of Education

MAP	INSTITUTION	T&F	TE	NS
1	Aultman Hosp Sch of Nursing Canton 44710	$ 3.2	N/A	200+
2	Christ Hosp Sch of Nursing Cincinnati 45219	$11.7	$14.2	189
3	Comm Hosp Sch of Nursing Springfield 45501	$ 2.7	$ 4.1	80
4	Fairview Gen Hosp Sch of Nursing Cleveland 44111	$ 1.6+	N/A	113
5	Good Samaritan Hosp Sch of Nursing Cincinnati 45220	$ 4.7	$ 7.3	276
6	Mansfield Gen Hosp Sch of Nursing Mansfield 44903	$ 2.8*	$ 6.7*	69
7	Mercy Sch of Nursing Toledo 43624	$ 4.9	$ 8.2	94
8	Meridia-Huron Rd. Hosp Sch of Nursing Cleveland 44112	$ 4.4	$ 7.8*	98
9	Metro-Health Med Center Sch of Nursing Cleveland 44109	$ 3.2	$ 3.2	117
10	Ohio Valley Hosp Sch of Nursing Steubenville 43952	$ 3.1	$ 4.0	129
11	Providence Hosp Sch of Nursing Sandusky 44870	$ 4.4	$ 5.0	90
12	St. Elizabeth Hosp Sch of Nursing Youngstown 44501	$ 3.5	$ 4.5	208
13	St. Thomas Med Center Sch of Nursing Akron 44310	$ 3.5	N/A	112
14	St. Vincent Med Center Sch of Nursing Toledo 43608	$ 6.2	$ 7.3	150

Continued on next page

Continued on next page

OHIO EDUCATION PROFICIENCY TESTS
State & School Districts
1992-93

Source - Ohio Dept of Education
May, 1993

A project of the Ohio Dept of Education in conjunction with all local school districts.

Students of the 9th, 10th and 11th grades in public schools are tested annually for achievement in Writing, Reading, Math and Citizen to assist the students and to improve teaching methods.

The tests are a Ninth Grade proficiency level, with those who do not pass it repeating it in the subsequent 10th grade and, if necessary, in the 11th grade. More than 125,000 students are tested for each grade.

The following results cover the state totals and each district of each county.

	% PASSED WRITING 9th/10th/11th	% PASSED READING 9th/10th/11th	% PASSED MATH 9th/10th/11th	% PASSED CITIZEN 9th/10th/11th
STATE TOTAL	83%/94%/99%	85%/93%/99%	64%/74%/79%	79%/85%/89%
ADAMS COUNTY				
District:				
Ohio Valley	56%/77%/86%	68%/80%/90%	46%/53%/66%	63%/67%/78%
ALLEN COUNTY				
District:				
Delphos	94%/100%/97%	83%/96%/94%	67%/80%/86%	85%/87%/94%
Lima	92%/98%/99%	72%/86%/90%	43%/58%/56%	73%/82%/79%
Bluffton	99%/95%/97%	94%/94%/99%	92%/89%/91%	94%/96%/88%
Allen	91%/92%/98%	91%/97%/94%	76%/82%/88%	90%/93%/94%
Bath	94%/95%/98%	89%/93%/94%	62%/76%/80%	73%/86%/88%
Elida	91%/97%/99%	95%/95%/98%	75%/86%/85%	86%/93%/95%
Perry	90%/91%/94%	81%/90%/99%	48%/76%/79%	73%/81%/90%
Shawnee	85%/97%/99%	90%/98%/99%	76%84%/85%	83%/97%/95%
Spencerville	95%/96%/97%	96%/94%/100	87%/93%/91%	96%/94%/91%
ASHLAND CONTY				
District:				
Ashland	95%/93%/93%	87%/93%/94%	77%/79%/78%	82%/85%/85%
Loudonville- Perrysville	85%/95%/97%	88%/97%/91%	73%/80%/82%	87%/95%/95%
Hillsdale	93%/99%/100%	88%/96%/99%	75%/84%/87%	83%/90%/94%
Mapleton	82%/94%/94%	91%/94%/95%	65%/87%/88%	78%/92%/88%
ASHTABULA COUNTY				
District:				
Ashtabula	76%/90%/95%	77%/89%/95%	43%/55%/68%	66%/75%/83%
Conneaut	84%/90%/93%	83%/90%/91%	65%/76%/74%	73%/82%/85%
Geneva	81%/91%/93%	89%/90%/93%	64%/78%/76%	82%/85%/87%
Buckeye	79%/88%/97%	91%/86%/97%	68%/70%/79%	83%/82%/95%
Grand Valley	80%/96%/94%	79%/95%/97%	57%/84%/83%	78%/95%/88%
Jefferson	87%/94%/94%	94%/96%/97%	76%/79%/84%	93%/92%/95%
Pymatuning Valley	86%/96%/94%	90%/95%/98%	77%/83%/80%	91%/90%/88%

Continued from preceeding page

	% PASSED WRITING 9th/10th/11th	% PASSED READING 9th/10th/11th	% PASSED MATH 9th/10th/11th	% PASSED CITIZEN 9th/10th/11th
STATE TOTAL	83%/94%/99%	85%/93%/99%	64%/74%/79%	79%/85%/89%
ATHENS COUNTY				
District:				
Athens	84%/94%/96%	87%/96%/94%	74%/89%/82%	80%/96%/87%
Nelsonville-				
York	85%/94%/96%	90%/89%/95%	58%/60%/78%	85%/76%/95%
Alexander	77%/92%/92%	83%/91%/92%	60%/68%/79%	82%/84%/92%
Federal				
Hocking	72%/93%/90%	75%/91%/97%	47%/58%/62%	75%/92%/84%
Trimble	78%/94%/85%	74%/87%/87%	38%/60%/59%	70%/75%/78%
AUGLAIZE COUNTY				
District:				
St Marys	83%/91%/100%	91%/90%/98%	73%/85%/85%	82%/85%/92%
Wapakoneta	90%/96%/95%	94%/96%/96%	66%/78%/80%	84%/85%/93%
Minster	93%/100%/100	89%/100%/100	94%/98%/98%	97%/96%/98%
New Bremen	96%/95%/98%	96%/97%/98%	91%/93%/91%	91%/98%/98%
New Knoxville	95%/100%/92%	95%/100%/96	87%/88%/88%	97%/100%/92
Waynesfield-				
Goshen	90%/93%/94%	100%/89%/94	78%/64%/74%	95%/73%/94%
BELMONT COUNTY				
District:				
Bellaire	67%/86%/93%	78%/96%/97%	58%/78%/88%	65%/81%/93%
Martins Ferry	88%/92%/98%	97%/94%/92%	67%/71%/73%	91%/81%/82%
Clairsville-				
Richland	87%/95%/98%	90%/97%/97%	69%/88%/89%	82%/94%/94%
Barnesville	88%/96%/100%	92%/92%/98%	62%/72%/93%	91%/82%/95%
Bridgeport	96%/96%/89%	94%/93%/90%	56%/75%/73%	79%/85%/80%
Shadyside	76%/90%/95%	94%/94%/92%	80%/84%/92%	84%/90%/88%
Union	84%/97%/89%	90%/96%/98%	69%/80%/85%	83%/88%/95%
BROWN COUNTY				
District:				
Georgetown	81%/75%/96%	89%/81%/85%	72%/84%/70%	87%/84%/73%
Eastern	91%/98%/94%	87%/97%/92%	71%/83%/80%	88%/90%/90%
Fayetteville-				
Perry	86%/90%/96%	89%/85%/96%	75%/82%/87%	89%/90%/93%
Ripley-Union-				
Lewis	72%/89%/82%	76%/79%/83%	51%/57%/63%	83%/70%/81%
Western Brown	79%/86%/96%	78%/91%/98%	56%/64%/72%	74%/83%/85%
BUTLER COUNTY				
District:				
Edgewood	86%/97%/95%	88%/92%/97%	77%/83%/87%	88%/87%/93%
Fairfield	82%/93%/96%	87%/93%/97%	77%/77%/79%	81%/85%/86%
Hamilton	84%/98%/99%	86%/95%/97%	58%/69%/73%	84%/87%/87%
Middletown	82%/96%/93%	86%/92%/96%	55%/71%/67%	84%/85%/80%
Talawanda	92%/89%/98%	86%/85%/96%	68%/73%/73%	85%/82%/82%
Lakota	92%/98%/99%	94%/98%/98%	86%/92%/90%	93%/97%/94%
Madison	90%/95%/98%	93%/92%/98%	63%/82%/83%	78%/83%/88%
New Miami	66%/83%/85%	82%/81%/85%	48%/54%/63%	54%/67%/66%
Ross	83%/95%/98%	87%/94%/98%	69%/80%/89%	78%/90%/97%

Continued on next page

Continued from preceeding page

	% PASSED WRITING 9th/10th/11th	% PASSED READING 9th/10th/11th	% PASSED MATH 9th/10th/11th	% PASSED CITIZEN 9th/10th/11th
STATE TOTAL	83%/94%/99%	85%/93%/99%	64%/74%/79%	79%/85%/89%
CARROLL COUNTY				
District:				
Carrollton	94%/97%/99%	96%/96%/95%	72%/83%/84%	91%/94%/93%
Brown	90%/92%/93%	88%/95%/99%	57%/81%/89%	75%/87%/93%
CHAMPAIGN COUNTY				
District:				
Urbana	76%/90%/88%	77%/80%/86%	55%/65%/68%	69%/74%/78%
Mechanicsburg	62%/83%/78%	79%/83%/85%	57%/65%/64%	62%/75%/80%
Graham	82%/88%/94%	81%/88%/97%	70%/75%/77%	82%/83%/84%
Triad	61%/78%/92%	77%/82%/86%	67%/62%/72%	71%/77%/79%
W Liberty-Salem	91%/94%/97%	77%/89%/93%	72%/82%/85%	71%/81%/87%
CLARK COUNTY				
District:				
Springfield	64%/82%/88%	74%/82%/89%	43%/48%/51%	57%/64%/72%
Mad River-				
Green	93%/92%/96%	85%/95%/92%	69%/87%/85%	85%/89%/90%
Northeastern	84%/99%/98%	91%/99%/100	77%/87%/87%	89%/94%/97%
Northwestern	82%/92%/95%	89%/94%/94%	76%/88%/78%	83%/89%/88%
Southeastern	82%/95%/93%	84%/89%/93%	66%/66%/80%	76%/89%/86%
Springfield	83%/95%/98%	88%/91%/98%	74%/81%/78%	81%/86%/88%
Tecumseh	71%/95%/94%	82%/94%/95%	58%/79%/70%	73%/79%/80%
CLERMONT COUNTY				
District:				
Milford	91%/94%/97%	94%/94%/99%	75%/78%/83%	86%/87%/93%
New Richmond	67%/86%/93%	72%/91%/89%	51%/65%/69%	67%/78%/84%
Batavia	85%/95%/95%	86%/88%/96%	66%/69%/82%	83%/85%/88%
Bethel-Tate	90%/83%/98%	93%/85%/94%	65%/72%/79%	80%/76%/95%
Clermont-				
Northeastern	77%/93%/92%	82%/93%/94%	52%/77%/81%	68%/89%/92%
Felicity-Franklin	67%/80%/92%	74%/88%/96%	54%/65%/69%	73%/85%/86%
Goshen	69%/85%/89%	81%/83%/93%	56%/67%/65%	73%/73%/78%
W Clermont	80%/93%/98%	78%/92%/96%	63%/72%/76%	67%/84%/87%
Williamsburg	94%/98%/97%	91%/91%/97%	74%/78%/76%	89%/81%/79%
CLINTON COUNTY				
District:				
Wilmington	85%/98%/98%	90%/93%/95%	61%/79%/82%	85%/86%/90%
Blanchester	81%/95%/93%	87%/94%/95%	63%/70%/76%	82%/81%/84%
Clinton-Massie	91%/99%/100%	87%/91%/97%	59%/63%/85%	87%/84%/90%
E Clinton	90%/98%/97%	80%/92%/96%	55%/71%/74%	68%/89%/86%
COLUMBIANA COUNTY				
District:				
E Liverpool	82%/86%/96%	83%/88%/97%	52%/57%/73%	80%/77%/87%
E Palestine	77%/91%/93%	95%/94%/96%	71%/84%/85%	85%/84%/91%
Salem	91%/95%/100%	92%/97%/98%	80%/87%/87%	86%/90%/93%
Columbiana	88%/94%/94%	95%/98%/88%	67%/81%/86%	79%/94%/89%
Leetonia	89%/100%/95%	88%/96%/94%	83%/88%/78%	89%/93%/90%
Lisbon	79%/95%/91%	82%/93%/90%	70%/70%/81%	75%/84%/89%

Continued on next page

	% PASSED WRITING 9th/10th/11th	% PASSED READING 9th/10th/11th	% PASSED MATH 9th/10th/11th	% PASSED CITIZEN 9th/10th/11th
STATE TOTAL	83%/94%/99%	85%/93%/99%	64%/74%/79%	79%/85%/89%
Beaver	73%/93%/91%	78%/97%/97%	65%/82%/79%	78%/93%/94%
Crestview	95%/92%/91%	95%/91%/97%	75%/76%/79%	91%/92%/87%
Southern	73%/89%/94%	83%/90%/91%	54%/60%/64%	79%/80%/83%
United	93%/94%/98%	90%/94%/95%	679%/80%/87%	83%/90%/90%
Wellsville	85%/97%/92%	92%/93%/100	64%/75%/83%	78%/91%/91%
COSHOCTON COUNTY				
District:				
Coshocton	76%/92%/96%	78%/86%/94%	61%/75%/76%	82%/79%/86%
Ridgewood	75%/82%/88%	84%/92%/100	57%/79%/78%	70%/88%/91%
River View	74%/85%/92%	85%/89%/94%	77%/80%/83%	84%/76%/88%
CRAWFORD COUNTY				
District:				
Bucyrus	84%/89%/98%	80%/86%/94%	65%/71%/66%	76%/80%/84%
Galion	86%/87%/93%	85%/85%/98%	55%/67%/66%	81%/85%/90%
Crestline	76%/88%/95%	76%/93%/90%	67%/80%/76%	78%/78%/95%
Buckeye	75%/94%/95%	92%/98%/95%	82%/88%/89%	85%/94%/97%
Colonel	83%/96%/94%	81%/98%/95%	68%/88%/78%	70%/92%/84%
Wynford	87%/94%/91%	89%/95%/96%	72%/84%/86%	87%/95%/97%
CUYAHOGA COUNTY				
District:				
Bay Village	94%/99%/100%	98%/99%/99%	88%/92%/93%	96%/96%/98%
Beachwood	99%/98%/99%	96%/98%/99%	90%/92%/95%	95%/97%/97%
Bedford	79%/95%/98%	80%/92%/98%	50%/64%/77%	71%/81%/89%
Berea	86%/95%/99%	91%/94%/98%	80%/86%/85%	89%/90%/94%
Brecksville- Broadview Hts	88%/96%/99%	95%/98%/99%	88%/91%/94%	90%/93%/96%
Brooklyn	84%/92%/97%	81%/92%/97%	69%/80%/76%	76%/81%/86%
Cleveland	65%/86%/92%	65%/80%/95%	28%/34%/44%	51%/44%/67%
Cleveland Hts- Univ Hts	83%/92%/98%	83%/89%/97%	45%/65%/58%	70%/78%/76%
E Cleveland	66%/91%/87%	63%/88%/84%	25%/29%/41%	64%/75%/70%
Euclid	83%/97%/97%	85%/92%/99%	56%/65%/72%	70%/81%/91%
Fairview Park	91%/95%/99%	95%/99%/99%	87%/88%/90%	96%/95%/97%
Garfield Hts	79%/90%/96%	84%/88%/97%	57%/70%/69%	75%/82%/85%
Lakewood	85%/97%/97%	86%/92%/98%	67%/77%/77%	80%/88%/87%
Maple Hts	81%/80%/93%	70%/81%/97%	47%/59%/68%	72%/66%/79%
Mayfield	87%/97%/96%	91%/96%/99%	79%/94%/92%	87%/94%/93%
N Olmsted	90%/97%/97%	92%/97%/99%	77%/82%/89%	86%/90%/96%
N Royalton	97%/99%/99%	95%/98%/99%	82%/90%/90%	92%/94%/95%
Olmsted Falls	94%/95%/99%	89%/97%/95%	82%/88%/88%	89%/91%/89%
Orange	93%/97%/98%	95%/99%/99%	82%/97%/95%	93%/95%/95%
Parma	81%/94%/99%	83%/95%/98%	66%/79%/82%	82%/91%/93%
Rocky River	93%/96%/100	95%/96%/98%	85%/88%/96%	92%/96%/97%
Shaker Hts	90%/97%/100%	89%/95%/99%	71%/77%/76%	88%/92%/92%
Solon	98%/99%/99%	97%/99%/100	92%/95%/96%	95%/97%/99%

Continued on next page

	% PASSED WRITING 9th/10th/11th	% PASSED READING 9th/10th/11th	% PASSED MATH 9th/10th/11th	% PASSED CITIZEN 9th/10th/11th
STATE TOTAL	83%/94%/99%	85%/93%/99%	64%/74%/79%	79%/85%/89%
S Euclid-				
Lyndhurst	87%/98%/94%	88%/95%/97%	73%/79%/87%	87%/89%/95%
Strongsville	96%/96%/98%	93%/95%/98%	85%/90%/90%	92%/92%/97%
Warrensville	85%/97%/99%	85%/94%/96%	52%/60%/64%	77%/82%/85%
Westlake	92%/96%/97%	93%/99%/98%	80%/90%/93%	88%/95%/97%
Chagrin Falls	99%/98%/97%	98%/100%/98	92%/95%/100	97%/97%/98%
Cuyahoga Hts	89%/97%/95%	89%/97%/97%	85%/88%/95%	85%/91%/97%
Independence	90%/100%/96%	90%/100%/99	79%/96%/91%	87%/97%/95%
Richmond Hts	92%/98%/100%	85%/98%/100	83%/88%/85%	77%/94%/94%
DARKE COUNTY				
District:				
Greenville	84%/88%/97%	85%/88%/98%	75%/79%/83%	80%/83%/86%
Versailles	91%/98%/97%	95%/99%/95%	87%/92%/91%	90%/97%/93%
Ansonia	98%/98%/100	95%/92%/94%	70%/79%/81%	73%/85%/94%
Arcanum Butler	97%/99%/99%	94%/99%/98%	82%/95%/84%	90%/93%/88%
Franklin-Monroe	100%/98%/98%	95%/98%/98%	98%/91%/93%	95%/96%/95%
Mississinawa				
Valley	100%/100%/100	92%/93%/97%	69%/75%/85%	88%/83%/90%
Tri-Village	86%/95%/96%	90%/94%/100	73%/85%/82%	94%/94%/93%
DEFIANCE COUNTY				
District:				
Defiance	86%/99%/99%	84%/93%/98%	63%/82%/85%	75%/90%/86%
Hicksville	80%/90%/91%	96%/100%/99	70%/80%/86%	85%/90%/93%
Ayersville	87%/93%/95%	90%/95%/92%	80%/80%/86%	85%/86%/95%
Central	80%/97%/96%	91%/97%/100	74%/91%/90%	82%/89%/91%
Northeastern	94%/89%/95%	94%/94%/96%	84%/79%/88%	81%/79%/91%
DELAWARE COUNTY				
District:				
Delaware	80%/89%/95%	86%/91%/97%	69%/74%/80%	81%/83%/86%
Big Walnut	96%/96%/99%	90%/95%/96%	78%/85%/84%	85%/89%/92%
Buckeye Valley	81%/89%/98%	84%/94%/96%	65%/78%/82%	89%/89%/95%
Olentangy	99%/98%/99%	95%/96%/96%	86%/89%/92%	89%/96%/95%
ERIE COUNTY				
District:				
Huron	96%/100%/97%	91%/98%/94%	69%/84%/81%	89%/93%/89%
Sandusky	77%/93%/96%	84%/90%/98%	60%/69%/77%	60%/71%/83%
Berlin-Milan	88%/97%/93%	92%/96%/100	77%/84%/88%	87%/94%/95%
Kelleys Island	100%/100%/50	100%/100/50%	100%/50%/0%	100%/100/0%
Margaretta	85%/92%/87%	92%/96%/92%	76%/88%/78%	87%/92%/87%
Perkins	87%/95%/98%	91%/97%/100	74%/82%/90%	80%/89%/93%
Vermilion	79%/90%/95%	84%/90%/96%	66%/74%/75%	79%/86%/87%
FAIRFIELD COUNTY				
District:				
Lancaster	72%/93%/96%	81%/90%/93%	65%/78%/78%	77%/85%/86%
Amanda-				
Clearcreek	73%/86%/95% •	82%/81%/95%	57%/71%/75%	80%/76%/83%
Berne Union	90%/95%/95%	92%/96%/99%	77%/78%/88%	82%/89%/93%
Bloom Carroll	84%/91%/91%	92%/93%/94%	58%/75%/77%	85%/84%/89%
Fairfield Union	82%/95%/92%	85%/90%/95%	70%/76%/73%	85%/87%/89%

Continued on next page

	% PASSED WRITING 9th/10th/11th	% PASSED READING 9th/10th/11th	% PASSED MATH 9th/10th/11th	% PASSED CITIZEN 9th/10th/11th
STATE TOTAL	83%/94%/99%	85%/93%/99%	64%/74%/79%	79%/85%/89%
Liberty Unionn-Thurston	92%/91%/91%	91%/94%/90%	84%/83%/83%	82%/91%/87%
Pickerington	91%/99%/98%	93%/97%/100	80%/89%/91%	92%/95%/96%
Walnut	63%/98%/89%	80%/93%/89%	53%/70%/70%	77%/87%/86%
FAYETTE COUNTY				
District:				
Washington Court House	95%/96%/98%	88%/92%/91%	69%/74%/77%	87%/94%/91%
Miami Trace	93%/98%/94%	83%/93%/96%	55%/77%/83%	73%/84%/88%
FRANKLIN COUNTY				
District:				
Bexley	97%/99%/98%	97%/100%/98	89%/97%/97%	96%/99%/98%
Columbus	70%/87%/98%	68%/80%/93%	35%/48%/55%	60%/65%/75%
Dublin	95%/99%/99%	95%/97%/99%	88%/95%/93%	91%/94%/95%
Gahanna-Jefferson	90%/96%/100	93%/98%/99%	78%/82%/85%	89%/90%/73%
Grandview Hts	99%/98%/99%	90%/100%/98	85%/89%/92%	95%/99%/98%
Hilliard	91%/98%/99%	89%/96%/97%	78%/86%/83%	86%/91%/89%
Renoldsburg	84%/96%/99%	90%/98%/98%	76%/87%/86%	92%/91%/92%
South-Western	79%/93%/98%	82%/92%/98%	60%/73%/76%	76%/83%/88%
Upper Arlington	99%/99%/100%	98%/98%/99%	95%/97%/96%	99%/99%/98%
Westerville	91%/96%/99%	92%/97%/97%	76%/85%/85%	90%/91%/91%
Whitehall	77%/93%/95%	77%/88%/97%	55%/69%/74%	71%/76%/83%
Worthington	92%/98%/99%	92%/97%/99%	85%/90%/92%	90%/93%/96%
Canal Winchester	94%/95%/97%	92%/93%/97%	79%/90%/89%	93%/92%/99%
Groveport Madison	80%/96%/99%	82%/92%/92%	63%/75%/70%	79%/85%/82%
Hamilton	83%/91%/93%	83%/85%/94%	61%/62%/66%	77%/83%/85%
Plain	88%/96%/95%	88%/96%/97%	82%/88%/89%	95%/97%/100
FULTON COUNTY				
District:				
Wauseon	91%/99%/97%	88%/95%/100	77%/91%/87%	86%/98%/95%
Archbold-Area	96%/98%/99%	96%/98%/97%	79%/90%/89%	89%/96%/98%
Evergreen	95%/91%/98%	86%/84%/94%	74%/69%/84%	90%/87%/93%
Gotham Fayette	85%/98%/95%	87%/87%/95%	61%/73%/82%	65%/73%/95%
Pettisville	93%/100%/91%	89%/95%/91%	85%/95%/94%	85%/95%/97%
Pike-Delta-York	89%/95%/95%	82%/95%/90%	64%/75%/74%	76%/85%/88%
Swanton	81%/96%/96%	87%/93%/95%	65%/65%/79%	89%/90%/94%
GALLIA COUNTY				
District:				
Gallipolis	78%/91%/85%	86%/93%/95%	64%/77%/80%	81%/88%/84%
Gallia	69%/81%/89%	79%/88%/94%	45%/57%/72%	71%/81%/90%
GEAUGA COUNTY				
District:				
Berkshire	94%/100%/99%	92%/99%/98%	88%/89%/83%	91%/93%/92%
Cardinal	80%/93%/97%	92%/95%/96%	92%/83%/87%	97%/92%/89%
Chardon	91%/99%/98%	91%/97%/99%	84%/86%/84%	89%/92%/91%

Continued on next page

Continued from preceeding page

	% PASSED WRITING 9th/10th/11th	% PASSED READING 9th/10th/11th	% PASSED MATH 9th/10th/11th	% PASSED CITIZEN 9th/10th/11th
STATE TOTAL	83%/94%/99%	85%/93%/99%	64%/74%/79%	79%/85%/89%
Kenston	97%/99%/99%	97%/97%/99%	88%/91%/93%	96%/96%/95%
Ledgemont	82%/88%/94%	90%/86%/96%	38%/73%/76%	77%/92%/84%
Newbury	91%/92%/95%	91%/95%/100	71%/86%/83%	80%/94%/94%
W Geauga	94%/99%/99%	91%/96%/95%	87%/94%/89%	91%/93%/93%
GREENE COUNTY				
District:				
Fairborn	87%/97%/98%	81%/89%/98%	64%/70%/78%	76%/83%/89%
Xenia	72%/95%/97%	89%/91%/98%	77%/77%/78%	81%/85%/91%
Yellow Springs	94%/98%/98%	88%/96%/98%	75%/90%/81%	81%/96%/92%
Beavercreek	93%/98%/98%	96%/98%/99%	85%/92%/95%	97%/98%/98%
Cedar Cliff	77%/89%/100%	95%/97%/96%	77%/86%/88%	89%/89%/92%
Greeneview	88%/95%/95%	91%/95%/95%	67%/77%/74%	74%/86%/90%
Sugarcreek	89%/99%/100%	93%/98%/97%	86%/90%/92%	92%/91%/98%
GUERNSEY COUNTY				
District:				
Cambridge	66%/95%/95%	79%/93%/98%	64%/76%/81%	76%/84%/83%
E Guernsey	78%/90%/90%	75%/90%/99%/	57%/72%/72%	69%/85%/92%
Rolling Hills	80%/90%/86%	79%/89%/93%	52%/70%/69%	76%/80%/85%
HAMILTON COUNTY				
District:				
Cincinnati	65%/77%/86%	64%/72%/84%	36%/42%/46%	54%/59%/63%
Deer Park	65%/95%/95%	82%/96%/91%	66%/71%/83%	79%/86%/88%
Lockland	91%/96%/100%	83%/93%/93%	68%/50%/76%	83%/72%/93%
Loveland	91%/97%/100%	89%/96%/98%	78%/87%/87%	87%/91%/93%
Madeira	97%/98%/100%	96%/98%/99%	91%/83%/96%	92%/93%/97%
Mariemont	91%/98%/97%	95%/100%/100	91%/91%/91%	92%/92%/97%
Mt Healthy	92%/91%/99%	84%/88%/97%	51%/57%/52%	70%/78%/81%
N College	66%/91%/95%	75%/85%/100	65%/74%/84%	77%/78%/93%
Norwood	73%/83%/95%	77%/85%/90%	58%/60%/58%	82%/76%/82%
Princeton	88%/98%/98%	87%/94%/98%	68%/71%/78%	81%/82%/88%
Reading	86%/94%/91%	81%/94%/97%	74%/72%/69%	82%/86%/84%
St Bernard				
Elmwood	90%/93%/99%	80%/83%/93%	65%/67%/77%	83%/71%/83%
Sycamore	92%/99%/98%	92%/97%/99%	89%/89%/93%	88%/95%/95%
Winton Woods	75%/88%/98%	84%/88%/97%	58%/76%/77%	79%/82%/89%
Wyoming	83%/99%/100%	94%/98%/98%	95%/97%/92%	98%/99%/95%
Indian Hill	100%/100%/100	95%/99%/98%	93%/92%/90%	94%/96%/97%
Finneytown	93%/99%/100%	94%/95%/98%	90%/90%/91%	89%/92%/93%
Forest Hills	95%/98%/99%	92%/99%/99%	81%/92%/90%	92%/96%/97%
Northwest	88%/97%/98%	85%/94%/99%	68%/78%/78%	83%/90%/90%
Oak Hills	95%/97%/99%	92%/96%/96%	78%/86%/87%	90%/93%/92%
Southwest	81%/93%/89%	78%/87%/92%	66%/74%/75%	77%/82%/82%
Three Rivers	81%/88%/99%	78%/80%/98%	65%/62%/80%	74%/82%/86%
HANCOCK COUNTY				
District:				
Findlay	84%/97%/95%	88%/94%/96%	70%/82%/83%	80%/91%/88%
Arcadia	93%/93%/96%	96%/88%/93%	89%/81%/88%	93%/84%/88%

Continued on next page

Continued from preceeding page

	% PASSED WRITING 9th/10th/11th	% PASSED READING 9th/10th/11th	% PASSED MATH 9th/10th/11th	% PASSED CITIZEN 9th/10th/11th
STATE TOTAL	83%/94%/99%	85%/93%/99%	64%/74%/79%	79%/85%/89%
Arlington	70%/89%/93%	92%/98%/98%	86%/85%/93%	86%/91%/93%
Cory-Rawson	92%/98%/97%	73%/90%/92%	90%/83%/92%	97%/83%/88%
Liberty-Benton	91%/96%/92%	84%/94%/92%	73%/85%/85%	77%/85%/83%
McComb	88%/92%/95%	90%/94%/90%	80%/83%/73%	86%/83%/81%
Van Buren	88%/90%/90%	91%/93%/85%	84%/93%/83%	91%/83%/82%
Vanlue	93%/86%/93%	89%/93%/96%	63%/90%/96%	85%/93%/100
HARDIN COUNTY				
District:				
Kenton	71%/96%/90%	81%/95%/96%	64%/82%/78%	78%/89%/91%
Ada	97%/100%/96%	91%/99%/93%	72%/78%/80%	92%/95%/83%
Hardin Northern	74%/89%/91%	83%/96%/91%	74%/84%/84%	83%/89%/91%
Ridgemont	71%/84%/92%	88%/95%/89%	61%/78%/76%	67%/81%/76%
Riverdale	89%/95%/81%	91%/95%/84%	70%/83%/69%	84%/91%/74%
Upper Scioto	75%/90%/86%	91%/95%/82%	52%/80%/70%	86%/93%/81%
HARRISON COUNTY				
District:				
Harrison Hills	83%/86%/93%	80%/92%/92%	62%/74%/81%	79%/85%/89%
Conotton Valley	91%/91%/96%	91%/96%/96%	83%/77%/77%	96%/91%/93%
HENRY COUNTY				
District:				
Napoleon	93%/95%/98%	87%/95%/97%	76%/86%/89%	88%/92%/96%
Holgate	98%/94%/94%	93%/96%/96%	83%/78%/84%	89%/88%/86%
Liberty Center	75%/78%/91%	88%/86%/89%	66%/80%/75%	88%/84%/90%
Patrick Henry	92%/98%/96%	95%/96%/95%	77%/84%/90%	92%/94%/99%
HIGHLAND COUNTY				
District				
Hillsboro	85%/90%/88%	87%/96%/93%	64%/78%/68%	79%/87%/79%
Greenfield	59%/92%/84%	63%/82%/88%	42%/56%/58%	59%/65%/75%
Bright	95%/83%/96%	89%/86%/92%	63%/58%/77%	84%/71%/83%
Fairfield	85%/98%/89%	81%/87%/93%	51%/60%/78%	68%/80%/96%
Lynchburg-Clay	89%/96%/99%	93%/96%/96%	67%/74%/83%	89%/86%/94%
HOCKING COUNTY				
District:				
Locan-Hocking	86%/94%/97%	84%/94%/95%	58%/73%/79%	81%/88%/91%
HOLMES COUNTY				
District:				
E Holmes	95%/100%/100	100%/97%/100	94%/95%/100	97%/99%/98%
W Holmes	95%/96%/97%	91%/92%/97%	80%/83%/87%	92%/90%/95%
HURON COUNTY				
District:				
Bellevue	83%/95%/96%	84%/96%/99%	75%/84%/92%	88%/89%/95%
Norwalk	77%/93%/90%	86%/91%/95%	61%/73%/81%	77%/85%/84%
Willard	78%/95%/96%	85%/94%/98%	70%/68%/79%	75%/82%/89%
Monroeville	87%/88%/92%	89%/94%/98%	74%/85%/87%	80%/93%/92%
New London	80%/89%/93%	84%/85%/96%	69%/70%/76%	85%/84%/85%
South Central	76%/91%/93%	89%/94%/96%	76%/77%/82%	73%/80%/81%
Western Reserve	62%/84%/94%	84%/83%/95%	60%/73%/84%	72%/77%/89%

Continued on next page

Continued from preceeding page

	% PASSED WRITING 9th/10th/11th	% PASSED READING 9th/10th/11th	% PASSED MATH 9th/10th/11th	% PASSED CITIZEN 9th/10th/11th
STATE TOTAL	83%/94%/99%	85%/93%/99%	64%/74%/79%	79%/85%/89%
JACKSON COUNTY				
District:				
Jackson	88%/97%/97%	85%/94%/94%	69%/73%/77%	78%/82%/85%
Wellston	79%/90%/97%	78%/86%/97%	48%/72%/70%	69%/85%/87%
Oak Hill Union	81%/91%/88%	82%/91%/85%	48%/61%/79%	74%/79%/76%
JEFFERSON COUNTY				
District:				
Steubenville	70%/84%/91%	91%/97%/99%	71%/88%/86%	82%/90%/91%
Toronto	80%/98%/99%	94%/98%/97%	66%/82%/83%	88%/94%/95%
Buckeye	89%/97%/97%	84%/98%/98%	64%/76%/88%	87%/93%/94%
Edison	80%/93%/95%	88%/94%/100	62%/77%/90%	88%/91%/97%
Indian Creek	89%/95%/94%	90%/96%/96%	72%/79%/85%	84%/87%/93%
KNOX COUNTY				
District:				
Mount Vernon	84%/90%/87%	89%/87%/90%	74%/75%/82%	86%/84%/88%
Centersburg	97%/89%/93%	89%/95%/98%	75%/89%/90%	89%/92%/97%
Danville	79%/89%/96%	92%/95%/96%	94%/88%/81%	92%/86%/91%
E Knox	80%/100%/96%	89%/98%/96%	77%/87%/88%	88%/91%/94%
Fredericktown	85%/97%/99%	94%/96%/94%	80%/84%/90%	87%/97%/90%
LAKE COUNTY				
District:				
Wickliffe	93%/92%/97%	89%/89%/98%	70%/80%/86%	89%/90%/92%
Willoughby-Eastlake	90%/97%/98%	90%/96%/98%	72%/80%/86%	87%/90%/94%
Fairport Harbor	85%/86%/80%	80%/89%/88%	71%/78%/66%	88%/81%/78%
Mentor	93%/96%/99%	94%/96%/99%	85%/88%/90%	90%/89%/95%
Kirtland	96%/94%/95%	94%/94%/96%	84%/81%/86%	90%/90%/93%
Madison	94%/99%/100%	88%/94%/94%	66%/81%/83%	81%/85%/87%
Painesville	78%/86%/98%	73%/76%/96%	52%/61%/65%	64%/69%/80%
Painesville Twp	86%/97%/96%	90%/97%/98%	71%/86%/86%	86%/93%/95%
Perry	99%/98%/97%	98%/98%/98%	86%/96%/94%	94%/97%/96%
LAWRENCE COUNTY				
District:				
Ironton	85%/93%/97%	85%/96%/95%	50%/67%/69%	75%/81%/88%
Chesapeake	82%/93%/100%	84%/90%/96%	61%/73%/79%	74%/79%/92%
Dawson-Bryant	79%/89%/90%	76%/85%/94%	63%/57%/67%	72%/78%/90%
Fairland	98%/99%/98%	96%/95%/96%	84%/82%/86%	90%/91%/93%
Rock Hill	91%/83%/88%	89%/78%/83%	56%/59%/49%	85%/71%/73%
S Point	83%/94%/98%	82%/87%/97%	54%/65%/80%	77%/82%/90%
Symmes Valley	55%/86%/83%	83%/92%/90%	64%/75%/73%	81%/84%/83%
LICKING COUNTY				
District:				
Heath	97%/96%/95%	89%/98%/93%	66%/78%/77%	78%/92%/90%
Newark	79%/96%/95%	80%/94%/95%	60%/76%/74%	73%/87%/84%
Granville	91%/98%/100%	99%/96%/98%	95%/91%/89%	97%/94%/95%
Johnstown-Monroe	93%/94%/97%	88%/95%/99%	61%/79%/84%	75%/81%/88%

Continued on next page

Continued from preceeding page

	% PASSED WRITING 9th/10th/11th	% PASSED READING 9th/10th/11th	% PASSED MATH 9th/10th/11th	% PASSED CITIZEN 9th/10th/11th
STATE TOTAL	83%/94%/99%	85%/93%/99%	64%/74%/79%	79%/85%/89%
Lakewood	80%/97%/95%	78%/86%/87%	56%/73%/69%	77%/87%/76%
Licking Hts	76%/91%/93%	86%/94%/96%	64%/71%/73%	88%/87%/92%
Licking Valley	76%/92%/93%	89%/96%/99%	63%/76%/91%	87%/93%/94%
N Fork	87%/91%/91%	86%/92%/95%	53%/71%/70%	79%/88%/80%
Northridge	87%/97%/100%	81%/92%/91%	58%/72%/81%	79%/88%/84%
Southwest	83%/96%/95%	89%/95%/97%	69%/80%/81%	81%/90%/89%
LOGAN COUNTY District:				
Bellefontaine	74%/88%/94%	77%/87%/97%	62%/74%/77%	67%/82%/85%
Benjamin Logan	78%/90%/94%	85%/90%/91%	65%/79%/79%	79%/86%/86%
Indian Lake	90%/96%/97%	88%/95%/93%	72%/69%/76%	88%/93%/86%
Riverside	76%/96%/93%	81%/91%/95%	74%/78%/80%	88%/88%/85%
LORAIN COUNTY District:				
Avon Lake	96%/100%/99%	89%/96%/100	84%/91%/90%	88%/96%/98%
Elyria	62%/82%/91%	71%/78%/93%	51%/56%/63%	64%/64%/75%
Lorain	57%/74%/75%	61%/70%/82%	34%/43%/47%	53%/60%/62%
N Ridgeville	91%/94%/98%	84%/90%/96%	68%/73%/78%	81%/80%/88%
Oberlin	80%/81%/94%	82%/89%/88%	66%/63%/68%	79%/77%/79%
Sheffield-Sheffield Lake	84%/94%/98%	79%/91%/97%	70%/81%/80%	79%/90%/87%
Amherst	95%/97%/97%	95%/96%/99%	77%/83%/92%	81%/87%/96%
Wellington	74%/89%/93%	87%/89%/95%	65%/83%/80%	70%/87%/89%
Avon	97%/99%/96%	96%/98%/99%	89%/90%/93%	95%/97%/99%
Clearview	87%/95%/97%	81%/92%/98%	41%/61%/71%	66%/75%/85%
Columbia	84%/98%/96%	85%/96%/98%	67%/75%/82%	77%/80%/88%
Firelands	81%/92%/95%	85%/91%/93%	77%/80%/78%	78%/83%/86%
Keystone	81%/96%/97%	84%/91%/99%	63%/70%/73%	73%/85%/90%
Midview	79%/89%/97%	76%/90%/95%	57%/68%/80%	63%/77%/86%
LUCAS COUNTY District:				
Maumee	88%/97%/96%	87%/96%/98%	79%/91%/85%	85%/92%/96%
Oregon	81%/94%/93%	80%/91%/94%	69%/83%/83%	78%/83%/89%
Sylvania	91%/99%/99%	91%/96%/98%	81%/93%/90%	90%/94%/94%
Toledo	69%/84%/94%	66%/80%/89%	37%/48%/50%	51%/64%/67%
Anthony Wayne	88%/97%/95%	89%/93%/99%	69%/82%/86%	85%/91%/94%
Ottawa	99%/98%/98%	99%/97%/100	97%/98%/96%	96%/98%/98%
Springfield	93%/97%/94%	80%/95%/94%	59%/76%/75%	74%/88%/86%
Washington	79%/91%/99%	82%/89%/97%	63%/73%/73%	69%/82%/86%
MADISON COUNTY District:				
London	86%/84%/96%	87%/86%/99%	70%/78%/71%	84%/80%/86%
Jefferson	90%/90%/96%	89%/94%/97%	72%/81%/85%	83%/84%/91%
Jonathan Alder	88%/96%/91%	87%/93%/95%	76%/84%/77%	89%/96%/90%
Madisonn-Plains	78%/93%/99%	89%/95%/90%	66%/67%/80%	94%/93%/92%

Continued on next page

Continued from preceeding page

District	% PASSED WRITING 9th/10th/11th	% PASSED READING 9th/10th/11th	% PASSED MATH 9th/10th/11th	% PASSED CITIZEN 9th/10th/11th
STATE TOTAL	83%/94%/99%	85%/93%/99%	64%/74%/79%	79%/86%/89%
MAHONING COUNTY				
District:				
Campbell	89%/96%/94%	89%/93%/98%	62%/70%/78%	80%/84%/90%
Struthers	94%/98%/98%	87%/95%/96%	69%/78%/90%	74%/82%/87%
Youngstown	73%/91%/98%	69%/83%/95%	34%/45%/50%	63%/69%/79%
Austintown	95%/99%/98%	93%/96%/99%	73%/80%/88%	87%/88%/95%
Boardman	95%/99%/99%	96%/98%/99%	79%/85%/89%	90%/95%/96%
Canfield	97%/100%/99%	96%/99%/98%	88%/86%/91%	97%/97%/94%
Jackson-Milton	91%/91%/95%	91%/92%/90%	69%/73%/78%	76%/86%/83%
Lowellville	97%/98%/97%	97%/98%/100	79%/91%/95%	97%/100/97%
Poland	98%/99%/99%	96%/99%/100	92%/94%/98	95%/97%/99%
Sebring	85%/96%/93%	83%/96%/94%	71%/77%/67%	77%/73%/83%
S Range	87%/95%/98%	88%/91%/97%	71%/87%/79%	92%/96%/92%
Springfield	91%/86%/98%	88%/98%/96%	79%/81%/91%	83%/89%/94%
W Branch	92%/98%/95%	95%/99%/96%	76%/82%/85%	89%/94%/97%
Western Reserve	98%/96%/97%	96%/89%/97%	88%/84%/93%	100/89%/94%
MARION COUNTY				
District:				
Marion	74%/86%/95%	81%/84%/92%	65%/68%/68%	68%/67%/81%
Elgin	78%/87%/89%	82%/89%/98%	65%/78%/83%	79%/91%/89%
Pleasant	89%/96%/93%	85%/88%/92%	67%/78%/88%	83%/91%/88%
Ridgedale	82%/90%/98%	87%/85%/89%	74%/78%/77%	86%/92%/81%
River Valley	80%/95%/97%	82%/95%/95%	54%/83%/81%	81%/95%/93%
MEDINA COUNTY				
District:				
Brunswick	88%/95%/99%	89%/95%/97%	72%/83%/82%	88%/94%/89%
Median	89%/99%/99%	93%/97%/100	76%/88%/88%	82%/91%/93%
Wadsworth	88%/100%/98%	90%/95%/97%	75%/87%/95%	80%/89%/97%
Black River	78%/81%/92%	90%/88%/97%	68%/78%/83%	84%/88%/93%
Buckeye	81%/95%/94%	95%/95%/97%	73%/85%/85%	89%/89%/91%
Cloverleaf	90%/98%/98%	90%/97%/97%	73%/85%/86%	90%/95%/94%
Highland	94%/99%/98%	95%/97%/99%	89%/89%/87%	95%/95%/91%
MEIGS COUNTY				
District:				
Eastern	74%/76%/85%	79%/90%/96%	46%/60%/65%	78%/77%/80%
Meigs	64%/85%/89%	71%/92%/98%	41%/66%/72%	63%/83%/82%
Southern	74%/94%/99%	86%/94%/88%	66%/71%/65%	77%/83%/76%
MERCER COUNTY				
District:				
Celina	87%/99%/98%	88%/94%/98%	81%/85%/88%	82%/88%/95%
Coldwater	97%/94%/100%	96%/97%/99%	90%/96%/98%	92%/97%/98%
Fort Recovery	75%/94%/97%	92%/97%/93%	93%/94%/90%	95%/96%/93%
Marion	91%/100%/87%	95%/100/76%	87%/100/53%	89%/100/60%
Parkway	89%/88%/97%	87%/93%/88%	70%/86%/81%	83%/96%/83%
St Henry	80%/96%/100%	89%/94%/100	89%/94%/99%	95%/99%/100

Continued on next page

Continued from preceeding page

	% PASSED WRITING 9th/10th/11th	% PASSED READING 9th/10th/11th	% PASSED MATH 9th/10th/11th	% PASSED CITIZEN 9th/10th/11th
STATE TOTAL	83%/94%/99%	85%/93%/99%	64%/74%/79%	79%/85%/89%
MIAMI COUNTY				
District:				
Piqua	83%/88%/90%	77%/87%/87%	64%/67%/73%	74%/77%/78%
Troy	83%/96%/96%	83%/94%/98%	66%/77%/79%	70%/84%/87%
Bradford	85%/93%/91%	75%/87%/94%	73%/61%/85%	75%/80%/87%
Covington	86%/97%/98%	92%/97%/94%	86%/87%/92%	80%/92%/98%
Milton-Union	87%/91%/96%	95%/95%/98%	77%/85%/88%	92%/90%/98%
Tipp	97%/99%/99%	95%/97%/99%	86%/91%/88%	89%/93%/93%
Bethel	95%/100%/100	85%/96%/100	70%/96%/93%	79%/91%/97%
Miami E	81%/100%/97%	91%/97%/99%	68%/85%/85%	80%/91%/93%
Newton	91%/100%/93%	93%/96%/95%	69%/87%/79%	84%/94%/93%
MONROE COUNTY				
District:				
Switzerland	79%/90%/94%	84%/92%/96%	66%/79%/79%	76%/85%/87%
MONTGOMERY COUNTY				
District:				
Centerville	93%/98%/97%	97%/99%/99%	89%/95%/94%	93%/96%/98%
Dayton	61%/73%/76%	62%/66%/80%	29%/33%/34%	50%/48%/49%
Huber Hts	84%/94%/98%	89%/95%/94%	63%/75%/79%	79%/92%/86%
Kettering	84%/97%/97%	95%/98%/98%	81%/87%/88%	91%/91%/94%
Miamisburg	79%/90%/97%	91%/96%/99%	70%/80%/89%	87%/92%/95%
Northmont	80%/92%/96%	89%/93%/98%	79%/87%/86%	82%/87%/93%
Oakwood	96%/99%/100%	95%/98%/100	96%/89%/99%	95%/95%/100
Trotwood- Madison	63%/85%/88%	73%/88%/95%	40%/46%/51%	56%/66%/72%
Vandalia-Butler	74%/95%/99%	85%/98%/97%	78%/86%/89%	85%/94%/93%
W Carrollton	89%/96%/98%	89%/95%/94%	68%/77%/80%	86%/87%/88%
Brookville	90%/97%/95%	96%/94%/96%	78%/82%/83%	94%/91%/94%
Jefferson	73%/97%/93%	82%/97%/96%	39%/51%/40%	79%/75%/72%
Mad River	81%/94%/95%	78%/90%/97%	51%/69%/65%	68%/87%/84%
New Lebanon	92%/98%/97%	86%/100%/96	76%/80%/92%	84%/93%/94%
Northridge	77%/93%/95%	85%/95%/98%	50%/70%/73%	85%/81%/84%
Valley View	98%/100%/99%	91%/98%/97%	78%/82%/85%	86%/91%/90%
MORGAN COUNTY				
District:				
Morgan	80%/82%/83%	80%/84%/95%	61%/70%/70%	71%/75%/81%
MORROW COUNTY				
District:				
Mt Gilead	81%/90%/92%	85%/90%/97%	63%/73%/78%	84%/89%/86%
Cardington- Lincoln	81%/90%/96%	82%/91%/95%	58%/82%/74%	77%/92%/84%
Highland	79%/91%/94%	75%/96%/94%	66%/74%/86%	70%/93%/92%
Northmor	83%/95%/94%	93%/97%/92%	73%/80%/77%	83%/91%/94%
MUSKINGUM COUNTY				
District:				
Zanesville	81%/89%/94%	70%/78%/94%	45%/52%/67%	77%/75%/81%
E Muskingum	86%/97%/98%	82%/95%/95%	66%/88%/89%	81%/94%/94%

Continued on next page

	% PASSED WRITING 9th/10th/11th	% PASSED READING 9th/10th/11th	% PASSED MATH 9th/10th/11th	% PASSED CITIZEN 9th/10th/11th
STATE TOTAL	83%/94%/99%	85%/93%/99%	64%/74%/79%	79%/85%/89%
Franklin	79%/90%/93%	82%/88%/94%	63%/71%/78%	79%/75%/84%
Maysville	78%/96%/94%	84%/91%/95%	61%/70%/71%	82%/91%/89%
Tri-Valley	80%/93%/95%	90%/94%/97%	73%/86%/90%	89%/89%/94%
W Muskingum	82%/95%/96%	86%/90%/97%	82%/84%/83%	85%/87%/94%
NOBLE COUNTY				
District:				
Caldwell	92%/90%/98%	90%/90%/93%	58%/72%/74%	70%/79%/85%
Noble	87%/94%/95%	87%/99%/95%	76%/93%/84%	83%/96%/89%
OTTAWA COUNTY				
District:				
Port Clinton	78%/94%/96%	91%/95%/97%	71%/75%/82%	78%/86%/93%
Benton Carroll	99%/99%/96%	97%/95%/95%	81%/88%/91%	91%/91%/95%
Danbury	92%/88%/86%	92%/90%/95%	90%/79%/88%	94%/92%/92%
Genoa	91%/97%/91%	89%/97%/96%	74%/84%/83%	91%/90%/93%
Put-in-Bay	71%/100%/100	100%/100/100	57%/100%/100	86%/100%/100
PAULDING COUNTY				
District:				
Paulding	77%/93%/98%	81%/94%/97%	71%/90%/85%	74%/92%/92%
Antwerp	72%/84%/100	95%/89%/100	77%/84%/94%	93%/94%/100
Wayne Trace	94%/96%/91%	94%/88%/95%	87%/83%/94%	79%/84%/83%
PERRY COUNTY				
District:				
New Lexington	69%/86%/96%	76%/87%/98%	54%/71%/75%	72%/77%/89%
Crooksville	76%/77%/92%	74%/82%/96%	60%/72%/83%	70%/75%/92%
Northern	87%/97%/99%	83%/96%/94%	68%/77%/78%	82%/91%/92%
Southern	85%/75%/77%	65%/80%/73%	43%/51%/59%	53%/65%/78%
PICKAWAY COUNTY				
District:				
Circleville	70%/87%/94%	70%/88%/95%	54%/74%/69%	73%/79%/89%
Logan Elm	75%/93%/97%	88%/92%/99%	63%/75%/83%	71%/81%/92%
Teays Valley	85%/96%/93%	90%/94%/93%	65%/78%/71%	85%/88%/83%
Westfall	85%/84%/96%	81%/84%/88%	55%/59%/61%	75%/69%/76%
PIKE COUNTY				
District:				
Waverly	79%/88%/96%	85%/95%/97%	50%/75%/80%	79%/89%/91%
Eastern	80%/79%/86%	61%/78%/88%	46%/58%/66%	54%/70%/78%
Scioto Valley	81%/82%/96%	86%/92%/91%	71%/73%/70%	89%/89%/79%
Western	84%/77%/92%	88%/77%/95%	63%/59%/68%	82%/82%/79%
PORTAGE COUNTY				
District:				
Aurora	90%/98%/100	94%/98%/99%	87%/89%/94%	97%/99%/99%
Kent	86%/95%/94%	93%/98%/99%	74%/85%/88%	89%/91%/93%
Ravenna	82%/97%/98%	88%/92%/98%	66%/71%/81%	79%/79%/90%
Streetsboro	73%/97%/92%	88%/96%/94%	57%/82%/69%	82%/91%/85%
Windham	93%/87%/96%	88%/85%/96%	67%/65%/70%	83%/76%/92%
Crestwood	69%/92%/93%	75%/92%/95%	68%/81%/87%	74%/75%/80%
Field	93%/98%/98%	92%/99%/95%	71%/74%/81%	83%/90%/87%

Continued on next page

Continued from preceeding page

	% PASSED WRITING 9th/10th/11th	% PASSED READING 9th/10th/11th	% PASSED MATH 9th/10th/11th	% PASSED CITIZEN 9th/10th/11th
STATE TOTAL	83%/94%/99%	85%/93%/99%	64%/74%/79%	79%/85%/89%
James A				
Garfield	81%/95%/98%	88%/92%/96%	59%/70%/80%	78%/73%/85%
Rootstown	91%/96%/96%	94%/97%/98%	82%/87%/81%	95%/94%/93%
Southeast	86%/99%/100	93%/95%/96%	72%/81%/85%	84%/85%/86%
Waterloo	80%/86%/98%	90%/92%/94%	60%/77%/77%	82%/80%/89%
PREBLE COUNTY				
District				
Eaton	81%/92%/96%	81%/92%/97%	67%/77%/77%	75%/83%/86%
C R Coblentz	65%/94%/88%	81%/89%/91%	56%/75%/74%	60%/83%/85%
Preble-Shawnee	77%/89%/93%	81%/91%/94%	58%/74%/68%	60%/77%/78%
Tri-County N	80%/96%/97%	94%/96%/95%	69%/79%/77%	91%/85%/86%
Twin Valley				
Community	87%/88%/91%	88%/86%/92%	61%/65%/71%	74%/77%/88%
PUTNAM COUNTY				
District				
Columbus Grove	92%/98%/95%	94%/98%/98%	77%/89%/90%	88%/94%/95%
Continental	90%/90%/89%	90%/94%/94%	75%/86%/88%	84%/92%/91%
Jennings	85%/97%/100	100%/97%/100	93%/97%/97%	100%/100/100
Kalida	97%/97%/97%	94%/97%/100	88%/97%/94%	89%/97%/98%
Leipsic	90%/98%/81%	92%/93%/84%	59%/74%/63%	76%/82%/77%
Miller City-				
New Cleveland	71%/92%/89%	97%/96%/98%	86%/94%/96%	86%/94%/96%
Ottawa-Glandorf	94%/93%/93%	89%/97%/98%	91%/92%/91%	92%/94%/90%
Ottoville	87%/96%/100	96%/100%/100	87%/98%/96%	94%/98%/100
Pandora-Gilboa	87%/96%/96%	92%/96%/100	77%/87%/92	89%/96%/92%
RICHLAND COUNTY				
District				
Mansfield	84%/93%/90%	77%/89%/90%	46%/50%/60%	66%/70%/77%
Shelby	74%/90%/98%	90%/97%/96%	80%/82%/87%	87%/83%/91%
Clear Fork Valley	77%/92%/99%	81%/94%/94%	69%/81%/84%	86%/89%/92%
Crestview	86%/98%/94%	87%/95%/94%	66%/78%/86%	87%/98%/90%
Lexington	94%/99%/100	94%/95%/96%	81%/84%/87%	87%/91%/91%
Lucas	88%/91%/95%	91%/90%/95%	73%/79%/85%	85%/95%/79%
Madison	82%/95%/98%	80%/89%/96%	62%/72%/77%	74%/77%/87%
Ontario	95%/97%/98%	93%/93%/97%	68%/81%/86%	96%/89%/93%
Plymouth	87%/84%/89%	81%/90%/88%	60%/65%/78%	63%/70%/82%
ROSS COUNTY				
District				
Chillicothe	74%/85%/89%	76%/82%/91%	57%/65%/70%	64%/79%/79%
Adena	92%/96%/92%	89%/99%/96%	72%/76%/73%	92%/91%/89%
Huntington	85%/94%/97%	88%/95%/96%	54%/64%/70%	85%/91%/91%
Paint Valley	84%/92%/99%	81%/89%/96%	57%/71%/80%	69%/82%/96%
Scioto Valley	86%/93%/100	86%/94%/97%	57%/69%/85%	81%/85%/95%
Union-Scioto	87%/94%/95%	84%/89%/94%	64%/64%/78%	79%/77%/92%
Zane Trace	96%/98%/98%	86%/94%/93%	54%/79%/77%	86%/94%/85%

Continued on next page

	% PASSED WRITING 9th/10th/11th	% PASSED READING 9th/10th/11th	% PASSED MATH 9th/10th/11th	% PASSED CITIZEN 9th/10th/11th
STATE TOTAL	83%/94%/99%	85%/93%/99%	64%/74%/79%	79%/86%/89%
SANDUSKY COUNTY				
District:				
Fremont	89%/95%/96%	88%/91%/96%	59%/73%/83%	78%/80%/90%
Clyde-Green				
Springs	86%/89%/95%	85%/90%/98%	66%/73%/77%	75%/84%/83%
Gibsonburg	77%/96%/93%	90%/99%/95%	70%/70%/86%	90%/91%/92%
Lakota	85%/82%/95%	84%/83%/95%	71%/70%/83%	88%/87%/93%
Woodmore	79%/88%/98%	83%/89%/96%	63%/74%/89%	78%/89%/94%
SCIOTO COUNTY				
District:				
Portsmouth	57%/83%/89%	63%/80%/95%	46%/57%/64%	57%/69%/75%
Bloom-Vernon	61%/79%/90%	83%/91%/95%	67%/73%/77%	61%/82%/89%
Clay	92%/96%/95%	82%/93%/92%	64%/62%/70%	84%/80%/79%
Green	71%/83%/98%	77%/92%/93%	41%/67%/79%	73%/86%/84%
Minford	77%/91%/94%	76%/91%/94%	59%/74%/80%	78%/76%/85%
New Boston	78%/92%/93%	83%/78%/97%	63%/58%/77%	83%/64%/80%
Northwest	73%/80%/83%	77%/85%/91%	61%/63%/65%	69%/73%/85%
Valley	93%/93%/99%	78%/90%/90%	62%/74%/76%	78%/81%/82%
Washington	56%/83%/93%	67%/85%/95%	40%/56%/65%	53%/65%/83%
Wheelersburg	76%/93%/96%	84%/90%/96%	51%/73%/81%	81%/83%/88%
SENECA COUNTY				
District:				
Fostoria	74%/85%/81%	73%/84%/82%	48%/72%/59%	76%/84%/77%
Tiffin	93%/97%/98%	92%/95%/97%	80%/83%/83%	88%/93%/92%
Bettsville	82%/97%/83%	96%/80%/93%	86%/77%/83%	86%/83%/87%
Hopewell-				
Loudon	100%/97%/99%	93%/97%/96%	83%/90%/87%	88%/95%/96%
New Riegel	89%/97%/100	95%/100/98%	79%/97%/88%	84%/97%/100
Old Fort	93%/100%/97%	98%/92%/100	95%/92%/92%	98%/89%/97%
Seneca East	93%/99%/100	89%/95%/95%	79%/85%/87%	85%/89%/91%
SHELBY COUNTY				
District:				
Sidney	79%/89%/93%	83%/89%/98%	67%/71%/75%	72%/78%/89%
Anna	93%/95%/96%	86%/91%/91%	77%/92%/96%	82%/88%/91%
Botkins	71%/91%/94%	88%/98%/100	81%/89%/98%	81%/91%/98%
Fairlawn	82%/94%/83%	75%/96%/83%	52%/69%/59%	84%/85%/85%
Fort Loramie	96%/97%/89%	93%/94%/89%	89%/82%/92%	87%/87%/92%
Hardin-Houston	86%/91%/93%	76%/93%/91%	61%/77%/78%	58%/77%/78%
Jackson Center	84%/96%/93%	86%/92%/100	86%/85%/81%	89%/94%/86%
Russia	89%/100%/91%	97%/100/94%	92%/100%/100	
92%/100%/97%				
STARK COUNTY				
District:				
Alliance	78%/93%/96%	79%/93%/94%	58%/63%/72%	69%/81%/83%
Canton	82%/98%/96%	84%/93%/94%	52%/66%/63%	73%/80%/79%
Louisville	95%/100%/99%	95%/98%/97%	83%/89%/94%	91%/96%/97%
Massillon	83%/90%/97%	78%/93%/96%	51%/72%/77%	76%/83%/86%

Continued on next page

Continued from preceeding page

	% PASSED WRITING 9th/10th/11th	% PASSED READING 9th/10th/11th	% PASSED MATH 9th/10th/11th	% PASSED CITIZEN 9th/10th/11th
STATE TOTAL	83%/94%/99%	85%/93%/99%	64%/74%/79%	79%/85%/89%
N Canton	90%/98%/99%	97%/99%/100	92%/89%/93%	97%/97%/97%
Canton	78%/96%/94%	86%/96%/97%	69%/95%/99%	82%/97%/95%
Fairless	86%/97%/85%	88%/99%/87%	79%/92%/75%	88%/96%/88%
Jackson	88%/93%/99%	95%/95%/99%	84%/87%/94%	95%/94%/98%
Lake	98%/98%/100	94%/98%/100	77%/90%/94%	95%/96%/99%
Marlington	91%/96%/98%	93%/97%/95%	71%/84%/81%	79%/92%/94%
Minerva	92%/95%/98%	88%/95%/95%	58%/81%/80%	83%/88%/89%
Northwest	79%/96%/95%	90%/97%/99%	69%/79%/88%	91%/94%/93%
Osnaburg	87%/93%/93%	100/95%/98%	80%/74%/84%	91%/91%/88%
Perry	91%/99%/98%	96%/99%/99%	88%/83%/82%	95%/96%/95%
Plain	88%/98%/99%	90%/97%/98%	78%/81%/88%	93%/95%/97%
Sandy Valley	93%/100%/90%	86%/93%/90%	75%/78%/71%	91%/88%/81%
Tuslaw	88%/93%/95%	89%/96%/97%	75%/81%/73%	82%/88%/83%
SUMMIT COUNTY District:				
Akron	74%/92%/93%	78%/91%/98%	43%/59%/68%	65%/75%/80%
Barberton	79%/90%/93%	81%/91%/97%	60%/59%/72%	77%/78%/82%
Copley-Fairlawn	99%/98%/99%	93%/94%/99%	79%/88%/93%	92%/93%/97%
Cuyahoga Falls	88%/97%/95%	86%/96%/98%	74%/83%/81%	80%/91%/92%
Nordonia Hills	89%/99%/99%	91%/96%/99%	78%/82%/88%	90%/95%/100
Norton	89%/95%/97%	92%/98%/97%	79%/86%/81%	90%/93%/93%
Stow	93%/96%/97%	94%/97%/100	83%/87%/88%	92%/91%/95%
Tallmadge	96%/99%/98%	93%/99%/97%	77%/88%/87%	89%/89%/96%
Twinsburg	88%/95%/97%	88%/97%/100	72%/84%/79%	91%/95%/91%
Coventry	89%/96%/99%	88%/94%/97%	62%/84%/87%	82%/91%/91%
Green	97%/94%/99%	91%/96%/98%	83%/85%/86%	89%/90%/90%
Hudson	96%/98%/98%	97%/99%/98%	95%/95%/96%	94%/96%/98%
Manchester	93%/96%/98%	96%/93%/98%	82%/81%/89%	90%/86%/96%
Mogadore	83%/91%/97%	92%/85%/93%	75%/76%/84%	89%/80%/93%
Revere	93%/99%/98%	97%/97%/100	93%/97%/94%	94%/96%/98%
Springfield	79%/87%/91%	82%/87%/90%	71%/68%/75%	76%/76%/78%
Woodridge	79%/95%/100	92%/96%/94%	80%/81%/85%	87%/94%/93%
TRUMBULL COUNTY District:				
Girard	89%/94%/96%	86%/90%/98%	71%/81%/76%	76%/84%/87%
Niles	79%/94%/99%	82%/92%/98%	67%/70%/79%	85%/84%/87%
Warren	71%/88%/89%	77%/89%/96%	46%/51%/56%	67%/72%/73%
Hubbard	83%/96%/97%	93%/96%/97%	79%/82%/85%	91%/89%/92%
Newton Falls	85%/90%/98%	89%/95%/94%	75%/79%/80%	72%/85%/84%
Bloomfield-Mespo	63%/82%/96%	80%/88%/96%	57%/79%/81%	83%/88%/96%
Bristol	88%/96%/95%	88%/98%/96%	71%/85%/93%	80%/93%/95%
Brookfield	96%/97%/99%	93%/94%/97%	64%/76%/83%	90%/92%/93%
Champion	84%/95%/97%	89%/97%/95%	69%/86%/84%	86%/96%/93%
Howland	94%/97%/95%	93%/98%/99%	75%/82%/86%	87%/93%/95%
Joseph Badger	85%/92%/95%	88%/92%/99%	67%/81%/79%	72%/87%/88%
LaBrae	79%/96%/93%	88%/94%/98%	62%/76%/79%	80%/89%/93%

Continued on next page

	% PASSED WRITING 9th/10th/11th	% PASSED READING 9th/10th/11th	% PASSED MATH 9th/10th/11th	% PASSED CITIZEN 9th/10th/11th
STATE TOTAL	83%/94%/99%	85%/93%/99%	64%/74%/79%	79%/85%/89%
Lakeview	96%/97%/97%	95%/96%/98%	79%/83%/86%	88%/85%/94%
Liberty	87%/97%/94%	91%/93%/99%	73%/77%/82%	85%/88%/94%
Lordstown	93%/94%/100	98%/98%/100	95%/87%/96%	98%/98%/100
Maplewood	90%/90%/87%	94%/93%/88%	76%/90%/81%	97%/92%/89%
Mathews	91%/96%/96%	89%/94%/100	73%/78%/90%	88%/86%/88%
McDonald	98%/100%/95%	98%/99%/98%	88%/99%/92%	98%/99%/98%
Southington	92%/89%/96%	90%/92%/96%	79%/78%/87%	85%/78%/85%
Weathersfield	92%/98%/100	91%/99%/95%	70%/90%/89%	88%/96%/88%
TUSCARAWAS COUNTY District:				
Claymont	87%/87%/86%	89%/87%/93%	65%/78%/63%	85%/80%/78%
Dover	88%/96%/98%	91%/95%/99%	69%/81%/84%	80%/85%/91%
New Philadelphia	77%/85%/95%	89%/90%/94%	59%/81%/81%	84%/81%/83%
Newcomerstown	85%/92%/93%	74%/89%/88%	65%/69%/75%	76%/78%/79%
Garaway	93%/97%/99%	94%/97%/99%	78%/87%/94%	88%/97%/97%
Indian Valley	71%/89%/94%	92%/94%/97%	76%/76%/86%	88%/89%/87%
Strasburg-Franklin	93%/96%/100	84%/96%/95%	75%/83%/84%	76%/94%/91%
Tuscarawas Valley	88%/91%/98%	92%/92%/94%	74%/75%/85%	89%/88%/94%
UNION COUNTY District:				
Marysville	82%/88%/92%	82%/86%/93%	65%/76%/73%	77%/82%/81%
Fairbanks	92%/94%/93%	89%/92%/98%	77%/94%/89%	83%/82%/89%
N Union	82%/94%/98%	87%/97%/94%	62%/87%/83%	74%/91%/86%
VAN WERT COUNTY District:				
Van Wert	95%/97%/97%	93%/94%/93%	72%/76%/78%	88%/88%/86%
Crestview	96%/99%/99%	91%/97%/100	83%/91%/96%	88%/97%/97%
Lincolnview	92%/92%/94%	96%/88%/96%	82%/78%/81%	92%/94%/84%
VINTON COUNTY District:				
Vinton	60%/76%/80%	88%/91%/93%	55%/73%/67%	78%/86%/89%
WARREN COUNTY District:				
Franklin	83%/94%/93%	86%/91%/93%	66%/73%/76%	86%/84%/86%
Lebanon	85%/97%/98%	93%/96%/96%	76%/87%/87%	91%/94%/90%
Mason	94%/93%/99%	92%/93%/98%	91%/93%/86%	95%/95%/88%
Springboro	87%/93%/98%	94%/95%/98%	74%/86%/88%	88%/97%/95%
Carlisle	84%/93%/97%	77%/89%/89%	58%/74%/77%	88%/93%/88%
Kings	87%/96%/95%	87%/92%/98%	73%/78%/87%	82%/88%/91%
Little Miami	77%/98%/93%	82%/92%/97%	61%/84%/88%	79%/90%/91%
Wayne	83%/99%/96%	81%/92%/100	69%/82%/88%	84%/97%/97%

Continued on next page

Continued from preceeding page

	% PASSED WRITING 9th/10th/11th	% PASSED READING 9th/10th/11th	% PASSED MATH 9th/10th/11th	% PASSED CITIZEN 9th/10th/11th
STATE TOTAL	83%/94%/99%	85%/93%/99%	64%/74%/79%	79%/85%/89%

WASHINGTON COUNTY

District:

Belpre	89%/92%/99%%	85%/94%/97%	74%/79%/88%	79%/84%/92%
Marietta	81%/86%/95%	78%/87%/96%	63%/70%/78%	74%/79%/86%
Fort Frye	80%/87%/94%	84%/89%/95%	69%/74%/85%	75%/82%/90%
Frontier	66%/94%/92%	89%/92%/95%	41%/64%/70%	75%/87%/84%
Warren	92%/97%/96%	95%/95%/98%	73%/82%/82%	86%/86%/90%
Wolf Creek	86%/83%/93%	88%/89%/95%	74%/80%/85%	80%/88%/91%

WAYNE COUNTY

District:

Orrville	88%/94%/93%	84%/95%/91%	69%/80%/76%	87%/85%/84%
Wooster	87%/98%/98%	92%/96%/98%	77%/77%/81%	86%/87%/89%
Rittman	90%/94%/90%	90%/91%/99%	66%/80%/71%	80%/84%/79%
Chippewa	92%/99%/99%	89%/94%/91%	74%/80%/84%	93%/90%/89%
Dalton	93%/99%/95%	94%/97%/99%	86%/86%/88%	92%/88%/93%
Green	97%/97%/94%	95%/97%/96%	86%/87%/89%	94%/95%/95%
N Central	82%/96%/94%	92%/91%/94%	68%/79%/81%	81%/88%/84%
Northwestern	95%/90%/91%	93%/98%/88%	79%/77%/77%	89%/91%/85%
Southeast	87%/97%/92%	89%/95%/99%	71%/78%/83%	72%/85%/90%
Triway	88%/95%/96%	94%/97%/98%	75%/84%/88%	86%/89%/92%

WILLIAMS COUNTY

District:

Bryan	96%/98%/94%	89%/98%/98%	76%/84%/86%	84%/89%/88%
Montpelier	81%/91%/94%	89%/93%/92%	73%/76%/78%	85%/80%/83%
Edgerton	91%/92%/93%	95%/87%/94%	80%/70%/74%	91%/80%/85%
Edon-Northwest	96%/98%/96%	88%/93%/92%	82%/88%/85%	86%/93%/96%
Millcreek-W Unity	88%/95%/95%	86%/95%/92%	81%/82%/93%	97%/95%/90%
N Central	82%/94%/87%	89%/92%/94%	76%/81%/81%	87%/93%/83%
Stryker	96%/100%/100	98%/91%/91%	81%/75%/78%	89%/81%/78%

WOOD COUNTY

District:

Bowling Green	91%/98%/99%	87%/95%/97%	75%/86%/88%	82%/92%/94%
Perrysburg	91%/94%/99%	91%/96%/98%	81%/86%/89%	94%/92%/94%
Rossford	94%/95%/92%	78%/92%/96%	70%/78%/81%	74%/87%/90%
Eastwood	77%/98%/90%	90%/95%/95%	70%/80%/77%	86%/89%/90%
Elmwood	87%/94%/95%	92%/92%/95%	78%/74%/74%	89%/91%/91%
Lake	89%/91%/96%	90%/89%/97%	71%/72%/86%	87%/88%/95%
N Baltimore	90%/88%/92%	83%/88%/83%	68%/67%/75%	83%/77%/88%
Northwood	82%/91%/92%	85%/87%/93%	73%/84%/90%	78%/88%/93%
Otsego	91%/98%/97%	94%/97%/97%	82%/75%/87%	90%/94%/92%

WYANDOT COUNTY

District:

Carey	93%/96%/100	90%/95%/98%	65%/72%/81%	81%/85%/94%
Upper Sandusky	93%/97%/99%	86%/97%/100	76%/80%/90%	87%/91%/96%
Mohawk	95%/95%/98%	96%/93%/95%	83%/78%/90%	92%/85%/94%

Source - Dept. Of Education

OBS	DISTRICT	COUNTY	TOTAL ENROLLMENT 1994	VALUATION PER 1994
1	Ohio Valley Local SD	Adams	5,460	$ 92,448
2	Delphos City SD	Allen	1,065	90,844
3	Lima City SD	Allen	6,252	41,759
4	Bluffton Ex Vill SD	Allen	1,174	63,259
5	Allen East Local SD	Allen	1,183	53,581
6	Bath Local SD	Allen	2,239	121,169
7	Elida Local SD	Allen	3,410	60,333
8	Perry Local SD	Allen	772	74,495
9	Shawnee Local SD	Allen	2,656	119,281
10	Spencerville Local SD	Allen	1,054	46,607
11	Ashland City SD	Ashland	4,517	60,132
12	Loudonville-Perrysville Ex Vil	Ashland	1,481	69,101
13	Hillsdale Local SD	Ashland	1,210	63,073
14	Mapleton Local SD	Ashland	1,086	41,770
15	Ashtabula Area City SD	Ashtabula	5,347	49,841
16	Conneaut Area City SD	Ashtabula	2,482	45,625
17	Geneva Area City SD	Ashtabula	3,208	44,281
18	Buckeye Local SD	Ashtabula	2,250	90,103
19	Grand Valley Local SD	Ashtabula	1,370	48,228
20	Jefferson Area Local SD	Ashtabula	2,196	46,532
21	Pymatuning Valley Local SD	Ashtabula	1,453	51,835
22	Athens City SD	Athens	3,243	69,800
23	Nelsonville-York City SD	Athens	1,621	30,747
24	Alexander Local SD	Athens	1,711	52,406
25	Federal Hocking Local SD	Athens	1,662	35,143
26	Trimble Local SD	Athens	1,110	18,086
27	St Marys City SD	Auglaize	2,581	53,454
28	Wapakoneta City SD	Auglaize	3,866	46,952
29	Minster Local SD	Auglaize	859	92,888
30	New Bremen Local SD	Auglaize	901	64,875
31	New Knoxville Local SD	Auglaize	491	51,882
32	Waynesfield-Goshen Local SD	Auglaize	565	36,815
33	Bellaire City SD	Belmont	1,938	36,087
34	Martins Ferry City SD	Belmont	1,703	52,857
35	Barnesville Ex Vill SD	Belmont	1,433	37,202
36	Bridgeport Ex Vill SD	Belmont	895	54,568
37	St Clairsville-Richland City S	Belmont	1,896	84,673
38	Shadyside Local SD	Belmont	912	98,293
39	Union Local SD	Belmont	1,720	36,710
40	Georgetown Ex Vill SD	Brown	1,120	44,843
41	Eastern Local SD	Brown	1,550	37,046
42	Fayetteville-Perry Local SD	Brown	865	35,440
43	Western Brown Local SD	Brown	3,052	30,286
44	Ripley-Union-Lewis Local SD	Brown	1,198	41,592
45	Hamilton City SD	Butler	10,681	54,304
46	Middletown City SD	Butler	9,895	85,354
47	Edgewood City SD	Butler	2,590	57,019
48	Fairfield City SD	Butler	8,499	79,916

Continued from preceeding page

OBS	DISTRICT	COUNTY	TOTAL ENROLLMENT 1994	VALUATION PER 1994
49	Lakota Local SD	Butler	11,840	$ 81,945
50	Madison Local SD	Butler	1,580	45,719
51	New Miami Local SD	Butler	984	35,145
52	Ross Local SD	Butler	2,693	52,818
53	Talawanda City SD	Butler	3,422	75,751
54	Carrollton Ex Vill SD	Carroll	2,999	48,114
55	Brown Local SD	Carroll	1,121	49,871
56	Urbana City SD	Champaign	2,535	67,419
57	Mechanicsburg Ex Vill SD	Champaign	807	40,526
58	Graham Local SD	Champaign	2,250	50,398
59	Triad Local SD	Champaign	943	36,461
60	West Liberty-Salem Local SD	Champaign	1,032	56,467
61	Springfield City SD	Clark	11,440	48,739
62	Mad River-Green Local SD	Clark	2,276	64,126
63	Tecumseh Local SD	Clark	3,761	46,343
64	Northeastern Local SD	Clark	3,078	79,845
65	Northwestern Local SD	Clark	1,997	68,693
66	Southeastern Local SD	Clark	856	60,260
67	Springfield Local SD	Clark	2,321	79,283
68	Milford Ex Vill SD	Clermont	5,689	67,526
69	New Richmond Ex Vill SD	Clermont	2,743	220,834
70	Batavia Local SD	Clermont	1,569	66,363
71	Bethel-Tate Local SD	Clermont	2,077	34,787
72	Clermont-Northeastern Local SD	Clermont	2,481	60,174
73	Felicity-Franklin Local SD	Clermont	1,336	23,215
74	Goshen Local SD	Clermont	2,651	35,892
75	West Clermont Local SD	Clermont	9,047	63,772
76	Williamsburg Local SD	Clermont	1,117	56,522
77	Wilmington City SD	Clinton	3,329	67,434
78	Blanchester Local SD	Clinton	1,874	33,381
79	Clinton-Massie Local SD	Clinton	1,510	39,488
80	East Clinton Local SD	Clinton	1,600	40,943
81	East Liverpool City SD	Columbiana	3,583	31,297
82	East Palestine City SD	Columbiana	1,625	40,139
83	Salem City SD	Columbiana	2,904	67,828
84	Wellsville City SD	Columbiana	1,229	24,342
85	Columbiana Ex Vill SD	Columbiana	1,087	67,883
86	Leetonia Ex Vill SD	Columbiana	890	38,939
87	Lisbon Ex Vill SD	Columbiana	1,290	39,416
88	Beaver Local SD	Columbiana	2,360	51,211
89	Crestview Local SD	Columbiana	1,211	44,593
90	Southern Local SD	Columbiana	1,156	39,154
91	United Local SD	Columbiana	1,604	39,714
92	Coshocton City SD	Coshocton	2,118	64,475
93	Ridgewood Local SD	Coshocton	1,584	43,317
94	River View Local SD	Coshocton	2,752	111,422
95	Bucyrus City SD	Crawford	2,039	54,498
96	Galion City SD	Crawford	2,649	45,902

Continued on next page

OBS	DISTRICT	COUNTY	TOTAL ENROLLMENT 1994	VALUATION PER 1994
97	Crestline Ex Vill SD	Crawford	1,031	$ 58,263
98	Buckeye Central Local SD	Crawford	637	55,881
99	Colonel Crawford Local SD	Crawford	1,092	79,054
100	Wynford Local SD	Crawford	1,248	50,128
101	Bay Village City SD	Cuyahoga	2,459	117,201
102	Beachwood City SD	Cuyahoga	1,447	332,211
103	Bedford City SD	Cuyahoga	3,827	164,792
104	Berea City SD	Cuyahoga	7,826	138,033
105	Brecksville-Broadview Heights	Cuyahoga	3,448	154,131
106	Brooklyn City SD	Cuyahoga	1,270	195,852
107	Cleveland City SD	Cuyahoga	71,358	69,450
108	Cleveland Hts-Univ Hts City SD	Cuyahoga	7,592	94,798
109	East Cleveland City SD	Cuyahoga	7,743	28,408
110	Euclid City SD	Cuyahoga	5,595	131,609
111	Fairview Park City SD	Cuyahoga	1,881	133,364
112	Garfield Heights City SD	Cuyahoga	2,944	100,752
113	Lakewood City SD	Cuyahoga	8,330	71,543
114	Maple Heights City SD	Cuyahoga	3,406	93,186
115	Mayfield City SD	Cuyahoga	3,904	207,054
116	North Olmsted City SD	Cuyahoga	5,061	108,755
117	North Royalton City SD	Cuyahoga	3,845	123,025
118	Parma City SD	Cuyahoga	13,296	123,855
119	Rocky River City SD	Cuyahoga	1,993	223,539
120	Shaker Heights City SD	Cuyahoga	4,972	121,734
121	South Euclid-Lyndhurst City SD	Cuyahoga	4,421	134,540
122	Strongsville City SD	Cuyahoga	6,343	113,250
123	Warrensville Heights City SD	Cuyahoga	3,087	98,829
124	Westlake City SD	Cuyahoga	3,833	181,230
125	Chagrin Falls Ex Vill SD	Cuyahoga	1,695	152,442
126	Cuyahoga Heights Local SD	Cuyahoga	744	583,916
127	Independence Local SD	Cuyahoga	903	370,867
128	Olmsted Falls City SD	Cuyahoga	2,691	73,828
129	Orange City SD	Cuyahoga	2,439	252,070
130	Richmond Heights Local SD	Cuyahoga	907	150,721
131	Solon City SD	Cuyahoga	3,949	192,618
132	Greenville City SD	Darke	3,882	65,354
133	Versailles Ex Vill SD	Darke	1,373	45,277
134	Ansonia Local SD	Darke	724	39,661
135	Arcanum Butler Local SD	Darke	1,186	45,543
136	Franklin-Monroe Local SD	Darke	747	40,600
137	Mississinawa Valley Local SD	Darke	916	35,095
138	Tri-Village Local SD	Darke	921	45,871
139	Defiance City SD	Defiance	3,325	48,573
140	Hicksville Ex Vill SD	Defiance	1,023	48,109
141	Ayersville Local SD	Defiance	850	84,753
142	Central Local SD	Defiance	1,237	44,352
143	Northeastern Local SD	Defiance	1,219	75,375
144	Delaware City SD	Delaware	3,891	70,318

Continued on next page

OBS	DISTRICT	COUNTY	TOTAL ENROLLMENT 1994	VALUATION PER 1994
145	Big Walnut Local SD	Delaware	2,534	$ 72,604
146	Buckeye Valley Local SD	Delaware	2,197	59,184
147	Olentangy Local SD	Delaware	2,578	161,682
148	Huron City SD	Erie	1,488	105,169
149	Sandusky City SD	Erie	4,722	67,726
150	Berlin-Milan Local SD	Erie	1,668	69,775
151	Kelleys Island Local SD	Erie	16	934,908
152	Margaretta Local SD	Erie	1,535	74,828
153	Perkins Local SD	Erie	2,040	115,605
154	Vermilion Local SD	Erie	2,598	95,254
155	Lancaster City SD	Fairfield	6,516	71,012
156	Amanda-Clearcreek Local SD	Fairfield	1,541	31,665
157	Berne Union Local SD	Fairfield	1,026	57,760
158	Bloom Carroll Local SD	Fairfield	1,605	57,250
159	Fairfield Union Local SD	Fairfield	1,888	39,772
160	Liberty Union-Thurston Local S	Fairfield	1,304	47,645
161	Pickerington Local SD	Fairfield	5,478	56,502
162	Walnut Township Local SD	Fairfield	690	75,933
163	Washington Court House City SD	Fayette	2,340	45,587
164	Miami Trace Local SD	Fayette	3,017	54,745
165	Bexley City SD	Franklin	2,314	101,807
166	Columbus City SD	Franklin	64,007	91,277
167	Grandview Heights City SD	Franklin	1,298	107,255
168	South-Western City SD	Franklin	16,515	75,759
169	Upper Arlington City SD	Franklin	5,382	140,135
170	Westerville City SD	Franklin	12,411	83,518
171	Whitehall City SD	Franklin	3,120	74,720
172	Worthington City SD	Franklin	10,623	113,866
173	Canal Winchester Local SD	Franklin	1,095	77,872
174	Hamilton Local SD	Franklin	2,349	51,538
175	Gahanna-Jefferson City SD	Franklin	6,827	92,630
176	Groveport Madison Local SD	Franklin	5,816	58,563
177	Plain Local SD	Franklin	722	164,215
178	Reynoldsburg City SD	Franklin	4,871	66,585
179	Hilliard City SD	Franklin	8,462	97,141
180	Dublin City SD	Franklin	8,985	133,872
181	Wauseon Ex Vill SD	Fulton	1,886	56,544
182	Archbold-Area Local SD	Fulton	1,457	99,787
183	Evergreen Local SD	Fulton	1,245	64,569
184	Gorham Fayette Local SD	Fulton	496	54,030
185	Pettisville Local SD	Fulton	456	51,587
186	Pike-Delta-York Local SD	Fulton	1,643	42,776
187	Swanton Local SD	Fulton	1,792	61,032
188	Gallipolis City SD	Gallia	2,657	48,536
189	Gallia County Local SD	Gallia	3,143	110,362
190	Berkshire Local SD	Geauga	1,276	71,704
191	Cardinal Local SD	Geauga	1,446	87,428
192	Chardon Local SD	Geauga	2,915	91,118

Continued on next page

OBS	DISTRICT	COUNTY	TOTAL ENROLLMENT 1994	VALUATION PER 1994
193	Kenston Local SD	Geauga	2,529	$106,988
194	Ledgemont Local SD	Geauga	702	59,369
195	Newbury Local SD	Geauga	853	107,581
196	West Geauga Local SD	Geauga	2,204	154,560
197	Fairborn City SD	Greene	6,627	53,239
198	Xenia City SD	Greene	5,952	59,619
199	Yellow Springs Ex Vill SD	Greene	640	84,878
200	Beavercreek Local SD	Greene	6,468	101,652
201	Cedar Cliff Local SD	Greene	740	51,256
202	Greeneview Local SD	Greene	1,669	46,903
203	Sugarcreek Local SD	Greene	2,125	80,542
204	Cambridge City SD	Guernsey	3,049	47,529
205	Rolling Hills Local SD	Guernsey	2,238	53,973
206	East Guernsey Local SD	Guernsey	1,137	44,966
207	Cincinnati City SD	Hamilton	49,438	96,781
208	Deer Park Community City SD	Hamilton	1,536	93,340
209	Winton Woods City SD	Hamilton	4,535	71,557
210	Lockland City SD	Hamilton	844	226,856
211	Loveland City SD	Hamilton	3,300	74,059
212	Madeira City SD	Hamilton	1,338	98,341
213	Mariemont City SD	Hamilton	1,546	108,569
214	Mount Healthy City SD	Hamilton	3,904	56,309
215	North College Hill City SD	Hamilton	1,341	75,241
216	Norwood City SD	Hamilton	3,783	57,912
217	Princeton City SD	Hamilton	6,743	205,169
218	Reading Community City SD	Hamilton	1,339	120,325
219	St Bernard-Elmwood Place City	Hamilton	1,279	173,460
220	Sycamore Community City SD	Hamilton	6,064	177,504
221	Wyoming City SD	Hamilton	1,613	87,294
222	Indian Hill Ex Vill SD	Hamilton	1,838	269,954
223	Finneytown Local SD	Hamilton	1,727	77,363
224	Forest Hills Local SD	Hamilton	7,877	97,112
225	Northwest Local SD	Hamilton	10,563	81,152
226	Oak Hills Local SD	Hamilton	8,446	85,193
227	Southwest Local SD	Hamilton	4,068	58,990
228	Three Rivers Local SD	Hamilton	2,109	131,921
229	Findlay City SD	Hancock	6,293	83,252
230	Arcadia Local SD	Hancock	602	80,824
231	Arlington Local SD	Hancock	700	53,086
232	Cory-Rawson Local SD	Hancock	783	93,289
233	Liberty Benton Local SD	Hancock	909	83,185
234	McComb Local SD	Hancock	839	65,836
235	Van Buren Local SD	Hancock	802	157,291
236	Vanlue Local SD	Hancock	330	51,184
237	Kenton City SD	Hardin	2,273	54,083
238	Ada Ex Vill SD	Hardin	900	41,571
239	Hardin Northern Local SD	Hardin	614	42,428
240	Ridgemont Local SD	Hardin	534	48,583

Continued on next page

Continued from preceeding page

OBS	DISTRICT	COUNTY	TOTAL ENROLLMENT 1994	VALUATION PER 1994
241	Riverdale Local SD	Hardin	1,225	$ 46,431
242	Upper Scioto Valley Local SD	Hardin	790	36,902
243	Harrison Hills City SD	Harrison	2,578	53,624
244	Conotton Valley Union Local SD	Harrison	600	57,791
245	Napoleon City SD	Henry	2,540	67,531
246	Holgate Local SD	Henry	656	39,672
247	Liberty Center Local SD	Henry	1,026	52,154
248	Patrick Henry Local SD	Henry	1,260	50,452
249	Hillsboro City SD	Highland	2,710	45,970
250	Greenfield Ex Vill SD	Highland	2,260	33,338
251	Bright Local SD	Highland	864	31,354
252	Fairfield Local SD	Highland	777	33,384
253	Lynchburg-Clay Local SD	Highland	1,214	29,246
254	Logan-Hocking City SD	Hocking	3,993	54,292
255	East Holmes Local SD	Holmes	2,039	76,979
256	West Holmes Local SD	Holmes	2,599	63,052
257	Bellevue City SD	Huron	2,400	63,886
258	Norwalk City SD	Huron	2,695	69,630
259	Willard City SD	Huron	2,338	59,356
260	Monroeville Local SD	Huron	698	62,776
261	New London Local SD	Huron	1,270	32,652
262	South Central Local SD	Huron	980	37,885
263	Western Reserve Local SD	Huron	1,339	36,535
264	Jackson City SD	Jackson	2,795	43,876
265	Wellston City SD	Jackson	1,872	36,173
266	Oak Hill Union Local SD	Jackson	1,364	42,510
267	Steubenville City SD	Jefferson	2,673	53,011
268	Toronto City SD	Jefferson	1,073	60,525
269	Buckeye Local SD	Jefferson	2,804	92,536
270	Edison Local SD	Jefferson	2,981	111,262
271	Indian Creek Local SD	Jefferson	2,843	76,903
272	Mount Vernon City SD	Knox	4,086	73,337
273	Centerburg Local SD	Knox	942	37,060
274	Danville Local SD	Knox	698	34,500
275	East Knox Local SD	Knox	905	69,316
276	Fredericktown Local SD	Knox	1,308	42,711
277	Painesville City SD	Lake	2,391	59,172
278	Wickliffe City SD	Lake	1,540	163,155
279	Willoughby-Eastlake City SD	Lake	8,834	125,621
280	Fairport Harbor Ex Vill SD	Lake	535	63,202
281	Mentor Ex Vill SD	Lake	11,134	88,900
282	Kirtland Local SD	Lake	846	185,045
283	Madison Local SD	Lake	3,454	48,085
284	Painesville Local SD	Lake	3,864	103,392
285	Perry Local SD	Lake	1,706	407,180
286	Ironton City SD	Lawrence	2,146	44,135
287	Chesapeake Union Ex Vill SD	Lawrence	1,504	37,551
288	Dawson-Bryant Local SD	Lawrence	1,336	24,280

Continued on next page

OBS	DISTRICT	COUNTY	TOTAL ENROLLMENT 1994	VALUATION PER 1994
289	Fairland Local SD	Lawrence	1,869	$ 34,534
290	Rock Hill Local SD	Lawrence	1,988	37,933
291	South Point Local SD	Lawrence	2,237	46,843
292	Symmes Valley Local SD	Lawrence	1,045	23,919
293	Heath City SD	Licking	1,310	108,011
294	Newark City SD	Licking	8,233	53,912
295	Granville Ex Vill SD	Licking	1,390	96,897
296	Johnstown-Monroe Local SD	Licking	1,288	58,488
297	Lakewood Local SD	Licking	2,229	86,462
298	Licking Heights Local SD	Licking	1,092	80,390
299	Licking Valley Local SD	Licking	1,899	38,453
300	North Fork Local SD	Licking	1,867	43,919
301	Northridge Local SD	Licking	1,278	62,530
302	Southwest Licking Local SD	Licking	2,916	53,424
303	Bellefontaine City SD	Logan	2,962	60,789
304	Benjamin Logan Local SD	Logan	1,949	91,725
305	Indian Lake Local SD	Logan	2,133	78,337
306	Riverside Local SD	Logan	831	34,108
307	Elyria City SD	Lorain	9,470	66,691
308	Lorain City SD	Lorain	11,158	45,561
309	North Ridgeville City SD	Lorain	3,624	65,694
310	Oberlin City SD	Lorain	1,310	70,989
311	Sheffield-Sheffield Lake City	Lorain	2,233	62,414
312	Amherst Ex Vill SD	Lorain	3,334	74,375
313	Wellington Ex Vill SD	Lorain	1,600	49,819
314	Avon Local SD	Lorain	1,085	105,098
315	Avon Lake City SD	Lorain	2,942	143,810
316	Clearview Local SD	Lorain	1,027	52,154
317	Columbia Local SD	Lorain	1,209	66,913
318	Firelands Local SD	Lorain	1,981	55,886
319	Keystone Local SD	Lorain	1,904	47,968
320	Midview Local SD	Lorain	3,162	57,489
321	Maumee City SD	Lucas	3,177	110,965
322	Oregon City SD	Lucas	3,854	112,360
323	Sylvania City SD	Lucas	7,295	105,796
324	Toledo City SD	Lucas	38,676	60,338
325	Anthony Wayne Local SD	Lucas	3,153	87,051
326	Ottawa Hills Local SD	Lucas	852	134,113
327	Springfield Local SD	Lucas	3,880	86,880
328	Washington Local SD	Lucas	7,256	102,611
329	London City SD	Madison	2,110	61,294
330	Jefferson Local SD	Madison	1,296	57,696
331	Jonathan Alder Local SD	Madison	1,514	55,743
332	Madison-Plains Local SD	Madison	1,778	59,093
333	Campbell City SD	Mahoning	1,507	37,437
334	Struthers City SD	Mahoning	2,330	34,699
335	Youngstown City SD	Mahoning	13,793	39,339
336	Austintown Local SD	Mahoning	5,261	65,015

Continued on next page

OBS	DISTRICT	COUNTY	TOTAL ENROLLMENT 1994	VALUATION PER 1994
337	Boardman Local SD	Mahoning	5,272	$ 94,369
338	Canfield Local SD	Mahoning	2,680	78,252
339	Jackson-Milton Local SD	Mahoning	1,161	68,855
340	Lowellville Local SD	Mahoning	451	47,753
341	Poland Local SD	Mahoning	2,386	69,445
342	Sebring Local SD	Mahoning	773	35,241
343	South Range Local SD	Mahoning	1,088	59,315
344	Springfield Local SD	Mahoning	1,401	41,581
345	West Branch Local SD	Mahoning	2,583	42,429
346	Western Reserve Local SD	Mahoning	753	55,093
347	Marion City SD	Marion	6,289	38,417
348	Elgin Local SD	Marion	1,601	59,835
349	Pleasant Local SD	Marion	1,320	61,328
350	Ridgedale Local SD	Marion	1,007	50,613
351	River Valley Local SD	Marion	1,811	91,747
352	Brunswick City SD	Medina	6,941	56,893
353	Medina City SD	Medina	5,633	79,995
354	Wadsworth City SD	Medina	3,832	72,420
355	Black River Local SD	Medina	1,300	49,083
356	Buckeye Local SD	Medina	2,181	82,131
357	Cloverleaf Local SD	Medina	3,726	57,223
358	Highland Local SD	Medina	2,059	98,422
359	Eastern Local SD	Meigs	862	39,193
360	Meigs Local SD	Meigs	2,571	45,999
361	Southern Local SD	Meigs	905	65,312
362	Celina City SD	Mercer	3,432	58,694
363	Coldwater Ex Vill SD	Mercer	1,516	52,175
364	Marion Local SD	Mercer	854	39,292
365	Parkway Local SD	Mercer	1,225	45,327
366	St Henry Consolidated Local SD	Mercer	1,066	38,476
367	Fort Recovery Local SD	Mercer	940	43,436
368	Piqua City SD	Miami	4,127	64,362
369	Troy City SD	Miami	4,759	96,898
370	Bradford Ex Vill SD	Miami	679	26,468
371	Covington Ex Vill SD	Miami	916	58,182
372	Milton-Union Ex Vill SD	Miami	1,887	55,722
373	Tipp City Ex Vill SD	Miami	2,508	74,232
374	Bethel Local SD	Miami	814	80,882
375	Miami East Local SD	Miami	1,444	54,148
376	Newton Local SD	Miami	581	49,481
377	Switzerland Of Ohio Local SD	Monroe	3,352	82,667
378	Centerville City SD	Montgomery	7,188	134,042
379	Dayton City SD	Montgomery	28,349	59,129
380	Kettering City SD	Montgomery	7,907	129,888
381	Miamisburg City SD	Montgomery	4,373	122,397
382	Oakwood City SD	Montgomery	1,540	116,983
383	Vandalia-Butler City SD	Montgomery	3,605	117,272
384	West Carrollton City SD	Montgomery	4,126	84,358

Continued on next page

OBS	DISTRICT	COUNTY	TOTAL ENROLLMENT 1994	VALUATION PER 1994
385	Brookville Local SD	Montgomery	1,606	$ 56,715
386	Jefferson Township Local SD	Montgomery	970	60,016
387	Trotwood-Madison City SD	Montgomery	4,053	53,196
388	Mad River Local SD	Montgomery	3,870	47,857
389	New Lebanon Local SD	Montgomery	1,443	40,383
390	Northmont City SD	Montgomery	6,108	59,456
391	Northridge Local SD	Montgomery	2,216	94,124
392	Valley View Local SD	Montgomery	1,913	56,084
393	Huber Heights City SD	Montgomery	7,869	54,045
394	Morgan Local SD	Morgan	2,703	49,882
395	Mount Gilead Ex Vill SD	Morrow	1,396	49,816
396	Cardington-Lincoln Local SD	Morrow	1,152	33,450
397	Highland Local SD	Morrow	1,732	28,677
398	Northmor Local SD	Morrow	1,155	51,658
399	Zanesville City SD	Muskingum	4,825	52,359
400	East Muskingum Local SD	Muskingum	2,275	43,319
401	Franklin Local SD	Muskingum	2,485	41,563
402	Maysville Local SD	Muskingum	2,053	35,384
403	Tri-Valley Local SD	Muskingum	2,860	42,045
404	West Muskingum Local SD	Muskingum	1,881	65,160
405	Caldwell Ex Vill SD	Noble	1,257	50,398
406	Noble Local SD	Noble	1,287	60,509
407	Port Clinton City SD	Ottawa	2,342	121,806
408	Benton Carroll Salem Local SD	Ottawa	2,014	258,636
409	Danbury Local SD	Ottawa	693	162,205
410	Genoa Area Local SD	Ottawa	1,641	50,360
411	North Bass Local SD	Ottawa	11	37,497
412	Put-In-Bay Local SD	Ottawa	75	409,081
413	Paulding Ex Vill SD	Paulding	2,119	42,913
414	Antwerp Local SD	Paulding	820	40,929
415	Wayne Trace Local SD	Paulding	1,320	42,039
416	New Lexington City SD	Perry	2,201	30,078
417	Crooksville Ex Vill SD	Perry	1,088	28,700
418	Northern Local SD	Perry	2,225	40,647
419	Southern Local SD	Perry	1,047	23,381
420	Circleville City SD	Pickaway	2,481	67,905
421	Logan Elm Local SD	Pickaway	2,240	75,257
422	Teays Valley Local SD	Pickaway	2,585	47,081
423	Westfall Local SD	Pickaway	1,737	47,543
424	Eastern Local SD	Pike	1,059	22,636
425	Scioto Valley Local SD	Pike	1,612	33,581
426	Waverly City SD	Pike	2,174	42,076
427	Western Local SD	Pike	964	17,374
428	Kent City SD	Portage	4,018	71,001
429	Ravenna City SD	Portage	3,432	58,423
430	Windham Ex Vill SD	Portage	1,208	23,100
431	Aurora City SD	Portage	1,700	126,537
432	Crestwood Local SD	Portage	2,598	51,869

Continued on next page

OBS	DISTRICT	COUNTY	TOTAL ENROLLMENT 1994	VALUATION PER 1994
433	Field Local SD	Portage	2,473	$ 62,808
434	James A Garfield Local SD	Portage	1,522	44,968
435	Rootstown Local SD	Portage	1,313	56,514
436	Southeast Local SD	Portage	2,361	38,772
437	Streetsboro City SD	Portage	1,699	63,271
438	Waterloo Local SD	Portage	1,362	49,344
439	Eaton City SD	Preble	2,420	51,210
440	C R Coblentz Local SD	Preble	1,379	45,726
441	Preble-Shawnee Local SD	Preble	1,911	36,701
442	Twin Valley Community Local SD	Preble	1,122	48,432
443	College Corner Local SD	Preble	109	52,260
444	Tri-County North Local SD	Preble	1,189	52,792
445	Columbus Grove Local SD	Putnam	951	45,487
446	Continental Local SD	Putnam	848	31,020
447	Jennings Local SD	Putnam	446	38,350
448	Kalida Local SD	Putnam	803	38,063
449	Leipsic Local SD	Putnam	719	44,651
450	Miller City-New Cleveland Loca	Putnam	520	33,343
451	Ottawa-Glandorf Local SD	Putnam	1,730	59,935
452	Ottoville Local SD	Putnam	648	38,445
453	Pandora-Gilboa Local SD	Putnam	662	47,619
454	Mansfield City SD	Richland	6,626	53,896
455	Shelby City SD	Richland	2,561	59,630
456	Clear Fork Valley Local SD	Richland	1,661	46,785
457	Crestview Local SD	Richland	1,197	38,746
458	Lexington Local SD	Richland	2,844	56,937
459	Lucas Local SD	Richland	613	63,755
460	Madison Local SD	Richland	4,118	54,214
461	Plymouth Local SD	Richland	1,061	32,849
462	Ontario Local SD	Richland	1,662	120,475
463	Chillicothe City SD	Ross	3,934	87,881
464	Adena Local SD	Ross	1,263	34,176
465	Huntington Local SD	Ross	1,278	16,976
466	Paint Valley Local SD	Ross	1,308	24,723
467	Scioto Valley Local SD	Ross	1,222	40,900
468	Union Scioto Local SD	Ross	1,704	31,145
469	Zane Trace Local SD	Ross	1,345	54,951
470	Fremont City SD	Sandusky	5,458	70,158
471	Clyde-Green Springs Ex Vill SD	Sandusky	2,437	53,295
472	Gibsonburg Ex Vill SD	Sandusky	1,073	41,575
473	Lakota Local SD	Sandusky	1,520	45,313
474	Woodmore Local SD	Sandusky	1,259	82,743
475	New Boston Local SD	Scioto	475	62,205
476	Portsmouth City SD	Scioto	3,797	47,660
477	Bloom Local SD	Scioto	1,224	24,741
478	Clay Local SD	Scioto	608	51,896
479	Green Local SD	Scioto	755	82,767
480	Minford Local SD	Scioto	1,687	25,618

Continued on next page

OBS	DISTRICT	COUNTY	TOTAL ENROLLMENT 1994	VALUATION PER 1994
481	Northwest Local SD	Scioto	2,029	$ 22,216
482	Valley Local SD	Scioto	1,223	28,479
483	Washington Local SD	Scioto	1,731	23,180
484	Wheelersburg Local SD	Scioto	1,701	44,814
485	Fostoria City SD	Seneca	2,918	57,273
486	Tiffin City SD	Seneca	3,908	58,549
487	Seneca East Local SD	Seneca	1,249	42,059
488	Bettsville Local SD	Seneca	348	34,325
489	Hopewell-Loudon Local SD	Seneca	878	62,609
490	New Riegel Local SD	Seneca	492	32,634
491	Old Fort Local SD	Seneca	526	47,972
492	Sidney City SD	Shelby	4,200	84,535
493	Anna Local SD	Shelby	1,003	131,442
494	Botkins Local SD	Shelby	678	53,217
495	Fairlawn Local SD	Shelby	535	40,581
496	Fort Loramie Local SD	Shelby	783	42,898
497	Hardin-Houston Local SD	Shelby	975	39,402
498	Jackson Center Local SD	Shelby	527	68,569
499	Russia Local SD	Shelby	373	50,384
500	Alliance City SD	Stark	4,064	44,306
501	Canton City SD	Stark	12,900	48,492
502	Massillon City SD	Stark	4,997	52,755
503	North Canton City SD	Stark	4,030	83,401
504	Canton Local SD	Stark	2,532	101,282
505	Fairless Local SD	Stark	1,942	52,779
506	Jackson Local SD	Stark	4,940	121,166
507	Lake Local SD	Stark	3,112	62,212
508	Louisville City SD	Stark	2,949	58,243
509	Marlington Local SD	Stark	2,503	64,840
510	Minerva Local SD	Stark	2,329	48,447
511	Northwest Local SD	Stark	2,378	50,427
512	Osnaburg Local SD	Stark	972	53,025
513	Perry Local SD	Stark	4,952	82,561
514	Plain Local SD	Stark	6,289	81,207
515	Sandy Valley Local SD	Stark	1,450	59,397
516	Tuslaw Local SD	Stark	1,174	65,516
517	Akron City SD	Summit	33,392	59,114
518	Barberton City SD	Summit	4,478	52,598
519	Cuyahoga Falls City SD	Summit	5,925	76,147
520	Norton City SD	Summit	2,439	62,391
521	Stow City SD	Summit	5,771	77,841
522	Tallmadge City SD	Summit	2,470	85,711
523	Woodridge Local SD	Summit	1,194	180,032
524	Copley-Fairlawn City SD	Summit	2,431	153,832
525	Coventry Local SD	Summit	1,705	86,923
526	Manchester Local SD	Summit	1,503	63,282
527	Green Local SD	Summit	3,409	80,976
528	Hudson Local SD	Summit	5,035	99,900

Continued on next page

OBS	DISTRICT	COUNTY	TOTAL ENROLLMENT 1994	VALUATION PER 1994
529	Mogadore Local SD	Summit	777	$ 84,096
530	Nordonia Hills City SD	Summit	3,098	115,478
531	Revere Local SD	Summit	2,690	145,444
532	Springfield Local SD	Summit	3,147	82,227
533	Twinsburg City SD	Summit	2,612	138,125
534	Girard City SD	Trumbull	1,764	51,797
535	Niles City SD	Trumbull	3,171	55,179
536	Warren City SD	Trumbull	7,091	55,130
537	Hubbard Ex Vill SD	Trumbull	2,394	50,654
538	Newton Falls Ex Vill SD	Trumbull	1,556	41,974
539	Bloomfield-Mespo Local SD	Trumbull	413	48,528
540	Bristol Local SD	Trumbull	995	35,664
541	Brookfield Local SD	Trumbull	1,616	54,948
542	Champion Local SD	Trumbull	1,710	57,868
543	Mathews Local SD	Trumbull	1,125	63,886
544	Howland Local SD	Trumbull	3,442	105,147
545	Joseph Badger Local SD	Trumbull	1,251	45,318
546	Lakeview Local SD	Trumbull	2,313	71,797
547	Liberty Local SD	Trumbull	1,807	90,974
548	Lordstown Local SD	Trumbull	801	152,774
549	Maplewood Local SD	Trumbull	1,166	33,087
550	McDonald Local SD	Trumbull	869	33,177
551	Southington Local SD	Trumbull	686	39,225
552	La Brae Local SD	Trumbull	1,738	47,849
553	Weathersfield Local SD	Trumbull	1,163	59,727
554	Claymont City SD	Tuscarawas	2,410	35,422
555	Dover City SD	Tuscarawas	2,792	78,225
556	New Philadelphia City SD	Tuscarawas	3,478	72,703
557	Newcomerstown Ex Vill SD	Tuscarawas	1,295	41,658
558	Garaway Local SD	Tuscarawas	1,286	70,661
559	Indian Valley Local SD	Tuscarawas	1,758	48,367
560	Strasburg-Franklin Local SD	Tuscarawas	646	52,916
561	Tuscarawas Valley Local SD	Tuscarawas	1,689	55,747
562	Marysville Ex Vill SD	Union	3,110	118,648
563	Fairbanks Local SD	Union	828	98,770
564	North Union Local SD	Union	1,512	43,758
565	Van Wert City SD	Van Wert	2,683	61,205
566	Crestview Local SD	Van Wert	976	46,947
567	Lincolnview Local SD	Van Wert	899	51,817
568	Vinton County Local SD	Vinton	2,429	46,014
569	Franklin City SD	Warren	3,146	61,306
570	Lebanon City SD	Warren	3,653	66,293
571	Carlisle Local SD	Warren	1,790	60,665
572	Springborough Community City S	Warren	2,583	89,785
573	Kings Local SD	Warren	3,191	82,888
574	Little Miami Local SD	Warren	2,202	64,487
575	Mason Local SD	Warren	2,957	95,426
576	Wayne Local SD	Warren	1,250	65,982

Continued on next page

OBS	DISTRICT	COUNTY	TOTAL ENROLLMENT 1994	VALUATION PER 1994
577	Belpre City SD	Washington	1,542	$ 87,619
578	Marietta City SD	Washington	4,066	65,742
579	Fort Frye Local SD	Washington	1,243	94,229
580	Frontier Local SD	Washington	1,089	31,708
581	Warren Local SD	Washington	2,728	67,772
582	Wolf Creek Local SD	Washington	662	118,610
583	Orrville City SD	Wayne	2,063	70,464
584	Wooster City SD	Wayne	4,277	85,731
585	Rittman Ex Vill SD	Wayne	1,408	47,399
586	Chippewa Local SD	Wayne	1,497	53,779
587	Dalton Local SD	Wayne	1,061	66,225
588	Green Local SD	Wayne	1,463	43,361
589	North Central Local SD	Wayne	1,497	41,291
590	Northwestern Local SD	Wayne	1,458	41,421
591	Southeast Local SD	Wayne	1,824	62,647
592	Triway Local SD	Wayne	2,288	55,521
593	Bryan City SD	Williams	2,353	76,040
594	Montpelier Ex Vill SD	Williams	1,241	40,314
595	Edgerton Local SD	Williams	765	53,109
596	Edon-Northwest Local SD	Williams	723	39,036
597	Millcreek-West Unity Local SD	Williams	807	40,736
598	North Central Local SD	Williams	852	53,518
599	Stryker Local SD	Williams	629	59,796
600	Bowling Green City SD	Wood	3,564	76,966
601	Perrysburg Ex Vill SD	Wood	3,845	86,026
602	Rossford Ex Vill SD	Wood	2,331	103,812
603	Eastwood Local SD	Wood	1,850	57,416
604	Elmwood Local SD	Wood	1,258	41,448
605	Lake Local SD	Wood	1,851	81,217
606	North Baltimore Local SD	Wood	846	52,859
607	Northwood Local SD	Wood	1,229	58,141
608	Otsego Local SD	Wood	1,646	50,645
609	Carey Ex Vill SD	Wyandot	934	50,007
610	Upper Sandusky Ex Vill SD	Wyandot	1,894	64,841
611	Mohawk Local SD	Wyandot	1,195	43,695

Trivia

QUESTION   Who founded the first permanent white
            settlement in Ohio?

ANSWER   General Rufus Putman (Marietta, Ohio)

QUESTION   Where was Ohio's first Capital?

ANSWER   Chillicothe

TEACHERS SALARY & STUDENT-TEACHER RATIO - BY COUNTY
1994

1 = Average teachers salary
2 = Student-teacher ratio

Source: Ohio Dept. of Education

COUNTY	1	2	COUNTY	1	2
Adams	$29,724	18.0	Logan	$31,560	16.5
Allen	31,059	16.7	Lorain	35,783	16.7
Ashland	32,843	17.2	Lucas	34,885	16.1
Ashtabula	34,272	17.8	Madison	28,894	15.8
Athens	29,789	17.7	Mahoning	34,817	16.9
Auglaize	$30,695	16.6	Marion	$32,172	16.1
Belmont	29,908	15.8	Medina	36,986	17.9
Brown	28,479	16.0	Meigs	27,619	16.2
Butler	32,945	16.5	Mercer	31,391	17.8
Carroll	33,955	13.8	Miami	33,318	17.7
Champaign	$30,535	19.2	Monroe	$34,615	16.3
Clark	32,255	20.4	Montgomery	35,201	16.4
Clemont	32,655	16.2	Morgan	29,638	16.8
Clinton	31,322	18.6	Morrow	28,858	18.1
Columbiana	31,221	24.2	Muskingum	30,800	17.1
Coshocton	$32,311	16.6	Noble	$27,188	19.4
Crawford	30,758	17.0	Ottawa	35,436	16.2
Cuyahoga	40,607	17.3	Paulding	29,630	17.0
Darke	30,030	17.6	Perry	27,595	17.9
Defiance	31,304	16.7	Pickaway	32,495	18.1
Delaware	$33,562	16.8	Pike	$30,087	18.1
Erie	33,930	15.6	Portage	35,391	17.1
Fairfield	34,895	18.9	Preble	28,679	17.4
Fayette	30,268	18.5	Putnam	28,010	16.4
Franklin	37,853	16.1	Richland	32,397	16.2
Fulton	$31,178	17.5	Ross	$32,397	17.2
Gallia	29,883	17.0	Sandusky	30,731	16.3
Geauga	37,229	16.5	Scioto	32,385	16.6
Greene	34,537	18.6	Seneca	29,267	17.4
Guernsey	29,686	15.9	Shelby	30,864	19.2
Hamilton	$37,658	18.2	Stark	35,432	17.7
Hancock	32,393	16.4	Summit	36,655	17.9
Hardin	28,276	18.6	Trumbull	34,077	17.4
Harrison	28,267	18.1	Tuscarawas	30,130	16.9
Henry	29,832	21.2	Union	34,255	17.4
Highland	$28,361	17.7	Van Wert	$30,873	15.0
Hocking	30,525	17.3	Vinton	27,885	18.8
Holmes	28,714	19.2	Warren	33,596	17.9
Huron	31,340	18.6	Washington	29,091	17.3
Jackson	29,963	15.9	Wayne	33,564	17.4
Jefferson	$33,056	16.6			
Knox	31,354	17.0	Williams	$29,784	17.4
Lake	39,742	17.3	Wood	33,152	16.0
Lawrence	29,681	17.6	Wyandot	29,989	17.2
Licking	30,784	16.7			

VOCATIONAL SCHOOLS IN OHIO - PRIVATE

ACADEMY OF TRAVEL, Highland Hts 44143, (216) 449-2907.
AKRON TESTING & WELDING SCH, Barberton 44203, (216) 753-2268.
AKRON MACHINING INST, Barberton 44203, (216)745-1111.
AKRON MED-DENTAL INST, Akron 44303, (216)762-9788
AL-WIN TRAINING, W Jefferson 43162, (614)852-1244.

ALEX. SCH OF FLORAL DESIGN, Bedford Hts 44146, (216)292-4500
AACR STENO MED TRANSC SCH, Kettering 45409, (513) 293-0006
ACA COL OF DESIGN, Cincinnati, 45206, (513) 751-1206
ACAD OF CT REPORTING, Akron, 44313, (216) 867-4030
ACAD OF CT REPORTING, Columbus, 43215, (614) 221-7770
ACAD OF CT REPORTING, Cleveland, 44113, (216)861-3222
AM INST FOR PARALGL ST, Middleburg Hts, 44130,(614)794-9100
AM TRVL TRNG CNTR, Boardman, 44512, (216) 758-0180
AM SCHL OF TECH, Columbus, 43229, (614) 436-4820
AM ACAD OF TRVL AGNT, Youngstown, 44507, (216) 788-8872
AM SCHL OF BRDCSTNG, Columbus, 43229, (614) 785-9272
AM INST FOR PARALGL ST, N Canton, 44720, (614) 794-9100
ANTONELLI INST ART & PHOTO,Cincinnati, 45202,(513)241-4338
ARISTOTLE INST MED & DENTL,Westerville, 43081, (800)282-0820
ART ADV ACAD, Cincinnati, 45211, (513) 574-1010
BARBIZON ACAD OF AKRON, Akron, 44313, (216) 867-4110
BARBIZON ACAD OF NE OHIO,Independence, 44131, (216) 781-5220
BETTE MASSIE, Centerville, 45459, (513) 435-3477
BLISS COLLEGE, Columbus, 43214, (614) 267-8355
BOHECKERS BUS COL, Ravenna, 44266, (216) 297-7319
BRADFORD SCHOOLS, Columbus, 43229, (614) 846-9410
BRYANT & STRATTON BUS INST, Parma, 44070, (216)265-3151
BRYANT & STRATTON BUS INST, Richmond Hts, 44143(216)461-3151
CARPET ACAD, Columbus, 43202, (614) 263-7480
CENTRVL BIBLE COL, Centerville, 45459, (513) 433-5016
CNTRL OHIO SCHL OF DOG GRMG, Columbus, 43223, (614) 279-7366
CHAMBER SCHL OF UPHOLSTERY, Youngstown, 44502,(216)743-8068
CHASE SCHL OF MED TRANS, Hudson, 44236, (216) 656-4008
CINCI SCHL OF CT REPORTING, Cincinnati, 45202,(513)241-1011
CINCI METRO COL, St Bernard, 45217, (513) 242-0202
CINCI ACAD OF DESIGN, Cincinnati, 45206, (513) 961-2484
CINCI SCHL OF HYPNOSIS, Milford, 45150, (513) 831-3600
CINCI FLORAL DESGN CNTR, Cincinnati, 45242, (513)791-4437
CLVLND INST OF TECH, Brooklyn Hts, 44131, (216)447-1095
CLVLND INST OF DEN-MED ASST, Cleveland, 44115,(216)241-2930
CLVLND INST ELECTRNCS, Clevelnad, 44114, (216) 781-9400
COL SCHL OF HYPNOSIS, Columbus, 43229, (614) 841-9944
COL PARA-PROF INST, Columbus, 43201, (614) 299-0200
CONN SCHL OF BRDCSTNG, Cincinnati, 45236, (513)281-6060
CONN SCHL OF BRDCASTNG, Independence, 44131,(216)447-9117
CROWN ACAD, Cleveland, 44111, (216) 671-2727
CROWN ACAD, Akron, 44313, (216) 671-2727
DAVID-CURTIS SCHL FLORAL DES, Centerville, 45459, (513)4330566
DAVIS JR COL, Toledo, 43623, (419) 473-2700
DAYTON SCHL OF CT REPORTING, Dayton, 45402, (513)228-4256
DE'ELEGANCE PROD MDLNG, Trotwood, 45420, (513) 837-5881
ELYRIA MACH INST, Elyria, 44035, (216)365-4178
ESI CAREER CTR, Euclid, 44117, (216)289-1299
ESI CAREER CTR, Sheffield, 44055, (216) 277-8832
ETI TECH COL, Cleveland, 44103, (216) 431-4300
ETI TECH COL, N Canton, 44720, (216) 494-1214
ETI TECH COL, Niles, 44446, (216) 652-9919
FINISHING TOUCHES SEC SCHL, Cincinnati, 45201(513)721-8500
FOLIO MODELS, Toledo, 43614, (419)841-1213
FRANTZ BUS COL, Toledo, 43624, (419) 244-0044
GT LKS DOG GMG ACAD, Toledo, 43609, (419) 385-7851
H & R BLOCK, Columbus, 43232, (614) 863-0202
HAMMEL COL, Akron, 44305, (216) 762-7491
HAMRICK TRUCK DRVNG SCHL, Medina, 44256, (216)239-2229
HIXON'S SCHL OF FLORAL DES, Lakewood, 44107, (216)521-9277

Continued on next page

Continued from preceeding page

HOBART INST OF WELDNG TECH, Troy, 45373, (513)332-5000
HONDROS CAREER CTRS, Mayfield Village, 44129, (216)461-7900
HONDROS CAREER CTRS, Columbus, 43229, (614) 888-7277
HONDROS CAREER CTRS, Dayton 45414, (800) 783-0094
HONDROS CAREER CTRS, Cincinnati, 45241, (800)783-0097
HONDROS CAREER CTRS, Independence, 44131, (800)783-0094
HOSPITALITY TRNG CTR, Hudson, 44236, (216) 653-9151
INTL BARTENDING, Cincinnati, 45223, (513) 541-3555
INTL BARTENDING INST, Columbus, 43214, (614) 885-9610
INTL BARTENDING SCHL, Dayton, 45414, (513) 878-4166
INST OF MED-DENTL TECH, Cincinnati, 45245, (513)753-5030
INST MED-DENTL TECH, Cincinnati, 45246, (513)851-8500
INTL COL OF BROADCASTNG, Dayton, 45431, (513)258-8251
ITT TECH INST, Youngstown, 44502, (216) 747-5555
JOHN RBTS POWERS, Columbus, 43229, (614)846-1047
JOHN CASABLANCAS MDL & CAR, Columbus, 43229,(614)847-0010
JOHN CASABLANCAS MDL & CAR, Cincinnati, 45241,(513)733-8998
KATHLEEN WELLMAN SCHL OF MDL, Cincinnati, 45202,(513)381-6996
LILLIAN GALLOWAY MDL ACAD, Cincinnati, 45213, (513)351-2700
MARYCREST COL, Toledo, 43623, (419)472-2115
MCKIM TECH INST, Akron, 44321, (216) 666-4014
MERIDIAN SCHL OF TRVL, Brooklyn Hts, 44131, (216) 749-6400
LINCOLN WELDING SCHL, Cleveland, 44117, (216)383-2259
SOUTHESTRN BUS COL, Sandusky, 44870, (419)627-8345
MARGARET O'BRIEN'S FNSHNG&MDL,Toledo, 43615,(419)536-5522
MTI BUS SCHLS, Cleveland, 44113, (216)621-8228
NATL EDUC CTR, Cleveland, 44125, (216)475-7520
MIAMI VALLEY SCHL OF CT REPRT, Dayton, 45402, (513)224-8511
AM INST FOR PARA LEGL,Dayton, 45401, (614)794-9100
AM INST FOR PARA LEGL, Columbus, 43219, (614)794-9100
MTC TRNG CTR, Niles, 44446, (216)544-1945
NATL ACAD FOR PARA STD, Columbus, 43210, (800)922-0771
NATL ACAD FOR PARA STD, Norwood, 45212, (800)27-LEGAL
NATL EDUC CTR, Cuyahoga Fls, 44221, (216)923-9959
NATL K-9 SCHL FOR DOG TRNRS,Columbus,43213,(614)864-0213
NONI AGENCY FINISHNG MDL SCHL, Columbus, 43215,(614)224-7217
OHIO ACAD OF HYPNOTHERAPY, Zenia, 45385, (513)427-0506
OHIO AUTO/DIESEL TECH, Cleveland, 44103, (216)881-1700
OHIO TECH, Chillicothe, 45601, (614)775-5669
OHIO ACAD OF HYPNOTHERAPY, Zenia, 45385, (513)427-0506
OHIO VALLEY BUS COL, E Liverpool, 43920, (216)385-1070
NORTHSHORE TECH INST, Cleveland, 44105, (216)883-2800
OHIO INST OF PHOTO & TECH, Dayton,45439,(513)294-6155
OHIO REAL ESTATE INST, Dayton, 45458, (513)435-1145
OHIO SCHL OF CULINARY ARTS, Euclid, 44123, (216)943-3208
OH VALLEY GOODWILL IND, Cincinnati, 45215, (513)771-4800
PENN-OHIO COL, Youngstown, 44507, (216)788-5084
PRESCOTT SCHL OF TRVL, Cleveland, 44114, (216)621-2264
PRESCOTT SCHL OF TRVL, Beachwood, 44122, (216)523-2232
PRESCOTT SCHL OF TRVL, Akron, 44333, (216)523-2232
PROF SKILLS INST, Toledo, 43615, (419)531-9610
PROG FASHION SCHL, Cleveland, 44113, (216)781-4595
PTC CAREER INST, Cleveland, 44115, (216)575-1100
RAEDEL COL & IND WELDING, Canton, 44702, (216)454-9006
RECORDING WORKSHOP, Chillicothe, 45601, (614)663-2544
RETS INST OF TECH, Toledo, 43612, (419)478-7387
RETS TECH CNTR, Centerville, 45459, (513)433-3410
SAWYER COL OF BUS, Cleveland, 44111, (216)941-7666
SAWYER COL OF BUS, Cleveland, 44118, (216)932-0911
SCHL OF ADVERTISING ART, Kettering, 45429,(513)294-0592
SCHL OF CLERICL TECH, Toledo, 43604, (419)255-0070
SHARKEY CAREER SCHL, Dayton, 45459, (513)434-4461
SOUTHEASTERN ACAD, Kissimmee, 34742, (407)847-4444
SOUTHEASTERN BUS COL, Gallipolis, 45631, (614)446-4367
SOUTHEASTERN BUS COL, Chillicothe, 45601, (614)774-6300
SOUTHEASTERN BUS COL, Jackson, 45640, (614)286-1554
SOUTHEASTERN BUS COL, New Boston, 45662, (614)456-4124
SOUTHEASTERN BUS COL, Lancaster, 43130, (614)687-6126

Continued on next page

Continued from preceeding page

SOUTHERN OHIO COL, Akron, 44312, (216)733-8766
SOUTHERN OHIO COLL, Cincinnati, 45327, (513)242-3791
SOUTHERN OHIO COL, Fairfield, 45104, (513)829-7100
SOUTHWESTERN COL OF BUS, Middletown, 45044, (513)423-3346
SOUTHWESTERN COL OF BUS, Cincinnati, 45246, (513)874-0432
SOUTHWESTERN COL OF BUS, Dayton, 45402, (513)224-0061
STAUTZENBERGER COL, Toledo, 43614, (419)866-0261
STAUTZENBERGER COL, Findlay, 45840, (419)423-2211
STENOTYPE INST, Springfield, 45502, (513)390-6005
TECH EDUC CTR, Columbus, 43213, (614)759-7700
TOLEDO TRVL SCHL, Toledo, 43614, (419)385-3161
TOTAL TECH INST, Parma Hts, 44130, (216)843-2323
TRAVL CAREERS, Dublin, 43107, (614)766-6315
TDDS, Diamond, 44412, (513)538-2216
TOLEDO ACAD OF BARTENDING, Toledo, 43615, (419)866-3753
CINCINNATI DNTL CAREERS, Cincinnati, 45224, (513)681-6220
DAVINCI TRVL ACAD, Akron, 44333, (216)666-7788

HONDROS CAREER CTR, Akron, 44319, (800)536-0094
PROF HOSPITALITY CTR, Grafton, 44044, (216)926-2608
SAFEGUARD SEC INST, Cleveland, 44114, (216)621-9724
MIDWEST SCHL OF TELECOM, Mansfield, 44901, (419)747-1175
FOLIO MODELS, Toledo, 43614, (419)841-1213
NATURES WORLD, Findlay, 45840, (419)423-2211
DENTAL CAREERS INST, Columbus, 43205, (614)253-0123
CINCI SCHL OF PHLEBOTOMY, Fairfield, 45104, (513)829-1505
DEVRY INST OF TECH, Columbus, 43209, (614)523-7291
TRAVELINE SCHL OF TRVL, Mentor, 44060, (216)951-8012
TRAVL AGENTS TRNG SCHL, Parma Hts, 44129, (216)845-0304
TRVL STATION TECH, Canton, 44702, (216)453-1600
TRAVELINE SCHL OF TRVL, Lakewood, 44107, (216)226-0380
TRI-STATE TRVL SCHL, Cincinnati, 45212, (513)841-5588
TRUMBULL BUS COL, Warren, 44482, (216)369-3200
URBANE ACAD, Cincinnati, 45202, (513)381-7371
VIRGINIA MARTI COL OF FASHION, Lakewood, 44107, (216)221-8584
VOCATIONAL GUIDANCE SERV, Cleveland, 44103, (216)431-7800
WEST SIDE INST OF TECH, Cleveland, 44102, (216)651-1656
WESTERN RESERVE TRNG CTR, Niles, 44446, (216)652-3323
WILLA SINGER STAR WORLD ACAD, Centerville, 45459, 513-4390220
WRITER'S DIGEST SCHL, Cincinnati, 45207, (513)531-2222

Trivia

QUESTION	Which is the first University founded in Ohio **and** the Northwest Territory?
ANSWER	Ohio University (1804)
QUESTION	When and where was the American Federation of Labor founded?
ANSWER	1886, in Columbus (Samuel Gompers was the first President)
QUESTION	How many acres does Ohio, the nation's leading greenhouse vegetable producer, have under glass?
ANSWER	750 Acres.

MEMORABLE DATES IN OHIO HISTORY

4000 - 5000 B.C.	Indians inhabited area, including what was to become Jefferson County.
1669-70	French explorer de La Salle first European to reach present-day Ohio.
1763	British gain control of Ohio area following the French and Indian War.
1788	The first permanent white settlement in Ohio was established at Marietta (April 7).
1789	Ft. Washington established by U.S. Army at Cincinnati site.
1794	Gen. "Mad Anthony" Wayne defeated massive Indian force at the Battle of Falling Timbers, resulting in the Indians ceding three-fourths of the Ohio area (Treaty of Greenville, 1795).
1796	Zane's Trail opened, the first formal road in the Ohio area (Jefferson City to Adams County).
1800	Chillicothe named Ohio Territory capital. Indiana Territory detached from Ohio. Connecticut and Virginia cede their claims to large part of Ohio area.
1801	First U.S. land-sale in Ohio Territory.
1803	Ohio granted statehood.
1804	Ohio University chartered as an academy.
1811	First steamboat on the Ohio River.
1812	Columbus named the state capital.
1813	Oliver Perry defeated British in naval battle on Lake Erie (Put-in-Bay), "We met the enemy and they are ours."
1817	First abolitionist newspaper in U.S. established at Mt. Pleasant.
1818	First steamboat on Lake Erie.
1820	Cincinnati (population 25,000) was the second largest city in the West (New Orleans was first).
1827	Cincinnati Daily Express was the first daily newspaper west of Philadelphia.
1832	Oho & Erie Canal completed (Cleveland to Portsmouth, Dec. 1).
1833	National Pike road reached Columbus (from Maryland).
1835	"Toledo War" ended without bloodshed when Michigan relinquished its claim to the Toledo area in exchange for much of its Upper Peninsula and statehood.
1837	Oberlin College became the first coeducational college in U.S.
1840	Ohio resident William Henry Harrison was elected President of the U.S.
1842	Last Indian tribe in Ohio moved west (Wyandots).
1846	Railroads connect the cities of Cleveland - Columbus - Cincinnati.
1850	Ohio led the U.S. in production of corn, horses, and sheep. Cincinnati led U.S. in production of carriages and wagons.
1861-65	More than half of Ohio's able bodied men fought in the Civil War.
1863	Confederate force under Gen. John Morgan invaded Ohio. Captured near Salineville (Columbiana County).
1866	Cincinnati Reds organized as world's first professional baseball team.
1869	First public weather service in U.S. established at Cincinnati.

Continued on next page

Continued from preceeding page

1870	John D. Rockefeller organized Standard Oil Co. (Cleveland) and became America's first billionaire.
1884	First electric street railway in U.S. opened in Cleveland.
1886	American Federation of Labor founded at Columbus, with Charles Gompers president. Charles Martin Hall discovered process of making aluminum (Oberlin).
1892	Ohio makes it illegal to dismiss a worker for union membership.
1896	First rubber automobile tire made by B.F. Goodrich (Akron).
1901	Nation's first county public library dedicated at Van Wert (Brumback Library).
1905	World's first successful blood transfusion performed (Dr. George Crile, Cleveland).
1912	Major revision of Ohio Constitution.
1913	Floods take more than 425 lives in Ohio ($250 million property damage).
1917-18	200,000 Ohioans served in World War I.
1920	National Football League organized (Columbus).
1929	Iron and steel was Ohio's leading industry.
1933	Great Depression rocked the U.S. and two of every three workers in Ohio were unemployed.
1934	Ohio adopted 3% sales tax.
1937	Ohio River flood left 750,000 homeless (Jan. 28).
1955	Ohio Turnpike (241 miles long) opened.
1959	St. Lawrence Seaway opened Ohio ports on Lake Erie to world trade.
1962	Ohioan John Glenn, Jr. was first American to orbit the earth.
1967	Carl Stokes elected mayor of Cleveland (first black elected mayor of a major U.S. city).
1969	Ohioan Neil Armstrong was first human to walk on the moon.
1970	Four Kent State University students killed (by National Guard) during anti-Vietnam protest demonstration.
1971	Ohio adopted state income tax.
1973	Ohio lottery adopted.
1980	Ohio became automobile manufacturing state second only to Michigan.

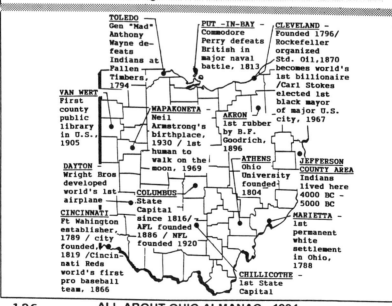

Ohio Presidents

Eight U.S. Presidents came from Ohio -- earning Ohio the nickname "the Mother of Presidents."

Source - Ohio Secretary of State

WILLIAM HENRY HARRISON
(1841)
9th President
Whig
Birthplace: Berkeley Plantation,
Virginia*

ULYSSES SIMPSON GRANT
(1869-1877)
18th President
Republican
Birthplace: Point Pleasant

RUTHERFORD BIRCHARD HAYES
(1877-1881)
19th President
Republican
Birthplace: Delaware

JAMES ABRAM GARFIELD
(1881)
20th President
Republican
Birthplace: Orange

* *Although born in Virginia, William Henry Harrison is considered an Ohio President because he settled on a farm in North Bend, Ohio after the War of 1812 and lived there when elected President.*

BENJAMIN HARRISON
(1889-1893)
23rd President
Republican
Birthplace: North Bend

WILLIAM MCKINLEY
(1897-1901)
25th President
Republican
Birthplace: Niles

WILLIAM HOWARD TAFT
(1909-1913)
27th President
Republican
Birthplace: Cincinnati

WARREN GAMILIEL HARDING
(1921-1923)
29th President
Republican
Birthplace: Corsica
          (now Blooming Grove)

BIRTHS - DEATHS - MARRIAGES - DIVORCES

*LIVE BIRTH RATES PER 1000 POPULATION
LOW BIRTH WEIGHT AND ILLEGITIMATE BIRTH RATES PER 1000 LIVE BIRTHS
TEEN BIRTH RATES PER 1000 FEMALE POPULATION 10-19 YEARS OF AGE
INFANT, NEONATAL, AND FETAL DEATH RATES PER 1000 LIVE BIRTHS
PERINATAL DEATH RATES PER 1000 LIVE BIRTHS PLUS FETAL DEATHS
MATERNAL DEATH RATES PER 10,000 LIVE BIRTHS
DEATHS, ALL CAUSES AND SELECTED CAUSES - RATES PER 100,000 POPULATION

SELECTED VITAL EVENTS: NUMBER & RATE, 1991

VITAL EVENT	NUMBER TOTAL	WHITE	BLACK	RATE* TOTAL	WHITE	BLACK
Total Live Births	165389	134797	28365	15.2	14.2	24.6
Low Birth Weight Births	12428	8343	3953	75.1	61.9	139.4
Illegitimate Births	50689	29028	21308	306.5	215.3	751.2
Teen Births	23020	15523	7298	30.1	23.9	73.8
Infant Deaths	1548	1067	464	9.4	7.9	16.4
Neonatal Deaths	955	654	290	5.8	4.9	10.2
Fetal Deaths**	1235	850	338	7.5	6.3	11.9
Perinatal Deaths**	2190	1504	628	13.1	11.1	21.9
Maternal Deaths	15	8	7	0.9	0.6	2.5
Deaths All Causes	100009	89144	10596	922.0	936.2	917.5
Heart Disease	34955	31783	3114	322.3	333.8	269.7
Malignant Neoplasms	24573	21871	2644	226.5	229.7	229.0
Cerebrovascular Diseases	6646	5998	631	61.3	63.0	54.6
Chr Obstructive Pulmonary Dis	4520	4217	295	41.7	44.3	25.5
Accidents	3549	3113	406	32.7	32.7	35.2
Marriages	94787					
Rate per 1,000 Population	8.7					
Divorces	52203					
Rate per 1,000 Population	4.8					

COUNTY - 1991
VITAL STATISTICS
ON NEXT PAGE

SELECTED VITAL EVENTS: NUMBER & RATE, 1981

VITAL EVENT	NUMBER TOTAL	WHITE	BLACK	RATE TOTAL	WHITE	BLACK
LIVE BIRTHS	166,971	142,260	23,050	15.5	14.8	21.4
Low Birthweight Births	11,253	8,147	2,998	67.4	57.3	130.0
Illegitimate Births	30,526	16,269	14,114	182.8	114.4	612.3
Teen Births	24,519	18,728	5,653	26.3	23.1	51.8
DEATHS ALL CAUSES	96,510	86,892	9,496	893.8	905.4	881.9
Diseases of Heart	38,577	35,421	3,124	357.3	369.1	290.1
Malignant Neoplasms	21,122	18,885	2,206	195.6	196.8	204.9
Cerebrovascular Diseases	7,817	7,139	667	72.4	74.4	61.9
Accidents	4,002	3,579	408	37.1	37.3	37.9
Ch. Obstructive Pulmonary Dis.	2,918	2,739	175	27.0	28.5	16.3
Infant Deaths	2,058	1,543	510	12.3	10.8	22.1
Neonatal Deaths	1,436	1,072	360	8.6	7.5	15.6
Fetal Deaths	1,380	1,094	270	8.3	7.7	11.7
Perinatal Deaths	2,816	2,166	630	16.7	15.1	27.0
Maternal Deaths	20	11	9	1.2	0.8	3.9
Marriages	99,959					
Rate per 1,000 Population	9.3					
Divorces	58,567					
Rate per 1,000 Population	5.4					

Continued on next page

COUNTY	LIVE BIRTHS Number	Rate*	TOTAL DEATHS Number	Rate*	MARRIAGES Number	Rate	DIVORCES Number	Rate
OHIO	165,389	15.2	100,009	9.2	94787	8.7	52203	4.8
Adams	362	14.3	283	11.2	245	9.7	170	6.7
Allen	1,772	16.1	960	8.7	893	8.1	639	5.8
Ashland	703	14.8	432	9.1	382	8.0	213	4.5
Ashtabula	1,419	14.2	1,037	10.4	951	9.5	530	5.3
Athens	659	11.1	457	7.7	460	7.7	260	4.4
Auglaize	689	15.5	368	8.3	294	6.6	205	4.6
Belmont	855	12.0	891	12.5	572	8.0	331	4.7
Brown	557	15.9	319	9.1	281	8.0	191	5.5
Butler	4,419	15.2	2,160	7.4	2610	9.0	1805	6.2
Carroll	324	12.2	220	8.3	192	7.2	131	4.9
Champaign	466	12.9	322	8.9	342	9.5	198	5.5
Clark	2,116	14.3	1,472	10.0	1158	7.8	916	6.2
Clermont	2,581	17.2	1,035	6.9	1537	10.2	611	4.1
Clinton	515	14.5	310	8.8	271	7.7	213	6.0
Columbiana	1,506	13.9	1,142	10.5	986	9.1	576	5.3
Coshocton	495	14.0	369	10.4	275	7.8	168	4.7
Crawford	651	13.6	515	10.8	425	8.9	316	6.6
Cuyahoga	23,069	16.3	15,245	10.8	10434	7.4	5774	4.1
Darke	706	13.2	513	9.6	542	10.1	265	4.9
Defiance	563	14.3	310	7.9	365	9.3	210	5.3
Delaware	910	13.6	481	6.9	503	7.5	353	5.3
Erie	1,059	13.8	780	10.2	742	9.7	335	4.4
Fairfield	1,421	13.7	834	8.1	845	8.2	571	5.5
Fayette	374	13.6	330	12.0	257	9.4	163	5.9
Franklin	16,401	17.1	7,341	7.6	9292	9.7	5091	5.3
Fulton	613	15.9	291	7.6	333	8.6	170	4.4
Gallia	398	12.9	287	9.3	258	8.3	206	6.7
Geauga	1,176	14.5	547	6.7	598	7.4	272	3.4
Greene	1,786	13.1	977	7.1	1079	7.9	652	4.8
Guernsey	515	13.2	459	11.8	396	10.1	180	4.6
Hamilton	14,242	16.4	8,174	9.4	6159	7.1	3199	3.7
Hancock	1,024	15.6	541	8.3	718	11.0	341	5.2
Hardin	400	12.9	323	10.4	226	7.3	182	5.9
Harrison	201	12.5	221	13.7	128	8.0	54	3.4
Henry	419	14.4	248	8.5	212	7.3	124	4.3
Highland	520	14.6	343	9.6	355	9.9	223	6.2
Hocking	399	15.6	230	9.0	219	8.6	127	5.0
Holmes	756	23.0	266	8.1	268	8.2	71	2.2
Huron	929	16.5	509	9.1	512	9.1	301	5.4
Jackson	434	14.4	325	10.8	330	10.9	183	6.1
Jefferson	955	11.9	940	11.7	721	9.0	338	4.2
Knox	642	13.5	471	9.9	399	8.4	227	4.8
Lake	2,957	13.7	1,758	8.2	1925	8.9	885	4.1
Lawrence	820	13.3	693	11.2	377	6.1	391	6.3
Licking	1,791	14.0	1,150	9.0	1135	8.8	751	5.9
Logan	692	16.4	424	10.0	429	10.1	289	6.8
Lorain	4,136	15.3	2,274	8.4	2255	8.3	1280	4.7
Lucas	7,855	17.0	4,379	9.5	7752	16.8	2132	4.6
Madison	527	14.2	311	8.4	306	8.3	165	4.5
Mahoning	3,685	13.9	3,030	11.4	1926	7.3	971	3.7
Marion	960	14.9	620	9.6	700	10.9	415	6.5
Medina	1,690	13.8	843	6.9	1027	8.4	543	4.4
Meigs	339	14.7	265	11.5	209	9.1	154	6.7
Mercer	662	16.8	336	8.5	354	9.0	126	3.2
Miami	1,297	13.9	844	9.1	904	9.7	491	5.3
Monroe	171	11.0	164	10.6	217	14.0	75	4.8
Montgomery	9,223	16.1	5,122	8.9	5013	8.7	3044	5.3
Morgan	181	12.8	170	12.0	150	10.6	66	4.6
Morrow	417	15.0	234	8.4	197	7.1	159	5.7
Muskingum	1,193	14.5	835	10.2	683	8.3	494	6.0
Noble	145	12.8	117	10.3	79	7.0	37	3.3
Ottawa	466	11.6	428	10.7	338	8.4	123	3.1
Paulding	219	10.7	149	7.3	137	6.7	117	5.7
Perry	478	15.1	309	9.8	242	7.7	158	5.0

ALL ABOUT OHIO ALMANAC - 1994

Continued from preceeding page

Pickaway	623	12.9	403	8.4	421	8.7	288	6.0
Pike	360	14.8	240	9.9	255	10.5	132	5.4
Portage	1,876	13.2	907	6.4	1068	7.5	700	4.9
Preble	453	11.3	345	8.6	235	5.9	201	5.0
Putnam	601	17.8	271	8.0	262	7.7	93	2.7
Richland	1,854	14.7	1,136	9.0	1103	8.7	701	5.6
Ross	878	12.7	664	9.6	691	10.0	348	5.0
Sandusky	971	15.7	542	8.7	356	5.7	322	5.2
Scioto	1,137	14.2	970	12.1	536	6.7	489	6.1
Seneca	875	14.6	541	9.1	454	7.6	272	4.6
Shelby	773	17.2	339	7.5	414	9.2	200	4.5
Stark	5,479	14.9	3,680	10.0	3253	8.8	1600	4.4
Summit	7,842	15.2	4,922	9.6	4500	8.7	2558	5.0
Trumbull	3,125	13.7	2,209	9.7	1695	7.4	1194	5.2
Tuscarawas	1,130	13.4	879	10.5	737	8.8	399	4.7
Union	500	15.6	277	8.7	289	9.0	205	6.4
Van Wert	357	11.7	262	8.6	261	8.6	148	4.9
Vinton	184	16.6	109	9.8	105	9.5	63	5.7
Warren	1,780	15.6	769	6.8	1055	9.3	706	6.2
Washington	805	12.9	580	9.3	642	10.3	318	5.1
Wayne	1,635	16.1	801	7.9	870	8.6	513	5.1
Williams	528	14.3	321	8.7	402	10.9	199	5.4
Wood	1,443	12.7	871	7.7	854	7.5	484	4.3
Wyandot	275	12.4	258	11.6	209	9.4	119	5.3

OHIO DEATHS FROM INFECTIOUS/PARASITIC DISEASE

	YEAR OF DEATH				
	1991	1990	1989	1988	1987

	NUMBER OF DEATHS				
TOTAL DISEASE	1537	1437	1337	1306	1183
TUBERCULOSIS	31	50	50	42	42
DIPTHERIA	0	0	0	0	0
WHOOPING COUGH	0	1	0	0	0
STREP THROAT	0	2	1	2	1
MENINGOCOCCAL(SPINAL MENINGITIS)	6	3	10	9	8
TETANUS	1	0	0	0	0
SEPTICEMA	790	709	707	830	792
HIV INFECTION	549	492	417	265	196
ACUTE POLIQ	2	5	2	2	3
CHICKEN POX	3	1	1	1	2
HERPES ZOSTER(SHINGLES)	2	5	1	8	5
HERPES SIMPLEX	4	8	7	5	6
MEASLES	0	0	1	0	0
RUBELLA	0	0	0	0	0
ARTHROPOD-BORNE ENCEPHALITIS	0	0	0	0	0
VIRAL HEPATITIS	38	47	42	22	36
MUMPS	0	0	0	0	0
SYPHILIS	5	6	0	2	1
ALL OTHER INFECTIOUS/PARA-SITIC RESIDUAL	106	104	97	115	89

AIDS (ACQUIRED IMMUNE DEFICIENCY) OHIO - U.S.

Ohio is significantly below the U.S. rate for AIDS.

The state rate for the period 1981 to January 1993 is 34 cases per 100,000 people compared to the national rate of 97. As shown on the accompanying map, only 7 counties exceed the state rate. Eighty-one counties are below the state rate, 3 have zero case and 16 have one case. In 1992 there were zero new cases in 30 counties.

In both Ohio and the United States the largest racial-ethnic groups with AIDS is white, but when the population size of each group is considered, the reverse is reported. The rate (cases per 100,000 people) among blacks is 89, among Hispanics it is 70, and among whites it is 28.

Male homosexual sex is the principal cause of transmission in both the state (72%) and nation (58%). Almost 90% is in the 20 - 49 age group, both in the state and nation. No age group is exempt, however, with 1% of cases 4 years or younger, and 1% of cases over 65 years.

Males outnumber female AIDS victims about 9 to 1 in both the state and nation. The death rate is significantly high in both Ohio and U.S. (66%).

While this epidemic continues, condoms are advocated for "safe" sex. It has been pointed out, however, that "safer" is more accurate than "safe".

There is a 16% chance of condom failure when used as a contraceptive, and the AIDS virus is 30 times smaller than one sperm.

CUMULATIVE AIDS CASES BY RESIDENCE AT DIAGNOSIS

1. New York	49154	8. Georgia	6755
2. California	44935	9. Pennsylvania	6681
3. Florida	23228	10. Maryland	4996
4. Texas	16709	11. Massachusetts	4857
5. New Jersey	14173	12. District of Columbia	3938
6. Puerto Rico	8117	13. Ohio	3719
7. Illinois	7654	14. Louisiana	3644

U.S. fatalities	160372 / 242146 (66%)
Ohio fatalities	2471 / 3719 (66%)

Continued on next page

Patient Description or Behavior	Ohio AIDS: 1981- 12/31/92			U.S. AIDS: 1981 - 9/30/92		
	Cases	Pct.	Rate[1]	Cases	Pct.	Rate[1]
GENDER						
Male	3,462	93%	66.4	214,315	89%	176.8
Female	257	7%	4.6	27,831	11%	21.8
TRANSMISSION						
Male-Male sex	2,624	72%	N/A	136,912	57%	N/A
Injecting Drug Use	301	8%	N/A	54,475	22%	N/A
Male-Male Sex/IDU	219	6%	N/A	15,203	6%	N/A
Blood Products[3]	84	2%	N/A	7,272	3%	N/A
Heterosexual[4]	154	4%	N/A	15,221	6%	N/A
Perinatal[5]	44	N/A	N/A	3,480	1%	N/A
Blood Transfusion	75	2%	N/A	4,833	2%	N/A
Undetermined[6]	205	6%	N/A	9,583	4%	N/A
AGE AT DIAGNOSIS						
0-12	57	2%	2.7	4,051	2%	
13-19	22	1%	1.6	912	<1%	
20-29	838	23%	43.8	46,476	19%	
30-39	1,657	45%	113.8	110,849	46%	
40-49	794	21%	72.3	55,038	23%	
50 and over	351	9%	12.4	24,820	10%	
RACE/ETHNICITY						
White	2,671	72%	28.0	127,317	53%	67.7
Black	951	26%	89.0	71,984	30%	246.4
Hispanic	84	2%	70.1	1,525	1%	21.9
Other/Unknown	13	<1%	16.0			
DEATHS	2,471	66%		160,372	66%	
TOTAL each group	3,719	34.4%	242,146	100%	97.4	

1Cumulative rates per 100,000 population are calculated using 1990 Census figures.   Populations and rates are not available (N/A)
2 U.S. figures are produced by Centers for Disease Control every three months.
3Includes patients infected from coagulation disorder (2,136 US) or transfusion
(5,136 US)blood products.
4A heterosexual partner is know to be: an injecting drug user (8,060 US), a bisexual man (789 US), a recipient of infected blood products (412 US), from a country where heterosexual transmission predominates (3,039 US), or HIV positive with unknown behavior history (2,921US).
5Perinatal transmission is from HIV + mother to infant, before birth.
6Patient risks are under investigation, or no risk was identified.

AIDS CASES BY COUNTY

Cumulative Ohio AIDS cases, by county,
1981 to 1-1-93.

Source - Ohio Dept of Health

Map by the Almanac

ONSET	CASES	FATAL	%FATAL
1981	2	2	100%
1982	7	7	100%
1983	26	25	96%
1984	57	54	95%
1985	118	109	92%
1986	204	192	94%
1987	392	351	90%
1988	526	448	85%
1989	610	466	76%
1990	625	394	63%
1991	647	313	48%
1992	505	110	22%

AIDS BY COUNTY - TOTAL, RATE, DEATHS

County	Total	Rate*	Dead	<1990	1990	1991	1992
Adams	2	8.2	0	2	0	0	0
Allen	25	22.3	21	15	5	4	1
Ashland	3	6.5	1	2	0	1	0
Ashtabula	8	7.7	6	3	2	2	1
Athens	10	17.7	8	8	2	0	0
Auglaize	1	2.3	1	0	0	1	0
Belmont	10	12.1	8	5	3	2	0
Brown	4	12.5	1	1	1	1	1
Butler	45	17.4	32	24	7	8	6
Carroll	2	7.8	2	1	0	1	0
Champaign	6	17.8	4	2	2	0	2
Clark	43	28.6	24	22	9	6	6
Clermont	18	14.0	9	8	1	3	6
Clinton	6	17.3	4	2	1	1	2
Columbiana	14	12.3	11	9	2	2	1
Coshocton	2	5.6	1	2	0	0	0
Crawford	8	16.0	5	5	1	2	0
Cuyahoga	908	60.6	575	463	139	180	126
Darke	5	9.1	5	4	0	1	0
Defiance	4	10.0	4	2	0	1	1
Delaware	9	16.7	5	5	1	2	1
Erie	21	26.4	16	15	0	4	2
Fairfield	20	21.3	14	11	3	3	3
Fayette	9	32.8	3	3	2	2	2
Franklin	707	81.3	493	388	111	114	94
Fulton	5	13.2	4	4	0	0	1
Gallia	1	3.3	1	1	0	0	0
Geauga	11	14.8	5	5	2	0	4
Greene	39	30.1	31	20	5	5	9
Guernsey	2	4.8	2	1	1	0	0
Hamilton	452	51.8	299	236	81	86	49
Hancock	11	17.0	9	5	3	3	0
Hardin	4	12.2	1	1	1	0	2
Harrison	1	5.5	1	1	0	0	0
Henry	3	10.6	2	1	1	0	1
Highland	4	11.9	2	2	0	1	1
Hocking	1	4.1	0	0	0	0	1
Holmes	1	3.4	1	1	0	0	0
Huron	6	11.0	5	2	3	0	1
Jackson	5	16.3	4	5	0	0	0
Jefferson	19	20.8	9	12	3	1	3
Knox	8	17.3	7	5	1	1	1
Lake	43	20.2	28	20	10	6	7

County	Total	Rate*	Dead	<1990	1990	1991	1992
Lawrence	8	12.5	6	5	3	0	0
Licking	28	23.1	19	12	6	0	10
Logan	6	15.3	3	2	2	1	1
Lorain	52	18.9	31	22	12	6	12
Lucas	182	38.6	110	79	45	30	28
Madison	10	30.3	7	3	5	1	1
Mahoning	75	25.9	52	45	14	11	5
Marion	16	23.5	10	9	1	3	3
Medina	9	8.0	6	5	0	2	2
Meigs	2	8.5	2	1	0	1	0
Mercer	5	13.0	4	2	1	1	1
Miami	16	17.7	9	10	3	2	1
Monroe	3	17.3	3	3	0	0	0
Montgomery	262	45.8	184	145	49	36	32
Morgan	1	7.0	0	0	0	0	1
Morrow	7	26.4	6	5	1	1	0
Muskingum	11	13.2	7	7	0	2	2
Ottawa	7	17.5	4	2	1	2	2
Paulding	2	9.4	1	2	0	0	0
Perry	4	12.9	2	2	1	1	0
Pickaway	30	68.7	14	12	5	7	6
Pike	7	30.7	5	4	1	1	1
Portage	21	15.5	14	12	5	2	2
Preble	6	15.7	3	3	1	0	2
Putnam	3	9.1	3	3	0	0	0
Richland	35	26.7	22	18	3	9	5
Ross	26	40.0	15	13	1	9	3
Sandusky	7	11.1	5	4	1	1	1
Scioto	13	15.4	7	6	2	4	1
Seneca	11	17.8	8	4	3	4	0
Shelby	9	20.9	7	6	3	0	0
Stark	74	19.5	58	41	12	14	7
Summit	161	30.7	101	77	20	36	28
Trumbull	34	14.1	26	18	6	4	6
Tuscarawas	4	4.7	4	3	1	0	0
Union	5	16.9	5	1	1	2	1
Warren	9	9.1	6	6	1	1	1
Washington	17	26.5	13	11	3	1	2
Wayne	11	11.3	8	6	1	4	0
Williams	7	19.2	4	3	2	1	1
Wood	14	13.0	10	5	4	3	2
Wyandot	3	13.2	3	1	2	0	0
MEDIAN RATE		15.5					

OHIO LEADS IN PRODUCTION OF:

Aircraft Lighting Equipment • Asphalt Roofing Tile • Automotive Air Brakes • Baseballs • Bathroom Fixtures • Batteries • Bee Supplies • Beeswax Candles • Bibles • Bolts • Bookmobiles • Bookplates • Bushings • Business Machines • Candy Canes • Canned Chinese Foods • Cash Registers • Ceramic Tile • Clay Pipe • Clothing Patterns • Coated Fabrics • Coffee Grinders - Commercial • Coffins • Coke • Cutlery • Dance Footwear • Dehumidifiers • Detergents • Dishwashers - Commercial and Home • Earth-Moving Equipment • Electric Equipment for Internal Combustion Engines • Electric Refrigerators and Stoves • Enamel • False Teeth Materials • Fertilizer • Fire Fighting Equipment • Fishing Lures, Reels and Rods • Footballs • Furnaces, Warm Air • Garden Hose • Gauging and Measuring Devices • Glass, Safety Plate • Glassware • Golf Balls and Clubs • Greeting Cards • Hand Shovels • Heavy Mill Machinery • Hose • Innertubes • Ironwork, Ornamental • Jet Turbine Engines • Lathes • Lawn Care Products and Seed • Liederkranz Cheese • Lime • Lithographed-stamped Metal Toys • Living Room Tables • Machine Tools • Manure Spreaders • Matches • Metal Kitchen Cabinets • Milk-Packaging Machinery • Mining Equipment • Nuts (metal) • Paint - House and Children's watercolors • Paper, Fine White • Paving Brick • Pig Iron Products • Plastic Housewares • Playground Equipment • Playing Cards • Porcelain Ware • Pottery • Pretzels • Pumps and Equipment • Punchpresses • Ranges • Refrigeration Controls • Rubber Products • Safes • Scales • School Buses • Sewer Tile • Shoelaces • Soap • Soybean Milk Processing • Spark Plugs • Steel Presses • Surface Grinders • Table Salt • Tapered Roller Bearings • Tires • Tomato Juice • Tools • Traveling Cranes • Truck Bodies • Twine • Upholstered Furniture • Vacuum Cleaners • Valve Cores - Tires • Varnishes • Vaults • Washers and Rivets • Washing Machines • Water Coolers • Water Softening Compounds • Welding Equipment • Whistles - Police and Athletic • Woven Steel Wire Outdoor Furniture.

CRIME IN OHIO
METRO AREAS, CITIES, RURAL
STATE AND RANK

Source - FBI 1992

Ohio ranks 7th in population among the states, but ranks 21st in total crime per 100,000 people, which means it has far less crime than might be expected by its size. It has similarly less crime in all major categories.

	POPULATION	CRIME INDEX TOTAL	VIOLENT CRIME	PROPERTY CRIME
Metropolitan Statistical Areas	8,963,351			
Area actually reporting	85.9%	417,735	51,130	366,605
Estimated totals	100.0%	459,625	54,096	405,529
Cities outside metro-politan areas	744,925			
Areas actually reporting	76.4%	27,241	1,892	25,349
Estimated totals	100.0%	35,659	2,476	33,183
Rural	1,307,724			
Area actually reporting	62.5%	11,687	854	10,833
Estimated totals	100.0%	18,668	1,363	17,305
State Total	11,016,000	513,952	57,935	456,017
Rate per 100,000 inhabitants		4,665.5	525.9	4,139.6
RANK	7	21	28	36

Continued on next page

OHIO LAW
VOTING – DRIVING –
MARRIAGE – DIVORCE

VOTING AGE – 18

VOTING REGISTRATION – 30 days before election

CONSUMER FINANCE LOAN RATES – 28% per year to $1,000/
22% per year to $5,000/
25% per year over $5,000,
plus fees

DRIVERS MINIMUM AGE – 16 with completion of drivers education course;
18 without course

MARRIAGE – minimum age with parental consent: Male 18
Female 16 (Younger in pregnancy or birth of child, or with parental consent and/or permission of judge)

Continued on next page

Continued from preceeding page

MURDER AND NON NEGLI-GENT MAN SLAUGHTER	FORCI-BLE RAPE	ROB-BERY	AGGRI-VATED ASSAULT	BURG-LARY	LAR-CENY THEFT	MOTOR VEH THEFT
637	4,842	20,542	25,109	85,737	234,507	46,361
662	5,212	21,403	26,819	93,443	262,591	49,495
27	247	315	1,303	4,101	20,181	1,067
35	323	412	1,706	5,368	26,418	1,397
17	128	69	640	3,472	6,739	622
27	204	110	1,022	5,546	10,765	994
724	5,739	21,925	29,547	104,357	299,774	51,886
6.6	52.1	199.0	268.2	947.3	2,721.3	471.0
24	12	16	30	32	38	24

Continued from preceeding page

OHIO LAW   MARRIAGE – DIVORCE

Age without parential consent: 18

Blood test for veneral diseases required 5 days (min) or 30 days (max) between exam and license (waiting period may be avoided).

License valid 60 days.

DIVORCE – Ohio resident 6 months.

Grounds for absolute divorce: adultery, cruelty, desertion 1 year, alcoholism, impotency, non-support, bigamy (annulment), separation 1 year, felony conviction or imprisonment, fraud, force, duress.

OHIO LOTTERY

Listed below are the winners, winning numbers and prizes for the 12-month period thru Nov. 1, 1993.

Annual proceeds from the lotto ($600 million +) are used for education, and represent about 7% of the Ohio education budget. The chance of winning one in eleven million. Even more interesting is the chance of winning twice is one in twenty billion, and it has been done twice!

M = millions

Source: Ohio Lottery Commission

DATE	WINNING NUMBER	PRIZE	WINNER	CITY
1993				
OCT				
30	33-34-35-43-45-46	$16M	A Heckathorn	Northwood,OH
16	10-12-33-38-41-42	$12M	M Scannell	Columbus, OH
			L Power	Carmel, IN
			T Scannell	Whitehall, OH
			T McDonald	Columbus, OH
			K Scannell	Columbus, OH
6	7-19-30-32-42-47	$ 4M	L Hirschbach	Lebanon, OH
2	10-15-16-17-18-42	$10M	T Bonfield	Cincinnati, OH
SEPT				
15	1-6-27-28-39-46	$ 8M	D Bays	Minford, OH
8	6-16-21-32-39-46	$ 8M	R Baksa	Austintown, OH
1	2-18-25-36-39-45	$ 4M	G Craft	Willoughby, OH
AUG				
28	2-3-11-40-44-45	$12M	G Keglovic	Maple Hts., OH
			D Burnett	Medina, OH
18	2-15-20-26-37-42	$ 6M	S Bowen	Cleveland, OH
			J Bowen	Cleveland, OH
7	24-27-28-29-35-44	$ 4M	B Nichols	New Philadelphia, OH
			C Nichols	New Philadelphia, OH
JUL				
28	7-19-17-24-32-36	$16M	J Fagel Jr.	Cleveland, OH
JUN				
30	3-7-30-32-36-39	$12M	M Fares	Youngstown, OH
			W Vesia	Diamond, OH
			R Vesia	Youngstown, OH
19	5-16-24-27-29-31	$18M	A Crawford II	Hamilton, OH
			R Crawford	Hamilton, OH
			A Crawford	Hamilton, OH
16	6-32-35-43-44-45	$26M	J Suschak	Mayfield Hts, OH
			M E Suschak	Mayfield Hts, OH
			J Suschak	N. Olmstead, OH
			B Suschak	N. Olmstead, OH
			M Martinis	Mayfield Hts, OH
			M A Martinis	Mayfield Hts, OH
MAY				
26	1-10-14-15-17-36	$ 4M	H Bassell	Springfield, OH
			J Hitchman	Mansfield, OH
19	10-26-27-37-40-44	$12M	E Freiberg	Franklin, OH
			L Freiberg	Franklin, OH
			R Freiberg	Middletown, OH
			C Oswald	Franklin, OH
8	8-11-13-14-36-41	$ 8M	R Hinkle	Crooksville, OH
			R Hinkle	Crooksville, OH
1	15-20-30-36-41-46	$ 8M	W Johnson	Cleveland, OH

Continued on next page

Continued from preceeding page

DATE	WINNING NUMBER	PRIZE	WINNER	CITY
APR				
24	10-22-27-32-33-39	$6.7M	K Harwood	Euclid, OH
			S O'Dell	Hubbard, OH
			F Fullerman	Youngstown, OH
			M Cirelli	Boardman, OH
			R Rothbauer	Poland, OH
			A Donatella	New Middletown, OH
			C O'Dell	Hubbard, OH
			C Hartsock	Youngstown, OH
			C Durkin	Boardman, OH
			J Griffiths	Hubbard, OH
			V Bechtler	Mansfield, OH
			S Bechtler	Mansfield, OH
7	2-22-24-33-34-39	$16M	T McNalley	Bryan, OH
			J McNalley	Bryan, OH
			T Zuver	Pioneer, OH
			S Baden	Sherwood, OH
MAR				
24	13-14-31-40-42-46	$12M	C Chase	Middleburg Hts, OH
			P Chase	Middleburg Hts, OH
13	6-8-23-26-30-31	$12M	14 Teachers	Youngstown, OH
3	3-14-40-43-44-45	$ 8M	J Randall	Xenia, OH
			F Krueger	Cincinnati, OH
			T Helterbran	Wilmington, OH
			W Evans	Tipp City, OH
			D Freeman	Beavercreek, OH
			B Nelson	Huber Hts, OH
			C McCallister	Vandalia, OH
			P Reese	Tipp City, OH
			N Jackson	Washington, OH
			J Flynn	Dayton, OH
			C Niarhos	Vandalia, OH
			T Anderson	Milledgeville, OH
			L Bey	Greenville, OH
			O Cousin	Dayton, OH
			J Saul	Dayton, OH
			C Sink Jr.	New Carlisle, OH
			H Jones	Vandalia, OH
			T Baker	Sabina, OH
			L Neff	Xenia, OH
FEB				
24	4-5-18-23-28-43	$12M	S James	Columbus, OH
			S Mankowski	Garfield Hts, OH
			K Mankowski	Garfield Hts, OH
			R Mankowski	Cal-Nev-Ari, NV
3	1-4-14-31-36-39	$16M	R & C McCullough	Middletown, OH
JAN				
20	1-5-8-10-37-42	$20M	E Barnum	Sandusky, OH
			L Barnum	Sandusky, OH
			L Perin	Sandusky, OH
			L Barnun Jr.	Sandusky, OH
			J Barnum	Sandusky, OH
2	3-8-16-31-33-38	$12M	P Watson	Chardon, OH

Continued on next page

Continued from preceeding page

1992
DEC

23	7-13-27-32-34-35	$12M	L & K Large	Toledo, OH
12	1-4-19-24-34-42	$20M	R & E Thomas	Columbus, OH

NOV

25	1-5-14-25-38-43	$16M	J & M McCallister	Richmond, OH
11	19-25-29-37-41-46	$10M	14 Michelin Tire Employees	Canton, OH
			C & C Mills	Columbus, OH

Lottery Profits Education Fund Group

		1992	1993
603	Vocational Education Consolidated	0	5,000,000
612	School Building Assistance	0	10,000,000
670	School Foundation Basic Allowance	565,151,931	554,500,000
671	Special Education	49,999,999	50,000,000
672	Vocational Education	30,508,930	30,000,000
677	Lottery Profits Educ Reserve	273,639	0

Source: Office of Legislative Information.

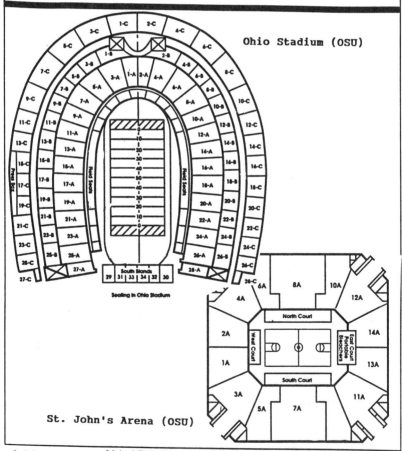

Ohio Stadium (OSU)

Seating in Ohio Stadium

St. John's Arena (OSU)

MAJOR LEAGUE BASEBALL

MAJOR LEAGUE BASEBALL CHAMPIONS
* Division playoffs began in 1969 when both leagues expanded to 12 teams.

Cincinnati

YEAR	PENNANT CHAMPION	WON	LOST	PCT.	PLAYOFF
1990	National League - West	102	60	.630	
	National League	4	2		over Pittsburgh
	WORLD SERIES	4	0		over Oakland
1979	National League - West	90	71	.559	
	--------------------→	0	3		lost N.L. to Pittsburgh
1976	National League - West	102	60	.630	
	National League	3	0		over Philadelphia
	WORLD SERIES	4	0		over New York
1975	National League - West	108	54	.667	
	National League	3	0		over Pittsburgh
	WORLD SERIES	4	3		over Boston
1973	National League - West	99	63	.611	
	--------------------→	3	2		lost N.L. to New York
1972	National League - West	95	59	.617	
	National League	3	2		over Pittsburgh
	--------------------→	3	4		lost W.S. to Oakland
1970*	National League - West	102	60	.630	
	National League	3	0		over Pittsburgh
	--------------------→	1	4		lost W.S. to Baltimore
1961	National League	93	61	.604	
	--------------------→	4	1		lost W.S. to New York
1940	National League	100	53	.654	
	WORLD SERIES	4	3		over Detroit
1939	National League	97	57		
	--------------------→	0	4		lost W.S. to New York
1919	National League	96	44	.686	
	WORLD SERIES	5	2		over Chicago

Continued on next page

ALL ABOUT OHIO ALMANAC - 1994

Cleveland

YEAR	PENNANT CHAMPION	WON	LOST	PCT.	PLAYOFF
1954	American League	111	43	.721	
	--------------------------→	0	4		lost W.S. to New York
1948	American League	97	58	.626	
	WORLD SERIES	4	2		over Boston
1920	American League	98	56	.636	
	WORLD SERIES	5	2		over Brooklyn

MAJOR LEGAUE BASEBALL PLAYER RECORDS

Cleveland Indians
A.L. ANNUAL HOME RUN CHAMPION

Year	Player	H.R.
1959	Rocky Colavito	42
1954	Larry Doby	32
1953	Al Rosen	43
1952	Larry Doby	37
1950	Al Rosen	37
1915	Robert Ruth	7

Cincinnati Reds
N.L. ANNUAL HOME RUN CHAMPION

Year	Player	H.R.
1978	George Foster	40
1977	George Foster	52
1972	Johnny Bench	40
1970	Johnny Bench	45
1954	Ted Kluszewski	49
1905	Fred Odwell	9

A.L. ANNUAL BATTING CHAMPION

Year	Player	PCT.
1954	Bobby Avila	.341
1944	Lon Boudreau	.327
1929	Lew Fonseca	.369
1916	Tris Speaker	.386
1905	Elmer Flick	.306
1904	Nap Lajoie	.381
1903	Nap Lajoie	.355

N.L. ANNUAL BATTING CHAMPION

Year	Player	PCT.
1973	Pete Rose	.338
1969	Pete Rose	.348
1968	Pete Rose	.335
1938	Ernie Lombardi	.342
1926	Gene Hargrave	.353
1919	Edd Roush	.341
1917	Edd Roush	.321
1916	Hal Chase	.339
1905	Cy Seymour	.377

A.L. ANNUAL STOLEN BASES CHAMPION

Year	Player	#
1993	Kenny Lofton	70
1992	Kenny Lofton	62
1946	George Case	28
1906	Elmer Flick	39
1904	Elmer Flick	42
1903	Harry Bay	45

N.L. ANNUAL STOLEN BASES CHAMPION

Year	Player	#
1970	Bobby Tolan	57
1940	Lonny Frey	22
1912	Bob Bescher	67
1911	Bob Bescher	81
1910	Bob Bescher	70
1909	Bob Bescher	54

Continued on next page

Continued from preceeding page

A.L. ANNUAL PITCHING LEADER, %				N.L. ANNUAL PITCHING LEADER, %			
Year	Pitcher	W-L	PCT.	Year	Pitcher	W-L	PCT.
1966	Sonny Siebert	16-8	.667	1991	Jose Rijo	15-6	.714
1960	Jim Perry	18-10	.643	1981	Tom Seaver	14-2	.875
1951	Bob Feller	22-8	.733	1979	Tom Seaver	16-6	.727
1937	Johnny Allen	15-1	.938	1975	Don Gullett	15-4	.789
1926	George Uhle	27-11	.711	1972	Gary Nolan	15-5	.750
1920	Jim Bagby	31-12	.721	1971	Don Gullett	16-6	.727
				1962	Bob Purkey	23-5	.821
				1941	Elmer Riddle	19-4	.826
				1939	Paul Derringer	25-7	.781
				1923	Dolf Luque	27-8	.771
				1922	Pete Donohue	18-9	.667
				1919	Dutch Ruether	19-6	.760

Cleveland Indians
A.L. ANNUAL EARNED RUN AVG., LEADER

Cincinnati Reds
N.L. ANNUAL EARNED RUN AVG., LEADER

Year	Player	E.R.A.	Year	Player	E.R.A.
1968	Luis Tiant	1.60	1944	Ed Heusser	2.38
1950	Early Wynn	3.20	1941	Elmer Riddle	2.24
1948	Gene Bearden	2.43	1940	Bucky Walters	2.48
1940	Bob Feller	2.61	1939	Bucky Walters	2.29
1933	Monte Person	2.33	1925	Dolf Luque	2.63
1923	Stan Coveleski	2.76	1923	Dolf Luque	2.16
1911	Vean Gregg	1.81			
1908	Addie Joss	1.16			
1904	Addie Joss	1.59			
1903	Earl Moore	1.77			

A.L. ANNUAL PITCHING LEADER STRIKEOUTS

N.L. ANNUAL PITCHING LEADER STRIKEOUTS

Year	Pitcher	S.O.	Year	Pitcher	S.O.
1985	Bert Blyleven	206*	1993	Jose Rijo	227
1981	Len Barker	127	1947	Ewell Blackwell	193
1980	Len Barker	187	1946	Johnny Schmitz	135
1970	Sam McDowell	304	1943	John Vander Meer	174
1969	Sam McDowell	279	1942	John Vander Meer	186
1968	Sam McDowell	283	1941	John Vander Meer	202
1966	Sam McDowell	225	1939	Bucky Walters	137*
1965	Sam McDowell	325	1901	Noodles Hahn	239
1957	Early Wynn	184			
1956	Herb Score	263		*Tied	
1955	Herb Score	245			
1950	Bob Lemon	170			
1948	Bob Feller	164			
1947	Bob Feller	196			
1946	Bob Feller	348			
1943	Allie Reynolds	151			
1941	Bob Feller	260			
1940	Bob Feller	261			
1939	Bob Feller	246			
1938	Bob Feller	240			
1920	Stan Covelski	133			

Continued on next page

Continued from preceeding page

A.L. ANNUAL MVP AWARD

Year	Player
1977	Al Rosen
1948	Lou Boudreau
1926	George Burns

N.L. ANNUAL MVP AWARD

Year	Player
1977	George Foster
1976	Joe Morgan
1975	Joe Morgan
1973	Pete Rose
1972	Johnny Bench
1970	Johnny Bench
1961	Frank Robinson
1940	Frank McCormick
1939	Bucky Walters
1938	Ernie Lombardi

Cleveland Indians
A.L. ROOKIE OF THE YEAR

Year	Player
1990	Sandy Alomar, Jr.
1980	Joe Cherboneau
1971	Chris Chambliss
1955	Herb Score

Cincinnati Reds
N.L. ROOKIE OF THE YEAR

Year	Player
1988	Chris Sabo
1976	Pat Zachry
1968	Johnny Bench
1966	Tommy Helms
1963	Pete Rose
1956	Frank Robinson

MAJOR LEAGUE ALL-STAR GAMES IN OHIO

YEAR	PLACE	WINNER (MANAGER)	SCORE	LOSER (MANAGER)
1988	Cincinnati	A.L. (Kelly)	2-1	N.L. (Hertzog)
1981	Cleveland	N.L. (Green)	5-4	N.L. (Frey)
1970	Cincinnati	N.L. (Hodges)	5-4	A.L. (Weaver)
1963	Cleveland	N.L. (Dark)	5-3	A.L. Houkl)
1954	Cleveland	A.L. (Stengel)	11-9	N.L. (Alston)
1953	Cincinnati	N.L. (Dressen)	5-1	A.L. (Stengel)
1938	Cincinnati	N.L. (Terry)	4-1	A.L. (McCarthy)
1935	Cleveland	A.L. (Cochrane)	4-1	N.L. (Frisch)

Continued on next page

INTERNATIONAL BASEBALL LEAGUE
Pennant Winners
Columbus & Toledo
Source: International League

Ohio has two pro-ball teams, the Columbus Clippers and the Toledo Mud Hens, in the Triple-A I.L. Columbus is affiliated with the N.Y. Yankees and Toledo is affiliated with the Detroit Tigers.

NOTE: The I.L. dates since 1884, and over time has had the teams from such current major league cities as Detroit, Baltimore, Montreal and Toronto.

Ohio teams have won the I.L. pennant in the following years:

YEAR	TEAM	MANAGER
1992	Columbus	Rick Down
1991	Columbus	Rick Down
1984	Columbus	Stump Merrill
1983	Columbus	Johnny Oates
1981	Columbus	Frank Verdi
1980	Columbus	Joe Altobelli
1979	Columbus	Gene Michael
1968	Toledo	Jack Tighe
1965	Columbus	Larry Shepard
1961	Columbus	Larry Shepard

PRO FOOTBALL HALL OF FAME

Source - Pro Football Hall of Fame

Eleven Ohio players and one coach are in the National Pro Football Hall of Fame. All were with the Cleveland Browns. One, the coach, also was with the Cincinnati Bengals.

Note: Before joining the NFL, the Cleveland Browns played in the new, rival "All America Football Conference", where the Browns won all four of the annual AAFC championships (1946-1949), before they (and the San Francisco 49ers) were accepted into the NFL. Seven of the Browns' Hall of Famers were on the Browns' AAFC team and continued with the Browns into the NFL. (Coach Paul Brown, Len Ford, Frant Gatski, Otto Graham, Lou Groza, Dante Laveill and Bill Willis).

PLAYER	POSITION	YEARS
Jim Brown	Fullback	1957-65
Paul E. Brown	Coach, Browns (1946-62) Bengals (1968-75)	1946-75
Len Dawson	Quarterback	1957-75*
Len Ford	End, Def. End	1948-58*
Frank Gatski	Offensive Lineman	1946-57
Otto Graham	Quarterback	1946-55
Lou Groza	Place-Kicker Tackle	1946-67
Dante Laveili	End	1946-56
Mike McCormack	Tackle	1951-62*
Bobby Mitchell	Wide Receiver	1958-68*
Paul Warfield	Wide Receiver	1964-74, 76-77 *
Bill Willis	Guard	1946-53

*Career included other teams

Continued on next page

GATEWAY - CLEVELAND'S NEW SPORTS COMPLEX

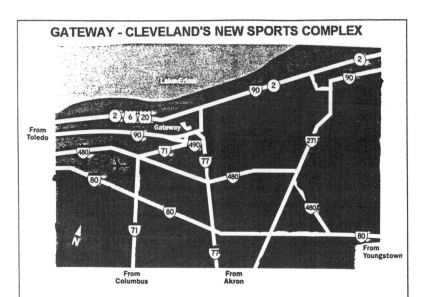

GATEWAY - CLOSE-UP

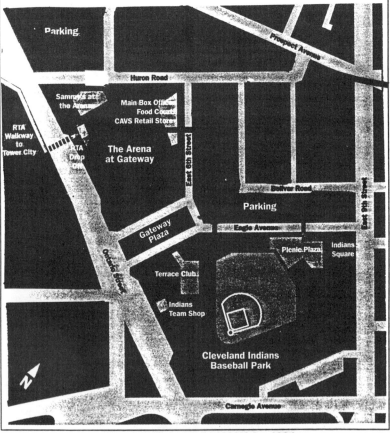

ALL ABOUT OHIO ALMANAC - 1994

GATEWAY - DOWNTOWN CLEVELAND

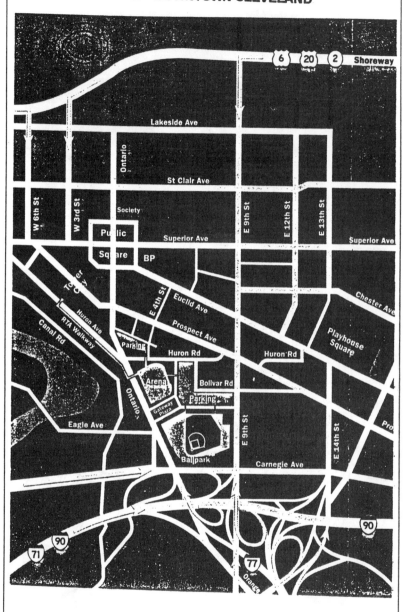

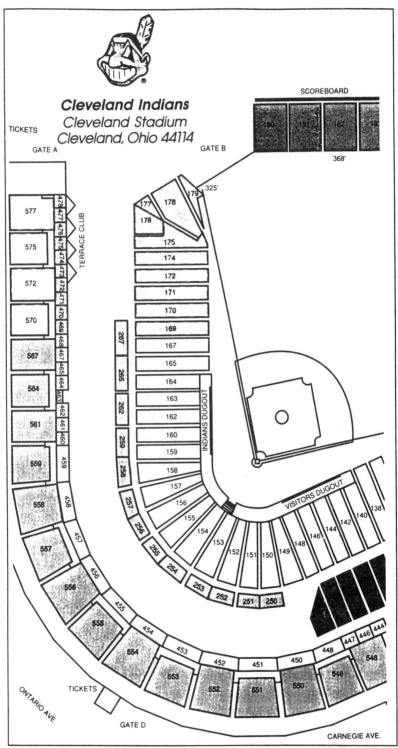

Cleveland Indians
Cleveland Stadium
Cleveland, Ohio 44114

TICKETS

GATE A

GATE B

SCOREBOARD

368'

325'

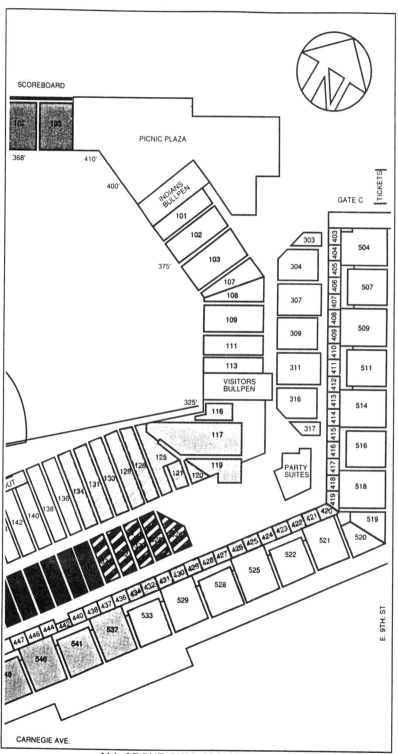

NBA BASKETBALL - OHIO

Cleveland Cavaliers, since 1970
Cincinnati Royals (1958 - 1972), now Sacramento (California) Kings

1993 CLEVELAND PLAYERS IN TOP NBA RANKINGS

Mark Price -
- NBA All-League guard
- NBA Free- Throw % (1st) .948%, 289 total
- NBA 3-Point Field Goad % (6th), .416%, 122 total
- NBA Assists(10th) 8.0 avg., 602 total

Bill Daugherty
- NBA Field-Goal % (r2nd) .571%, 520 total
- NBA Rebounds (15th) 10.2 avg., 726 total
- NBA Scoring (19th) 20.2 avg., 1432 total

Larry Nance
- NBA Field Goal % (7th) .549%, 533 total
- NBA Blocked Shots (10th) 2.57 avg. 198 total

NBA MOST VALUABLE PLAYER
1969 - Oscar Robinson, Cincinnati

NBA COACH OF THE YEAR
1976 - Bill Fitch, Cleveland

NBA ROOKIE OF THE YEAR
1963 - Jerry Lewis, Cincinnati
1961 - Oscar Robertson, Cincinnati

NBA ANNUAL LEADER
1971 - Johnny Green, Field Goal %, .587%
1970 - Johnny Green, Field Goal %, .589%
1969 - Oscar Robinson, Assists, 9.7 avg., 690 total
1966 - Oscar Robinson, Assists, 11.1 avg., 847 total
1965 - Oscar Robinson, Assists, 11.5 avg., 861 total
1964 - Oscar Robinson, Assists, 11.0 avg., 868 total
1964 - Jerry Lucas, Field Goal %, .527%
1962 - Oscar Robinson, Assists, 11.4 avg., 899 total
1961 - Oscar Robinson, Assists, 9.7 avg., 690 total
1958 - Jack Twyman, Field Goad %, .452%

Note: The above players were with Cincinnati

$ VALUE OF OHIO SPORT FRANCHISES

Ohio has five major league franchises, with a total value of $525 million (Financial World magazine, May, 1993).

FRANCHISE	VALUE
Cincinnati Reds (baseball)	$103 million
Cleveland Indians (baseball)	$81 million
Cleveland Cavaliers (basketball)	$81 million
Cleveland Browns (football)	$133 million
Cincinnati Bengals (football)	$128 million

Continued on next page

OHIO COLLEGE FOOTBALL CHAMPIONS
MAJOR CONFERENCES

Big Ten

NOTE: There are 11 schools in the conference (Illinois, Indiana, Iowa, Michigan, Michigan St, Minnesota, Northwestern, Ohio St, Penn St, Purdue and Wisconsin). Ohio St has won the title 25 times, which is exceeded only by Michigan's 37.

* Tied

YEAR	COLLEGE	WON-LOST RECORD	YEAR	COLLEGE	WON-LOST RECORD
1986	Ohio St	7-1	1961	Ohio St	6-0
1984	Ohio St	7-2	1957	Ohio St	7-0
1981	Ohio St *	6-2	1955	Ohio St	6-0
1979	Ohio St	8-0	1954	Ohio St	7-0
1977	Ohio St *	7-1	1949	Ohio St	4-1-1
1976	Ohio St *	7-1	1944	Ohio St	6-0
1975	Ohio St	8-0	1942	Ohio St	5-1
1974	Ohio St *	7-1	1939	Ohio St	5-1
1973	Ohio St *	7-0-1	1935	Ohio St *	5-0
1972	Ohio St *	8-0	1920	Ohio St	5-0
1970	Ohio St	7-0	1917	Ohio St	4-0
1969	Ohio St *	6-1	1916	Ohio St	4-0
1968	Ohio St	7-0			

Mid-America

NOTE: There are 10 schools in the conference (Akron, Ball St, Bowling Green, Central Mich, Eastern Mich., Kent, Miami (Ohio), Ohio Un., Toledo and Western Mich). Miami (Ohio) leads the conference.

* Tied

YEAR	COLLEGE	WON-LOST RECORD	YEAR	COLLEGE	WON-LOST RECORD
1992	Bowling Green	8-0	1974	Miami (Ohio)	5-0
1991	Bowling Green	8-0	1973	Miami (Ohio)	5-0
1990	Toledo *	7-1	1972	Kent St	4-1
1986	Miami (Ohio)	6-2	1971	Toledo	5-0
1985	Bowling Green	9-0	1970	Toledo	5-0
1984	Toledo	7-1-1	1969	Toledo	5-0
1982	Bowling Green	7-2	1968	Ohio Un	6-0
1981	Toledo	8-1	1967	Ohio Un *	5-1
1977	Miami (Ohio)	5-0		Toledo *	5-1
1975	Miami (Ohio)	6-0	1966	Miami (Ohio)	5-1

Continued on next page

YEAR	COLLEGE	WON-LOST RECORD	YEAR	COLLEGE	WON-LOST RECORD
1965	Bowling Green *	5-1	1955	Miami (Ohio)	5-0
	Miami (Ohio)	5-1	1954	Miami (Ohio)	4-0
1964	Bowling Green	5-1	1953	Miami (Ohio) *	5-0-1
1963	Ohio Un	5-1		Ohio Un *	3-0-1
1962	Bowling Green	5-0-1	1952	Cincinnati	3-0
1961	Bowling Green	5-1	1951	Cincinnati	3-0
1960	Ohio Un	6-0	1950	Miami (Ohio)	4-0
1959	Bowling Green	6-0	1949	Cincinnati	4-0
1958	Miami (Ohio)	5-0	1948	Miami (Ohio)	4-0
1957	Miami (Ohio)	5-0	1947	Cincinnati	3-1
1956	Bowling Green *	5-0-1			
	Miami (Ohio) *	4-0-1			

COLLEGE FOOTBALL
HALL OF FAME

Source - College Football Hall of Fame

Eleven Ohio college players are in the Hall of Fame. All played at Ohio State University.

Note: The Hall, located at Kings Island, Ohio, will re-open in 1995 at its new home in South Bend, Indiana.

PLAYER	LAST COLLEGE YEAR
Aming, Warren	Ohio State, 1946
Cassady, Howard	Ohio State, 1955
Daniell, James	Ohio State, 1941
Fesler, Wesley	Ohio State, 1930
Griffin, Archie	Ohio State, 1975
Harley, Chick	Ohio State, 1919
Horvath, Les	Ohio State, 1944
Janowicz, Vic	Ohio State, 1951
Jones Gormer	Ohio State, 1935
Parker, James	Ohio State, 1956
Stillwagon, Jim	Ohio State, 1970
Thomas, Aurelius	Ohio State, 1957
Willis, William	Ohio State, 1945
Zarnas, Gus	Ohio State, 1937

COLLEGE FOOTBALL BOWLS

Ohio State University

YEAR	BOWL	PLACE	WINNER	LOSER
1993	Florida Citrus	Orlando	Georgia 21	Ohio State 14
1992	Hall of Fame	Tampa	Syracuse 24	Ohio State 17
1990 Dec.	Liberty	Memphis	Air Force 23	Ohio State 11
1990 Jan.	Hall of Fame	Tampa	Auburn 31	Ohio State 14
1987	Cotton	Dallas	Ohio State 28	Texas A & M 12
1985	Rose	Pasadena	USC 20	Ohio State 17
1984	Fiesta	Tempe	Ohio State 28	Pittsburgh 23
1982 Dec.	Holiday	San Diego	Ohio State 47	Brigham Young 17
1981 Dec.	Liberty	Memphis	Ohio State 31	Navy 28
1980 Dec.	Fiesta	Tempe	Penn State 31	Ohio State 19
1980 Jan.	Rose	Pasadena	USC 17	Ohio State 16
1978 Dec.	Gator	Jacksonville	Clemson 17	Ohio State 15
1978 Jan.	Sugar	New Orleans	Alabama 35	Ohio State 6
1977	Orange	Miami	Ohio State 27	Colorado 10
1976	Rose	Pasadena	UCLA 23	Ohio State 10
1975	Rose	Pasadena	USC 18	Ohio State 17
1974	Rose	Pasadena	Ohio State 42	USC 21
1973	Rose	Pasadena	USC 42	Ohio State 17
1971	Rose	Pasadena	Stanford 27	Ohio State 17
1969	Rose	Pasadena	Ohio State 27	USC 16
1958	Rose	Pasadena	Ohio State 10	Oregon 7
1955	Rose	Pasadena	Ohio State 20	USC 7
1950	Rose	Pasadena	Ohio State 17	California 14
1921	Rose	Pasadena	California 28	Ohio State 0

Bowling Green St. Un.

1992	Las Vegas	Las Vegas	Bowling Green 35	Nevada 34
1991	Las Vegas	Las Vegas	Bowling Green 28	Fresno St. 21
1985	Las Vegas	Las Vegas	Fresno St. 51	Bowling Green 7
1982	Las Vegas	Las Vegas	Fresno St. 29	Bowling Green 28

Un. Cincinnati

1951	John Hancock * El Paso		W Texas St 14	Cincinnati 13
1947	John Hancock * El Paso		Cincinnati 18	Virginia Tech 6
	*formerly the Sun Bowl			

Ohio Un.

| 1963 | John Hancock * El Paso | | W Texas St 15 | Ohio Un 14 |
| | *formerly the Sun Bowl | | | |

Un. of Toledo

1984 *	Las Vegas	Las Vegas	*U Las Vegas 30	*Toledo 13
1991	Las Vegas	Las Vegas	Toledo 27	San Jose S. 25
	*U of LV later forfeited game to Toledo for ineligible players			

1993-94 STATE HIGH SCHOOL CHAMPIONS

Source: Ohio High School Athletic Association

Sport	Div.	School
Golf - Boys	III	Gates Mills Gilmour Academy
	II	Kettering Alter
	I	Upper Arlington
Golf - Girls	I	Toledo Notre Dame
Tennis - Girls	II	Singles - Celena McCoury, Louisville St. Thomas Aquinas
		Doubles - Cassidy Landes-Jessica Landes, Huron
	I	Singles - Lilia Osterioh, Groveport-Madison
		Doubles - Amee Hathaway-Brooke Hart, Cincinnati Anderson
Cross Contry - Boys	III	New London
	II	Salem
	I	Cleveland St. Ignatius
Cross Country - Girls	II	Elmore Woodmore
	I	Cleveland Hts. Beaumont
Field Hockey - Girls	I	Toledo Ottawa Hills
Volleyball - Girls	IV	New Washington Buckeye Central
	III	Pemberville Eastwood
	II	Cincinnati St. Ursula Academy
	I	Cincinnati Ursuline Academy
Soccer - Boys	II	Bay Village Bay
	I	Broadview Hts. Brecksville
Soccer - Girls	I	Cincinnati St. Ursula
Football - Boys	V	Steubenville Catholic Central
	IV	Versailles
	III	Wauseon
	II	St. Marys Memorial
	I	Cleveland St. Ignatius

1992-93 STATE HIGH SCHOOL CHAMPIONS

Source: Ohio High School Athletic Association

Sport (First Tournament)	Div.	School
Baseball - Boys (1928)	IV	Cincinnati Country Day
	III	Campbell Memorial
	II	Hebron Lakewood
	I	Cincinnati Moeller
Basketball - Boys (1923)	IV	Fort Loramie
	III	Campbell Memorial
	II	Girard
	I	Cincinnati
Basketball - Girls (1976)	IV	McGuffey Upper Scioto Valley
	III	Baltimore Liberty Union
	II	Urbana
	I	Pickingerton
Cross Country - Boys (1928)	III	Caldwell
	II	Bay Village Bay
	I	Sylvania Southview
Cross Country - Girls (1978)	II	Elmore Woodmore
	I	Worthington Thomas Worthington

Continued on next page

Continued from preceeding page

Field Hockey - Girls (1979)	I	Toledo Ottawa Hills
Football - Boys	V	St. Henry
	IV	Cincinnati Academy of P.E.
	III	Mentor Lake Catholic
	II	St. Marys Memorial
	I	Cleveland St. Ignatius
Golf - Boys	III	Gates Mills Gilmour Acad.
	II	Kettering Alter
	I	Upper Arlington
Gymnastics - Boys (1926-1937, 1965-)	I	Columbus DeSales
Gymnastics - Girls (1973)	I	Rocky River Magnificat
Ice-Hockey - Boys (1979)	I	Shaker Heights
Soccer - Boys (1976)	II	Columbus DeSales
	I	Broadview Hts. Brecksville
Soccer - Girls (1985)	I	Westerville North
Softball, Fast Pitch - Girls (1978)	III	Loudonville
	II	Tallmadge
	I	Akron Springfield
Swimming & Diving - Boys (1928)	I	Cincinnati St. Xavier
Swimming & Diving - Girls (1977)	I	Cincinnati St. Ursula
Tennis - Boys (1920)	II	Singles - Justin O'Neal, Lima Shawnee Doubles - Scott Seelbach-Carlin Wiegner Chagrin Falls Univ. School
	I	Singles - Matt Pledger, Middletown Doubles - Scott Marshall-Brad Goldberg Cincinnati Sycamore
Tennis - Girls (1976)	II	Singles - Chris Lucia, Gates Mills Hawken Doubles - Leslie Wargo- Cassidy Landes Huron
	I	Singles - Sora Moon, Centerville Doubles - Katherine Rhee-Tina Danielak Centerville
Track & Field - Boys (1908)	III	Yellow Springs
	II	Akron Hoban
	II	Bedford
Track & Field - Girls (1975)	III	* Elmore Woodmore
		* Middletown Fenwick
	II	Sandusky Perkins
	I	Rocky River Magnificat
Volleyball - Girls (1975)	IV	Antwerp
	III	Tontogany Otsego
	II	Akron Hoban
	I	Stow
Wrestling - Boys (1938)	III	Akron Coventry
	II	Ravenna
	I	Stow Walsh Jesuit
		* Co-Champions

BOYS STATE CROSS COUNTRY INDIVIDUAL RECORDS — DIVISION I

2.0 Miles	Alan Scharsu, Youngstown Austintown-Fitch	9:15.7	1975
2.5 Miles	George Nicholas, Dayton Meadowdale	11:36.7	1980
5000 Meters	Bob Mau, Rocky River	14:58.6	1982

BOYS STATE CROSS COUNTRY INDIVIDUAL RECORDS — DIVISION II

2.0 Miles	Bruce Smith, Martins Ferry	9:33.4	1975
2.5 Miles	Mitch Bentley, McArthur Vinton	12:03.4	1980
5000 Meters	Scott Fry, Sandusky Perkins	14:50.2	1984

BOYS STATE CROSS COUNTRY INDIVIDUAL RECORDS — DIVISION III

2.0 Miles	Dan Zoeller, Tipp City Bethel	9:49.9	1968
2.5 Miles	Earl Zilles, West Liberty-Salem	12:06.7	1978
5000 Meters	Bob Burley, New Albany	15:19.3	1982

GIRLS STATE CROSS COUNTRY INDIVIDUAL RECORDS — DIVISION II

2.5 Miles	C.J. Robinson, Cincinnati Reading	13:33.9	1981
5000 Meters	Patty Metzler, North Jackson Jackson-Milton	17:17.8	1982

GIRLS STATE CROSS COUNTRY INDIVIDUAL RECORDS — DIVISION I

2.5 Miles	Ann Henderson, Broadview Heights Brecksville	13:46.2	1978
5000 Meters	Kristy Orre, Clayton Northmont	17:15.6	1982

BOYS STATE TOURNAMENT SWIMMING AND DIVING RECORDS

200 YARDS MEDLEY RELAY
Cincinnati St. Xavier — 1:33.39 — 1992
Mike Andrews, Jon Maddux, Dod Wales, Shawn Trokhan

200 YARDS FREESTYLE
Joe Hudepohl, Cincinnati St. Xavier — 1:34.96 — 1991 N

200 YARDS INDIV. MEDLEY
Mark Rhodenbaugh, Cincinnati Oak Hills — 1:48.974 — 1982

50 YARDS FREESTYLE
Joe Hudepohl, Cincinnati St. Xavier — :20.01 — 1991 N

ONE METER DIVING
Randy Chambers, North Canton Hoover — 528.35 — 1978

100 YARDS BUTTERFLY
David Wilson, Cincinnati Anderson — :49.013 — 1979

100 YARDS FREESTYLE
Joe Hudepohl, Cincinnati St. Xavier — :43.43 — 1992 N

500 YARDS FREESTYLE
David Fairbanks, Cincinnati Sycamore — 4:26.567 — 1985

200 YARDS FREESTYLE RELAY
Cincinnati St. Xavier — 1:24.06 — 1992
Joe Hudepohl, Jason Davis, Lee Kammerer, Shawn Trokhan

100 YARDS BACKSTROKE
Mike Andrews, Cincinnati St. Xavier — :49.64 — 1992

100 YARDS BREASTSTROKE
Glen Mills, Cincinnati Finneytown — :55.442 — 1980

400 YARDS FREESTYLE RELAY
Cincinnati St. Xavier — 3:02.92 — 1992
Mike Andrews, Jason Davis, Dod Wales, Joe Hudepohl

N — National Record

Continued on next page

GIRLS STATE TOURNAMENT
SWIMMING AND DIVING RECORDS

200 YARDS MEDLEY RELAY
Cincinnati Oak Hills — 1:46.51 — 1991
Michelle McCarthy, Cynthia Janssen,
Amy Fritsch, Denise McCarthy

200 YARDS FREESTYLE
Beth Washut, Ashtabula St. John — 1:47.652 — 1981

200 YARDS INDIV. MEDLEY
Rachel Gustin, Cincinnati Seven Hills — 2:03.20 — 1991

50 YARDS FREESTYLE
Aimee Berzins, Centerville — :22.943 — 1984

ONE METER DIVING
Nancy Hauck, Sylvania Northview — 476.40 — 1979

100 YARDS BUTTERFLY
Sarah Weis, Sylvania Northview — :55.20 — 1988

100 YARDS FREESTYLE
Beth Washut, Ashtabula St. John — :49.977 — 1982

500 YARDS FREESTYLE
Katherine Creighton, Gates Mills Hawken — 4:49.49 — 1988

200 YARDS FREESTYLE RELAY
Kettering Fairmont — 1:38.24 — 1992
Kami Runzo, Carrie Houston, Erin Warner
Lisa Eck

100 YARDS BACKSTROKE
Sheri White, Worthington — :56.00 — 1989

100 YARDS BREASTSTROKE
Kim Rhodenbaugh, Cincinnati Oak Hills — 1:02.498 — 1982

400 YARDS FREESTYLE RELAY
Gates Mills Hawken: — 3:30.98 — 1987
Melissa Burovac, Melanie Valerio
Sarah Dykstra, Katherine Creighton

N — National Record

1992 DIVISION I BOYS STATE TRACK AND FIELD TOURNAMENT RECORDS

100 METER DASH
Mario Allmon, Cincinnati Princeton . . . . — 10.51 — 1990
Jonathan Burrell, Cleveland John Marshall . . . . . . — 10.51 — 1991

100 METER 39" HURDLES
Chris Nelloms, Dayton Dunbar . . . . — 13.57 — 1990

300 METER 36" HURDLES
Glenn C. Terry, Jr., Cincinnati Sycamore . . . . — 36.38 — 1988

200 METER DASH
Chris Nelloms, Dayton Dunbar . . . . — 20.47 — 1990

400 METER DASH
Chris Nelloms, Dayton Dunbar . . . . — 45.59 — 1990

800 METER RUN
Mike Huber, Cleveland St. Ignatius . . . . — 1:51.46 — 1984

1600 METER RUN
Robert O. Kennedy, Jr., Westerville North . . . . . . — 4:05.13 — 1988

3200 METER RUN
John Zishka, Lancaster . . . . — 8:57.5 — 1980

4 × 100 M. RELAY
Cleveland John Marshall . . . . — 41.48 — 1992
Dorian Green, Archie White, Elige Longino,
Jonathan Burrell

4 × 400 M. RELAY
Cleveland John Adams . . . . — 3:13.57 — 1984
Paul Thomas, Melran Leach, Don Taylor,
Harold Madox

4 × 800 M. RELAY
Cleveland John Adams . . . . — 7:44.29 — 1991
Thurman Tyus, Westley Edrington,
Charles Weaver, Donte Johnson

Continued on next page

Continued from preceeding page

DISCUS
Charles Moye, Akron Ellet . . . . 201'11" 1987
HIGH JUMP
Mark Cannon, Elyria . . . . 7'2¼" 1987
LONG JUMP
Todd Bell, Middletown . . . . 24'6¾" 1977
POLE VAULT
Justin Daler, Toledo St. John's . . . . 16'0" 1989
SHOT PUT
Barron Walker, Lancaster . . . . 67'2½" 1982

1992 DIVISION II BOYS STATE TRACK AND FIELD TOURNAMENT RECORDS

100 METER DASH
Voren Hughes, Leavittsburg LaBrae 10.69 1986
110 METER 39" HURDLES
Dan Oliver, Wooster Triway 13.3 1976
300 METER 36" HURDLES
Clinton Davis, Cincinnati Forest Park 37.35 1988
200 METER DASH
Dennis Mosley, Youngstown Rayen 21.3 1976
400 METER DASH
Laron Brown, Dayton Roth 47.54 1982
800 METER RUN
Alonzo Hatchette, Jefferson Area 1:53.42 1987
1600 METER RUN
Scott Fry, Sandusky Perkins 4:08.03 1985
3200 METER RUN
Scott Fry, Sandusky Perkins 8:49.40 1985
4 × 100 M. RELAY
Dayton Jefferson 41.79 1981
Ronnie Bonner, Brian Britton, Stephon Johnson,
Lorenzo Payne

4 × 400 M. RELAY
Youngstown East 3:18.5 1980
James Bryant, Brian Grizzard, Vernon Stone,
Charles Jones
4 × 800 M. RELAY
Genoa 7:48.40 1991
Jon Scheffer, John Elmers, Chris Lau, Bill Werner
DISCUS
Andy Pentecost, Uhrichsville Claymont . . . . 194'10" 1985
HIGH JUMP
Kevin Bryant, Bellbrook . . . . 7'0" 1977
LONG JUMP
Leigh Grey, Columbus Hartley . . . . 24'2½" 1986
POLE VAULT
John Coyne, Medina Buckeye . . . . 16'4" 1986
SHOT PUT
David Bzovi, Wauseon . . . . 60'7½" 1982

1992 DIVISION III BOYS STATE TRACK AND FIELD TOURNAMENT RECORDS

100 METER DASH
Tony Lee, Dayton Jefferson 10.67 1988
110 METER 39" HURDLES
Roland James, Jamestown Greeneview 13.8 1976
300 METER 36" HURDLES
Chris Miller, Summit Station Licking Heights 37.73 1987
200 METER DASH
Tony Lee, Dayton Jefferson 21.63 1988

Continued on next page

400 METER DASH
Joe Bradley, East Canton 47.94 1981
800 METER RUN
Byron Arbaugh, Lucasville Valley 1:54.1 1978
1600 METER RUN
Jerry Walker, Cortland Maplewood 4:13.4 1980
3200 METER RUN
Brian Hesson, Caldwell 9:21.02 1991
4 × 100 METER RELAY
Dayton Jefferson 42.31 1986
Clifford Clack, Paul Williams, Tony Lee,
Jamiel Trimble

4 × 400 M. RELAY
Bluffton 3:21.71 1986
Travis Douce, Dan Staley, J. R. Fox, Troy Joliff
4 × 800 M. RELAY
Caldwell 7:54.83 1992
Bryan Carna, Steve Carna, Jason Vensel,
Brian Hesson
DISCUS
Ken Scarbrough, McDonald .... 184'2" 1956
HIGH JUMP
Otis Winston, Toronto .... 7'0" 1992
LONG JUMP
Chris Bean, Cleveland Heights Lutheran East ... 23'9¾" 1984
Lincoln Cobb, Pettisville .... 23'9¾" 1991
POLE VAULT
Matt Vermillion, Lewisburg Twin Valley North ... 16'0" 1982
SHOT PUT
Larry Kolic, Smithville .... 62'¾" 1981

BOYS STATE GOLF Division I Record: Alex Antonio, Hubbard - 142, 1946

1992 DIVISION I GIRLS STATE TRACK AND FIELD TOURNAMENT RECORDS

100 METER 33" HURDLES
Terry Robinson, Columbus Northland 13.95 1987
300 METER 30" HURDLES
Terry Robinson, Columbus Northland 42.24 1987
100 METER DASH
D'Andre Hill, Cincinnati Mt. Healthy 11.77 1990
200 METER DASH
Brenda Morehead, Toledo Scott 24.1 1975
400 METER DASH
Vicky Davis, Youngstown Woodrow Wilson 54.86 1981
800 METER RUN
Lisa Breiding, Alliance Marlington 2:11.07 1984
1600 METER RUN
Laurie Gomez, Youngstown Boardman 4:53.39 1988
3200 METER RUN
Kristy Orre, Clayton Northmont 10:27.74 1985
4 × 100 METER RELAY
Cleveland Hts. Beaumont 47.28 1987
Richelle Webb, Tammy Leach, Martha Meaker,
Kathy DiFranco

4 × 200 METER RELAY
Cleveland Hts. 1:39.74 1991
Adrienne Bundy, Meka Rembert, Tara Williams,
Shawn Clark
4 × 400 METER RELAY
Cleveland Hts. Beaumont 3:49.14 1987
Martha Meaker, Richelle Webb, Treva Offutt,
Kathy DiFranco

Continued on next page

Continued from preceeding page

4 × 800 METER RELAY
Rocky River Magnificat 9:08.75   1985
Beth Crowley, Dawn Crowley, Joanna Butts,
Judy Crowley
HIGH JUMP
Peggy Odita, Upper Arlington . . . . 5'10"   1985
LONG JUMP
Laura Kirkham, Centerville . . . . 20'1"   1984
DISCUS
Katie Smith, Logan . . . . 157'6"   1992
SHOT PUT
Katie Smith, Logan . . . . 46'3½"   1992

1992 DIVISION II GIRLS STATE TRACK AND FIELD TOURNAMENT RECORDS

100 METER 33" HURDLES
Ebonita Williams, Cleveland Hts. Beaumont 14.62   1990
Beth Harris, Thornville Sheridan 14.5   1991
300 METER 30" HURDLES
Michelle Hite, Cleveland Hts. Beaumont 43.10   1992
100 METER DASH
Theresa Diggs, Columbus Hartley 12.03   1984
200 METER DASH
Judy Ratliff, Thornville Sheridan 24.63   1986
400 METER DASH
Jennifer Ridgley, Columbus Bexley 55.57   1991
800 METER RUN
Theresa Dunn, Springfield Catholic Central 2:12.38   1983
1600 METER RUN
Connie Robinson, Cincinnati Reading 4:53.39   1982
3200 METER RUN
Michelle Sica, Cincinnati Roger Bacon 10:47.99   1985
4 × 100 M. RELAY
Girard 49.0   1980
Batrese Jones, Karen Griggs, Jackie Jones,
Terry Murray

4 × 200 M. RELAY
Columbus Hartley 1:42.29   1986
Ronda Nutt, Tiffany Smith, Allyson Williams,
Shelley Joyce
4 × 400 M. RELAY
Cleveland Hts. Beaumont 3:54.80   1990
Richelle Webb, Gina Jefferson, Ebonita Williams,
Nancy Hackett
4 × 800 M. RELAY
Cleveland Hts. Beaumont 9:14.64   1990
Monica McHenry, Nancy Hackett, Missy Supler,
Gina Jefferson
HIGH JUMP
Shelley Jorgenson, New Lexington . . . .   5'10"   1983
LONG JUMP
Theresa Diggs, Columbus Hartley . . . .   19'2½"   1984
DISCUS
Teresa Sherman, South Point . . . .   157'10"   1988
SHOT PUT
Tammy Stahl, Kansas Lakota . . . .   43'9¾"   1988

Continued on next page

Continued from preceeding page

1992 DIVISION III GIRLS STATE TRACK AND FIELD TOURNAMENT RECORDS

100 METER 33" HURDLES
Erin Ebner, North Robinson Colonel Crawford . . .   14.59   1992
300 METER 30" HURDLES
Chris McGee, Zanesville Rosecrans 43.92   1985
100 METER DASH
Kathy Mobley, Dayton Miami Valley 12.2   1980
Julie Shade, Stryker 12.35   1990
200 METER DASH
Angie Shoulders, Cleveland Hgts. Lutheran East .   25.0   1975
Chris McGee, Zanesville Rosecrans 25.12   1985
400 METER DASH
Lori Albers, Maria Stein Marion Local . . . . ˊ   56.48   1989
800 METER RUN
Susan Nash, Zanesville Rosecrans 2:12.76   1983
1600 METER RUN
Patty Metzler, North Jackson Jackson-Milton 4:55.64   1983
3200 METER RUN
Rachel Sauder, Archbold 11:02.10   1990
4 × 100 M. RELAY
Cincinnati Academy of Physical Education 49.14   1986
Trina Pate, Tyra Gordon, Jacqueline Jordan,
Michelle McGruder

4 × 200 M. RELAY
Lorain Clearview 1:44.95   1987
Tracie Bradley, Vanessa Tower, Sandy Hitchens,
Francine Woods
4 × 400 M. RELAY
Zanesville Rosecrans 3:56.70   1984
Lisa Young, Chris McGee, Kelly Long, Susan Nash
4 × 800 M. RELAY
Columbus School for Girls 9:20.75   1987
Karen Saah, Tia Chapman, Maggie McLeod,
Jibs Thorson
HIGH JUMP
Julie Brueggemeier, Old Fort . . . .   5'7½"   1992
LONG JUMP
Patty Harris, Frankfort 'Adena . . . .   18'7¾"   1980
DISCUS
Mary J. Reighard, Liberty Center . . . .   150'8"   1986
SHOT PUT
Angie Draper, Mt. Blanchard Riverdale . . . .   42'6½"   1989

Continued on next page

CONTINUED FROM PAGE 77   FISHING

Central Ohio (Division One Wildlife Office (614) 481-6300)
• Alum Creek Lake: saugeye, crappie, bluegill, white bass
• Buckeye Lake: bluegill, largemouth bass, crappie, channel catfish, carp, hybrid striped bass
• Deer Creek Lake: channel catfish, saugeye, crappie, white bass
• Delaware Lake: crappie, largemouth bass, channel catfish, saugeye
• Hoover Reservoir: largemouth bass, crappie, walleye, blue gill, white bass
• Indian Lake: largemouth bass, crappie, channel catfish
• Knox Lake: largemouth bass, bluegill, channel catfish

Continued on page 186

STATE INTERSCHOLASTIC TRACK AND FIELD RECORDS

BOYS
DIVISION III

Event	Mark	Name	City	Year
100 M. DASH	10.67	Tony Lee, Dayton Jefferson	Columbus	1988
	10.4	Tony Lee, Dayton Jefferson	Dayton	1988
110 M. 39" HURDLES	13.8	Roland James, Jamestown Greeneview	Columbus	1976
300 M. 36" HURDLES	37.73	Chris Miller, Summit Station Licking Heights	Columbus	1987
200 M. DASH	21.63	Tony Lee, Dayton Jefferson	Columbus	1988
	21.1	Tony Lee, Dayton Jefferson	Dayton	1988
400 M. DASH	47.6	Gary Linstedt, Kent State High	Mansfield	1968
800 M. RUN	1:54.1	Byron Arbaugh, Lucasville Valley	Columbus	1978
1600 M. RUN	4:13.4	Jerry Walker, Cortland Maplewood	Columbus	1980
3200 M. RUN	9:13.8	John Jones, Marion Elgin	Worthington	1967
4 X 100 M. RELAY	42.31	Clifford Clack, Paul Williams, Tony Lee, Jamiel Trimble — Dayton Jefferson	Columbus	1986
4 x 400 M. RELAY	3:21.71	Travis Douce, Dan Staley, J. R. Fox, Troy Jolliff — Bluffton	Columbus	1986
4 x 800 M. RELAY	7:54.83	Bryan Carna, Steve Carna, Jason Vensel, Brian Hesson — Caldwell	Columbus	1992
DISCUS	188'½"	John Casler, Ashland Crestview	Mansfield	1967
HIGH JUMP	7'0"	Richard Paul Dunwoodie Jr., West Alexandria Twin Valley S	Eaton	1987
	7'0"	Otis Winston, Toronto	Shadyside	1992
	7'0"	Otis Winston, Toronto	Dublin	1992
	7'0"	Otis Winston, Toronto	Columbus	1992
LONG JUMP	23'11"	Martin Maize, Dayton Jefferson	Dayton	1988
POLE VAULT	16'¾"	Matt Vermillion, Lewisburg Twin Valley North	West Alexandria	1982
SHOT PUT (12 lbs.)	64'9"	Larry Kolic, Smithville	Cuyahoga Hts.	1981

DIVISION II

Event	Mark	Name	City	Year
100 M. DASH	10.69	Voren Hughes, Leavittsburg LaBrae	Columbus	1986
110 M. 39" HURDLES	13.3	Dan Oliver, Wooster Triway	Columbus	1976
300 M. 36" HURDLES	37.35	Clinton Davis, Cincinnati Forest Park	Columbus	1988
200 M. DASH	21.2	Matt Thiry, Warren Champion	Andover	1992
400 M. DASH	47.22	Laron Brown, Dayton Roth	Dayton	1982
800 M. RUN	1:51.0	John Anich, Akron Hoban	Ft. Wayne, Ind	1976
1600 M. RUN	4:08.03	Scott Fry, Sandusky Perkins	Columbus	1985
3200 M. RUN	8:46.7	Scott Fry, Sandusky Perkins	Oak Harbor	1985
4 x 100 M. RELAY	41.79	Ronnie Bonner, Brian Britton, Stefan Johnson, Lorenzo Payne — Dayton Jefferson	Columbus	1981
4 x 400 M. RELAY	3:14.57	Quinthony Brown, Michael McCray, Juan Mosby, Laron Brown — Dayton Roth	Dayton	1982
4 x 800 M. RELAY	7:48.40	John Scheffer, John Elmers, Chris Lau, Bill Werner — Genoa	Columbus	1991
DISCUS	194'10"	Andy Pentecost, Uhrichsville Claymont	Columbus	1985
HIGH JUMP	7'¼"	Scott Wall, Springfield Shawnee	Troy	1979
	7'¼"	Jaye Bailey, Columbus Wehrle	Dayton	1982
LONG JUMP	24'2½"	Leigh Grey, Columbus Hartley	Columbus	1986
POLE VAULT	16'4"	John Coyne, Medina Buckeye	Columbus	1986
SHOT PUT (12 lbs.)	60'7½"	David Bzovi, Wauseon	Columbus	1982

DIVISION I

Event	Mark	Name	City	Year
100 M. DASH	10.48	Mario Allmon, Cincinnati Princeton	Dayton	1990
110 M. 39" HURDLES	13.30	Chris Nelloms, Dayton Dunbar	Dayton	1990
300 M. 36" HURDLES	36.38	Glenn C. Terry, Jr., Cincinnati Sycamore	Columbus	1988
200 M. DASH	20.47	Chris Nelloms, Dayton Dunbar	Columbus	1990
400 M. DASH	45.59	Chris Nelloms, Dayton Dunbar	Columbus	1990
800 M. RUN	1:51.46	Mike Huber, Cleveland St. Ignatius	Columbus	1984
1600 M. RUN	4:05.13	Robert O. Kennedy, Jr., Westerville North	Columbus	1988
3200 M. RUN	8:45.8	Alan Scharsu, Youngstown Austintown-Fitch	Kent	1977
4 x 100 M. RELAY	41.48	Dorian Green, Archie White, Elige Longino, Jonathan Burrell Cleveland John Marshall	Columbus	1992
	41.4	Craig Thompson, Carlos Britton, Paris Carter, Mario Allmon Cincinnati Princeton	Dayton	1989
4 x 400 M. RELAY	3:13.57	Paul Thomas, Melran Leach, Donald Taylor, Harold Madox - Cleveland John Adams	Columbus	1984
4 x 800 M. RELAY	7:44.29	Thurman Tyus, Westley Edrington, Charles Weaver, Donte Cleveland John Adams	Columbus	1991
DISCUS	204'5"	Charles Moye Jr., Akron Ellet	Austintown	1987
HIGH JUMP	7'2¼"	Mark Cannon, Elyria	Columbus	1987
LONG JUMP	25'5"	Todd Bell, Middletown	Mansfield	1976
POLE VAULT	16'0"	Les West, Dayton Wayne	Bowling Green	1975
	16'0"	Justin Daler, Toledo St. John's	Columbus	1989
SHOT PUT (12 lbs.)	70'6¼"	Charles Moye Jr., Akron Ellet	Mansfield	1987

Continued on next page

STATE INTERSCHOLASTIC TRACK AND FIELD RECORDS

GIRLS

DIVISION III

Event	Mark	Athlete	City	Year
100 M. 33" HURDLES	14.59	Erin Ebner, North Robinson Colonel Crawford	Columbus	1992
300 M. 30" HURDLES	43.92	Chris McGee, Zanesville Rosecrans	Columbus	1985
100 M. DASH	12.2	Kathy Mobley, Dayton Miami Valley	Columbus	1980
200 M. DASH	25.0	Angie Shoulders, Cleveland Hts. Lutheran East	Columbus	1975
400 M. DASH	56.48	Lori Albers, Maria Stein Marion Local	Columbus	1989
800 M. RUN	2:12.76	Susan Nash, Zanesville Rosecrans	Columbus	1983
1600 M. RUN	4:55.64	Patty Metzler, North Jackson Jackson-Milton	Columbus	1983
3200 M. RUN	11:02.10	Rachel Sauder, Archbold	Columbus	1990
4 x 100 M. RELAY	49.14	Trina Pate, Jacqueline Jordan, Tyra Gordon, Michelle McGruder Cincinnati Academy of Physical Education	Columbus	1986
4 x 200 M. RELAY	1:44.95	Tracie Bradley, Vanessa Tower, Francine Woods, Sandy Hitchens Lorain Clearview	Columbus	1987
4 x 400 M. RELAY	3:56.70	Lisa Young, Chris McGee, Kelly Long, Susan Nash — Zanesville Rosecrans	Columbus	1984
4 x 800 M. RELAY	9:20.75	Karen Saah, Tia Chapman, Maggie McLeod, Jibs Thorson — Columbus School for Girls	Columbus	1987
DISCUS	150'8"	Mary Jane Reighard, Liberty Center	Columbus	1986
HIGH JUMP	5'8"	Pam Deaton, New Paris National Trail	Tipp City	1985
LONG JUMP	18'7¾"	Patty Harris, Frankfort Adena	Columbus	1980
SHOT PUT (4kg)	44'10½"	Beverly Obringer, Maria Stein Marion Local	Minster	1984

DIVISION II

Event	Mark	Athlete	City	Year
100 M. 33" HURDLES	14.62	Ebonita Williams, Cleveland Hts. Beaumont	Columbus	1990
	14.5	Beth Harris, Thornville Sheridan	Columbus	1991
300 M. 30" HURDLES	43.10	Michelle Hite, Cleveland Hts. Beaumont	Columbus	1992
100 M. DASH	12.03	Theresa Diggs, Columbus Hartley	Columbus	1984
200 M. DASH	24.63	Judy Ratliff, Thornville Sheridan	Columbus	1986
400 M. DASH	55.57	Jennifer Ridgley, Columbus Bexley	Columbus	1991
800 M. RUN	2:12.17	Kristi Grooms, Springboro	Dayton	1983
1600 M. RUN	4:52.23	Connie Robinson, Reading	Dayton	1982
3200 M. RUN	10:47.99	Michelle Sica, Cincinnati Roger Bacon	Columbus	1985
4 x 100 M. RELAY	48.63	Sheila Ballado, Richelle Webb, Heather Wilson, Nancy Hackett Cleveland Hts. Beaumont	Kent	1989
4 x 200 M. RELAY	1:42.29	Allyson Williams, Shelley Joyce, Tiffany Smith, Ronda Nutt — Columbus Hartley	Columbus	1986
4 x 400 M. RELAY	3:54.80	Richelle Webb, Gina Jefferson, Ebonita Williams, Nancy Hackett Cleveland Heights Beaumont	Columbus	1990
4 x 800 M. RELAY	9:14.64	Monica McHenry, Nancy Hackett, Missy Supler, Gina Jefferson Cleveland Heights Beaumont	Columbus	1990
DISCUS	170'8"	Teresa Sherman, South Point	Ironton	1989
HIGH JUMP	5'10"	Shelly Jorgenson, New Lexington	Columbus	1983
LONG JUMP	19'2½"	Theresa Diggs, Columbus Hartley	Columbus	1984
SHOT PUT (4kg)	43'9¾"	Tammy R. Stahl, Kansas Lakota	Columbus	1988

DIVISION I

Event	Mark	Athlete	City	Year
100 M. 33" HURDLES	13.95	Terry Robinson, Columbus Northland	Columbus	1987
300 M. 30" HURDLES	42.24	Terry Robinson, Columbus Northland	Columbus	1987
100 M. DASH	11.6	Kellie Simpson, Columbus Mifflin	Whitehall	1982
	11.77	D'Andre Hill, Cincinnati Mt. Healthy	Columbus	1990
200 M. DASH	24.1	Brenda Morehead, Toledo Scott	Columbus	1975
	24.12	Latrice Joyner, Toledo Scott	Columbus	1987
400 M. DASH	54.86	Vicky Davis, Youngstown Woodrow Wilson	Columbus	1981
800 M. RUN	2:11.07	Lisa Breiding, Alliance Marlington	Columbus	1984
1600 M. RUN	4:48.59	Laurie Gomez, Youngstown Boardman	Arcadia, CA.	1988
3200 M. RUN	10:27.74	Kristy Orre, Clayton Northmont	Columbus	1985
4 x 100 M. RELAY	47.28	Richelle Webb, Martha Meaker, Tammy Leach, Kathy DiFranco Cleveland Hts. Beaumont	Columbus	1987
4 x 200 M. RELAY	1:39.74	Adrienne Bundy, Meka Rembert, Tara Williams, Shawn Clark — Cleveland Hts.	Columbus	1991
4 x 400 M. RELAY	3:49.14	Martha Meaker, Treva Offutt, Kim Liggins, Kathy DiFranco — Cleveland Heights Beaumont	Columbus	1987
4 x 800 M. RELAY	9:08.75	Beth Crowley, Judy Crowley, Joanna Butts, Dawn Crowley — Rocky River Magnificat	Columbus	1985
DISCUS	160'2"	Julie Victor, Youngstown Austintown-Fitch	Kent	1989
HIGH JUMP	5'10"	Peggy Odita, Upper Arlington	Columbus	1985
LONG JUMP	20'1"	Laura Kirkham, Centerville	Columbus	1984
SHOT PUT (4kg)	46'3½"	Katie Smith, Logan	Columbus	1992

CITY MAPS

Source - Dept. Of Transportation

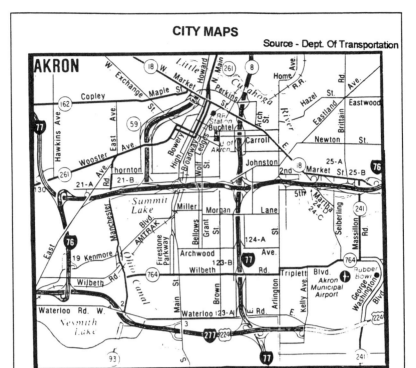

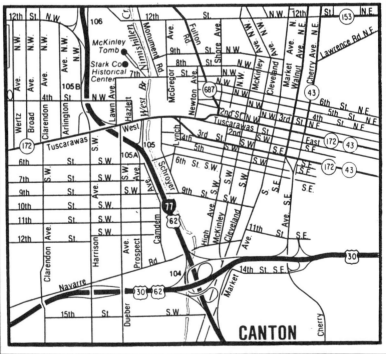

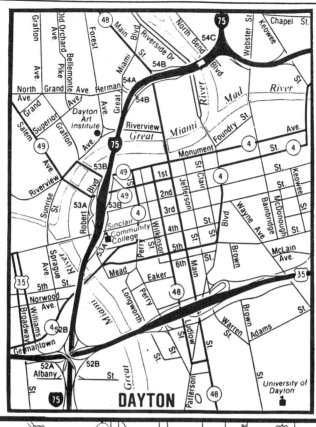

DAYTON

YOUNGSTOWN

CINCINNATI & DOWNTOWN MAP

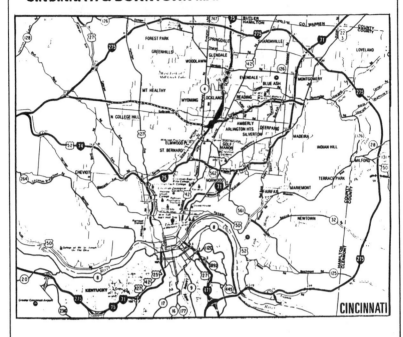

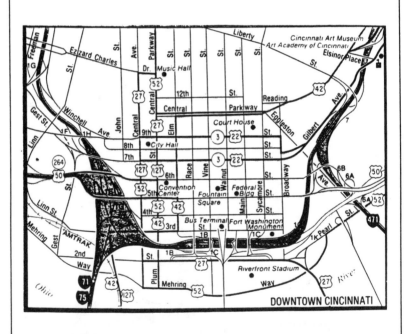

CLEVELAND & DOWNTOWN MAP

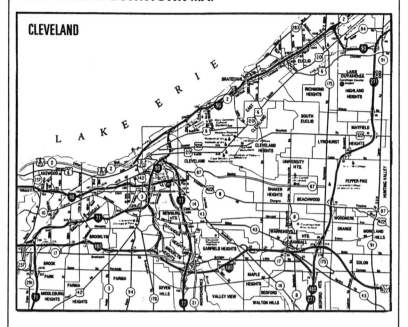

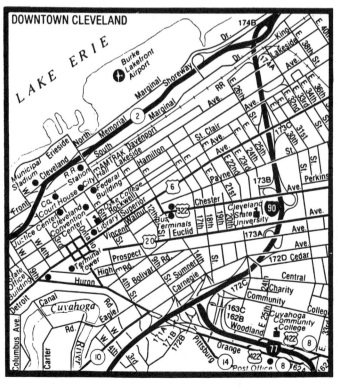

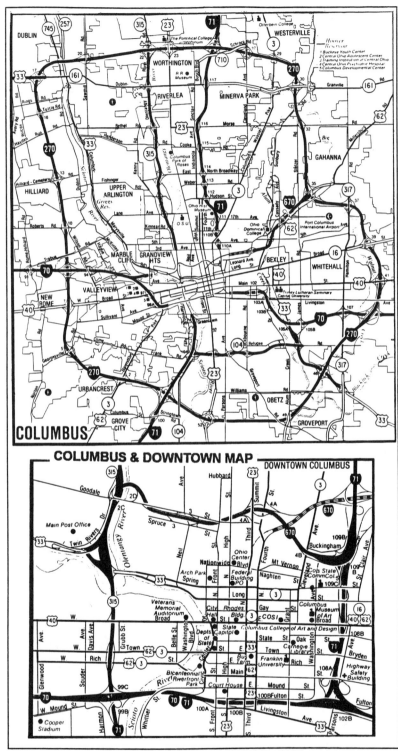

COLUMBUS & DOWNTOWN MAP

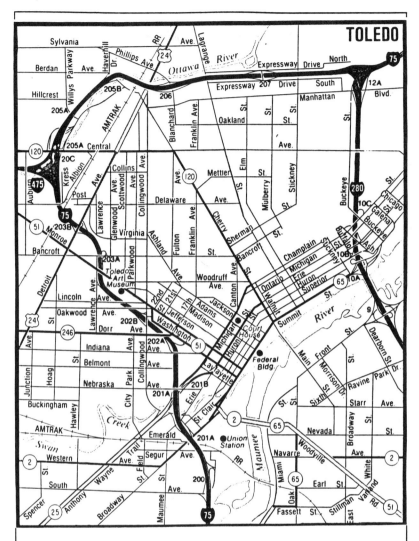

TOLEDO

Trivia

QUESTION In which city was the first dental school in the U S founded?

ANSWER Bainbridge, Ohio (in 1928 by Dr John Harris)

QUESTION In which city and year was the Nation's first interracial, coeducational college founded?

ANSWER Oberlin, Ohio, in 1833.

CITIES & PLACES IN OHIO

ZIP, POPULATION, COUNTY LOCATION

Incomplete zips, such as 454xx, are given for some large cities and places which are served by more than one zip. The last two digits for a specific address in such city or place is available from your local post office or library.

Some small places have no zips and are served by adjoining post offices.

Compiled by the Almanac. Sources - U.S. Census 1990, U.S. Postal Service 1993, Ohio Data Users Center.

PLACE, COUNTY,ZIP	C = CITY V = VILLAGE T = TOWNSHIP	1990 POPULATION

Continued on next page

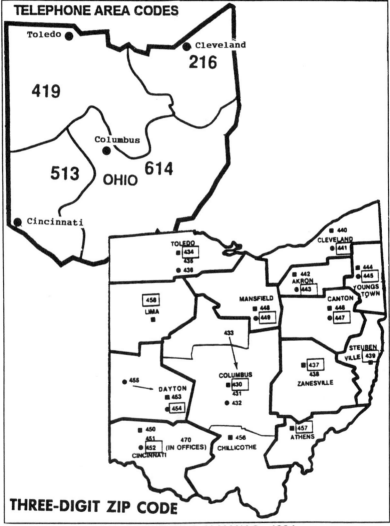

TELEPHONE AREA CODES

THREE-DIGIT ZIP CODE

PLACE, COUNTY,ZIP

C = CITY
V = VILLAGE
T = TOWNSHIP,

1990
POPULATION

Aberdeen, Brown, 45101/ V 1,329
Ada, Hardin, 45801/ V 5,413
Adamsville, Muskingum, 43802/ V 151
Addyston, Hamilton, 45001/ V1,198
Adelphi, Ross 43101/ V 398
Adena, Jefferson 43901/ V 842
Akron, Summit, 43xxx/ C 223,019
Albany, Athens, 45710/ V 795
Alexandria, Licking, 43001/ V 468
Alger, Hardin, 45812/ V 864
Alliance, Stark, 44601/ C 23,376
Alvordon, Williams, 43501/ V 298
Amanda, Fairfield, 43102/ V 729
Amberley, V 3,108
Amelia, Clermont, 45102/ V 1,837
Amesville, Athens, 45711/ V 250
Amherst, Lorain, 44001/ C 10,332
Amherst T, Lorain, 44001/ V 7,060
Amsterdam, Jefferson, 43903/ V 669
Andover, Ashtabula, 44003/ V 1,216
Anna, Shelby, 45302/ V 1,164
Ansonia, Darke, 45303/ V 1,279
Antioch, Woodsfield, 43793/ V 68
Antwerp, Paulding, 45813/ V 1,677
Apple Creek, Wayne, 44606/ V 860
Aquilla, V 360
Arcardia, Hancock, 44804/ V 546
Archbold, Fulton, 43502/ V 3,440
Arlington, Hancock, 45814/ V 1,267
Ashland, Ashland, 44805/ C 20,079
Ashley, Deleware, 43003/ V 1,059
Ashtabula, Ashtabula, 44004/ C 21,633
Ashville, Pickway, 43103/ V 2,254
Athalia, V 346
Athens, Athens, 45701/ C 21,265
Attica, Seneca, 44807/ V 944
Aurora, Portage, 44202/ V 9,192
Avon, Lorain, 44011/ C 7,337
Avon Lake, Lorain, 44012/ C 15,066
Bailey Lakes, V 367
Bainbridge, Ross, 45612/ V 968
Bairdstown, V 130
Ballville, T 6,049
Baltic, Tuscarawas, 43804/ V 659
Baltimore, Fairfield, 43105/ V 2,971
Barberton, Summit, 44203/ C 27,623
Barnesville, Belmont, 43713/ V 4,326
Barnhill, V 313
Batavia, Clermont, 45103/ T 13,673
Batesville, V 95
Bath, Summit, 44210/ T 9,015
Bay View, V 739
Bay V, Cayahoga, 44119/C 17,000
Beach City, Stark, 44608/ V 1,051
Beachwood, Cayahoga, 44122/ C10,677
Beallsville, Monroe, 43716/ V 464
Beaver, Pike, 45613/ V 336
Beaver T, Pike, 45613/ T 5,433
Beavercreek, Mont. 45431/T33,626
Beavercreek, T 35,536
Beaverdam, Allen, 45808/ V 467
Bedford, Cayahoga, 44146/C14,822
Bedford Hgts, C 12,131
Bellaire, Belmont, 43906/ C6,028
Bellbrook, Greene, 45305/ C6,511
Belle Cntr, Logan, 43310/ V 796
Belle V, Noble, 43717/ V 267

Bellefontaine, Logan, 43311/C12,142
Bellevue, Huron, 44811/ C 8,146
Bellville, Richland, 44813/V 1,568
Belmont, Belmont, 43718/ V 471
Belmore, Putman, 45815/ V 161
Beloit, Mahoning, 44609/ V 1,037
Belpre, Washington, 45714/ C6,796
Bentleyville, Adams, 45105/ V 674
Benton Ridge, Hancock, 45816/V351
Berea, Cuyahoga, 44017/ C 19,051
Bergholz, Jefferson, 43908/ V 713
Berkley, Lucas, 43504/ V 264
Berlin Hts, Erie, 44814/ V 691
Bethel, Clermont, 45106/ V 2,407
Bethel Twp, T 19,580
Bethesda, Belmont, 43719/ V 1,161
Bethlehem, T 5,803
Bettsville, Seneca, 44815/ V 752
Beverly, Washington, 45715/ V1,444
Bexley, Franklin, 43209/ C 13,088
Blakeslee, Williams, 43505/ V 128
Blanchester, Clinton, 45107/ V 4,206
Blendon Twp, T 11,194
Bloom Twp, T 5,788
Bloomdale, Wood, 44817/ V 632
Bloomingburg, Fayette, 43106/V769
Bloomingdale, Jefferson, 43910/V227
Bloomville, Seneca, 44818/ V 949
Blue Ash, C 11,860
Bluffton, Allen, 45817/ V 3,367
Boardman Twp, C 41,796
Bolivar, Tuscarawas, 44612/ V 914
Boston Hgts, V 733
Botkins, Shelby, 45306/ V 1,340
Bowerton,Harrison 44695/ V 343
Bowersville, Greene, 45307/ V225
Bowling Green, Wood, 43402/28,176
Bradford, Miami, 45308/ V 2,005
Bradner, Wood, 43406/ V1,093
Brady Lake, Portage, 44211/V 490
Bratenahl, V 1,356
Brecksville, Clvlnd, 44141/V11,818
Bremen, Fairfield, 43107/ V 1,386
Brewster, Stark, 44613/ V 2,307
Briarwood Beach, V 682
Brice, Franklin, 43109/ V 109
Bridgeport, Belmont, 43912/V2,318
Brilliant, Jefferson, 43913/V1,672
Brimfield,Twp, T 8,389
Broadview Ht,Cuyahoga, 44147/C12,219
Brook Pk, Cuyahoga,44142/ C22,865
Brookfield Twp, T 10,562
Brooklyn, Cuyahoga, C 11,706
Brooklyn Hgts, V 1,450
Brookside, V 703
Brookville, Mont. 45309/ V 4,621
Broughton, V 151
Brown Twp, T 7,958
Brownhelm Twp, T7,060
Brunswick, Medina, 44212/ C28,230
Bryan, Williams, 43506/ C 8,348
Buchtel, Athens, 45716/ V 640
Buckeye Lk, Licking,43008/V2,986
Buckland, Auglaize, 45819/V 239

Continued on next page

Continued on next page

Continued from preceeding page

Dupont,Putnam, 45837/V 279
E Canton,Cuyahoga,44112/V1,742
E Cleveland, Cuyahoga, 44112/
　　　　　　　　　C 33,096
E Liverpool, Columbiana,43920/
　　　　　　　　　C13,654
E Palestine, Columbiana,44413/
　　　　　　　　　C 5,168
E Sparta, Stark, 44626/V771
E Union Twp, T 5,833
Eastlake, C21,161
Eaton, Preble, 45320/C 7,396
Eaton Twp, C8,821
Edgerton, Williams, 43517/V1,896
Edison, Morrow, 43320/ V488
Edon, Williams,43518/ V 880
Eldorado, Preble,45321/V549
Elgin, Van Wert, 45838/V 71
Elida, Allen, 45807/V 1,486
Elmore, Ottava,43416/1,334
Elmwood Place, V 2,937
Elyria, Lorain, 440XX/C56,746
Empire, Jefferson,43926/V364
Englewood, Mont.45322/C11,432
Enon,Clark, 45323/V 2,605
Etna Twp, C 6,439
Euclid, Cuyahoga,44117/
　　　　　　　　　C54,875
Evendale, C 3,175
Fairborn, Greene,45324/C31,300
Fairfax,Butler,45014/V 2,029
Fairfield,Butler, 45014/ C39,729
Fairfield Twp, Butler, T 49,373
Fairfield Twp, Columbiana,T8,981
Fairlawn, C 5,779
Fariport Harbor, Painsville, 44077
　　　　　　　　　V 2,978
Fairview, Guernsey,43736/V 79
Fairview Park, Cuyahoga,44126/
　　　　　　　　　C18,028
Falls, Hocking, T10,878
Falls, Muskinghum,T8,524
Farmersville, Mont.45325/V932
Fayette, Fulton, 43521/V1,248
Fayette Twp, T 9,181
Fayetteville, Brown,45118/V393
Felicity, Clermont,45120/V856
Findlay, Hancock, 45840/C35,703
Fletcher, Miami, 45326/V545
Florida, V 304
Flushing,Belmont, 43977/V 1,042
Forest, Hardin, 45843/V 1,594
Forest Park, Montgomery,
　　　　　　　　　45045/C18,609
Fort Jennings, Putnam, 45844/
　　　　　　　　　V436
Ft Lorramie, Shelby,45845/V1,042
Ft Recovery,Mercer, 45846/V1,313
Ft Shawnee, V 4,128
Fostoria, Seneca,44830/C14,983
Frankfort, Ross, 45628/V 1,065
Franklin, Warren,45005/C11,026
Frnklin Twp, Franklin,T 14,757
Franklin, Portage, T34,968
Franklin Twp, Summit, T 14,910
Franklin Twp, Warren, T 27,476
Frazeyburg, Muskingum,43822/V1,165
Fredericksburg, Wayne,44627/V 502
Frederickstovn, Knox,43019/V2,443
Freeport, Harrison,43973/V 475
Fremont, Sandusky,43420/C17,648
Fulton, Morrow, 43321/V 325
Fultoham,Muskingham,43738/V178
Gahanna, Franklin, 43230/C27,791
Galena,Delaware,43021/V 361
Galion,Crawford,44833/C11,859
Gallipolis,Galia,45631/C 4,831
Gallipolis Twp, T 6,500

Gambier, Knox, 43022/V2,073
Gann, V 179
Garfield Hts, Cuyahoga, 44125/
　　　　　　　　　C 31,739
Garrettsville, Portage,44231/
　　　　　　　　　V2,014
Gates Mills, Cuyahoga,44040/
　　　　　　　　　V2,508
Geneva, Ashtabula,44041/
　　　　　　　　　C6,597
Geneva Twp, T 11,912
Geneva-on the Lake, V1,626
Genoa, Ashtabula, 44125/
　　　　　　　　　V2,262
Georgetown, Brown, 45121/
　　　　　　　　　V3,627
German Twp, Clark, T7,467
German Twp,Fulton, T 5,477
German Twp, Montgomery,T7,712
Germantovn,Mont.45327/C4,916
Gettysburg, Darke,45328/V539
Gibsonburg, Sandusky,43431/V2,579
Gilboa, Ottava, 45875/V 208
Gilead, T 5,512
Girard, Trumbull, 44420/C11,304
Glandorf, Putnam.45848/ V 829
Glendale, V 2,445
Glenford, Perry,43739/V 208
Glenmont, Holmes,44628/V233
Glenvillow, V 455
Gloria Glens Park, V446
Glouster, Athens, 45732/V2,001
Gnadenhutten,Tuscaravas,44629/
　　　　　　　　　V1,226
Golf Manor, V 4,154
Gordon, Darke, 45329/ V206
Goshen Twp, Clermont,T12,697
Goshen Twp, Tuscaravas, T 5,718
Grafton, Lorain, 44044/ V 3,344
Grand Rapids, Wood, 43522/V 955
Grand River, Lake, 44045/ V 297
Grandview Hgts, C 7,010
Granville, Licking, 43023/V 4,353
Granville Twp, T 7,819
Gratiot, Licking, 43740/ V 195
Gratis, Preble, 45330/ V 998
Graysville, Monroe,45734/V89
Green, V 3,553
Green Camp, Marion, 43322/V 393
Green Creek Twp, T 9,792
Green Springs, V 1,446
Green Twp, Galia, T 5,189
Green Twp, Hamilton, T 52,687
Green Twp, Summit, T19,179
Green Twp, Wayne, T 11,356
Greenfield, Highland, 45123/C5,172
Greenhills, V 4,393
Green Springs, Seneca, 44836/
　　　　　　　　　V1,446
Greenville, Darke, 45331/
　　　　　　　　　C12,863
Greenville Twp T 17,302
Greenwich, Huron, 44837/V1,442
Grove City, Franklin, 43123/
　　　　　　　　　C19,661
Groveport, Franklin, 43125/V 2,948
Grover Hill, Paulding,45849/V 518
Hamden, Vinton, 45634/V 877
Hamersville, Brown,45130/V 586
Hamilton, Butler, 450XX/C61,368
Hamilton Twp, Franklin, T 9,746
Hamilton Twp, Warren, T 5,900
Hamler, Henry, 43524/V 623
Hanging Rock, V 306
Hanover, V 803
Hanover Twp, T 7,653
Hanoverton, Columbiana, 44423/V434
Harbor View, Lucas, 43434/ V 122
Hardy Twp, T 5,261

Continued on next page

Continued on next page

Continued from preceeding page

Lowell, Washington, **45744/V** 617
Lowellville, Mahoning,**44436/**
    V 1,349
Lower Salem, Washington, **45745/**
    V 103
Lucas, Richland, **44843/V**730
Luckey, Wood, **43443/** V 848
Ludlow Fl,Miami, **45339,V**300
Lynchburg, Highland, **45142/V**1,212
Lyndhurst, Cuyahoga, **44124/**
    C.15,982
Lyons,Fulton, **43533/V** 579
McArthur, Vinton, **45651/V**1,541
McClure, Henry, **43534/V**781
McComb, Hancock, **45858/V** 1,544
Mc Connelsville, Morgan,**43756/**
    V 1,804
Macedonia, Summit, **44056/C**7,509
Macksburg, Washington,**45746/**
    V 218
Mad River Twp, Clark, T11,819
Mad River Twp, Mont, T 30,195
Madeira, Hamilton, **45243/C**9,141
Madison, Lake, **44057/** V2,477
Madison Twp, Butler, T 8,547
Madison Twp, Franklin, T 18,749
Madison Twp, Highland, T 6,987
Madison Twp, Lake, T 17,954
Madison Twp, Montgomery,T29,421
Madison Twp, Richland, T13,286
Magnetic Springs, Union,**43036/V**373
Magnolia, Stark, **44643/** V 937
Maineville, Warren,**45039/V** 359
Malinta, Henry,**43535/V** 2S4
Malta, Morgan, **43758/** V802
Malvern, Carroll, **44644/V**1,112
Manchester, Adams, **45144/V**2,223
Mansfield, Richland, **449XX/**
    C50,627
Mantua, Portage, **44255/V**1,178
Mantua Twp, T 5,596
Maple Hgts, Cuyahoga, **44137/**
    C 27,089
Marble Cliff,V 633
Marblehead, Lakeside, **43440/**
    V 745
Marengo, Morrow, **43334/V**393
Margaretta Twp, T 6,255
Mariemont, V3,118
Marietta, Washington,**45750/**
    C 15,026
Marion, Marion, **43302/C**34,075
Marion Twp, Allen, T 6,676
Marion Twp, Clinton, T 5,184
Marion Twp, Marion, T 43,564
Marseilles, V 130
Marshallville, Wayne, **44645/V**758
Martinsburg, Knox, **43037/V** 213
Martins Ferry,Belmont, **43935/**
    C7,990
Martinsville, Clinton, **45146/**
    V 476
Marysville, Union, **43040/C** 9656
Mason, Warren, **45040/C** 11,452
Massillon, Stark, **44646/C**31,007
Matamoras, V 1,002
Maumee, Lucas,**43537/C** 15,561
Mayfield, V 3,462
Mayfield Hgts, C 19,847
McDonald, Trumbull, **44437/**
    V 3,526
McGuffey, Hardin, **45859/V**550
Mead, T 6,166
Mechanicsburg, V,1,803
Medina, Medina, **44256/C**19,231
Melrose, Paulding,**45861/V**307
Mendon, Mercer,**45862/V** 717
Mentor, Lake, **44060/C**47,358

Mentor-on-the-Lake, C 8,271
Metamora, Fulton, **43540/V**543
Meyers Lake, V 493
Miami Twp, Clemont, T 28,199
Miami Twp, Greene, T 5,162
Miami Twp, Hamilton, T11,552
Miami Twp, Montgomery,T 40,700
Miamisburg, C 17,834
Middleburg Hgts, C 14,702
Middlefield, Geauga, **44062/**
    V 1,898
Middle Point, Van Wert, **45863/**
    V 639
Middlefield Twp, T 6,009
Middleport, Meigs, **45760/V**2,725
Middletown, Butlert, **45042/**
    C46,022
Midland, Clinton,**45148/V**319
Midvale, Tuscaravas, **44653/V**575
Midway, V 289
Mifflin, V162
Mifflin Twp, Franklin, T28,449
Mifflin Twp, Richland, T 6,859
Milan, Erie, **44846/V** 1,464
Milford, Clermont, **45150/C**5,660
Milford Center, V 651
Mill Twp, T 10,315
Millbury, Wood, **43447/** V1,081
Milledgeville, Fayette,**43142/V**120
Miller Cty, Putnam,**45864/V**173
Millersburg, Holmes, **44654/V**3,051
Millersport, Fairfield, **43046/V**1,010
Millville, V 755
Milton Cntr, Wood, **43541/V**200
Milton Twp, T 9,023
Miltonsburg, V 56
Mineral City, Tuscaravas,**44656/V**725
Minerva, Stark, **44657/V**4,318
Minerva Park, V 1,463
Mingo Jnctn, Jefferson, **43938/C**4,297
Minster, Auglaize, **45865/V**2,650
Mogadore, Summit, **44260/V**4,008
Monroe, Butler, **45050/V**4,490
Monroe Twp, Clemont,T 7,762
Monroe Twp, Licking,T5,151
Monroe Twp, Miami, T 12,690
Monroeville, Huron, **44847/V** 1,381
Montezuma, Mercer, **45866/V**199
Montgomery, C 9,752
Montpelier, Williams, **43543/V**4,299
Moorfield Twp, T 9,621
Moraine, C 5,989
Moreland Hills, V 3,354
Morral, Marion, **43337/** V373
Morristown, Belmont, **43759/V**296
Morrow, Warren, **45152/V** 1,206
Moscow, Clermont, **45153/V**279
Mt Blanchard, Hancock, **45867/V**491
Mt Cory, Hancock, **45868/V**245
Mt Eaton, Wayne, **44659/V**236
Mt Gilead, Morrow, **43338/V**2846
Mt Healthy, Hamltn, **45231/C**7580
Mt Orab,Brown, **45154/V**1,929
Mt Pleasant, Jefferson, **43939/**
    V 498
Mt Sterling, Madison, **43143/**
    V 1,647
Mt Vernon, Knox, **43050/C**14,550
Mt Victory, Hardin,**43340/V**551
Mowrystown,Highland, **45155/V**460
Munroe Fls, Summit, **44262/V**5,359
Munson Twp, T 5,775
Murray Cty, Hocking,**43144/V**499
Mutual, V 126
Napolean,Henry,**43545/C**8,884
Napolean Twp, T 10,033
Nashville, Holmes, **44661/V**181
Navarre, Stark, **44662/** V1,635
Nellie, V 130

Continued on next page

Nelsonville, Athens, 45764/C4,563
Nevada,Wyandot,44849/V849
Neville, Clermont, 45156/V226
New Albany, Franklin, 43054/V1,621
New Alexander, V257
Newark, Licking, 43055/V148
New Athens, Harrison, 43981/V370
New Bavaria, Henry, 43548/V 92
New Bloomington, Marion, 43341/V282
New Boston, Portsmouth, 45662/
          V 2,717
New Bremen, Auglaize, 45869/V2,558
Newburgh, Cuyahoga, 44105/V2,310
Newbury Twp, T5,611
Newcomerstown, Tuscarawas,43832/
          V 4,012

New Carlisle, Clark,45344/C6,049
New Concord, Muskingum,43762/
          V 2,086
New Holland, Pickaway,43145/
          V 841
New Knoxville, Auglaize,45871/
          V 838
New Lebanon, Montgomery,45345/
          V4,323
New Lexington, Perry, 43764/
          V 5,117
New London, Huron, 44851/V2,642
New Madison, Darke, 45346/V928
New Miami, V 2,555
New Middleton, Mahoning, 44442/
          V 1,912
New Paris, Preble, 45347/V1,801
New Philadelphia, Tuscarawas,
          44663/C 15,698
New Richmond, Clermont, 45157/
          V 2,408
New Riegel, Seneca, 44853/V298
New Rome, V 111
New Straitsville, Perry, 43766/
          V865
Newton Fls, Newton, C 4,866
Newton Twp, Muskingum, T 5,205
Newton Twp, Trumbull, T 9,541
Newtonsville, Clermont, 45158/V427
Newtown,Hamilton, 45244/V1,589
New Vienna, Clinton,45159/V932
New Washington, Crawford,44854/
          V 1,057
New Waterford, Columbiana, 44445/
          v 1,278
New Weston, Darke, 45348/V148
Ney, Defiance, 43549/V 331
Niles, Trumbull, 44446/C21,128
Nimishillen Twp, T 9,492
Noble Twp, T 6,249
N Baltimore, Wood, 45872/V3,139
N Bend,hamilton, 45052/V 541
N Canton, Stark, 44720/C14,748
N College Hill, C 11,002
N Fairfield, Huron, 44855/V504
N Hampton, Clark, 45349/V417
N Kingsville, Ashtabula, 44068/
          V 2,672
N Lewisburg, Champaign, 43060/
          V 1,160
N Olmsted, Cuyahoga, 44070/
          C34,204
N Perry, V 824
N Randall, V 977
N Ridgeville, Lorain, 44039/
          C21,564
N Robinson, Crawford, 44856/
          V216
N Royalton, Cuyahoga, 44133/
          C 23,197

North Star, Darke, 45350/V246
Northfield, T 3,624
Northwood, Wood, 43619/C5,506
Norton, Barberton, 44203/C11,477
Norwalk, Huron, 44857/C14,731
Norwich, Muskingum, 43767/V133
Norwich Twp, T15,960
Norwood, Wood, 43619/C23,674
Oak Harbor, Ottawa, 43449/V2,637
Oak Hill, Jackson, 45656/V1,831
Oakwood, Paulding, 45873/V3,392
Oakwood City, C 8,957
Oakwood Village, V 709
Oberlin, Lorain, 44074/C8,191
Obetz,V 3,167
Octa, V 78
Ohio City, Van Wert, 45874/V899
Ohio Twp, T 5,310
Old Washington, Guernsey, 43768/V281
Olmsted Fls, Cuyahoga, 44138/V6,741
Olmsted Twp, T 8,380
Ontario, Richland, 44862/V4,026
Orange, V 2,810
Orangeville, Trumbull, 44453/V253
Oregon, Lucast, 43616/C18,334
Orient, Pickaway,43146/V273
Orrville, Wayne,44667/C7,712
Orwell, Ashtabula,44076/V1,258
Osgood, Darke, 45351/V255
Osnaburg, T5,781
Ostrander, Delaware,43061/V431
Ottawa,Putnam, 45875/V3,999
Ottawa Hills, V 4,543
Ottawa Twp, T 7,589
Ottoville, Putnam,45876/V842
Otway, Scioto,45667/V105
Owensville, Clermont, 45160/V1,019
Oxford, Butler, 45056/C18,937
Oxford Twp, Butler, T23,092
Oxford Twp, Tuscarawas,T5,149
Painesville, Lake, 44077/C15,699
Painesville Twp, T16,493
Palestine, Darke, 45352/V197
Pandora, Putnam, 45877/V1,009
Paris Twp, T 5,907
Paris Twp, Union, T 12,024
Parma, Cuyahoga, 44129/C87,876
Parma Hgts, C 21,448
Parral, V255
Pataskala, Licking, 43062/V3,046
Patterson, Forest, 45843/V 145
Paulding,Paulding, 45679/V2,605
Payne, Paulding, 45880/V1,244
Pease Twp, T 16,368
Pee Pee Twp, c 7,481
Peebles, Adams, 45660/V1,782
Pemberville, Wood, 43450/V1,279
Peninsula, Summit, 44264/V562
Pepper Pike, C6,185
Perkins Twp, T 10,793
Perry, Lake, 44081/V1,012
Perry Twp, Columbiana, T 17,215
Perry Twp, Franklin, T5,933
Perry Twp, Lake, T6,780
Perry Twp, Lawrence, T 6,584
Perry Twp, Montgomery, T 6,172
Perry Twp, Stark, T 30,307
Perrysburg, Wood, 43551/C12,551
Perrysburg Twp, T 13,176
Perrysville, Ashland, 44864/V691
Phillipsburg, Montgomery,45354/
          V644
Philo, Muskingum, 43771/V810
Pickerington, Fairfield, 43147/
          V5,668
Pierce Twp, T9,589
Pike Twp, T 6,821
Piketon, Pike, 45661/V1,717

Continued on next page

Pioneer, Williams,43554/V1,287
Piqua, Miami,45356/C20,612
Pitsburg, Darke,45358/V425
Plain City, Madison, 43064/V2,278
Plain Twp, T49,181
Plainfield, Coshocton,43836/V178
Pleasant City, Guernsey, 43772/V419
Pleasant Hill, Miami, 45359/V1,066
Pleasant Plain, Warren, 45162/V138
Pleasant Twp, Fairfield, T 5,623
Pleasant Twp, Franklin, T 6,678
Pleasant Twp, Hardin, T 8,469
Pleasant Twp, Van Wert, T 11,237
Pleasantville, Fairfield, 43148/V926
Plymouth, Richland, 44865/V1,942
Poland, Mahoning, 44514/V2,992
Poland Twp, T 13,993
Polk, Ashland, 44866/V355
Pomeroy, Meigs, 45769/V2,259
Portage, Wood, 43451/V469
Port Clinton, Ottawa, 43452/C7,106
Port Jefferson, Shelby, 45360/V381
Port Washington, Tuscarawas, 43837/
V513
Port William, Clinton, 45164/V242
Portsmouth, C 22,676
Porter Twp, T 9,687
Potsdam Miami, 45361/V250
Powell, Delaware, 43065/V2,154
Powhatan.Point, Belmont, 43942/
V1,807
Prairie Twp, T16,945
Proctorville, Lawrence, 45669/V765
Prospect, Marion, 43342/V1,148
Pultney Twp, T11,107
Put-in-Bay, Ottawa, 43456/V141
Quaker City, Guernsey, 43773/V560
Quincy, Logan, 43343/V697
Racine, Meigs, 45771/V729
Randolph,Twp, T 30,458
Rarden, Scioto, 45671/V184
Ravenna, Portage, 44266/C12,069
Ravenna Twp, T 21,030
Rawson, Hancock, 45881/V482
Rayland, Jefferson, 43943/V490
Reading, C 12,038
Reminderville, Aurora, 44202/V2,163
Rendville, V32
Republic, Seneca, 44867/V611
Reynoldsburg, Franklin, 43068/
C25,748
Richfield, Summit, 44286/V3,117
Richfield Twp, T 5,010
Richland Twp, Allen,T5,494
Richland Twp, Belmont, T11,318
Richmond, Jefferson, 43944/V446
Richmond Hgts, Cuyahoga, 44143/C9611
Richwood, Union, 43344/V2,186
Ridgeway, Hardin, 43345/V378
Rio Grande, Gallie, 45674/V995
Ripley, Brown, 45167/V1,816
Risingsun,Wood, 43457/V659
Rittman, Wayne, 44270/V6,147
Riverlea, V503
Riverside, v1,471
Roaming Shores, V775
Rochester, V206
Rock Creek, Ashtabula, 44084/V553
Rockford, Mercer, 45882/V1,119
Rocky Ridge, Ottawa, 43458/V425
Rocky River, Cuyahoga, 44143/
C20,410
Rogers, Columbiana, 44455/V247
Rome, Ashtabula, 44085/V99
Rome Twp, T 7,579
Rootstown Twp, T6,612
Roseville, Muskingum,43777/V1,847

Ross Twp, T 6,383
Rossburg, Darke, 45362/V250
Rossford, Wood, 43460/C5,861
Roswell, V257
Rushsylvania, Logan, 43347/V573
Rushville, Fairfield, V229
Russell Twp, T5,765
Russells Point, Logan, 43348/
V1,504
Russellville, Brown,45168/V459
Russia, Shelby, 45363/V442
Russia Twp, T10,661
Rutland, Meigs, 45775/V469
Sabina, Clinton, 45169/V2,662
St Bernard, St Clair, C 5,344
St Clair, Butler, T 7,718
St Clair, Columbiana, T7,705
St Clirsville, C5,162
St Henry, V1,907
St Louisville, V372
St Martin, V141
St Marys, C8,441
St Marys Twp, T 11,562
St Paris, V1,842
Sagamore Hills Twp, T6,503
Salem, Columbiana, 44460/
C12,233
Salem Twp, Columbiana, T5,523
Salem Twp, Ottawa, T5,064
Salesville, Guernsey, 43778/V84
Salineville, Columbiana, 43945/
V1,474
Salisbury Twp, T7,227
Sandusky, Erie, 44870/C29,764
Sarahsville, Noble, 43779/V162
Sardinia, Brown, 45171/V792
Savannah, Ashland, 44874/V363
Saybrook Twp, T10,164
Scio, Harrison, 43988/V856
Scioto Twp, Pickaway,T8,231
Scioto Twp, Ross, T30,654
Scott, Van Wert, 45886/V339
Seaman, Adams, 45679/V1,013
Sebring, Mahoning, 44672/C4,848
Senecaville, Guernsey,43780/V434
Seven Hills, C12,339
Seven Mile, Butler, 43780/V804
Seville, Medina, 44273/V1,810
Shadyside, Belmont, 43947/V3,934
Shaker Hgts,C30,831
Shalersville Twp, T5,270
Sharon Twp, Franklin, T17,493
Sharon Twp, Richland, V9,812
Sharonville, Hamilton, 45241/T13,153
Shawnee, Perry, 43782/V742
Shawnee Hills, Powell,43065/V423
Shawnee Twp, T12,133
Sheffield, V1,943
Sheffield Lake, Lorain, 44054/C9825
Shelby, Richland, 44875/V828
Sherwood, Defiance, 43556/V828
Shiloh, Richland, 44878/V778
Shreve, Wayne, 44676/V1,584
Sidney, Shelby, 45365/C18,710
Silver Lake, Cuyahoga Fls, 44224/
V3,052
Silverton, C5,859
Sinking Spring, Highland, 45172/V189
Smithfield, Jefferson, 43948/V722
Smithville, Wayne, 44677/V1,354
Solon, C18,548
Somerset, Perry, 43783/V1,390
Somerville, Butler, 45064/V279
S Amherst, V1,765
S Bloomfield, V900
S Charleston, Clark, 45368/V1,626
S Euclid, Cleveland, 44121/C23,856
S Lebanon, Warren, 45965/V2,696

Continued on next page

OHIO COUNTIES
Location, Population, Seat, Area, Density, Year Organized

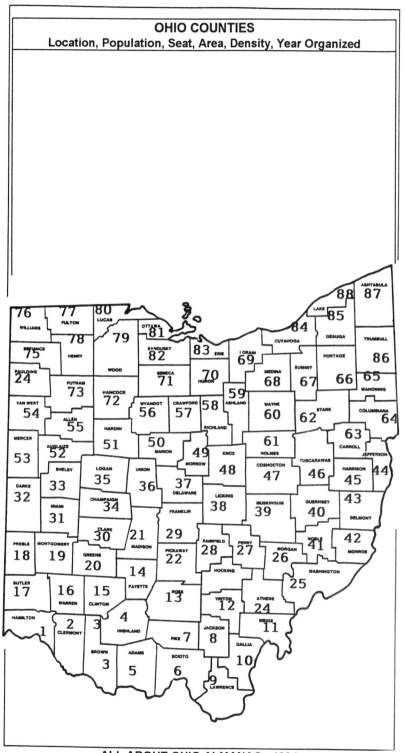

COUNTY	MAP NO.	POPULATION	COUNTY SEAT	SQ. MILES	DEN- SITY	ORGAN- IZED
Adams	5	25,371	West Union	586	43	1797
Allen	55	109,755	Lima	405	271	1820
Ashland	59	47,507	Ashland	424	112	1848
Ashtabula	87	99,821	Jefferson	703	141	1807
Athens	24	59,549	Athens	508	117	1805
Auglaize	52	44,595	Wapakoneta	398	112	1848
Belmont	43	71,074	St Clairsvll.	537	132	1801
Brown	3	34,966	Georgetown	493	70	1819
Butler	17	291,479	Harrison	470	620	1803
Carroll	63	26,521	Carrollton	393	67	1833
Champaign	34	36,019	Urbana	429	83	1805
Clark	30	147,548	Springfield	398	370	1818
Clermont	2	150,167	Batavia	456	329	1800
Clinton	15	35,417	Wilmington	410	86	1810
Colombiana	64	108,276	Lisbon	534	202	1803
Coshocton	47	35,427	Coshocton	566	62	1810
Crawford	57	47,870	Bucyrus	403	118	1820
Cuyahoga	84	1,412,140	Cleveland	459	3,076	1807
Darke	32	53,619	Greenville	600	89	1809
Defiance	75	39,350	Defiance	414	95	1845
Delaware	37	66,929	Delaware	443	151	1807
Erie	83	76,779	Sandusky	264	290	1838
Fairfield	28	103,461	Lancaster	506	204	1800
Fayette	14	27,466	Wash Ct Hs	405	67	1810
Franklin	29	961,437	Columbus	543	1,770	1803
Fulton	77	38,498	Wauseon	407	94	1850
Gallia	10	30,954	Gallipolis	471	65	1803
Geauga	85	81,129	Chardon	408	198	1806
Greene	20	136,731	Xenia	416	328	1803
Guernsey	40	39,024	Cambridge	522	74	1810
Hamilton	1	866,228	Cincinnati	412	2,102	1790
Hancock	72	65,536	Findlay	532	123	1820
Hardin	51	31,111	Kenton	471	66	1820
Harrison	45	16,085	Cadiz	400	40	1813
Henry	78	29,108	Napoleon	415	70	1820
Highland	4	35,728	Hillsboro	553	64	1805
Hocking	23	25,533	Logan	423	60	1818
Holmes	61	32,849	Millersburg	424	77	1824
Huron	70	56,240	Norwalk	494	113	1809
Jackson	8	30,230	Jackson	420	71	1816
Jefferson	44	80,298	Steuberville	410	195	1797
Knox	48	47,473	Mt Vernon	529	89	1808
Lake	88	215,499	Painesville	231	932	1840
Lawrence	9	61,634	Ironton	457	134	1815
Licking	38	128,300	Newark	686	187	1806
Logan	35	42,310	Bellefontain	458	92	1786
Lorain	69	271,126	Elyria	459	547	1822
Lucas	80	462,361	Toledo	341	1,355	1835
Madison	21	37,068	London	467	793	1810
Mahoning	65	264,806	Youngstown	417	634	1846
Marion	50	64,274	Marion	403	159	1820
Medina	68	122,354	Medina	422	289	1812
Meigs	11	22,987	Pomeroy	432	53	1819
Mercer	53	39,443	Celina	457	84	1812
Miami	31	93,182	Troy	410	227	1807

Continued on next page

Monroe	42	15,497	Woodsfield	457	39	1813
Montgomery	19	573,809	Dayton	458	1,252	1803
Morgan	26	14,194	McConnetsv	420	33	1817
Morrow	49	27,749	Mt Gillead	406	68	1848
Muskingum	39	82,068	Zanesville	654	125	1804
Noble	41	11,336	Caldwell	399	28	1851
Ottawa	81	40,029	Pt Clinton	253	158	1840
Paulding	74	20,488	Paulding	419	48	1820
Perry	27	31,557	New Lexingtor	412	76	1818
Pickaway	22	48,244	Circleville	503	95	1810
Pike	7	24,249	Waverly	443	54	1815
Portage	66	142,585	Ravenna	493	289	1807
Preble	18	40,113	Eaton	426	94	1808
Putnam	73	33,819	Ottawa	484	69	1820
Richland	58	126,137	Mansfield	497	253	1808
Ross	13	69,330	Chillicothe	692	100	1796
Sandusky	82	61,963	Fremont	409	151	1820
Scioto	6	80,327	Portsmouth	613	131	1803
Seneca	71	59,733	Tiffin	553	108	1820
Shelby	33	44,915	Sidney	409	109	1819
Stark	62	367,585	Canton	574	640	1808
Summit	67	514,990	Akron	412	1,249	1840
Trumbull	86	227,813	Warren	612	372	1800
Tuscarawas	46	84,090	New Phil.	570	147	1808
Union	36	31,969	Marysville	437	73	1820
Van Wert	54	30,464	Van Wert	410	74	1820
Vinton	12	11,098	McArthur	414	26	1850
Warren	16	113,927	Lebanon	403	282	1803
Washington	25	62,254	Marietta	640	97	1788
Wayne	60	101,461	Wooster	557	182	1796
Williams	76	36,956	Bryan	422	87	1820
Wood	79	113,269	Bowling Gr	619	182	1820
Wyandot	56	22,254	Upper Sand	406	54	1845

Trivia

QUESTION Which is the only place in Ohio (and one of less than ten in the U.S.) with a zip code consisting of the identical five numbers?

ANSWER Newton Falls (a small city in Trumbull County). The zip is 44444.

QUESTION Of the 12 pitchers in major league baseball history who threw **perfect games** (no runner of the opposing team reached base), how many were from Ohio teams?

ANSWER Three. Addie Jones (1908) and Lem Barker (1981), both of the Cleveland Indians, and Tom Browning (1988) of the Cincinnati Reds

COUNTIES WITH OVER 100,000 POPULATION
And 5 Smallest

Source - U.S. Bureau of the Census
Compiled by the Almanac

Twenty-five of Ohio's 88 counties have a population of 100,000 or more (1990 U.S. Census).

Three counties joined the list since the 1980 census (Fairfield, Warren and Wayne), with a growth of 4% to 14%. One county (Ashtabula) left the list with a 4% decline (1990 census 99,821)

The name of the place with the largest population in the county is also listed.

Counties which had population growth between 1990 and 1980 are identified with an asterisk *, and with their % growth in parenthesis ().

	COUNTY	POPULATION	MAJOR PLACE
1	Cuyahoga	1,412,140	Cleveland
2	Franklin * (10.6%)	961,439	Columbus
3	Hamilton	866,328	Cincinnati
4	Montgomery * (0.4%)	573,809	Dayton
5	Summit	514,909	Akron
6	Lucus	462,341	Toledo
7	Stark	367,585	Canton
8	Butler * (12.6%)	291,479	Hamilton
9	Lorain	271,126	Lorain
10	Mahoning	264,806	Youngstown
11	Trumbull	227,813	Warren
12	Lake * (1.3%)	215,499	Mentor
13	Clermont * (16.9%)	150,187	Union Twp.
14	Clark	147,548	Springfield
15	Portage * (5.0%)	142,585	Franklin Twp.
16	Greene * (5.4%)	136,731	Bath Twp.
17	Licking * (6.0%)	128,300	Newark
18	Richland	126,137	Mansfield
19	Medina * (8.1%)	122,354	Medina
20	Warren * (14.7%)	113,909	Deerfield Twp.
21	Wood * (5.5%)	113,267	Bowling Green
22	Allen	109,755	Lima
23.	Columbiana	108,276	Perry Twp.
24	Fairfield * (10.4%)	103,467	Lancaster
25	Wayne * (4.2%)	101,461	Wooster

And 5 Smallest Counties

88	Vinton	11,098
87	Morgan	14,194
86	Monroe	15,497
85	Harrison	16,085
84	Paulding	20,488

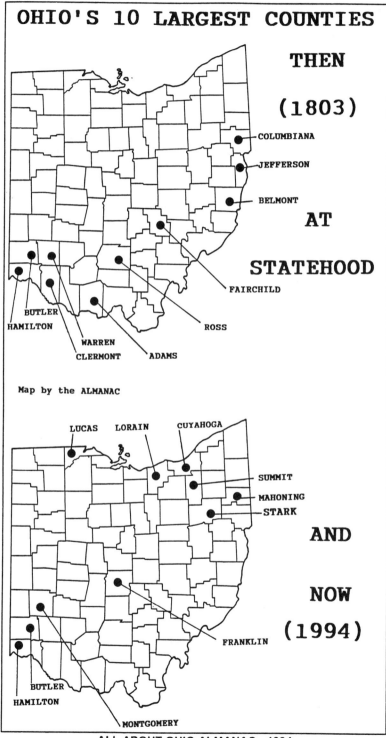

OHIO'S 10 LARGEST COUNTIES

THEN

(1803)

COLUMBIANA

JEFFERSON

BELMONT

AT

STATEHOOD

FAIRCHILD

ROSS

BUTLER

HAMILTON

WARREN

CLERMONT

ADAMS

Map by the ALMANAC

LUCAS   LORAIN   CUYAHOGA

SUMMIT

MAHONING

STARK

AND

NOW

(1994)

FRANKLIN

BUTLER

HAMILTON

MONTGOMERY

ALL ABOUT OHIO ALMANAC - 1994

185

16 RICHEST PEOPLE IN OHIO - FORBES 400

Sixteen people of Ohio are listed in the 9th annual Forbes 400. The magazine has published its new list of the 400 wealthiest people in the U.S. 10-18-93.

RANK	PERSON or FAMILY	RESIDENCE	AGE	WORTH*	PRIMARY SOURCE
1	Scripts (E.W.) family	Cincinnati		$1,600	Inheritance (Newspapers)
2	Wexner, Leslie Herbert	New Albany		$1,600	The Limited
3	Gund family	Cleveland		$1,300	Inheritance (Sanka, Banking)
4	Lennon, Fred A.	Chagrin Falls	87	$900	Valves
5	Lerner, Alfred	Shaker Hts.	60	$770	Banking
6	Linder, Carl Henry**	Cincinnati	74	$650	Insurance
7	Cafaro, Wm. Michael**	Hubbard	80	$630	Shopping Malls
8	Schottenstein family	Columbus		$525	Dept. Stores
9	Lewis, Peter Benjamin	Mayfield Village	59	$500	Progressive Corp.
10	Mandel, Morton Leon	Shaker Hts.	72	$490	Premier Industrial Corp.
11	Mandel, Jack N.	Shaker Hts.	81	$475	Premier Industrial Corp.
12	Mandel, Jos. C.	Lyndhurst	79	$460	Premier Industrial Corp.
13	Farmer, Richard T.	Indian Hills	58	$420	Cintas Corp.
14	Schiff family	Cincinnati		$400	Cincinnati Financial Corp.
15	Wexner, Bella	Columbus	84	$390	The Limited
16	Jacobs, Richard E.	Lakewood	68	$300	Shopping Centers

*   in millions
** and family

CONTINUED FROM PAGE 163 **FISHING**

Southeast Ohio (District Four Wildlife Office (614) 594-2211)
- Belmont Lake: bluegill, largemouth bass, channel catfish, golden trout, bullhead
- Burr Oak Lake: largemouth bass, channel catfish, bullhead, saugeye
- Dillon Reservoir: crappie, bluegill, largemouth bass, channel catfish, bullhead
- Jackson City Reservoir: channel catfish, sunfish, golden trout, largemouth bass
- Lake Logan: saugeye, channel catfish, largemouth bass
- Piedmont Lake: crappie, bluegill, largemouth bass, small mouth bass, saugeye, channel catfish, muskellunge, flathead catfish
- Ross Lake: channel catfish, largemouth bass, sunfish, bluegill
- Salt Fork Lake: muskellunge, channel catfish, walleye, large mouth bass
- Seneca Lake: bluegill, channel catfish, crappie, largemouth bass
- Wellston City Reservoir: crappie, sunfish, channel catfish, largemouth bass

Continued on next page

OHIO COMPANIES IN FORTUNE 500

RANK		500 SALES RANK	SALES $ millions	PROFITS $ millions	HEADQUARTERS	
OHIO 36 COMPANIES						
1	PROCTER & GAMBLE	13	29,890.0	1,872.0	1 P&G Plaza, Cincinnati 45202	513-983-1100
2	GOODYEAR TIRE	38	11,923.6	(658.6)	1144 E. Market St., Akron 44316	216-796-2121
3	TRW	64	8,311.0	(156.0)	1900 Richmond Rd., Cleveland 44124	216-291-7000
4	LTV	102	5,425.3	598.7	P.O. Box 6778, Cleveland 44115	216-622-5000
5	DANA	108	5,036.1	(382.0)	4500 Dofr St., Toledo 43697	419-535-4500
6	MEAD	114	4,703.2	71.6	Courthouse Plaza N.E., Dayton 45463	513-495-6323
7	CHIQUITA BRANDS	115	4,534.1	(284.0)	250 E. Fifth St., Cincinnati 45202	513-784-8000
8	EATON	121	4,109.0	(128.0)	Eaton Center, Cleveland 44114	216-523-5000
9	OWENS-ILLINOIS	135	3,718.4	(134.2)	1 SeaGate, Toledo 43666	419-247-5000
10	OWENS-CORNING	167	2,878.0	73.0	Fiberglas Tower, Toledo 43659	419-248-8000
11	SHERWIN-WILLIAMS	172	2,759.5	62.9	101 Prospect Ave. N.W., Cleveland 44115	216-566-2000
12	B.F. GOODRICH	186	2,530.6	(295.9)	3925 Embassy Parkway, Akron 44333	216-374-2000
13	PARKER HANNIFIN	192	2,382.0	11.2	17325 Euclid Ave., Cleveland 44112	216-531-3000
14	GENCORP	222	1,937.0	22.0	175 Ghent Rd., Fairlawn 44333	216-869-4200
15	RUBBERMAID	235	1,810.3	164.1	1147 Akron Rd., Wooster 44691	216-264-6464
16	TRINOVA	248	1,695.5	14.4	3000 Strayer Rd., Maumee 43537	419-867-2200
17	TIMKEN	254	1,642.3	4.5	1835 Dueber Ave. S.W., Canton 44706	216-438-3000
18	AMERICAN GREETINGS	263	1,573.1	97.5	10500 American Rd., Cleveland 44144	216-252-7300
19	LUBRIZOL	265	1,559.3	124.6	29400 Lakeland Blvd., Wickliffe 44092	216-943-4200
20	RELIANCE ELECTRIC	266	1,553.0	26.0	6065 Parkland Blvd., Cleveland 44124	216-266-5800
21	NACCO INDUSTRIES	274	1,481.5	(85.9)	5875 Landerbrk. Dr., Mayfield Hgts. 44124	216-449-9600
22	M.A. HANNA	286	1,337.9	19.0	1301 E. Ninth St., Cleveland 44114	216-589-4000
23	E.W. SCRIPPS	306	1,263.4	83.9	312 Walnut St., Cincinnati 45202	513-977-3000
24	COOPER TIRE & RUBBER	317	1,176.0	43.2	Lima & Western Avenues, Findlay 45840	419-423-1321
25	FIGGIE INTERNATIONAL	318	1,172.8	28.3	4420 Sherwin Rd., Willoughby 44094	216-953-2700
26	FERRO	330	1,107.4	58.8	1000 Lakeside Ave., Cleveland 44114	216-641-8580
27	WORTHINGTON INDUSTRIES	362	974.2	55.5	1205 Dearborn Dr., Columbus 43085	614-438-3210
28	LINCOLN ELECTRIC	393	862.3	(45.3)	22801 St. Clair Ave., Cleveland 44117	216-481-8100
29	CINCINNATI MILACRON	412	792.1	21.5	4701 Marburg Ave., Cincinnati 45209	513-841-8100
30	A. SCHULMAN	427	738.9	43.8	3550 W. Market St., Akron 44333	216-666-3751
31	STANDARD REGISTER	440	705.2	26.0	600 Albany St., Dayton 45408	513-443-1000
32	HUFFY	441	703.6	4.2	7701 Byers Rd., Miamisburg 45342	513-866-6251
33	STANDARD PRODUCTS	459	657.7	23.3	2130 W. 110 St., Cleveland 44102	216-281-8300
34	SEALY	463	654.2	10.0	1228 Euclid Ave., Cleveland 44115	216-522-1310
35	REYNOLDS & REYNOLDS	465	647.5	39.2	115 S. Ludlow St., Dayton 45402	513-443-2000
36	EAGLE-PICHER INDUSTRIES	485	612.2	28.9	580 Walnut St., Cincinnati 45202	513-721-7010
TOTAL			114,858.4	1,458.2		
MEDIAN			1,566.2	24.7		

CONTINUED FROM PAGE 186 **FISHING**

Southwest Ohio (Division Five Wildlife Office
(513) 426-4961)
- C.J. Brown Reservoir: walleye, channel catfish
- Caesar Creek Lake: bluegill, largemouth bass, white bass, saugeye
- Cowan Lake: bullhead, channel catfish, crappie, largemouth bass
- East Fork Lake (Harsha Lake): channel catfish, crappie, hybrid striped bass
- Grand Lake St. Marys: bullhead, channel catfish, crappie
- Paint Creek Lake: channel catfish, saugeye, crappie
- Rocky ForkLake: channel catfish, crappie, muskellunge

HOME PRICES & SALES -- OHIO
7 Major Areas
21 Counties

Source - Ohio Association of Realtors

Area	1992 Total Sales	1991 Total Sales	% Change 1992/1991	1992 Average Price	1991 Average Price	% Change 1992/1991
AKRON Counties: Portage Stark Summit	20,327	18,886	+7.62%	$70,766	$64,694	+9%
CINCINNATI Counties: Butler Clermont Hamilton Warren	31,862	28,241	+12.82%	$93,812	$89,059	+5%
CLEVELAND Counnties: Cuyahoga Lake Lorain Medina Portage	36,975	34,473	+7.25%	$89,568	$83,838	+7%
COLUMBUS Counties: Delaware Fairfield Franklin Licking Madison Pickaway	30,929	27,424	+12.78%	$87,543	$84,039	+4%
DAYTON Counties: Darke Greene Miami Montgomery Warren	21,306	18,643	+14.28%	$80,763	$74,740	+8%
TOLEDO Counties: Lucas Ottawa Sandusky Wood	12,488	10,962	+13.92%	$64,793	$61,849	+5%
YOUNGSTOWN Counties: Mahoning Trumbull	8,179	7,490	+9.19%	$52,876	$48,668	+9%

Motor Vehicle Manufacturers' Plants & Employment

Final Assembly Plants 10
Final Assembly Plant Employment 33,008
Parts Plants* 46
Parts Plant Employment* 77,990
* Includes Administrative/Engineering.

1991 Model Year Production by City

City	Cars	Truck & Bus	Total
Chillicothe	0	5,946	5,946
Liberty	95,171	0	95,171
Lorain	146,795	142,905	289,700
Lordstown	380,102	59,198	439,300
Marysville	344,595	0	344,595
Moraine	0	329,361	329,361
Orrville	0	3,866	3,866
Springfield	0	68,113	68,113
Toledo	0	146,347	146,347
Total	966,663	755,736	1,722,399

1993 Model Final Assembly Plants

City	Products
Avon Lake	Ford/Nissan Products: Mercury Villager and Nissan Quest passenger minivans.
Chillicothe	PACCAR Products: Kenworth heavy-duty trucks.
Liberty	Honda Products: Honda Civic 4-dr. sedan.
Lorain	Ford Products: Ford Thunderbird, Mercury Cougar; Ford Econoline and Club Wagon passenger and cargo vans.
Lordstown	GM Products: Chevrolet Cavalier, Pontiac Sunbird 2-dr., 4-dr. sedans and wagons.
Marysville	Honda Products: Honda Accord 2-dr. coupe, 4-dr. sedan and wagon.
Moraine	GM Products: Chevrolet S-Blazer, GMC S-Jimmy and Oldsmobile Bravada 2 and 4-dr. sport/utility vehicles; postal vehicles.
Orrville	Volvo GM Products: Volvo GM heavy-duty trucks.
Springfield	Navistar Products: Navistar medium and heavy-duty trucks.

Continued on next page

1993 Model Final Assembly Plants (con't.)

City   Products

Toledo ....   Chrysler Products: Jeep Cherokee 2 and 4-dr. sport/utility vehicles; Jeep Wrangler small-size sport/utility vehicle.

1991 New Motor Vehicle Registrations

Passenger Cars 377,998
Trucks 171,730
   Total 549,728

1991 Estimated Total Motor Vehicle Registrations

Passenger Cars 6,843,000
Trucks 1,616,000
   Total 8,459,000

1991 New Car Dealerships

Establishments 1,090
Sales $12,927,000,000
Employees 39,000
Annual Payroll $940,000,000

Automotive Establishments

Motor Vehicle & Equipment
   Manufacturing 288
Gasoline Service Stations 5,362
Automotive Wholesale 2,082
Automotive Repair & Service 6,538
Automotive Retail 9,109

Automotive Related Employment

Automotive Sales & Service 159,978
Road Construction & Maintenance 25,903
Petroleum Refining & Wholesaling.........5,869
Passenger Transportation 7,365
Truck Drivers & Others 337,408

State Profile

Resident Population 10,847,115
Licensed Drivers 7,524,000
   Male 3,804,000
   Female 3,720,000
Gross State Product $211,545,000,000
Public Road & Street
   Mileage 113,600
Vehicle Miles of Travel 86,972,000,000
State Motor Use Tax
   Revenue $1,382,333,000
Highway Capital Outlay
   & Maintenance $1,021,072,000
Government Owned Vehicles 106,948

KENWORTH

NAVISTAR

LABOR FORCE STATUS - OHIO

Source - U.S. Bureau of the Census 1990

Persons 16 years and over	8,349,183
In labor force	5,298,073
Percent in labor force	63.5%
Civilian labor force	5,279,995
Employed	4,931,357
Unemployed	348,638
Percent unemployed	6.6%
Armed Forces	18,078
Not in labor force	3,051,100

Males, 16 years and over	3,945,025
In labor force	2,887,807
Percent in labor force	73.2%
Civilian labor force	2,871,991
Employed	2,673,217
Unemployed	198,774
Percent unemployed	6.9%
Armed Forces	15,816
Not in labor force	1,057,218

Females 16 years and over	4,404,158
In labor force	2,410,266
Percent in labor force	54.7%
Civilian labor force	2,408,004
Employed	2,258,140
Unemployed	149,864
Percent unemployed	6.2%
Armed Forces	2,262
Not in labor force	1,993,892

Females 16 years and over	4,404,158
With own children under 6 years	654,773
Percent in labor force	57.7%
With own children 6 to 17 years only	763,182
Percent in labor force	72.9%
Own children under 6 years in families and subfamilies	920,679
All parents present in household in labor force	502,792

Own children 6 to 17 years in families and subfamilies	1,787,335
All parents present in household in labor force	1,174,821

Persons 16 to 19 years	641,127
Not enrolled in school and not high school graduate	56,910
Employed or in Armed Forces	20,488
Unemployed	10,692
Not in labor force	25,730

Continued on next page

Continued from preceeding page

Commuting to Work

Workers 16 years and over	4,843,205
Percent drove alone	80.3%
Percent in carpools	10.8%
Percent using public transportationn	2.5%
Percent using other means	0.7%
Percent walked or worked at home	5.7%
Mean travel time to work (minutes)	20.7%

Occupation

Employed persons 16 years and over	4,931,357
Executive, administrative, and managerial occupations	564,573
Professional specialty occupations	658,219
Technicians and related support occupations	181,350
Sales occupations	559,858
Administrative support occupations, including clerical	786,808
Private household occupations	14,011
Protective service occupations	73,084
Service occupations, except protective and household	560,332
Farming, forestry, and fishing, occupations	82,076
Precision production, craft, and repair occupations	569,771
Machine operators, assemblers, and inspectors	443,500
Transportation and material moving occupations	218,740
Handlers, equipment cleaners, helpers, and laborers	219,035

Continued on next page

Trivia

QUESTION Which Ohio port is the nation's largest shipper of coal?

ANSWER Toledo.

QUESTION For how many decades was a place in Ohio the center of the U.S. population?

ANSWER Three. (1860,1870, 1880) Constantly moving West, it started in Maryland(1790), and is now in Missouri.

Continued from preceeding page

Industry

Employed persons 16 years and over	4,931,357
Agriculture, forestry, and fisheries	92,543
Mining	21,007
Construction	254,208
Manufacturing, nondurable goods	358,704
Manufacturing, durable goods	782,679
Transportation	197,362
Communications and other public utilities	118,829
Wholesale trade	218,445
Retail trade	869,821
Finance, insurance, and real estate	285,524
Business and repair services	213,750
Personal services	122,683
Entertainment and recreation services	56,545
Health services	453,452
Educational services	405,388
Other professional and related services	295,463
Public administration	184,954

Class of Worker

Employed persons 16 years and over	4,931,357
Private wage and salary workers	4,008,904
Government workers	622,824
Local government workers	333,190
State government workers	170,754
Federal government workers	118,880
Self-employed workers	281,124
Unpaid family workers	18,505

Continued on next page

QUESTION Which county ranks first in more farming categories than any other county in Ohio?

ANSWER Wayne County. It ranks first in all-hay, oats, all-cattle and milk cows.

QUESTIO Which county ranks among the top 10 in the most farm categories?

ANSWER Darke County. It is 1st in corn-for-grain, soybeans and hogs, 5th in all-cattle, 9th in milk cows, and 10th in wheat and processing tomatoes.

Unemployment Rates
Ohio and U.S.

Percent

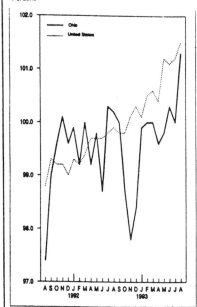

Indexes of Total Employment
Ohio and U.S.

Index (1990 = 100)

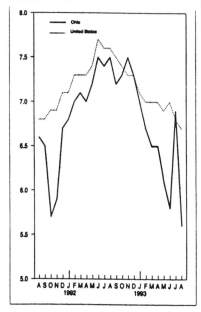

Continued on next page

QUESTION What is Blue Hole of Castalia?

ANSWER An artesia well in Castalia (Erie County) that is fed, 7,500 gallons per minute by an underground river and is capable of meeting the needs of a city of 75,000.

QUESTION What is the highest and lowest temperature ever recorded in Ohio?

ANSWER High 13º F (July 21,1934 at Centreville, Gallia County) and -39º F (February 10,1899 at Milligan, Perry County).

QUESTION In which U.S. census did Ohio pass one million in population?

ANSWER 150 years ago. (1840, Ohio had a population of 1,519,467.

Continued from preceeding page

**Ohio Civilian
Labor Force Estimates**
(in thousands)

	Civilian Labor Force			Unemployment Rates	
	Total	Employed	Unemployed	Ohio	U.S.
1982	5,114	4,474	640	12.5	9.7
1983	5,099	4,478	621	12.2	9.6
1984	5,089	4,609	480	9.4	7.5
1985	5,135	4,680	455	8.9	7.2
1986	5,232	4,806	425	8.1	7.0
1987	5,253	4,886	367	7.0	6.2
1988	5,322	5,002	320	6.0	5.5
1989	5,419	5,118	300	5.5	5.3
1990	5,433	5,126	307	5.7	5.5
1991	5,440	5,094	346	6.4	6.7
1992	5,490	5,093	396	7.2	7.4
1992					
August	5,635	5,246	389	6.9	7.3
September	5,531	5,183	347	6.3	7.2
October	5,475	5,104	371	6.8	6.8
November	5,417	5,048	369	6.8	7.0
December	5,406	5,024	381	7.1	7.0
1993					
January	5,437	4,991	447	8.2	7.9
February	5,420	4,997	423	7.8	7.7
March	5,438	5,040	398	7.3	7.3
April	5,416	5,063	353	6.5	6.8
May	5,444	5,115	329	6.0	6.7
June	5,521	5,190	331	6.0	7.1
July	5,608	5,240	368	6.6	6.9
August	5,590	5,307	283	5.1	6.5

Continued on next page

QUESTION In which Ohio city and year was the game
played with the largest attendance record
in major league baseball history?

ANSWER Cleveland, Sept. 12, 1954. 84,587 people
attended the double header between the
Indians and the New York Yankees.

QUESTION Which was the first and last counties
organized in Ohio?

ANSWER Washington (1788) and Noble (1851).

| | Employment (in thousands) | Change (in thousands) | Percent Change |
| | | | |

Civilian Labor Force and Nonagricultural Wage and Salary Employment Estimates for Ohio

Seasonally Adjusted

	Aug. 1993	From Last Year	From Last Year
Wholesale Trade	259	1	.5
Wholesale Trade-Durable Goods	159	0	.0
Wholesale Trade-Nondurable Goods	100	1	1.1
Retail Trade	905	2	.3
Building Materials and Garden Supplies ..	33	0	-.1
General Merchandise Stores...........	127	2	1.2
Food Stores.........................	138	-1	-.6
Automotive Dealers and Service Stations .	93	0	-.5
Apparel and Accessory Stores	48	1	1.7
Furniture and Homefurnishings Stores ...	33	0	1.2
Eating and Drinking Places	312	0	-.0
Miscellaneous Retail	121	1	.7
Finance, Insurance, and Real Estate......	258	1	.2
Finance	121	1	.8
Depository Institutions..............	87	0	-.2
Insurance..........................	90	0	-.3
Real Estate	46	0	-.3
Services...........................	1,265	29	2.3
Hotels and Other Lodging Places	35	-1	-2.7
Personal Services	56	0	.9
Business Services...................	228	9	3.9
Amusements, Including Motion Pictures ..	59	-1	-1.0
Health Services	438	11	2.6
Legal Services......................	30	1	2.1
Educational Services.................	69	2	3.0
Social Services	93	5	5.3
Membership Organizations	92	2	2.0
Engineering and Management Services ..	85	0	.6
Government.........................	735	-1	-.1
Federal Government	90	-3	-3.3
State Government	163	-1	-.6
State Government Education	85	-1	-.9
Local Government...................	483	3	.7
Local Government Education	277	4	1.5

Continued on next page

Civilian Labor Force and Nonagricultural Wage and Salary Employment Estimates for Ohio Seasonally Adjusted	Employment (in thousands)	Change (in thousands)	Percent Change
	Aug. 1993	From Last Year	From Last Year

Household Survey Data

Civilian Labor Force	5,502	-47	-.8
Employment.	5,193	59	1.1
Unemployment.	309	-106	-25.5
Unemployment Rate	5.6		

Employer Survey Data

Total.	4,860	19	.4
Goods–Producing Industries.	1,231	-9	-.8
Mining	14	-1	-6.1
Coal Mining.	5	-1	-12.7
Oil and Gas Extraction	5	0	-3.5
Construction	182	0	.2
General Building Contractors	43	0	.5
Heavy Construction, Except Building	22	1	2.8
Special Trade Contractors	117	0	-.3
Manufacturing	1,035	-9	-.9
Durable Goods	675	-11	-1.6
Lumber and Wood Products	22	0	-.9
Furniture and Fixtures	14	1	5.7
Stone, Clay, and Glass Products.	41	-2	-3.9
Primary Metal Industries	90	-2	-2.0
Fabricated Metal Products.	118	-3	-2.4
Industrial Machinery and Equipment . . .	147	-1	-.8
Electronic and Other Electric Equipment	73	-2	-2.1
Transportation Equipment	129	-2	-1.3
Instruments and Related Products.	27	-1	-4.3
Nondurable Goods	360	2	.5
Food and Kindred Products	61	0	.8
Apparel and Other Textile Products. . . .	14	0	-1.2
Paper and Allied Products	35	-1	-2.3
Printing and Publishing	74	0	-.3
Chemicals and Allied Products	68	2	2.6
Rubber and Misc. Plastics Products . . .	92	1	.6
Service–Producing Industries	3,630	29	.8
Transportation and Public Utilities.	208	-4	-1.7
Transportation	125	1	.5
Communications, Electric, Gas Services .	83	-4	-4.7

Continued on next page

OHIO

Hours and Earnings of Production or Nonsupervisory Workers

Not Seasonally Adjusted

	Average Weekly Earnings	Average Weekly Hours	Average Hourly Earnings
	Aug. 1993	Aug. 1993	Aug. 1993
Goods-Producing Industries	$611.24	42.3	$14.45
Mining	632.58	44.8	14.12
Coal Mining	728.82	43.1	16.91
Construction	673.28	40.1	16.79
General Building Contractors	575.52	39.5	14.57
Heavy Construction, Except Building	788.66	43.5	18.13
Special Trade Contractors	675.45	39.5	17.10
Manufacturing	597.37	42.7	13.99
Durable Goods	630.81	43.0	14.67
Lumber and Wood Products	356.61	39.8	8.96
Millwork, Plywood & Structural Members	449.19	43.4	10.35
Furniture and Fixtures	423.61	41.9	10.11
Stone, Clay, and Glass Products	540.91	43.1	12.55
Primary Metal Industries	760.16	44.9	16.93
Blast Furnace and Basic Steel Products	790.40	45.9	17.22
Iron and Steel Foundries	842.53	46.6	18.08
Nonferrous Rolling and Drawing	756.58	41.8	18.10
Nonferrous Foundries	552.89	43.5	12.71
Fabricated Metal Products	599.81	42.6	14.08
Fabricated Structural Metal Products	494.38	42.4	11.66
Metal Forgings and Stampings	811.72	44.6	18.20
Industrial Machinery and Equipment	598.23	43.1	13.88
Construction and Related Machinery	502.54	40.3	12.47
Metalworking Machinery	574.64	44.0	13.06
Special Industry Machinery	583.84	44.5	13.12
General Industrial Machinery	659.80	42.9	15.38
Computer and Office Equipment	575.53	42.6	13.51
Refrigeration and Service Machinery	664.70	41.7	15.94
Electronic and Other Electric Equipment	504.66	40.6	12.43
Electrical Industrial Apparatus	465.41	40.4	11.52
Household Appliances	501.86	39.3	12.77
Electric Lighting and Wiring Equipment	555.29	40.8	13.61
Electronic Components & Accessories	383.76	41.0	9.36
Transportation Equipment	837.39	44.9	18.65
Motor Vehicles and Equipment	875.88	45.5	19.25
Aircraft and Parts	716.81	43.0	16.67
Instruments and Related Products	419.35	39.9	10.51
Measuring and Controlling Devices	431.54	39.7	10.87
Nondurable Goods[g]	527.10	42.0	12.55
Food and Kindred Products	510.87	41.5	12.31
Dairy Products	560.28	43.5	12.88
Preserved Fruits and Vegetables	536.80	40.3	13.32
Bakery Products	537.99	38.9	13.83
Apparel and Other Textile Products	345.98	40.8	8.48

Continued on next page

Hours and Earnings
of Production or
Nonsupervisory Workers

Not Seasonally Adjusted

	Average Weekly Earnings	Average Weekly Hours	Average Hourly Earnings
	Aug. 1993	Aug. 1993	Aug. 1993
Paper and Allied Products	577.69	44.2	13.07
Paperboard Containers and Boxes	500.55	43.3	11.56
Misc. Converted Paper Products	509.35	42.2	12.07
Printing and Publishing	511.43	39.8	12.85
Newspapers	410.51	32.4	12.67
Commercial Printing	519.99	41.8	12.44
Chemicals and Allied Products	623.36	43.5	14.33
Plastics Materials and Synthetics	757.32	43.7	17.33
Rubber and Misc. Plastics Products	475.68	41.8	11.38
Tires and Inner Tubes	722.86	42.1	17.17
Miscellaneous Plastics Products	462.84	42.0	11.02
Service—Producing Industries	....	....	.....
Transportation and Public Utilities	....	....	.....
Communications, Electric, Gas Services	733.72	44.2	16.60
Communications	686.84	44.0	15.61
Electric, Gas, and Sanitary Services	787.21	44.5	17.69
Wholesale Trade	454.72	39.2	11.60
Wholesale Trade-Durable Goods	454.72	39.2	11.60
Motor Vehicles, Parts, and Supplies	393.95	38.1	10.34
Metals and Minerals, Except Petroleum	515.01	41.6	12.38
Wholesale Trade-Nondurable Goods	454.34	39.1	11.62
Retail Trade	$200.90	29.2	$ 6.88
General Merchandise Stores	206.31	29.6	6.97
Department Stores	215.52	30.1	7.16
Finance, Insurance, and Real Estate	405.86	....	.....
Finance	380.81	....	.....
Depository Institutions	311.54	....	.....
Commercial Banks	295.26	....	.....
Insurance	488.95	....	.....
Insurance Carriers	494.15	....	.....
Life Insurance	466.76	....	.....
Fire, Marine, and Casualty Insurance	537.62	....	.....,
Services	....	....	.....
Business Services	293.37	33.3	8.81
Health Services	358.07	31.8	11.26
Nursing and Personal Care Facilities	249.74	32.1	7.78
Hospitals	418.26	32.6	12.83
Engineering and Management Services	507.10	37.9	13.38
Engineering and Architectural Services	605.61	39.3	15.41
Research and Testing Services	425.15	35.4	12.01

THE GOVERNOR'S AWARDS

Source: Governor's Office

Awarded annually since 1949 "in recognition of excellence of achievement and outstanding dedication to improving the quality of life for all Ohioans."

The 1992 awardees were:

Ayers, Randy, of Columbus: basketball coach for the Ohio State University.

Collet, Ritter, of Dayton: sports editor emeritus of the <u>Dayton Daily News</u> and Baseball Hall of Fame inductee.

Conrad, Ron, of Toledo: Labor leader and chairman of the U.A.W.. unit at Jeep Corporation in Toledo.

Moss, Dr. Rev. Otic, Jr., of Cleveland: minister and civil rights leader.

Parham, Marjorie, of Cincinnati: publisher of the <u>Cincinnati Herald</u> and community activist.

Sauder, Erie, of Stryker: founder of Sauder Woodworking Co. and Sauder Village.

Trueman, Barbara, of Amlin: owner and C.E.O. of Red Roof Inns, Inc. and community activist.

Preceding awardees are listed below. The year awarded is identified by superscript as defined below.

1	1949	16	1964	31	1979
2	1950	17	1965	32	1980
3	1951	18	1966	33	1981
4	1952	19	1967	34	1982
5	1953	20	1968	35	1983
6	1954	21	1969	36	1984
7	1955	22	1970	37	1985
8	1956	23	1971	38	1986
9	1957	24	1972	39	1987
10	1958	25	1973	40	1988
11	1959	26	1974	41	1989
12	1960	27	1975	42	1990
13	1961	28	1976	43	1991
14	1962	29	1977		
15	1963	30	1978		

4-H Clubs of Ohio [19]

•Adams, Lee [25] Mansfield: Lyricist for Broadway musicals as "Bye Bye Birdie" and "Applause"

Advent, John [33] Columbus: Co-founder Governors Awards Program

Alden, Dr. Vernon R. [20] Athens: President, Ohio University

All-Ohio State Fair Band: [33] Omar P. Blackman - Director

All-Ohio State Fair Choir: [33] Glenville Davies Thomas - Director

Allyn, Stanley, C. [11] Dayton: President, National Cash Register Company

Alston, Walter "Smokey" [11] Darrtown: Manager, World Series winner, the Los Angeles Dodgers

Continued on next page

Continued from preceeding page

Alter, Most Reverend Karl J. [19] Cincinnati: Archbishop

American Legion Buckeye Boys State [19]

American Legion Buckeye Girls State [19]

Ames, Edward C. [20] Toledo: President, Ohio State Board of Education

Andrica, Theodore: [25] Retired Nationalities Editor, Cleveland Press

Arcaro, Eddie [32] Cincinnati: Horse racing jockey

Armstrong, Neil A. [18] Wapakoneta: NASA Astronaut

Armstrong, Neil A. [27] Wapakoneta: First man to land a craft on the moon, first to take a step on its surface

Aronoff, Stanley J. [33] Cincinnati: State legislative leader

Arquette, Cliff [12] Toledo: Better known as "Charlie Weaver" of radio and TV fame

Auburn, Dr. Norman P. [20] Akron: President, The University of Akron

Bailey, Pearl: [37] Entertainer, author, humanitarian; Special Advisor to the U.S. Mission to the United Nations

Baker, Dr. John, C.: [37] Humanitarian; past president, Ohio University - Athens

Baker, Jim [1] Columbus: Cartoonist, The Columbus Dispatch

Baker, John C. [10] Athens: President, Ohio University

Barlow, Howard [7] Plain City: Conductor for the "Voice of Firestone" radio and television programs

Bartien, Dewey F. [18] Marietta: Governor of Oklahoma

Battelle Memorial Institute [4] Columbus: For research work

Bearss, Russell L. [20] Perrysburg: Plant manager, Chrysler Corporation

Becker, Marion Rombauer [28] Cincinnati: Author, conservationist, and patron of the arts (posthumous award)

Bench, Johnny [24] Cincinnati: Renowned catcher, Cincinnati Reds baseball team

Bernardin, Most Reverend Joseph L. [28] Cincinnati: Archbishop of Cincinnati

Bischoff, Tina Marie [28] Columbus: Long distance swimmer

Bishop, Howard [15] Youngstown: Retired industrialist-civic leader

Blair, Claude M. [17] Cleveland: President, Ohio Bell Telephone Company

Blubaugh, C.D. [2] Lucas: Master conservationist

Blumberg, Rena J. [34] Cleveland: Author; Community Relations Director of WWWE-AM/WDOK-FM

Boehm, William C. [28] Cleveland: Choral director

Boeschenstein, Harold [18] Perrysburg: Chairman of the Board, Owens-Corning Fiberglas Corporation

Bohn, Ernest J. [7] Cleveland: Authority on public housing

Bombeck, Erma [28] Dayton: Columnist and author

Borch, Fred J. [15] Cleveland: President, General Electric Co.

Borgman, Jim, [41] Cincinnati native: Editorial cartoonist, Cincinnati Enquirer, whose work is nationally distributed by King Features

Born Free Program: [41] City-wide program to identify pregnant crack users and help them achieve a healthy delivery of crack-free babies, Dr. Lewis Buttino - Founder

Continued on next page

Continued from preceeding page

Bowen, Dr. William G. [39] Cincinnati native: Educator; President, Andrew Mellon Foundation; former president, Princeton University

Bowling Green State University [12] Bowling Green

Boy Scouts of America [19]

Boyd, William [3] Cambridge: Cowboy movie star, "Hopalong Cassady"

Boyer, Ernest L. [29] Dayton: U.S. Commissioner of Education

Branche, Christine F. [23] Cleveland: Education

Branson, Dr. Herman R. [20] Wilberforce: President, Central State University

Braun, Bob [33] Cincinnati: Television host

Bray, Mr. & Mrs. Billy [29] Youngstown: "The Wonder Dancers"

Brennan, Doris [38] Cleveland: Advocate for disabled persons; Director of the Lutheran Employment Awareness program

Brewer, Teresa [11] Toledo: Singer

Bricker, John W. [26] Madison County: Governor of Ohio from 1939 to 1945; former United States Senator

Briggs, Dr. Paul W. [20] Cleveland: Superintendent, Cleveland Public Schools

Brighton, Dr. Stayner [20] Columbus: Executive Secretary, Ohio Education Association

Briley, John Marshall [20] Toledo: Senior Vice-President, Owens-Corning Fiberglas Corp.

Brinkman, R.O. [20] Springfield: Director, Clark County Technical Institute

Bromfield, Louis [1] Mansfield: Novelist

Brooks, Dr. Gildden L. [20] Toledo: President, Medical College of Ohio

Brower, William A. [42] Toledo: Award winning reporter and columnist, The Toledo Blade

Brown, Joe E. [6] Holgate: Stage, screen and TV entertainer

Brown, John W. [26] Medina: Governor of Ohio from January 3 to January 14, 1957; former member of the Ohio House of Representatives and the Ohio Senate

Brown, Paul E. [30] Cincinnati: Pro football coach and general manager

Brown, Ruby Clark [5] Urbana: National Mother of the Year

Browning, Bruce C. [2] New Philadelphia: Founder, Muskingum Conservancy District

Bruce, Earle [31] Columbus: Head football coach, The Oho State University

Bruening, Joseph M. [26] Cincinnati: President and Founder, Bearings, Inc.

Bryne, John H. [3] Cleveland: Conservationist

Bryner, Gary B: [23] Labor

Burcham, Lester A. [16] Lancaster: President, F.W. Woolworth Company

Burick, S.I.: [21] Sports Editor, Dayton Daily News

Burke, Honorable Thomas A. [16] Cleveland: Attorney-at-law; former mayor of Cleveland and former U.S. Senator

Burroughs, Reverend Nelson M.: [19] Bishop, Episcopal Diocese of Ohio

Continued on next page

Continued from preceeding page

Cadden, Father Thomas J. [39] Columbus: Humanitarian; Vicar for Catholic Charities and Social Services; Founder, Joshua Foundation for Victims of AIDS

Camp Fire Girls of Ohio [19]

Caniff, Milton [8] Hillsboro: Cartoonist

Caplan, Dr. Benjamin [25] Columbus: Associate Editor, New York Times

Carlson, Dr. William S. a[20] Toledo: President, The University of Toledo

Carney, The honorable Charles J. [20] Columbus: Senator, Ohio Senate

Cassady, Howard "Hopalong" [7] Columbus: All-America football player for 1954 & 1955

Casstevens, Bill J. [28] Cleveland: Director, United Auto Workers - Region 2

Chapman, Dr. Charles E. [20] Cleveland: President, Cuyahoga Community College

Chevrolet Motor Division: [2] Sponsor of All-American Soap Box Derby at Akron

Christian, Richard C. [29] Dayton: Chief Executive Officer, Marsteller, Inc.

Cincinnati Gas & Electric Co.: [3] Industrial ads

Cincinnati Reds Baseball [27] Cincinnati: 1975 World Series Champions

Cleveland Browns [1] Cleveland: Champions of pro football

Cleveland Electric Illumination Co. [1] Cleveland: Industrial advertising program

Cleveland Indians [1] Cleveland: World Series winners

Cole, Joseph E. [29] Cleveland: Founded Cole National Corporation, key manufacturers

Collier, Howard [33] Toledo: State Finance Director

Collier, Howard L.: [20] Director, Department of Finance, State of Ohio

Cooper, Martha Kinney [5] Cincinnati: Founder, Ohioana Library

Cordier, Dr. Andrew W. [13] Canton: Under Secretary, United Nations

Craig, Eugene W.:[21] Cartoonist, The Columbus Dispatch

Crile, Jr., George M.D. [29] Cleveland: Emeritus consultant, Cleveland Clinic

Crum, Jimmy [30] Columbus: TV sports director; humanitarian

Cullman, Dr. W. Arthur: [38] Ohio State University professor emeritus from the College of Administrative Science

Curtis, Charlotte, [25] Columbus: Associate Editor, New York Times

D'Angelo, Beverly, [32] Columbus: Actress

Dale, Francis L. [18] Cincinnati: President and Publisher, Cincinnati Enquirer; President, Cincinnati Reds

Daugherty, Paul J.:[21] Executive Vice-President, Ohio Chamber of Commerce

Davis, Edward E. [26] Oak Hill: President of Ohio, Davis and Cambria Brick Companies

Continued on next page

Continued from preceeding page

Davis, Sgt. Sammy L. [24] Dayton: Congressional Medal of Honor recipient for service in South Vietnam

Davis, Sister Mary Humbert [35] Columbus: Coordinator of programs of Elderly in Diocese of Columbus

Dayton International Air Show and Trade Exposition

De Bartolo, Edward [36] Youngstown: Chairman of the Board and Chief Executive Officer, The Edward J. DeBartolo Corporation

de Souza, Bertram [43] Youngstown: Political writer, The Vindicator

Deford, Diane E. [40] Columbus: Co-investigator, Ohio Reading Recovery Program; Associate Professor, The Ohio State University

DeLancey, William J. [28] Cleveland: President, Republic Steel Corporation

Deschler, Lewis [22] Chillicothe: U.S. House of Representatives parliamentarian for 35 years, served under seven speakers

Devenow, Chester [32] Toledo: President and Chief Executive Officer, Sheller-Glove Corporation

DeVore, Earl, D. [9] Seaman: Brought World Plowing Matches to Ohio

DeYoung, Russell [18] Akron: Chairman of the Board, Goodyear Tire and Rubber Company

Dillard, Harrison [4] Cleveland: Track star, Olympic winner

Diller, Phyllis [28] Lima: Comedienne

Dinitz, Simon: [37] Criminologist, professor at The Ohio State University since 1951

DiSalle, Micheal [26] Columbus: Governor of Ohio from 1959 to 1963; former member of the Ohio House of Representatives and mayor of the city of Toledo

Dix, Raymond E. [27] Wooster: Publisher, The Daily Record; President, Inter American Press Association (IAPA)

Doan, Dr. Charles A. [14] Nelsonville: A nationally recognized blood expert and authority on leukemia; Dean emeritus of College of Medicine at Ohio State University

Dodd, Edwin D. [31] Toledo: Chairman of the Board and Chief Executive Officer, Owens-Illinois, Inc.

Donnell, II, James C. [12] Findlay: President, Ohio Oil Co.

Dove, Rita [39] Akron native: Poet, winner of Pulitzer Prize for Thomas and Beulah; Professor of Creative Writing, Arizona State University

Downs, Hugh [25] Akron: Former host of the "Today" TV program

Drayton, Otis Paul [16] Cleveland: Olympic Gold Medal Winner

Duerk, James A. [33] Columbus: State Development Director

Duerk, Rear Admiral Alene B. [24] Holgate: First woman to attain the rank of Flag Officer in any navy

Duncan, The Honorable Robert M. [43] Columbus: Ohio's first African-American state supreme court justice

Durbin, Robert J. [20] Archbold: Executive Director, Four County Technical Institute

Eakin, Thomas C. [30] Shaker Heights: Founder-Director, Cy Young Baseball Museum - Newcomerstown

Ealey, Charles [23] Portsmouth: University of Toledo football star

Eby, Vincent B. [33] Cincinnati: Labor leader

Continued on next page

Continued from preceeding page

Eckley, Frederick R. [17] Delaware: Executive Vice-President, American Telephone & Telegraph

Edgerton, Art J.: [21] University of Toledo

Eisele, Donn F. [18] Columbus: NASA Astronaut

Elde, Randolph [1] Cleveland: President, Ohio Bell Telephone Company

Enarson, Dr. Harold L. [20] Cleveland: President, Cleveland State University

Endres, Eugene [33] New Philadelphia: Florist

Essex, Dr. Martin [20] Columbus: Superintendent, Ohio Department of Education

Estes, Elliot M. "Pete" [31] Cincinnati: President, General Motors Corporation

Evans, Bob [29] Rio Grande: Established Bob Evans Farms, sausage and restaurant business

Evans, Helen W. [31] Columbus: Director of Industrial Relations, State of Ohio

Fairless, Benjamin F. [6] Pigeon Run: President U.S. Steel Corporation

Farr, Jamie [30] Toledo: Comedian and television star

Fawcett, Dr. Novice G. [20] Columbus: President, The Ohio State University

Ferger, Roger [2] Cincinnati: Editor Cincinnati Enquirer

Findlay College Football Team [31] Findlay: 1979 national champions of small college football

Finsterwald, Dow [10] Athens: Top money winner in professional golf

Firestone, Raymond [16] Akron: President, Firestone Tire and Rubber Company

Flemming, Dr. Arthur S. [9] Delaware: Secretary of U.S. Department of Health, Education & Welfare and former president of Ohio Wesleyan University

Folkman, Dr. Jerome D. [19] Columbus: Rabbi, Temple Israel

Forbes, George L. [28] Cleveland: President, Cleveland City Council

Frederick, Byron A. [5] Columbus: Master, Ohio State Grange

Fuldheim, Dorothy [30] Cleveland: Television news analyst

Future Farmers of America [19]

Galbreath, Daniel M. [31] Columbus: President, 1979 World Champion Pittsburgh Pirates; associate partner to John W. Galbreath & Co.

Galbreath, John W. [8] Mt. Sterling: Sportsman, one of nation's largest real estate brokers and city developers

Garrett, Alfred B. [15] Glencoe: Former professor and chairman of Department of Chemistry, vice-president for research at Ohio State University

Gault, Stanley C. [42] Wooster: C.E.O. of Rubbermaid, Inc. and nationally acclaimed business manager

Geismann, Robert [6] New Washington: Artist, creator of Ohio's official decal and poster

Gerstacker, Carl A. [18] Cleveland: Board Chairman, Dow Chemical Company

Gillman, Sid [33] Columbus: Football coach

Gillmor, Paul E. [31] Tiffin: Minority Leader, Ohio Senate

Continued on next page

Gingher, Paul [8] Columbus: President, Ohio State Automobile Assn.

Gingher, Paul R. [27] Lancaster: Trial lawyer, insurance executive and civic leader

Girl Scouts of Ohio [19]

Gish, Lillian [15] Massillon: Star of stage, screen and TV

Gish, Lillian [27] Springfield: "First Lady of the Silent Screen"; Winner of honorary Academy Award, 1971

Glenn, Jr., Colonel John H. [14] New Concord: First American to orbit the earth

Glennan, T. Keith [10] Cleveland: Head of NASA

Glueck, Dr. Nelson [17] Cincinnati: President, Rockefeller Foundation

Golding, Dr. Brage [20] Dayton: President, Wright State University

Gooding, Floyd E. [21] Columbus: President, Gooding Amusement Company

Goodman, Dody [31] Columbus: Television and stage star

Gordon, John F.: [16] President, General Motors Corporation

Grabner, George J. [21] Cleveland: President, Weather-head Corporation

Graham, Albert B. [4] **Columbus:** In 1902, he founded 4-H Clubs of America - Springfield

Graham, Martin F. [20] Columbus: Secretary-Treasurer, Ohio State Building and Construction Trades Council

Gray, The Honorable Theodore M. [20] Columbus: President pro tempore, Ohio Senate

Greene, Bob [37] Columbus: Syndicated columnist, best selling author and national magazine writer

Greer, Robert O. [24] Columbus: Assistant State Superintendent of public instruction for urban education

Griffin, Archie [27] Columbus: Two-time Heisman Trophy winner, Halfback with Ohio State Buckeyes

Griffin, James and Margaret [26] Columbus: Parents of Archie Griffin, Heisman Trophy winner

Grimes, Warren G. [27] Tiffin: World leader in the field of aircraft lighting; Founder and Chairman of the Board, Grimes Manufacturing Company - Urbana (posthumous award)

Groza, Lou [16] Martins Ferry: Member, Cleveland Browns. Greatest place kicker and leading scorer in pro football

Gushman [18] John S. [18] Lima: President, Anchor Hocking Glass Corporation

Haas, Ed [3] Marietta: Promoter, Collegiate Rowing Regatta

Hamilton, Margaret [29] Cleveland: Actress

Harden, Ned W. [27] Circleville: Promoter of tourism and nationally acclaimed Circleville Pumpkin Show

Harlow, James [28] Cincinnati: Executive secretary, Greater Cincinnati Building Trades Council

Hartinger, Gen. James B. [33] Middleport: Commander-in-Chief, North American Air Defense Command

Hatcher, Harlan [2] Ironton: Historian; writer; President of The University of Michigan

Hayes, Ben: [21] Columnist, <u>Columbus Citizen-Journal</u>

Continued on next page

Continued from preceeding page

Hayes, W.W. "Woody" [9] Columbus: Football coach at Ohio State University and Coach of the Year

Hays, The Honorable Wayne [22] Flushing: United States Congressman

Heckart, Eileen [28] Columbus: Actress

Heimlich, Dr. Henry J. [31] Cincinnati: Surgeon; author

Helmuth, Al and Amanda [25] Plain City: Operators of the Sunny-haven Children's Home

Henrich, Tommy [2] Canton: Most valuable player, baseball

Herda, Spec.4 Frank A. [24] Parma: Congressional Medal of Honor Recipient for service in South Vietnam

Herget, Dr. Paul [24] Cincinnati: Director, University of Cincinnati's Observatory

Herrmann, Most Rev. Edward J.: [34] Bishop of Columbus

Hess, Col. Dean Elmer [8] Marietta: Famous air ace of the Korean War

Hess, William [20] Athens: Head football coach, Ohio University

Hickey, Bishop James A. [29] Cleveland: Bishop of Cleveland

Hinkle, Clarke [33] Toronto: Pro football player

Hobart, Edward A. [31] Troy: President of the Hobart Brothers company

Holiday, Jr. Harry [28] Middletown: President, Armco Steel Corporation

Holl, Barton A. [18] Logan: President, Logan Clay Products Company

Holzer, Dr. Charles E. [4] Gallipolis: Physician; civic promoter

Hook, Charles R. [7] Middletown: Chairman of the Board, Armco Steel Corporation

Hope, Bob [1] Cleveland: Radio, movie and TV entertainer

Hughes, Bill and Betty: [21] Travel Editors, Cleveland Press

Hughes, Martin [33] Cleveland: Labor leader

Ireland, Mrs. R. Livingston [10] Cleveland: Director, Ohio Dept. of Welfare

Irwin, Josephine S. [34] Lakewood: Women;s rights leader; social activist

Izant, Grace Goulder [1] Hudson: Historian; writer for the Cleveland Plain Dealer

Jakes, John [28] Dayton: Novelist

James, Ollie: [21] Chief Editorial Writer, Cincinnati Enquirer

Jeffers, Dean W. Woodsfield: [26] Woodsfield: General Chairman and Chief Executive Officer, Nationwide Insurance organization

Jennings, Edward H. [33] Columbus: President, Ohio State University

Jerome, III, Dr. William Travers: [20] President, Bowling Green State University

Johnson, Thomas R.: [21] Executive Director, Ohio Manufacturers Association

Jones, Johnny [18] Oak Hill: Columnist, The Columbus Dispatch

Jordan, Harold D. [42] Akron: Educator and high school principal

Kaltenbach, Jerry [21] Columbus: Manager, Ohio State Fair

Kaull, George H. [28] Ashtabula: Chairman, Premix, Inc.

Kellstadt, Charles A. [10] Columbus: President, Sears Roebuck & Company

Continued on next page

Continued from preceeding page

Kent State University [12] Kent

Kent State University: [3] For photographic short course

Kenty, Hilmer James [32] Columbus: 1980 Lightweight Champion of the World

Kerr, R. Kenneth [1] Lancaster: Publisher, <u>Lancaster Gazette</u>

Ketchum, Alton [17] Cleveland: Author of several prize-winning articles about free enterprise

Kettering, Charles F. [2] Loudonville: Inventor; Vice-President, General Motors Corp.

Kilgour, Frederick G. [37] Columbus: Founder trustee, Online Computer Library Center, Inc. - Dublin

King, Admiral Ernest J. [7] Lorain: Commander-in-Chief, U.S. Flyer during World War II

King, The Honorable Frank [20] Columbus: Senator, Ohio Senate

Kiplinger, Willard M. [14] Bellefontaine: Editor and publisher <u>Changing Times</u> and <u>The Kiplinger Washington Letter</u>

Kirk, Willard C. [6] Fayette County: Twice world champion corn producer

Kiser, William S. [32] Cleveland: Chairman of the Board, Governors of the Cleveland Clinic Foundation

Klaric, Betty [27] Yorkville: Staff member, <u>Cleveland Press</u> and internationally recognized environmental writer

Knight, John S. [16] Akron: Publisher, <u>Akron Beacon Journal</u>

Knudson, Marvin C. [20] Dayton: President, Sinclair Community College

Kochan, Bernice [22] Cleveland: Free-lance artist; designer of a Christmas seal and two U.S. commemorative postage stamps which were all issued the same year

Koklowsky, Rev. Alvert: [24] For his humanitarian efforts on behalf of the poor and underprivileged while serving in the Cleveland and Lorain areas

Krol, Cardinal John [27] Cleveland: Cardinal of Roman Catholic Church and Archbishop of Philadelphia

Kuekes, Edward [5] Olmsted Falls: Cartoonist

Kurfess, The Honorable Charles F. [20] Columbus: Senator, Ohio House of Representatives

Lambing, Ellen [43] Cincinnati: Founder of Operation Orange Ribbon; activist in support of America's military personnel and veterans

Langsam, Dr. Walter C.: [20] President, University of Cincinnati

Larlham, Richard and Hattie [24] Mantua: For their concern and commitment to the plight of mentally handicapped children

Laslo, John [35] Martins Ferry: Mayor of Martins Ferry; civic leader

Laughter, Bob [29] Dayton: Laughter Corporation, largest die shop in Ohio

Laughter, Robert C. "Cy" [32] Dayton: President, Laughter Corporation

Lausche, Frank J. [26] Cleveland: Governor of Ohio for five two year terms, from 1945 to 1947 and from 1949 to 1957; former United States Senator

Lauterbach, Stephen (Honored Guest) [32] Dayton: American hostage in Iran for 14 months

Continued on next page

Lavelli, Dante [33] Hudson: Pro football player

Lawrence, Jerome [24] Cleveland: Playwright; co-producer of such plays as "Inherit the Wind" and "Auntie Mame"

Lawrence, Mary Wells [28] Youngstown: Chairman of Wells, Rich, Green, Inc. - New York City

Lee, Robert E. [24] Elyria: Producer of plays acclaimed here and abroad in collaboration with Jerome Lawrence

LeMay, Gen. Curtis [6] Columbus: World War II hero, commander of U.S. Strategic Air Command

Leonard, Sister Joan [40] Cincinnati: Founder, Arts and Humanities Resource Center; creator of cultural and educational programs for the elderly

Lerner, Dr. Max J. [20] Elyria: President, Lorain County Community College

Lewis, Ted [10] Circleville: Band leader and famous entertainer

Lima/Troy UAW-CAP Council: [25] The Community Action program Council of the United Auto Workers

Lin, Maya [36] Athens: Designed the Vietnam Veterans Memorial in Washington D.C.

Lindner, Carl H. [29] Cincinnati: Chief Executive Officer, American Financial Corporation; Cincinnati Enquirer publisher

Long, Melvin [23] Toledo: University of Toledo football star

Lowry, Howard: [9] Ohio Foundation of Independent Colleges

Lupica, Sebastian [27] Cleveland: Executive secretary, Cleveland AFL-CIO

Lynde, Paul [22] Mt. Vernon: State, motion picture and television comedian

Lyons, Carol A. [40] Columbus; Coordinator, Ohio Reading Recovery Program; The Ohio State University

Lyons, Ruth [16] Cincinnati: Radio and TV personality

MacDonald, William E. [33] Columbus: President and Chief Executive Officer, Ohio Bell Telephone Company

Macklin, Gordon S. [30] Cleveland: President of the National Association of Securities Dealers, Inc.

Mancini, Henry [38] Cleveland native: composer and conductor, world-renowned for film scores and television themes

Mandle, Roger: [34] Director of the Toledo Museum of Art

Mandry, Robert [17] Cleveland: First man to sail from America to England in 13-ft. boat

Marona, Vincent G. [30] Bedford Heights: Inventor and manufacturer of "Mr. Coffee" coffeemaker

Marsh, Milan [29] Girard: President, Ohio AFL-CIO

Marshall, Jim [29] Columbus: Minnesota Vikings defensive captain

Marzocchi, Dr. Alfred [31] Granville: Inventor and researcher

Masters, Michael [23] Groveport: First prize winner, International Cello Competition in Estoril, Portugal

Mayer, Jacquelyn [14] Sandusky: "Miss America"

Mayfield, Harry [36] Canton: Free trade union movement leader

McConnell, John [31] Worthington: Chairman and Chief Executive Officer, Worthington Industries, Inc.

Continued on next page

Continued from preceeding page

McCulloch, The Honorable William M. [22] Piqua: United States Congressman

McDonald, The Honorable John. [20] Columbus: Member, Ohio House of Representatives

McElroy, Neil H. [9] Cincinnati: Soap manufacturer; Secretary of Defense

McGovern, Maureen [41] Youngstown native: Gold record winner, recording artist for CBS records

McMaster, Harold A. [39] Perrysburg: Businessman and entrepreneur; Founder of GlassTech, Inc., holder of 72 patents for glass processing

Mears, Amos C. [21] Medina: Industrial developer

Meckstroth, J.A. [16] Columbus: Former editor of the Ohio State Journal

Meckstroth, J.A. "Jake" (Honored Guest) [30] Columbus: Editor and editor emeritus, Ohio State Journal

Medoris, General John B. [11] Millford: U.S. Missile Chief

Meeker, David A. [21] Troy: Chairman, Hobart Manufacturing Company

Meiling, Dr. Richard L. [21] Columbus: Director, Ohio State University Medical School

Mercer, Ruby [38] Athens native: Former Metropolitan Opera star and Broadway performer

Merz, Charles [6] Sandusky: Editor, New York Times

Meshel, Harry [33] Youngstown: State legislative leader

Miami University Redskins [27] Oxford: Captured the Mid-American Conference title for the third consecutive year

Miller, ELdon [31] Gnadenhutten: Head basketball coach, The Ohio State University

Miller, Samuel H. [28] Cleveland: Vice Chairman, Forest City Enterprises, Inc.

Millett, Dr. John D. [20] Columbus: Chancellor, Board of Regents

Millett, John [11] Oxford: President, Miami University

Minter, Steven [42] Cleveland: First U.S. Under Secretary of Education; leader in education reform

Mitchell, Doren [15] Columbus: Head of Satellite Systems Studies Department of Bell Telephone Laboratories; helped to develop Telstar

Mock, Jerrie, [16] Columbus: First woman to fly a single engine plane solo around the world

Modell, Arthur [17] Cleveland: Owner, Cleveland Browns

Moore, Bert (Honored Guest) [32] Mt. Vernon: American hostage in Iran for 14 months

Mora, Don C.: [3] Farmer of the year

Morgan, Joe: [27] Cincinnati Reds Baseball Team: Named the National League's Most Valuable Player for 1975 by America's baseball writers

Moritz, Dr. Timothy B. [32] Portsmouth: Director, Ohio Department of Mental Health and Mental Retardation

Motley, Marion [33] Canton: Pro football player

Moundbuilders Babe Ruth League, Inc. [33] Newark: International boys baseball league

Mulford, Raymon H. [24] Toledo: Chairman of the Board of Directors, Owens-Illinois, Inc.

Continued on next page

Munoz, Anthony [42] Cincinnati: All-star offensive tackle for the Cincinnati Bengals

Munson, Thurman [29] Canton: Catcher, New York Yankees

Murphy, Betty Southard [30] Columbus: Member and Chairman, National Labor Relations Board

Nance, James J. [9] Ironton: General manager of the Mercury-Edsel-Lincoln division of Ford Motor Company

Narduzzi, William E. [31] East Canton: Head football coach, Youngstown State University

Neal, Marguerite [25] Columbus: Lawyer

Neikirk Earl D. [28] Elyria: Investigative reporter, Chronicle-Telegram

Neuenschwander, F.P. [18] Wooster: Director, State of Ohio, Development Department

New Futures Program [41] Dayton: Identifies "at risk" students and works to keep them in school through graduation and prepare them for jobs or college

Newman, Steve M.: [39] "The World Walker"; First human being to complete solo walk around the world, in four years

Newsome, Ozzie: [41] All-Pro tight end for the Cleveland Browns, fourth leading receiver of all time in pro football

Nicklaus, Jack [16] Columbus: Golf pro

Nixon, Corwin M. [31] Lebanon: Minority Leader, Ohio House of Representatives

Noble, Donald E. [30] Wooster: Chairman and Chief Executive Officer, Rubbermaid, Inc.

Nutter, Zoe Dell Lantis [43] Xenia: Community leader and supporter of numerous civic charities

O'Brien, Hugh, [29] Cincinnati: Actor

O'Neill, C. William [26] Marietta: Chief Justice, Ohio Supreme Court; the only person in the history of Ohio to have held the top; position in all three branches of government - legislative, executive and judicial

O'Neill, Chief Justice C. William [23] Marietta: Only Ohioan to have served in the highest office of all three branches of state government; the executive, the judicial and the legislative

O'Neill, Francis J. "Steve" [33] Cleveland: Trucking executive and Chairman of the Board, Cleveland Indians

O'Neill, M.G. [17] Akron: President, General Tire & Rubber Company

Ocasek, Oliver, [31] Bedford: President Pro Tempore, Ohio Senate

Oelman, Robert S. [21] Dayton: Chairman, National Cash Register Company

Oertel, William J. [30] Columbus: Executive Director, Ohio Newspaper Association

Ohio Broadcasters Association: [4] For promotional work

Ohio Council of Urban Leagues [21]

Ohio Jaycees [21]

Ohio Newspaper Association: [34] Celebrated its 50th anniversary in 1983

Ohio Power Company [2] Canton: Industrial ads

Ohio State Buckeyes-Ohio State University: [27] Columbus: Football champions, 1975 team can boast of nine All-Americans

Ohio State Junior Grange [19]

Continued on next page

Continued from preceeding page

Ohio State University [6] Columbus: For outstanding medical research
Ohio State University Basketball Team [12] Columbus: National champions
Ohio University [30] Athens: Founded in 1804, oldest university in Ohio and the first university in the Northwest Territory
Ohio's Veterans of Operation Desert Storm [43]

Ott, Conrad C. [38] Superintendent, Akron Public Schools
Outdoor Writers of Ohio, Inc.: [31] Conservation organization
Owen, Ferris, [7] Newark: U.S. agricultural envoy to Russia
Owens, Jesse B. [27] Cleveland: "World's Fastest Human;" Internationally recognized Olympic athlete and member of the National Track and Field Hall of Fame
Pace, Angela [43] Columbus: WCMH-TV news anchor, and civic leader
Page, Jerry [36] Columbus: Gold Medal Olympic Boxing Champion
Palmer, Ray: [21] Publisher, Barnesville Enterprise
Panan, Thomas F. Cleveland: President, Republic Steel Corporation
Panerson, Grove [3] Toledo: Publisher, The Toledo Blade
Parker, Jim [33] Columbus: Pro football player
Parseghian, Ara [30] Akron: Head football coach, Notre Dame
Paycheck, Johnny [29] Greenfield: Country-western singer
Peale, Norman Vincent [6] Bowersville: Journalist, author,, minister
Peale, Norman Vincent [27] Bowersville: Minister, author and publisher of inspirational literature
Peppe, Mike [15] Columbus: Ohio State University swimming coach and world-renowned swimming figure
Perkins, Susan [29] Middletown: Miss America 1978
Pete, Dr. Louis E. [16] Ashland: Founder and leader, Ohio's All-Boys State Band
Peters, Mike [36] Beavercreek: Political cartoonist
Peters, Thomas Huntley [35] Lorain: Founder, Betterway Inc.; youth service leader
Petrofsky, Dr. Jerrold S.: [34] Professor of biomedical engineering, Wright State University
Picking Robert B [32] Bucyrus: Owner, Picking Copper Kettle Works
Pierce, Elijah [33] Columbus : Sculptor, wood-carver
Ping, Dr. Charles J. [43] Athens: President of Ohio University, and nationally recognized educator
Pinzone, Charles R. [31] Cleveland: Executive Secretary, Cleveland Building and Construction Trades Council
Pitzer, Betty [33] Springfield: Services for the elderly
Pitzer, Rev. Charles A. [23] Portsmouth: Community service
Plumb, Eugene [1] Cleveland: Producer of Sohio's movie about Ohio
Pollock, Sam [24] Cleveland: Chairman, Community Services Committee (Ohio AFL-CIO)
Ponitz, Doris Humes [42] Dayton: Community volunteer and leader in numerous civic organizations
Porter, Phillip W. [18] Shaker Heights: Former editor of Cleveland Plain Dealer

Continued on next page

Continued from preceeding page

Power, Donald C. [10] Columbus: President, General Telephone Company

Premix/EMS, Inc. [35] Lancaster: Outstanding employer and innovator of employment programs

Pubsley, Dr. A.L.: [20] President, Youngstown State University

Pugliese, Gilbert [23] Cleveland: Millwright; civic responsibility

Rahal, Bobby [39] Medina native: Champion race car driver, Winner of Indianapolis 500, 1986. Two time Indy Car Champion

Ramsdell, Robert W. [21] Cleveland: Chairman, East Ohio Gas Company

Randies, Christine [24] Cleveland: Director, Homes for Hough - Hough Development Corporation

Ransohon, Daniel J. [23] Cincinnati: Humanities

Ratner, Max [32] Cleveland: Chairman of the Board, Forest City Enterprises, Inc.

Rennie, Ysabel [23] Columbus: Humanitarianism

Reston, James B. "Scotty" [11] Dayton: Chief <u>New York Times</u> Washington bureau

Rhodes, The Honorable James A. [43] Columbus: Ohio's longest serving governor

Rickenbacker, Cap. Eddie [4] Columbus: Aviator, World War I ace; Chairman of the Board, Eastern Air Lines

Riffe, Vern [31] Portsmouth: Speaker of the Ohio House of Representatives

Riklis, Meshulam :[23] Business

Robbins, Dr. Frederick Chapman [23] Cleveland: Medicine

Roberts, Sgt. Gordon R. [24] Middletown: Congressional Medal of Honor recipient for service in South Vietnam

Robinson, Barbara S. [42] Bratenahl: Chair of the Ohio Arts Council; national leader in the support of the arts

Robinson, Norman [35] Cincinnati: President, R/P International Technologies; outstanding entrepreneur

Rodgers, Shannon [33] Cleveland: Fashion designer

Rose, Pete [25] Cincinnati: Star outfielder for Cincinnati Reds baseball team

Ross, Ray [29] Springfield: Director, United Auto Workers - Region 2A

Rubenstein, Rabbi Samuel W. [32] Columbus: Senior rabbi of Columbus

Rudolf, Max: [19] Music director, Cincinnati Symphony Orchestra

Ruhlman, Randall M. [14] Youngstown: Founder, Lake Erie International Vacationland Association

Ruthven, John A. Georgetown: [30] : Conservationist and wildlife artist

Sabin, Albert B. [27] Cincinnati: Microbiologist and physician; discoverer of oral vaccine for polio

Sabin, Dr. Albert B. [16] Cincinnati: Developer of oral polio vaccine

Safford William C. [17] Cincinnati: President, The Western & Southern Life Insurance Company

Santmeyer, Helen H. [36] Xenia: Author

Saunders, John A. [21] Youngstown: President, General Fireproofing Company

Continued on next page

Continued from preceeding page

Sawyer, Charles, [15] Cincinnati: Former Secretary of Commerce

Saxbe, William B. [26] Mechanicsburg: United States Ambassador to India; former United States Attorney General; Speaker of the Ohio House of Representatives and Attorney General of Ohio

Sayre, Morrie [41] Cleveland: Founded Shoes for Kids in 1969, which has distributed new shoes, gloves, scarves, and hats to over 650,000 Cleveland-area children

Scali, John A. [24] Canton: U.S. Ambassador to the United Nations

Schlemmer, Jim [2] Akron: Founder, All-American Soap Box Derby

Schlesinger, Jr., Arthur M. [25] Columbus: Humanities professor, City University of New York

Schott, Marge [27] Cincinnati: Business woman and civic leader

Schottenheimer, Marty: [38] Head Coach, Cleveland Browns

Schroeder, Paul Edward [28] Elyria: Investigative reporter, Chronicle-Telegram

Schul, Robert [16] West Milton: Olympic gold medal winner; first American to win 5,000 meter race

Scripps, Charles E. [18] Cincinnati: Publisher, Scripps Howard Newspapers

Seasongood, Murray [23] Cincinnati: Public service

Sedivy, Joseph F. [32] Lorain: President, Ohio State Building and Construction Trades Council and Vice President of the Ohio AFL-CIO

See, Dr. Jacob [20] Perrysburg: President, Penta-County Technical Institute

Seiberling, John F. [39] Akron: Public servant and former congressman, protector of natural areas and wildlife, advocate of conservation

Seibert, Donald V. [32] Hamilton: Chairman of the Board and Chief Executive officer, J.C. Penney, Inc.

Seltzer, Louis B. [17] Cleveland: Newspaper editor

Shaffer, Raymond P. [18] Sebring: Governor, Commonwealth of Pennsylvania

"Shavers, Ernie [29] Warren: World Heavyweight Champion contender

Sherard, Jr., Earel S., M.D. [28] Columbus: Pediatrician; professor of pediatrics at the Ohio State University

Shocknessy, James W. [16] Columbus: Chairman, Ohio Turnpike Commission

Shoemaker, Byrl R. [20] Columbus: Director, Vocational education

Shoemaker, Byrl R. [32] Columbus: Director of Vocational Education, Oho Department of Education

Shoemaker, Myrl H. [33] Chillicothe: State legislator and Lieutenant Governor

Shriver, Dr. Phillip R. [20] Oxford: President, Miami University

Shula, Don [24] Painesville: Head coach of Miami Dolphins

Siedel, Frank [1] Cleveland: Publisher, Writer of "Ohio Story" series

Silver, Dr. Abba Hillel [12] Cleveland: Rabbis of the largest reform Jewish congregation in America; one of the founders of Israel

Smith, Curtis Lee [21] Cleveland: President, National Copper &n Smelting Company

Continued on next page

Smoot, Sr., Lewis R. [34] Columbus: President and Chief Executive Officer, Sherman R. Smoot Company

Smucker, Paul H. [30] Orrville: President, J.M. Smucker Company; grandson of company's founder

Snyder, Robert H. [28] Columbus: Columbus Bureau Chief, <u>Cleveland Plain Dealer</u>

Sockman, Dr. Ralph W. [8] Mt. Vernon: Author, lecturer, minister

Staab, Charles W. [20] Cincinnati: Executive Vice-President, <u>Cincinnati Enquirer</u>

Stahler, Jeff: [41] Award-winning editorial cartoonist for <u>The Cincinnati Post</u>, nationally distributed by NEA

Stanton, Dr. Frank [13] Dayton: President, The Columbia Broadcasting System, Inc.

Stanton, Sister Mary: [41] Executive Director of Bethany Shelter House, a volunteer organization committed to caring for the homeless of Cincinnati

Staubach, Roger [31] Cincinnati: Heisman Trophy winner; NFL quarterback of the Dallas Cowboys

Steinbrenner, George M., III [29] Cleveland: Principal owner of N.Y. Yankees

Steinem, Gloria [23] Toledo: For her journalistic efforts in the area of women's rights

Stouffer, Vernon B. [18] Cleveland: President and Chairman of the Board, Stouffer Foods Corporation; owner, Cleveland Indians

Stover, James R. [43] Cleveland: Retired Chairman of the Board of Eaton Corporation, and civic leader

Szell, George: [19] Musical director & conductor, Cleveland Orchestra

Taber, Louis F. [8] Mt. Pleasant: Master, National Grange

Taft, Robert A. [5] Cincinnati: Lawyer; Ohio senator and U.S. senator; "Mr. Republican" (posthumous award)

Talbott, Dr. G. Douglas [40] Dayton: Founder, Talbott Recovery Services; specialist in addictionology and treatment of drug addicts and alcoholics

Talbott, Strobe [38] Dayton native: Washington Bureau Chief for <u>TIME</u> Magazine

Tatsch, Clinton E. [20] Columbus: Executive Director, Columbus Technical Institute

Taylor, Orrin R. [31] Archbold: Journalist and editor emeritus, <u>Archbold Buckeye</u>

Tebelak, John Michael [23] Berea: Theatre

Thomas, Bill [21] Cincinnati: Free-lance travel writer

Thomas, E.J. [14] Akron: Chairman of the Board and Chief Executive, Goodyear Tire & Rubber Co.

Thomas, Lowell [27] Darke County: Author, lecturer, adventurer and radio commentator for forty-six continuous years

Thomas, R. David [33] Columbus: Founder, Wendy's

Thornburg, Richard: [21] Editor emeritus, <u>Cincinnati Plain Dealer</u>

Timkin, Jr., W.R. [29] Canton: Director, The Timken Corp.

Continued on next page

Tomasi, Joseph [35] Toledo: Regional Director, United Auto Workers Region 2B; civic leader

Trabert, Tony [5] Cincinnati: National tennis champion

Trott, Richard W. [37] Columbus: Chairman of the Board and Director, Trott & bean Architects, Inc.

Ullery, Dr. John C. [20] Columbus: Professor of medicine, The Ohio State University

University of Cincinnati Basketball Team [13] Cincinnati: National champions

University of Dayton Football Team: [32] 1980 Winner of the NCM Division III football championship

Vail, Thomas [33] Cleveland: Editor and publisher, Cleveland Plain Dealer

Vall, Iris Jennings [28] Cleveland: Civic accomplishments and community betterment

Verity, Jr., C. William [18] Middletown: President, Armco Steel Corporation

Wagner, Richard [33] Cincinnati: President and Chief Executive Officer, Cincinnati Reds

Walter, Franklin B. [32] Columbus: Director of Vocational Education, Ohio Department of Education

Warfield, Paul D. [37] Warren: Director of Player Relations, Cleveland Browns; members the Pro Football Hall of Fame

Warner, Marvin L. [21] Cincinnati: Delegate to the United Nations General Assembly

Warther, Ernest "Mooney" [17] Dover: "World's Master Carver"

Weiskopf, Tom [29] Massillon: Golf pro

Westheimer, Irvin F. [28] Cincinnati: Founder, Big Brothers

Wexner, Leslie H. [37] Columbus: Founder, President and Chairman of the Board, The Limited, Inc.

White, Charles M. [10] Cleveland: President, Republic Steel Corporation

White, Dr. Robert I. [20] Kent: President, Kent State University

White, Dr. Robert J. [36] Shaker Heights: Professor Neurosurgery at Case Western Reserve University and the Brain Research Laboratory at Cleveland Metropolitan General Hospital

White, Dr. Stanley C. [13] Lebanon: Chief, National Aeronautics and Space Administration's Life System Division

Whitefield, Mal [4] Cleveland: Olympic winner

Wilkes, Reverend William R.: [19] Bishop, African Methodist Episcopal Church

Wilson, Charles E. [5] Minerva: President of General Motors, Secretary of Defense

Wilson, Dr. Judson, D. [21] Columbus: For work with crippled children

Wilson, Earl [1] Rockford: Nationally known columnist, radio commentator, author

Wilson, Earl [27] Rockford: Author and syndicated daily columnist reporting the adventures of show business celebrities

Wilson, Nancy [18] Cillicothe: Top female recording star

Continued on next page

Continued from preceeding page

Winter, Jonathan [40] Dayton native: Comedian, author, artist, actor

Witt, Mel J. [31] Cleveland: President of the Cleveland AFL-CIO; Executive Director, United Labor Agency, Inc.

Wittenberg Tigers-Wittenberg University [27] Springfield: Captured the NCAA Division III national football championship for the second time in three years

Wolfe, Preston: [19] Publisher, The Columbus Dispatch

Wren, Bob [33] Athens: Ohio University baseball coach

Yoder, George N. [20] Steubenville: Director, Jefferson County Technical Institute

Young, George C. [34] Cincinnati: President, Cincinnati Better Business Bureau

Zollinger, Robert M., M.D. [17] Millersport: Former president of top three societies of surgeons

ASSOCIATIONS AND ORGANIZATIONS

Compiled by the Almanac from multi-sources

AFL-CIO-Ohio, 271 E State St, Columbus (614) 224-8271·

AAA-Ohio Motor Club, 90 E Wilson Bridge, Worthington, (614) 431-7800

Abortion Alternatives, 22 E Gay St, Columbus (614) 221-0005

Adult Daycare-Ohio Assn of, 36 W Gay St, Columbus (614) 221-2882

Advertising Assn of Ohio-Outdoor, 12222 Plaza Dr, Parma, (216) 676-4321

Aggregates Assn Ohio, 20 S Front St, Columbus (614) 224-2717

Agribusiness Assn-Ohio, 6641 N High St, Columbus (614) 885-1067

Agricultural Marketing Assn-Ohio, Columbus (614) 249-2421

Aids Serv Connection, 1066 N High St, Columbus (614) 291-2300

AIDS, 2456 W Broad St, Columbus (614) 870-6460

Air Conditioning Contractors of Ohio, P.O... Box 627, Worthington, (614) 436-3371

Alcohol & Drug Abuse & Mental Health Servs Boards-Ohio Assn of, 42 E Gay St, Columbus (614) 224-1111

Alcohol Problems-Ohio Council on, 501 E Broad St, Columbus (614) 221-1410

Alliance for Cooperative Justice, 505 S High St, Columbus (614) 224-1890

Ambulance Assn- Ohio, 1161 Francisco Rd, Columbus (614) 457-7971

Ambulance Assn-Ohio, 6436 Reflections Dr, Columbus (614) 791-1503

American Legion Dept of Ohio, 4060 Indianola, Columbus (614) 268-7072

Amusement Ride Safety Officials-Intl Assn of, 6161 Busch Bl, Columbus (614) 888-9774

AMVETS Dept of Ohio, 65 S Front, Columbus (614) 221-1527

Animal Technicians-Ohio Assn of, 1350 W 5 Av, Columbus (614) 488-5084

Anti-Defamation League of B'nai Brith, 527 E Engler, Columbus (614) 621-0601

Apt Association-Ohio, 1200 W 1 Av, Columbus (614) 294-4222

Area Agcies on Aging-Ohio Assn of, 1335 Dublin Rd, Columbus (614) 481-3511

Arts Council-Ohio, 727 E Main, Columbus (614) 466-2613

Arts Education-Ohio Alliance for, 61 Jefferson Av, Columbus (614) 224-1060

Asbestos Council-Ohio, Columbus (614) 785-0094

Assault Prevention Ctr-Natl, 33 Warren St, Columbus (614) 291-2540

Assn Executives-Ohio Soc of, 33 N High St, Columbus (614) 461-6026

Auctioneers Assn-Ohio, 17 S High St, Columbus (614) 221-1900

Auto & Trucks Recyclers Assn Ohio, 85 E Gay St, Columbus (614) 221-4373

Auto Workers Comm Action Program-Ohio State United, 133 E Livingston, Columbus (614) 464-2055

Automatic Merchandising Assn-Ohio, 50 W Broad, St, Columbus (614) 221-7833

Continued on next page

Continued from preceeding page

Automobile Dealers Alliance of Ohio, 7870 Olentangy River Rd, Columbus (614) 436-3393

Automobile Dealers Assn-Ohio, 1366 Dublin Rd, Columbus (614) 487-9000

Automotive Wholesalers Assn-Ohio, 1560 Fishinger Rd, Columbus (614) 451-0573

Automtv Wholesalers Assn-Ohio, 4645 Leap Ct, Columbus (614) 777-7373

Aviation-Space Writers Assn, 17 S High St, Columbus (614) 221-1900

Bakers Assn-Ohio, 50 W Broad St, Columbus (614) 221-7833

Bank Servicers-Natl Assn of, 5008 Pine Creek Dr, Columbus (614) 895-1208

Bankers Assn-Ohio, 17 S High St, Columbus (614) 221-5121

Baptist Missionary Evang Assn, 3493 S Hamilton Rd Columbus (614) 833-0488

Bar Assn-Ohio State, 1700 Lake Shore Dr, Columbus (614) 487-2050

Beef Council-Ohio, 283 S State St, Columbus (614) 898-7771

Beer & Wine Assn of Ohio-Wholesale, 37 W Broad St, Columbus (614) 224-3500

Bicycle League Natl, 211 Bradenton Av, Columbus (614) 766-1625

Blind of Ohio, Am Council of, 2678 Edgevale, Columbus (614) 221-6688

Blind Vendors-Ohio, 209 S High St, Columbus (614) 221-1558

Blindness, Ohio Affil-Natl Soc to Prevent, 1500 W 3 Av, Columbus (614) 464-2020

Broadcasters-Ohio Assn of , 88 E Broad St, Columbus (614) 227-4052

Builders & Contractors-Assoc, 1372 Grandview Av, Columbus (614) 487-9100

Building & Construction Trades Council-Ohio, 236 E Town St, Columbus (614) 221-3682

Bus Assn-Ohio, 1723 Washington Av, Columbus (614) 443-5051

Business & Professional Women-Ohio Fed of, 4758 Middletowne, Columbus (614) 459-3888

Business Professionals of Amer, 5454 Cleveland Av, Columbus (614) 895-7277

Businessman's Assn-Ohio, 2708 Delcane Dr, Columbus (614) 442-6500

Businessman's Assoc-Ohio, 1631 Northwest Professional Pl, Columbus (614) 442-6500

Cable Television Assn-Ohio, 50 W Broad, Columbus (614) 461-4014

Campground Owners Assn-Ohio, 3386 Snouffer Rd, Columbus (614) 764-0279

Cancer Research Societies of Ohio, 50 W Broad St, Columbus (614) 224-1127

Cardiology-Ohio Chapter of Amer College of, 17 S High St, Columbus (614) 221-1900

Care Council-Ohio Continuum of, 101 E Wilson Bridge Rd, Columbus (614) 888-4515

Continued on next page

Continued from preceeding page

Carpenters-Ohio State Council of, 236 E Town St, Columbus (614) 461-4700

Cast Metals Assn-Ohio, 6990 Rieber St, Columbus (614) 848-8152

Casting Industry Suppliers Assn, 6990 Rieber St, Columbus (614) 848-8199

Casualty Insurers-Ohio Burr of, 172 E State St, Columbus (614) 228-1593

Catholic War Veterans, 65 S, Front St, Columbus (614) 221-7601

Cattle Club-Amer Jersey, 6486 E Main St, Columbus (614) 861-3636

Cattlemen's Assn-Ohio, 283 S State, Columbus (614) 898-7771

Cemeteries Ethics Committee-Ohio, 50 W Broad St, Columbus (614) 221-0139

Cert Residential Specialists-Ohio Chapter, 252 W 5 Av, Columbus

Certified Public Accountants-Ohio Soc of, 535 Metro Pl, Columbus (614) 764-2727

Chamber of Commerce-Ohio, 35 E Gay St, Columbus (614) 228-4201

Chemical Council-Ohio, 17 S High St, Columbus (614) 224-1730

Chemical Dependency Counselors Credentialing-Ohio, 740 Lakeview Plaza Bl, Columbus (614) 847-0330

Chemical Recyclers Assn-Ohio, 88 E Broad St, Columbus (614) 461-6272

Chiefs of Police-Ohio Assn of, 6277 Riverside Dr, Columbus (614) 761-0330

Child Caring Agcies-Ohio Assn of, 400 E Town St, Columbus (614) 461-0014

Children Servs Assn of Ohio-Public, 400 E Town St, Columbus (614) 224-5802

Children's Hospitals-Assn of Ohio, 21 W Broad St, Columbus (614) 228-2844

Chiropractic Assn-Ohio State, 1115 Bethel Rd, Columbus (614) 442-2610

Choices for Victims of Domestic Violence, (614) 258-6080

Christian Values Coalition (614) 337-2201

Church Developmt Fund-Ohio, 700 Morse Rd, Columbus (614) 785-1855

Churches-Ohio Council of, 89 E Wilson Bridge, Columbus (614) 885-9590

Citizen Action-Ohio, 691 N High St, Columbus (614) 224-4111

Civil Liberties Union-Am, 85 E Gay St, Columbus (614) 228-8951

Civil Trial Attorneys-Ohio Assn of, 17 S High St, Columbus (614) 221-1900

Cleaners Assn-Ohio, 17 S High St, Columbus (614) 221-1900

Coal & Energy Assn-Ohio, 3600 Olentangy River Rd, Columbus (614) 457-5423

Coin Machine Assn-Ohio, 6161 Busch Bl, Columbus (614) 888-9772

College Assn-Ohio, 45 W 11 Av, Columbus (614) 292-80441

Colleges & Schools-Ohio Council of Priv, 3770 N High, Columbus (614) 263-1799

Continued on next page

Continued from preceeding page

Commodores Assoc of Ohio, 88 E Broad St, Columbus (614) 621-0827

Common Cause Ohio, 16 E Broad St, Columbus (614) 461-0733

Community Action Agcies-Ohio Assn of, 85 E Gay St, Columbus (614) 224-8500

Community Connection for Ohio Offenders, 1717 Bethel Rd, Columbus (614) 451-9902

Community Dev Finance Fund-Ohio, 85 E Gay St, Columbus (614) 221-1114

Community Mental Health Boards-Ohio Assn of, 35 E Gay St, Columbus (614) 224-1111

Community Support-Society for, 1335 Dublin Rd, Columbus (614) 488-9233

Concrete Block Assn-Ohio, 17 S High St, Columbus (614) Columbus (614) 221-1900

Concrete Pipe Mfrs Assn-Ohio, 4924 Reed Rd, Columbus (614) 459-2385

Consumer Education Welfare Rights-Ohio State, 700 Bryden Rd, Columbus (614) 221-8333

Consumer Finance Assn-Ohio, 88 E Broad St, Columbus (614) 221-7527

Contract Management Assn-Natl, Columbus (614) 846-3328

Contractors Assn-Ohio, 1313 Dublin Rd, Columbus (614) 488-0724

Convenience Stores-Ohio Assn of, 50 W Broad St, Columbus (614) 221-7833

Coroners Assn-Ohio State, 2514 Summit St, Columbus (614) 461-4700

Counseling & Development-Ohio Assn for, 5295 Refugee Rd, Columbus (614) 577-1942

County Commissioner's Assn of Ohio, 175 S 3 St, Columbus (614) 221-5627

County Engineers Assn of Ohio, 175 S 3 St, Columbus (614) 221-0707

Court Reporters Assn-Ohio, 1024 Dublin Rd, Columbus (614) 488-0617

Credit Union League-Ohio, 1201 Dublin Rd, Columbus (614) 486-2917

Crime Prevention Assn- Ohio, 1560 Fishinger Rd, Columbus (614) 459-0580

Crime Prevention Practitioners-Internat Soc of, 1560 Fishinger Rd, Columbus (614) 451-8837

Dairy Products Assn-Ohio, 1429 King, Columbus (614) 486-6000

DARE Officers Assn-Ohio, 6277 Riverside Dr, Columbus (614) 761-9498

Dental Assn-Ohio, 1370 Dublin Rd, Columbus (614) 486-2700

Dental Hygienists Assn-Ohio, 1631 Northwest Professional Pl, Columbus (614) 451-7651

Developmentally Disabled -Assn for, 1395 W 5th Av, Columbus (614) 486-4361

Continued on next page

Dietetic Assn-Ohio, 5008 Pine Creek Dr, Columbus (614) 895-1253

Displaced Homemaker Network-Ohio, 51 Jefferson Av, Columbus (614) 461-8914

Donors Forum of Ohio, 200 W Henderson Rd, Columbus (614) 459-0820

Easter Seal Society-Ohio, 2204 S Hamilton Rd, Columbus (614) 868-9126

Economic Awareness-Intl Designs for, 6172 Busch Bl, Columbus (614) 846-5582

Education Assn-Ohio, 225 E Broad, Columbus (614) 228-4526

Education of Handicapped Children-Ohio Coalition for the, 933 High St, Columbus (614) 431-1307

Education of Young Children-Ohio Assn for, 5131 Sassafras Rd, Columbus (614) 436-4686

Education-Congress of Christian, 48 Parkwood, Columbus (614) 253-5563

Educational Library-Media Assn-Ohio, 67 Jefferson Av, Columbus (614) 221-9057

Electric Utility Institute-Ohio, 175 S 3 St, Columbus (614) 221-3422

Emergency Number Assn-Natl, 1500 W 3 Av, Columbus (614) 488-9115

Emergency Physicians-Am College of, 3510 Snouffer Rd, Columbus (614) 792-6506

Employees Serv Assn of Ohio, 16 E Broad.St, Columbus (614) 365-9030

Engineers Foundation of Ohio, 445 King Av, Columbus (614) 424-6645

Engineers-Natl Assn of Power, 140 E Town St, Columbus (614) 228-3018

Engineers-Ohio Assn of Consulting, 50 W Broad St, Columbus (614) 463-1151

Engineers-Ohio Soc of Professional, 445 King Av, Columbus (614) 424-6640

Enrolled Agents-Ohio Soc of, 1631 Northwest Professional Pl, Columbus (614) 459-0452

Entertainment Agcies-Ohio, 4954 Olde Coventry Rd W, Columbus (614) 866-2540

Environment-Ohio Alliance for the, 445 King Av, Columbus (614) 421-7819

Environmental Council-Ohio, 400 Dublin Av, Columbus (614) 224-4900

Epilepsy Assn of Ohio, 986 Goodale Bl, Columbus (614) 299-5166

Executive Housekeepers Assn-Natl, 1001 Eastwind Dr, Columbus (614) 895-7166

Fair Plan Underwriting Assn-Ohio, 5230 Busch Bl, Columbus (614) 436-4530

Family Developmt-Ohio Center for, 7729 Eagle Creek Dr, Columbus (614) 864-5552

Family Physicians-Ohio Acad of, 4075 N High St, Columbus (614) 267-7867

Family Service Council of Ohio, 125 E Broad St, Columbus (614) 461-1476

Continued on next page

Continued from preceeding page

Farm & Power Equipmt Assn of Ohio, 6124 Avery Rd, Columbus (614) 889-1309

Farm Bureau Federation-Ohio, 2 Nationwide Pl, Columbus (614) 249-2400

Farmers Union-Ohio, 20 S 3 St, Columbus (614) 221-9520

Federation of Teachers AFL-CIO-Ohio, (800) 821-1722

Fire Fighters-Ohio Assn of Prof, 236 E Town St, Columbus (614) 224-1415

Florists' Assn-Ohio, 2130 Stella Ct, Columbus (614) 487-1117

Food Processors Assn-Ohio, 993 Kilbourne Dr, Columbus (614) 885-6045

Forestry Assn-Ohio, 1301 Worthington Woods Bl, Columbus (614) 846-9456

Freedom of Choice Ohio, 760 E Broad St, Columbus (614) 221-6655

Fruit Growers Society-Ohio, Columbus (614) 249-2424

Funeral Directors Assn-Ohio, 2501 North Star, Columbus (614) 486-5339

Furniture Rental Assn of Amer, 5008 Pine Creek Dr, Columbus (614) 895-1273

Gas Assn-Ohio, 50 W Broad St, Columbus (614) 224-1036

General Contractors-Assoc, 1124 Goodale, Columbus (614) 294-2948

Girl Scout Seal of Ohio Council, 1295 Hubbard Rd, Columbus (614) 878-1382

Golfers Assn-Southern Ohio Professional, 17 S High St, Columbus (614) 221-7194

Gov Finance Officers Assn-Ohio, 17 S High St, Columbus (614) 221-1900

Grain & Feed Assn-Ohio, 17 S High St, Columbus (614) 221-1900

Grain & Feed Assn-Ohio, 6641 N High St, Columbus (614) 885-4429

Grape Industries-Ohio, 6877 N high St, Columbus (614) 885-3529

Grocers Assn-Ohio, 1564 W 1 Av, Columbus (614) 487-9991

Handicapped Children-Ohio Coalition for the Education of, 933 High St, Columbus (614) 431-1307

Handicapped-Ohio Industries for the, 4795 Evanswood Dr, Columbus (614) 846-4877

Handicapped-Ohio Resource Ctr for Low Incidence & Severely, 470 Glenmont Av, Columbus (614) 262-6131

Hardware Assn-Ohio, 1540 W 5 Av, Columbus (614) 486-5278

Harness Horseman Assn-Ohio, 471 E Broad St, Columbus (614) 221-3650

Head Injury Foundation-Natl, 751 Northwest Bl, Columbus (614) 424-6967

Health Care Assn-Ohio, 50 North Woods Bl, Columbus (614) 436-4154

Health Care Employees Union 1199 AFL-CIO-Ohio State, 475 E Mound St, Columbus (614) 461-1199

Health Information Mgmt Assn-Ohio, Columbus (614) 792-0488

Health Underwriters-Ohio Assn of, 3811 Chevington Rd, Columbus (614) 451-1313

Continued on next page

Continued from preceeding page

Heating & Air Conditioning Wholesalers Assn-North Amer, 1389 Dublin Rd, Columbus (614) 488-1835

High School Athletic Assn-Ohio , 4080 Roselea Pl, Columbus (614) 227-2502

Higher Education-Ohio Consortium for Ministry in Public, 89 E Wilson Bridge Rd, Columbus (614) 888-3844

Historical Society-Ohio, I-71 & E 17 Av, Columbus (614) 297-2439

HMO Assn-Ohio, 65 E State St, Columbus (614) 460-3503

Home Bldrs Assn-Ohio, 16 E Broad, Columbus (614) 228-6647

Home Care-Ohio Council for, 1335 Dublin Rd, Columbus (614) 481-3580

Home Economics Assn-Ohio, 1787 Neil Av, Columbus (614) 292-1583

Homeless-Ohio Coalition for the, 1066 N High St, Columbus (614) 291-1984

Homes for the Aging-Assoc of Ohio Philanthropic, 855 E Wall St, Columbus (614) 444-2882

Hospice Organization-Ohio, 3294 W Broad St, Columbus (614) 274-9513

Hospital Assn-Ohio, 155 E Broad St, Columbus (614) 221-7614

Hospital Pharmacists-Ohio Soc of, Columbus (614) 265-8855

Hotel & Motel Assn-Ohio, 692 N High St, Columbus (614) 461-6462

Housing Coalition- Ohio, 1066 N High St, Columbus (614) 299-0544

Human Services Directors Assn-Ohio, 175 S 3 St, Columbus (614) 221-3688

Humane Education Assn-Ohio, Columbus (614) 875-1810

Humanities Council-Ohio, 695 Bryden Rd, Columbus (614) 461-7802

Hunger Network in Ohio, 82 E 16 Av, Columbus (614) 424-6203

Hunger Task Force-Ohio, 80 S 6 St, Columbus (614) 464-1956

Ice Cream Retailers Assn-Natl, 1429 King Av, Columbus (614) 486-1444

Independent Business Ohio-Natl Federation of, 50 W Broad St, Columbus (614) 221-4107

Independent Colleges & Universities of Ohio-Assoc of, 17 S High St, Columbus (614) 228-2196

Independent Colleges-Ohio Foundation of, 21 E State St, Columbus (614) 469-1950

Insurance Agents Assn of Ohio-Independent, 1330 Dublin, Columbus (614) 464-3100

Insurance Agents Assn of Ohio-Professional, 3059 E Mound St, Columbus (614) 239-9634

Iron & Steel Institute-Amer, 49937 W Broad, Columbus (614) 878-6600

Irrigation Assn of Ohio, 2586 Oakstone Dr, Columbus (614) 523-3344

Jewelers Assn-Ohio, 50 W Broad St, Columbus (614) 221-7833

Jewish Family Services, 2831 E Main St, Columbus (614) 231-1890

Jewish Women-Natl Council of, 3667 E Broad St, Columbus (614) 235-4133

Kiwanis Intl-Ohio District, 65 Ceramic Dr, Columbus (614) 447-0630

Continued on next page

Labor Relations Assn-Ohio Motor Carriers, 50 W Broad St, Columbus (614) 224-8244

Laborers' District Council of Ohio, 8 E Long, Columbus (614) 221-6519

Land Surveyors of Ohio-Professional, 2865 W Dublin-Granville Rd, Columbus (614) 761-2313

Land Title Assn-Ohio, 2375 E Main St, Columbus (614) 235-5001

Landscape Archtcts-Ohio Chapter Amer Soc of, 420 W Whittier St, Columbus (614) 443-0938

Legal Servs Assn-Ohio State, 861 N High St, Columbus (614) 299-2114

Libertarian Campaign Finance Committee, 2325 Agler Rd, Columbus (614) 476-6773

Liberty Foundation, 338 S High St, Columbus (614) 224-7300

Library Assn-Ohio, 67 Jefferson Av, Columbus (614) 221-9057

Library Trustee Assn-Ohio, 67 Jefferson Av, Columbus (614) 221-9057

Library- Media Assn-Ohio Educational, 67 Jefferson Av, Columbus (614) 221-9057

Licensed Beverage Assn-Ohio, 692 High St, Columbus (614) 224-3840

Life Underwriters-Ohio Assn of, 17 S High St, Columbus (614) 221-1900

Lions-Ohio, 4442 Professional Pkwy, Columbus (614) 836-1052

Lumbermen's Assn-Ohio, 41 Croswell Rd, Columbus (614) 267-7816

Lung Assn of Ohio, Am 1700 Arlingate Ln, Columbus (614) 279-1700

Manufactured Housing Assn-Ohio, 906 E Broad St, Columbus (614) 258-6642

Marine Corps League Dept of Ohio, 65 S Front St, Columbus (614) 469-1775

Medical Equipment Companies-Ohio Assn of Durable, 6015 Frantz Rd, Columbus (614) 889-0450

Medical Professional Liability Underwriting Assn-Ohio, 6230 Busch Bl, Columbus (614) 436-4530

Medical Record Assn-Ohio, 5608 Parker Hill Ln, Columbus (614) 792-0488

Mental Health Assn in Ohio, 5 E Long St, Columbus (614) 221-5383

Mental Retardation-Ohio Assn of County Boards of, 73 E Wilson Bridge Rd, Columbus (614) 431-0616

Metal Finishers-Ohio Assn of, 5281 Melody Ln, Willoughby, (216) 953-1530

Mfrs Assn-Ohio, 33 N High St, Columbus (614) 224-5111

Middle School Assn-Natl, 4807 Evanswood Dr, Columbus (614) 848-8211

Military Order of the Purple Heart Dept of Ohio, 65 S Front St, Columbus (614) 228-8250

Mining & Reclamation Assn-Ohio, 50 S Young St, Columbus (614) 228-6336

Continued on next page

Continued from preceeding page

Monument Assn-Amer, 933 High St, Columbus (614) 885-2713

Mortgage Bankers Assn-Ohio, 2586 Oakstone Dr, Columbus (614) 891-4242

Mothers Against Drunk Driving, State of Ohio, 471 E Broad St, Columbus (614) 461-6233

Motor Bus Assn-Ohio, 33 S Grant Av, Columbus (614) 221-1498

Motor Carriers Labor Relations Assn-Ohio, 50 W Broad, St, Columbus (614) 224-8244

Motor Freight Tariff Committee-Ohio, 3341 W Broad, Columbus (614) 279-8659

Motorcycle Dealers Assn-Ohio, 3386 Snouffer Rd, Columbus (614) 764-0042

Motorcyclists Assn-Amer, 33 College View Rd, Westerville, (614) 891-2425

Municipal League-Ohio, 175 S 3 St, Columbus (614) 221-4349

Municipal Power-Amer, 601 Dempsey Rd, Columbus (614) 890-2805

NAACP-Ohio St Conference of Branches, 233 S High St Columbus (614) 221-5187

Narcotics Anonymous-Ohio Regional Serv Ofc, 2729 Winchester Pke, Columbus (614) 236-8787

Native American Indian Center, 1862 Parsons Av, Columbus (614) 443-6120

Natl Guard Assns-Ohio, 577 W 2 Av, Columbus (614) 294-6642

NEED Project-Ohio, 577 Wickham Way, Columbus (614) 471-7975

Negro College Fund-United, 50 W Broad St, Columbus (614) 221-5309

New Direction-Youth Leadership Program, 651 Harmon Av, Columbus (614) 469-0647

Newspaper Assn-Ohio, 1225 Dublin Rd, Columbus (614) 486-6677

Nurse Anesthetists-Ohio State Assn of, 17 S High St, Columbus (614) 221-1900

Nursery Stock Marketing Program-Ohio, 2021 E Dublin-Granville Rd, Columbus (614) 431-0457

Nurserymen's Assn-Ohio, 2021 E Dublin-Granville Rd, Columbus (614) 431-2452

Nurses & Health Professionals Federation of, 1015 E Main, Columbus (614) 258-6742

Nurses Assn-Ohio, 4000 E Main, Columbus (614) 237-5414

Nurses Testing Serv-Ohio, 4000 E Main St, Columbus (614) 237-8922

Nursing Homes-Ohio Acad, 8 E Broad St, Columbus (614) 461-1922

Ohio Democratic Party, 37 W Broad St, Columbus (614) 221-6563

Oil & Gas Assn-Ohio, P.O. Box 535 Granville, (614) 587-0444

Operating Engineers Health & Welfare Plan-Ohio, 1180 Dublin Rd, Columbus (614) 488-0708

Opthalmological Society-Ohio, 8 E Broad St, Columbus (614) 464-1985

Optical Publishing Assns, 7001 Discovery Bl, Columbus (614) 793-9660

Opticians Assn of Ohio, 1024 Dublin Rd, Columbus (614) 488-0617

Optometric Assn-Ohio, 169 E Livingston Av, Columbus (614) 224-2600

Continued on next page

Continued from preceeding page

Orthopaedic Society-Ohio, 8 E Broad St, Columbus (614) 464-2878
Orthopaedic Surgeons and Sports Medicine-Ohio, 1405 Dublin Rd, Columbus (614) 488-1816
Osteopathic Assn-Ohio, 53 W 3, Columbus (614) 299-2107
Parents & Teachers-Ohio Congress of, 427 E Town, Columbus (614) 221-4844
Parents Anonymous (614) 899-4700
Parents for Drug-Free Youth-Ohio, 1875 Morse Rd, Columbus (614) 268-6255
Parents Without Partners (614) 421-0044
Parking Assn-Ohio State, 50 W Broad St, Columbus (614) 224-7489
Parks & Recreation Assn Ohio, 420 Whittier, St, Columbus (614) 443-2322
Pastoral Care-Ohio Institute of, 4889 Sinclair Rd, Columbus (614) 885-2431
Peace March-Ohio, 1066 N High St, Columbus (614) 291-9255
Peace March-Ohio, 1101 Bryden Rd, Columbus (614) 252-9255
Pediatrics-Ohio Chap-Amer Acad of, 411 Highgate Av, Columbus (614) 846-6258
People's Rights Organization, 5 E Long St, Columbus (614) 268-0122
Pest Control Assn-Ohio, P.O.Box 716, Brunswick, (614) 225-9393
Petroleum Council-Ohio, 88 E Broad, Columbus (614) 221-5439
Petroleum Marketers Assn-Ohio, 6631 Commerce Pkwy, Columbus (614) 792-5212
Petroleum Producers Assn-Ohio, 85 E Gay St, Columbus (614) 461-8305
Pharmaceutical Assn-Ohio State, 395 E Broad St, Columbus (614) 464-1874
Pharmacists Assn-Ohio, 6037 Frantz Rd, Dublin, (614) 798-0037
Photographers of Ohio-Professional, 1024 Dublin Rd, Columbus (614) 488-0617
Physical Therapy Assn Ohio Chapter-Amer, 4355 N High St, Columbus (614) 267-7000
Physicians Effectiveness Program-Ohio, 525 Metro Pl N, Columbus (614) 766-2252
Physicians Ohio-Am College of, 5008 Pine Creek Dr (614) 895-1905
Physicians-Ohio Academy of Family, 4075 N High, Columbus (614) 268-7867
Planned Parenthood Affil of Ohio, 16 E Broad St, Columbus (614) 224-0761
Planning Conference, -Ohio, 129 S Southampton, Columbus (614) 274-3516
Plumbers & Pipe Fitters Ohio State Assn, 1240 Kinnear Rd, Columbus (614) 481-8055
Plumbing, Heating, & Cooling Contractors-Ohio St Assn of, 17 S High St, Columbus (614) 221-1900
Podiatric Medical Assn-Ohio, 5310 Kitrick Bl, Columbus (614) 457-6269
Police & Fire Retirees of Ohio, 2101 S Hamilton Rd, Columbus (614) 866-1352

Continued on next page

Continued from preceeding page

Police-Fraternal Order of Ohio, 222 E Town St, Columbus (614) 224-5700

Pork Producers Council-Ohio, 135 Allview Rd, Columbus (614) 882-5887

Potato Growers Assn-Ohio, 4680 Indianola Av, Columbus (614) 261-6834

Poultry Assn-Ohio, 674 W Lane Av, Columbus (614) 292-2089

Pregnancy Aid, 22 E Gay St, Columbus (614) 221-0844

Printing Industry-of Ohio, 88 Dorchester Sq, Westerville, (614) 221-7539

Private Detective Agencies-Ohio Assn of, 5310 E Main St, Columbus (614) 759-7420

Private Residential Assn-Ohio, 199 S 5 St, Columbus (614) 224-6772

Professionals Guild of Ohio, 1015 E Main, Columbus (614) 258-6742

Propane Gas Assn-Ohio, 17 S High St, Columbus (614) 221-1900

Prosecuting Attorneys Assn-Ohio, 42 E Gay St, Columbus (614) 221-1266

Psychological Assn-Ohio, 400 E Town St, Columbus (614) 224-0034

Public Accountants Soc of Ohio, 1395 E Dublin-Granville, Columbus (614) 846-4500

Public Education & Religious Liberty-Ohio Assn for, 203 King Av, Columbus (614) 299-9116

Public Expenditure Council-Ohio, 37 W Broad St, Columbus (614) 221-7738

Public Facilities Maintenance Assn-Ohio, 17 S High St, Columbus (614) 221-1900

Public Interest Research Group-Ohio, 2060 N High St, Columbus (614) 299-7474

Public Radio-Public TV-Ohio, State House Bldg, Columbus (614) 221-1811

Public School Employees-Ohio Assn of , 6805 Oak Creek Dr, Columbus (614) 890-4770

Race Track Chaplaincy of America-Ohio Div, 5755 Feder Rd, Columbus (614) 878-0123

Radiological Society-Ohio State, 1500 Lake Shore Dr, Columbus (614) 484-2401

Railroad Assn-Ohio, 17 High St, Columbus (614) 224-4010

Railroad Passengers-Ohio Assn of 489 Overwood Rd, Akron, (216) 867-5507

Ready Mixed Concrete Assn-Ohio, 1900 E Dublin-Granville Rd, Columbus (614) 891-0210

Realtors-Ohio Assn of, 200 E Town ST, Columbus (614) 228-6675

Rehabilitation Facilities-Ohio Assn of, 17 S High St, Columbus (614) 221-1900

Republican Finance Committee-Ohio, Columbus (614) 228-6683

Republican Headquarters-Ohio Fed of, 172 E State St, Columbus (614) 228-2481

Republican Women-Ohio Sate, 172 E State St, Columbus (614) 228-2481

Restaurant Assn-Ohio, 1335 Dublin Rd, Columbus (614) 488-3848

Retail Merchants-Ohio Council of , 50 W Broad St, Columbus (614) 221-7833

Continued on next page

Continued from preceeding page

Retail Permit Holders Assn-Ohio, 692 N High St, Columbus (614) 241-2216

Retarded Citizens-Council for, 777 Neil Av, Columbus (614) 221-9115

Retired Senior Volunteer Program, 673 Mohawk St, Columbus (614) 443-3844

Retired Teachers Assn-Ohio, 750 Brooksedge Bl, Columbus (614) 891-1377

Retirement Study Commission-Ohio, 88 E Broad, Columbus (614) 228-1346

Rural Electric Cooperatives-Ohio, 6677 Busch Pl, Columbus (614) 846-5757

Rural Water Systems-Ohio Assn of, 3669 Broadway, Columbus (614) 871-2725

Savings & Loan League-Ohio, 88 E Broad, Columbus (614) 224-6244

School Administrators-Buckeye Assn of, 750 Brooksedge Bl, Columbus (614) 891-5330

School Administrators-Ohio Assn of Elementary, 750 Brooksedge Bl, Columbus (614) 891-2810

School Business Officials-Ohio Assn of, 750 Brooksedge Bl, Columbus (614) 891-2215

School Counselor Assn-Ohio, 1821 Misty Way, Columbus (614) 863-6722

School Discipline-Ohio Center for More Effective, 155 W Main St, Columbus (614) 221-8829

School Employee Retirees of Ohio, 666 High St, Columbus (614) 431-0387

School Principals-Ohio Assn of Secondary, 750 Brooksedge, Columbus (614) 891-4733

School Psychologists' Assn-Ohio, 750 Brooksedge, Columbus (614) 891-2524

School Superintendents' Assn-Ohio County, 88 E Broad St, Columbus (614) 621-0502

Schools-Natl Assn for Neighborhood, 2778 Board St, Columbus (614) 2756267

Science-Ohio Acad of, 1500 W 3 Av, Columbus (614) 488-2228

Scrap Recycling Industries-Institute of, 4334 W Central, Toledo, (419) 531-4625

Second Chance Foundation, 1970 Village Green Dr, Columbus (614) 471-5112

Secretaries Internatl-Professional, 8 E Long St, Columbus (614) 221-8207

Security & Investigation Services-Ohio Assn of, 5310 Main St, Columbus (614) 759-7435

Seed Improvemt Assn-Ohio, 6150 Avery Rd, Columbus (614) 889-1136

Self-Insurers Assn-Ohio, 88 E Broad, Columbus (614) 221-8850

Senior Centers-Ohio Assn of, 36 WE Gay St, Columbus (614) 221-2882

Serv Staten & Automotive Repair Assn-Indep, 17 S High St, Columbus (614) 221-1900

Sewing Mach Dealers Assn-Indep, 615 Hilliard & Rome Rd, Columbus (614) 870-7211

Continued on next page

Continued from preceeding page

Sexual Assault-Ohio Coalition on, 65 S 4 St, Columbus (614) 469-0011

Sheep Improvement Assn-Ohio, 270 Bradenton Av, Columbus (614) 792-6742

Sheet Metal & Roofing Contractors Assn, 2210 Arbor Blvd, Dayton, (513) 294-0023

Sheriff's Assn Buckeye State, 6230 Busch Bl, Columbus (614) 431-5500

Shorthand Reporters Assn-Ohio, 1024 Dublin Rd, Columbus (614) 488-0617

Sickle Cell & Health Assn-Ohio, 370 S 5 St, Columbus (614) 228-0157

Social Workers Ohio Chapter-Natl Assn of, 40 W Long, Columbus (614) 461-4484

Social Workers Union, 1015 E Main, Columbus (614) 258-6742

Society for Training & Development-Amer, (614) 337-2783

Society of Enrolled Agents-Ohio, 163 Northwest Professional Pl, Columbus (614) 459-0452

Soft Drink Assn-Ohio, P.O.Box 1008, Columbus (614) 464-5617

Soybean Assn-Ohio, Columbus (614) 249-2422

Spa & Pool Institute- Natl, 2999 Silver Dr, Columbus (614) 261-0791

Speakers Forum-Ohio, 17 S High St, Columbus (614) 221-1900

Special Olympics-Ohio, 3303 Winchester Pke, Columbus.(614) 239-7050

Speech & Hearing Assn-Ohio, 9331 S Union Rd, Dayton, (513) 866-4972

Sportsmen-League of Ohio, 3953 Indianola Av, Columbus (614) 268-9924

Standardbred Breeders & Owners Assn-Ohio, 6797 N High St, Columbus (614) 885-8040

State County & Municipal Employees AFSCME-AFL-CIO,AM FED OF, 400 E Mound St, Columbus (614) 228-3900

State Grange-Ohio, 1031 E Broad, Columbus (614) 258-9569

State Medical Assn-Ohio, 1500 Lake Shore Dr, Columbus (614) 486-2401

Steel Service Ctr Institute, 1600 Terminal Tower, Cleveland, (216) 694-3630

Subcontractors Assn-Amer, 2871 Wellesley Dr, Columbus (614) 488-8447

Tax Assn-Natl, 5310 E Main St, Columbus (614) 864-1221

Teachers-Amer Federation of, 1015 E Main, Columbus (614) 258-6742

Technical & Community College Assn-Ohio, 65 E State St, Columbus (614) 460-3510

Teen Pregnancy Network, 206 E State St, Columbus (614) 224-2235

Telephone Assn-Ohio, 17 S High St, Columbus (614) 221-3231

Testing-Am Soc for Non-Destructive, 1711 Arlingate Ln, Columbus (614) 274-6003

Theatre Owners of Ohio-Natl Assn, 1024 Dublin Rd, Columbus (614) 488-3904

Tobacco & Candy Distribrs-Ohio Assn of, 16 E Broad St, Columbus (614) 224-3435

Continued on next page

Continued from preceeding page

Township Assn-Ohio, 5969 E Livingston Av, Columbus (614) 863-0045

Tractor Pullers Assn-Natl, 6969 Worthington-Galena Rd, Columbus (614) 436-1761

Travel Assn-Ohio, Columbus (614) 895-1931

Trial Lawyers-Ohio Acad of, 400 Dublin Av, Columbus (614) 341-6800

Troopers Coalition-Ohio, 222 E Town St, Columbus (614) 228-4815

Trotting Assn-US, 750 Michigan, Columbus (614) 224-2291

Trucking Assn-Ohio, 50 W Broad St, Columbus (614) 221-5375

Ukrainian Cultural Assn of Ohio, Columbus (614) 267-7036

United Nations Assn of the USA, 57 Jefferson Av, Columbus (614) 228-4010

United Way-Ohio, 16 E Broad St, Columbus (614) 224-8146

University Community Business Assn, 1714 N High St, Columbus (614) 299-2866

University Professors-Am Assn of, Columbus (614) 885-2287

Veterans of Foreign Wars, 65 S Front St, Columbus (614) 224-1838

Veterans of World War One of the USA, Dept of Ohio, 65 S Front St, Columbus (614) 221-1839

Veterinary Medical Assn-Ohio, 1350 W 5 Av, Columbus (614) 486-7253

Visitor's Council-Intl, 4600 International Gateway, Columbus (614) 231-9610

Vocational Assn-Ohio, 5080 Sinclair Rd, Columbus (614) 885-1881

Vocational Education-Ohio Council on, 750 Brooksedge Bl, Columbus (614) 891-4764

Walking Assn-US, 2142 Wesleyan Dr, Columbus (614) 459-9255

Waterwell Assn-Natl, 6375 Riverside Dr, Columbus (614) 761-1711

Welfare Conference-Ohio, 5 E Long St, Columbus (614) 224-5767

Woman's Christian Temperance Union-Ohio, 1444 E Broad St, Columbus (614) 258-7212

Women Martial Artists Tae Kwon Do Self Defense, (614) 268-6873

Women Voters of Ohio-League of, 65 S 4, Columbus (614) 469-1505

Women's & Children's Apparel Club of Ohio, 3635 Weston Pl, Columbus (614) 267-5888

Women-Ohio Fed of Business & Professionals, 4758 Middletowne, St, Columbus (614) 459-3888

Women-Ohio, 65 S 4 St, Columbus (614) 463-9558

YMCAs-Natl Council of, 40 W Long St, Columbus (614) 224-2225

Youth Advocate Program-Ohio, 1460 W Lane Av, Columbus (614) 486-6797

Youth Services Network-Ohio, 500 S 4th St, Columbus (614) 461-1354

OHIO AGRICULTURE

* Contributes $40.8 billion to Ohio's economy.

* Represents 12% of total output, 15% of employment, and 10% of value-added products.

* Statistics from The Ohio State University College of Agriculture

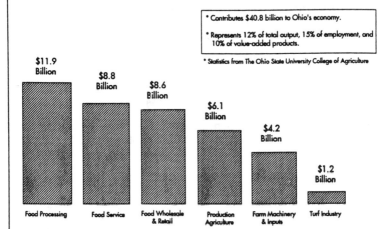

$11.9 Billion	$8.8 Billion	$8.6 Billion	$6.1 Billion	$4.2 Billion	$1.2 Billion
Food Processing	Food Service	Food Wholesale & Retail	Production Agriculture	Farm Machinery & Inputs	Turf Industry

OHIO: "STACK UP" ON THE NATIONAL LEVEL

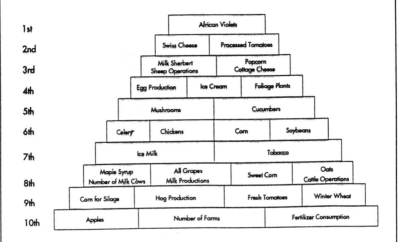

1st	African Violets
2nd	Swiss Cheese / Processed Tomatoes
3rd	Milk Sherbert, Sheep Operations / Popcorn, Cottage Cheese
4th	Egg Production / Ice Cream / Foliage Plants
5th	Mushrooms / Cucumbers
6th	Celery / Chickens / Corn / Soybeans
7th	Ice Milk / Tobacco
8th	Maple Syrup, Number of Milk Cows / All Grapes, Milk Productions / Sweet Corn / Oats, Cattle Operations
9th	Corn for Silage / Hog Production / Fresh Tomatoes / Winter Wheat
10th	Apples / Number of Farms / Fertilizer Consumption

Continued on next page

AG FACTS AND FIGURES

Agriculture contributes more than $40 billion to Ohio's economy.

Ohio agriculture employs one out of every seven people.

Ohio's top commodities are: soybeans, corn, milk, hogs, cattle, poultry, wheat, greenhouse/nursery items, vegetables and hay.

1992 Ohio Poultry Production was valued at $286 million, including 5.0 billion eggs, 145 million pounds of turkey, and 162.7 million pounds of chicken.

Ohio is a leader in the production of apples with more than 15 different varieties produced.

In 1992, Ohio produced more than 507 million bushels of corn, valued at over $1 billion. One bushel of corn (56 pounds) can be used to make 31.5 pounds of starch, 33 pounds of corn sweetener, or 2.5 gallons of pure ethanol.

Ohio's 42 wineries produce approximately 1.7 million gallons of wine per year.

Tomato juice became the official state beverage in 1965.

Exports

Every other row of soybeans and every 5th row of corn in Ohio is exported.

For every $1 billion in farm exports, 27,000 jobs are created. About one-third of those are non-farm jobs in food processing, manufacturing, marketing, transportation and other services.

One American farmer produces enough food to feed 128 people worldwide.

An average of 4 1/2 acres is farmed for every man, woman, and child in America (one acre is about the size of a football field).

In 1992 there were 78,000 farms in Ohio with an average size of 197 acres. On a national level, the average farm is 468 acres with assets of $400,000 and debt of about $66,000.

The averdge age of the U.S. farmer is 52 years.

Nearly five percent of Ohio's farms are operated by women.

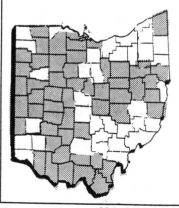

Counties shown in shadow are the principal farm counties of Ohio. Each ranks among the top 10 in one or more farm categories, as shown on the next page.

Continued on next page

Ohio Crops, Record Highs & Lows:
Harvested Acres, Yield and Production

Crop	Series began	Record[1]	Harvested Area		Yield		Total Production		Unit
			Thou. Acres	Year	Yield	Year	Thou. Units	Year	
Corn for grain	1919	High	4,030	1985	143.0	1992	511,810	1985	Bu.
		Low	2,537	1961	27.5	1930	75,598	1924	Bu.
Corn for silage	1919	High	285	1981	20.0	1992	4,000	1982	Ton
		Low	106	1935	5.4	1930	823	1933	Ton
Soybeans for beans	1924	High	4,080	1979	41.5	1985	160,605	1985	Bu.
		Low	17	1925	11.5	1926	207	1926	Bu.
Wheat	1866	High	3,209	1899	62.0	1985	79,650	1990	Bu.
		Low	800	1987	6.0	1900	9,000	1866	Bu.
Oats	1866	High	2,374	1928	85.0	1985	92,400	1912	Bu.
		Low	160	1986	20.0	1890	9,000	1988	Bu.
Rye	1866	High	200	1913	43.0	1985	2,700	1913	Bu.
		Low	4	1985	10.0	1896	150	1981	Bu.
Alfalfa hay	1919	High	1,052	1955	4.00	1990	2,800	1990	Ton
		Low	93	1920	1.30	1930	188	1919	Ton
Other hay	1964	High	1,080	1968	2.60	1990	2,160	1989	Ton
		Low	700	1991	1.49	1965	1,328	1965	Ton
All hay	1866	High	3,553	1908	3.30	1990	4,898	1916	Ton
		Low	1,260	1983	0.60	1895	1,755	1895	Ton
Apples	1934	High					7,886	1937	Bu.
		Low					780	1945	Bu.2/
Peaches	1899	High					3,800	1901	Bu.
		Low					15	1982	Bu.3.
Grapes[4]	1909	High					34.4	1935	Ton
		Low					4.9	1945	Ton
Potatoes-total	1866	High	225.0	1895	270	1985	12,269	1909	Cwt
		Low	6.0	1992	27	1881	1,425	1991	Cwt
Sugar beets[5]	1924	High	51.0	1938	21.7	1971	896	1971	Ton
		Low	9.5	1931	5.8	1937	72	1943	Ton
Burley tobacco	1919	High	25.0	1919	2,680	1970	28,350	1982	Lb.
		Low	6.7	1971	715	1935	6,435	1935	Lb.
All tobacco	1866	High	106	1909	2,496	1970	94,575	1918	Lb.
		Low	7.35	1987	620	1875	12,044	1987	Lb.

[1] In case of ties, most recent year designated as record year. [2] 42 lbs. [3] 48 lbs. [4] Utilized production. [5] No acres contracted in 198

Ohio County Ranking

Rank	Corn for grain	Soybeans	Wheat	All Hay	Oats	Processing Tomatoes
1	Darke	Darke	Wood	Wayne	Wayne	Sandusky
2	Pickaway	Wood	Hancock	Holmes	Stark	Putnam
3	Fayette	Madison	Seneca	Muskingum	Holmes	Fulton
4	Madison	Van Wert	Henry	Columbiana	Mercer	Wood
5	Clinton,	Pickaway	Putnam	Carroll	Columbiana	Henry
6	Wood	Hancock	Wyandot	Tuscarawas	Ashtabula	Seneca
7	Fulton	Seneca	Paulding	Ashtabula	Ashland	Ottawa
8	Preble	Fayette	Pickaway	Stark	Shelby	Miami
9	Champaign	Hardin	Hardin	Mercer	Portage	Hancock
10	Mercer	Marion	Darke	Belmont	Seneca	Darke

Rank	All Cattle	Milk Cows	Hogs	Sheep	Burley Tobacco	Sugar Beets
1	Wayne	Wayne	Darke	Muskingum	Brown	Sandusky
2	Mercer	Mercer	Mercer	Knox	Adams	Seneca
3	Holmes	Holmes	Clinton	Coshocton	Gallia	Erie
4	Clark	Stark	Fulton	Licking	Clermont	Ottawa
5	Darke	Columbiana	Preble	Harrison	Highland	Wood
6	Ashland	Ashtabula	Greene	Union	Scioto	
7	Muskingum	Tuscarawas	Putnam	Seneca	Lawrence	
8	Shelby	Ashland	Auglaize	Ashland	Pike	
9	Stark	Darke	Fayette	Morrow	Jackson	
10	Tuscarawas	Auglaize	Holmes	Logan		

1/ Crops are ranked on 1992 production. Hogs are ranked on year-end inventory. Cattle & sheep ranked Jan. 1.

Continued from preceeding page

Profile of Ohio Agriculture 1992

Commodity	Unit	Rank[2]	Ohio Prod. or inventory[3]	State ranked first State[2]	Prod. or inventory
			Thousand		Thousand
Field Crops					
Corn for grain	Bu.	6	507,650	Iowa	1,903,650
Corn for silage	Ton	9	3,600	Wisconsin	10,320
Oats	Bu.	8	12,070	S. Dakota	42,900
Winter wheat	Bu.	9	59,095	Kansas	363,800
Rye	Bu.	18	175	S. Dakota	1,666
Soybeans	Bu.	6	147,200	Illinois	405,490
All hay (baled)	Ton	15	4,550	Texas	9,800
Sugarbeets	Ton	12	328	Minnesota	6,845
All potatoes	Cwt.	26	1,440	Idaho	121,380
Tobacco	Lb.	7	22,680	N. Carolina	595,500
Fresh vegetables					
Sweet corn	Cwt.	9	697	Florida	4,781
Tomatoes	Cwt.	9	450	Florida	19,513
Celery	Cwt.	7	56	California	13,875
Storage onions	Cwt.	10	158	Oregon	8,371
Total fresh vegetables	Cwt.	17	2,631	California	169,870
Processing vegetables					
Tomatoes	Ton	2	374.68	California	7,932.00
Cucumbers	Ton	5	42.73	Michigan	111.80
Total processing vegetables	Ton	6	430.7	California	8,060.92
Fruit					
Apples	Lb.	10	115,000	Washington	4,900,000
All grapes	Ton	8	10.3	California	5,480
Processed grapes	Ton	7	10.2	California	4,702
Peaches	Lb.	14	14,000	California	1,825,000
Strawberries	Cwt.	8	71	California	10,296
Poultry and poultry products					
Chicken inventory 12/1/92	Head	6	23,160	California	31,500
Chicken sold	Lb.	8	45,720	Georgia	88,172
Broiler production	Lb.	21	117,030	Arkansas	4,499,000
Turkey production	Lb.	11	144,560	N. Carolina	1,320,600
Egg production 12/91-11/92 (million)	No.	4	5,021	California	7,007
Livestock and livestock products					
Hog and pig inventory 12/1/92	Head	9	1,750	Iowa	16,000
Hog and pig production	Lb.	9	771,622	Iowa	6,481,210
Cattle and calf inventory 1/1/93	Head	23	1,610	Texas	14,300
Cattle and calf production	Lb.	27	463,565	Texas	6,386,600
Beef cow inventory 1/1/93	Head	30	355	Texas	5,570
Milk cow inventory 1/1/93	Head	8	315	Wisconsin	1,625
Sheep and lamb inventory 1/1/93	Head	15	190	Texas	2,000
Sheep and lamb production	Lb.	14	13,335	Texas	110,500
Wool	Lb.	14	1,523	Texas	17,600
Cattle slaughtered	Head	14	197.0	Nebraska	6,582.4
Hogs slaughtered	Head	8	2,832.3	Iowa	29,684.4
Calves slaughtered	Head	4	121.9	New York	233.7
Sheep and lambs slaughtered	Head	11	22.8	Colorado	1,623.7
Red meat production	Lb.	16	670,653	Iowa	6,744,836
Livestock slaughter plants 1/1/93	No.	5	207	Texas	232
Not in thousands					

Do Ohio Proud

help consumers to identify products grown in Ohio...

Continued on next page

Farm Assets, Debts and Ratios, Ohio 1988-1991, U.S. 1990,1991[1]

| | Ohio | | | | United States | |
	12/31/88	12/31/89	12/31/90	12/31/91	12/31/90	12/31/91
			Million Dollars			
Farm Assets:						
Real Estate	19,900.6	19,961.7	20,190.0	20,550.0	711,400	705,600
Livestock & Poultry	1,249.3	1,277.5	1,305.8	1,217.8	70,900	68,400
Machinery & Motor Vehicles	3,255.0	3,454.4	3,398.7	3,264.7	88,600	88,000
Crops	810.6	882.8	941.4	864.4	22,800	23,600
Purchased Inputs	98.5	66.5	76.9	71.5	2,800	2,500
Household equipment & furnishings	1,469.8	1,675.9	1,880.7	2,099.6	46,400	50,400
Financial Assets	2,100.6	2,210.0	2,356.8	2,356.8	60,800	65,600
Total Farm Assets	**28,884.4**	**29,440.3**	**30,003.6**	**30,424.8**	**1,003,600**	**1,004,100**
Farm Debt:						
Real Estate Debt	2,166.4	2,101.5	2,024.7	2,040.5	78,400	79,100
Non-real Estate Debt	1,348.9	1,351.9	1,351.3	1,342.3	66,700	67,800
Total Farm Debt [2]	**3,515.4**	**3,453.3**	**3,376.0**	**3,382.8**	**145,100**	**147,000**
Equity	**25,369.1**	**25,987.0**	**26,627.6**	**27,042.0**	**858,500**	**857,100**
Debt/Asset Ratio	12.2	11.7	11.3	11.1	14.5	14.6
Debt/Equity Ratio	13.9	13.3	12.7	12.5	16.9	17.1
Net Cash Farm Income/Debt Ratio [3][4]	30.6	44.0	43.9	31.2	47.4	42.2

[1] Includes operator households. [2] Excludes CCC loans. [3] Net farm income after inventory adjustment. [4] Calculated using end of year debt.

Number of Farms, Average Size of Farm and Land in Farms Ohio and United States, 1990-1992

| Year | Number of farms [1] | | Average Size Farm | | Land in farms | |
	Ohio	U.S.	Ohio	U.S.	Ohio	U.S.
	Number		Acres		Thousand acres	
1990	84,000	2,140,000	187	461	15,700	987,420
1991	80,000	2,105,000	196	467	15,700	982,576
1992	78,000	2,096,000	197	468	15,400	980,083

[1] A farm is defined as a place with annual sales of agricultural commodities of $1,000 or more.

Index Numbers of Crop and Livestock Production in Ohio 1985-1992[1]

	1985	1986	1987	1988	1989	1990	1991	1992
Crops								
Feed grains	134	123	97	66	89	108	84	131
Food grains	81	67	68	64	87	110	73	82
Soybeans	132	120	118	82	103	111	111	121
Other field crops	79	72	64	64	64	83	86	87
Seed crops and hay	129	121	120	100	100	130	89	128
All vegetables	122	124	107	83	101	116	111	96
Fruit	179	120	196	136	162	158	155	169
Total crops	127	116	105	76	98	112	95	121
Livestock and livestock products								
Meat animals	108	108	110	117	112	126	106	100
Poultry and poultry products	158	170	194	200	204	227	230	247
Milk	109	111	109	107	102	105	105	105
Wool	59	60	60	57	56	56	57	47
Total livestock and products	114	116	119	123	118	128	120	119
Total all commodities	**123**	**116**	**110**	**92**	**105**	**117**	**104**	**120**

[1] Base year 1977 = 100

Continued on next page

WORLD FAMOUS ENTERTAINERS
BORN IN OHIO

Mentioning some of Ohio's most famous entertainers by their original names would produce the following:

Doris von Kappelhoff, Phyllis Driver, Joe Katz, Dino Crocetti and Leonard Stye.

Not impressed?

Let's list them again, using their stage names:

Doris Day, Phyllis Diller, Joel Gray, Dean Martin and Roy Rogers.

They, together with the following, make up an impressive list of Ohio natives who are among the world's most famous entertainers.

NAME	BIRTHPLACE	BIRTH DATE
Ballard, Kaye	Cleveland, Oh.	11/20/26
Battle, Kathleen	Portsmouth, Oh.	6/13/48
Brewer, Teresa	Toledo, Oh.	5/7/31
Carmen, Eric	Cleveland, Oh.	8/11/49
Conway, Tim	Willoughby, Oh.	12/15/33
D'Angelo, Beverly	Columbus, Oh.	11/15/54
Day, Doris	Cincinnati, Oh.	4/3/24
Dee, Ruby	Cleveland, Oh.	10/27/23
Diller, Phyllis	Lima, Oh.	7/17/17
Donahue, Phil	Cleveland, Oh.	12/21/35
Downs, Hugh	Akron, Oh.	2/14/21
Dullea, Keir	Cleveland, Oh.	5/30/36
Farr, Jamie	Toledo, Oh.	7/1/34
Feinstein, Michael	Columbus, Oh.	9/7/56
Garr, Teri	Lakewood, Oh.	12/11/45
Grey, Joel	Cleveland, Oh.	4/11/32
Hall, Arsenio	Cleveland, Oh.	2/12/55
Harewood, Dorian	Dayton, Oh.	8/6/51
Heckart, Eileen	Columbus, Oh.	3/29/19
Holbrook, Hal	Cleveland, Oh.	2/17/25
Hunter, Ross	Cleveland, Oh.	5/6/21
Ingram, James	Akron, Oh.	2/16/56
Jump, Gordon	Dayton, Oh.	4/1/32
Kane, Caropl	Cleveland, Oh.	6/18/52
King, Perry	Alliance, Oh.	4/30/48
Levine, James	Cincinnati, Oh.	6/23/43
Mancini, Henry	Cleveland, Oh.	4/16/24
Martin, Dean	Steubenville, Oh.	6/17/17
McGovern, Maureen	Youngstown, Oh.	7/27/49
Mercer, Marian	Akron, Oh.	11/26/35
Meredith, Burgess	Cleveland, Oh.	11/16/08
Newman, Paul	Cleveland, Oh.	1/26/25
O'Connell, Helen	Lima, Oh.	5/23/21

Continued on next page

Continued from preceeding page

NAME	BIRTHPLACE	BIRTH DATE
Paar, Jack	Canton, Oh.	5/1/18
Parker, Sarah Jessica	Nelsonville, Oh.	3/25/65
Paycheck, Johnny	Greenfield, Oh.	5/31/41
Perry, Luke	Fredericktown, Oh.	10/11/-
Poston, Tom	Columbus, Oh.	10/17/27
Rogers, Roy	Cincinnati, Oh.	11/5/12
Sandy, Gary	Dayton, Oh.	12/25/45
Sheen, Martin	Dayton, Oh.	8/3/40
Spielberg, Steven	Cincinnati, Oh.	12/18/47
Thomas, Philip Michael	Columbus, Oh.	5/16/49
Urich, Robert	Toronto, Oh.	12/19/46
Weston, Jack	Cleveland, Oh.	8/21/24
Williams, Hal	Columbus, Oh.	12/14/38
Wilson, Nancy	Chillicothe, Oh.	2/20/37
Winger, Debra	Cleveland, Oh.	5/16/55
Winters, Jonathan	Dayton, Oh.	11/11/25

SOME OTHER FAMOUS OHIOANS

Source - Ohio Chamber of Commerce

Johnny Appleseed (John Chapman)......................................Folk Hero
Neil Armstrong...First Man on the Moon
Walter Austin...Baseball Manager
Warner Baxter...Motion Picture Star
Clyde Beatty...........................Big Game Hunter and Animal Trainer
Ambrose Bierce.............................Journalist, Short Story Writer
Erma Bombeck...Syndicated Columnist
Louis Bromfield...................................Novelist and Farmer
Joe E. Brown..Movie Comedian
John Brown...........................Made raid on Harper's Ferry, 1861
Paul Brown.................Founder, Cleveland Browns and Owner, Cincinnati
Bengals
Alice Cary...................First President of First Women's Club in America
Bernie Casey..Artist, Poet, Actor, Athlete
Hopalong Cassady (William Boyd)...........................Cowboy Movie Star
Dr. Arthur H. Compton....................Physicist, Educator, Philosopher and
Humanitarian
Jay Cooke.................................Financier of the Civil War
J. S. Cox..................................Organized Coxey's Army
George A. Custer.........................General and Indian Fighter
Clarence Darrow..Criminal Lawyer
Charles Dawes..........................Vice President of U. S. under Hoover
Doris Day..Movie Star
Phyllis Diller..Comedienne
Phil Donahue.......................................TV Show Host
Hugh Downs......................................TV Show Host
Paul Laurence Dunbar..Poet
Allan W. Eckert......................................Historian, Author
Daniel Decatur Emmett..............................Author of ''Dixie''
Jamie Farr..TV Star of ''M*A*S*H''
Ted Lewis (Friedman)...................................Band Leader
Clark Gable...Motion Picture Star
John Galbreath..........................Realtor, Builder, Sportsman
Dorothy and Lillian Gish..................................Movie Stars

Continued on next page

John H. Glenn...Astronaut, U.S. Senator
Dody Goodman...TV Star
William Green..........................President, American Federation of Labor
Zane Grey..Author
Archie Griffin.................................Two-Time Heisman Trophy Winner
Charles M. Hall....................Discoverer of Process of Making Aluminum
Margaret Hamilton...Movie Star
Scott Hamilton...............................World Champion Figure Skater
Benjamin R. Hanby.......................Author of "Darling Nellie Gray"
Woody Hayes..Football Coach
Hal Holbrook...TV and Stage Personality
Bob Hope..TV and Motion Picture Star
Henry Howe...Historian
William Dean Howells...Novelist
John Jakes...Author
Elsie Janis...Actress
Ban Johnson..Educator
Sammy Kaye...Band Leader
Maya Lin.............Designer, Vietnam War Memorial in Washington, D.C.
Henry Mancini...Orchestra Leader
Horace Mann...................Educator and Founder of Antioch College
Dean Martin..............................TV and Motion Picture Star
William Holmes McGuffey...........................Author, School Textbooks
Burgess Meredith...TV Star
Toni Morrison...Author
Paul Newman..Motion Picture Star
Jack Nicklaus....................1976 Winner of First World Series of Golf
Annie Oakley..Sharpshooter
Adolph S. Ochs...Publisher of New York Times
Frederick B. Opper...Cartoonist
Jesse Owens...Track Star
Jacob Parrott..................First Congressional Medal of Honor Winner
Norman Vincent Peale...........................Journalist, Author, Minister
George Pendleton...................................Sponsored Civil Service Act
James Raye...First President of Liberia
Whitelaw Reid...New York Tribune Publisher
Judith Resnik..._Challenger_ Astronaut
Roy Rogers...King of Movie "Westerns"
Pete Rose..Baseball Player
Wilson Shannon........................First Native Son to be Elected Governor
Philip H. Sheridan...General, Civil War
John Sherman.........................The "Ralph Nader" of his day
William Tecumseh Sherman....................................General, Civil War
Platt Rogers Spencer..............Authored Spencerian System of Penmanship
Edward M. Stanton.....................Secretary of State under Lincoln
Harriet Beecher Stowe...........................Author of "Uncle Tom's Cabin
Rosalynn Summers.................................World Champion Figure Skater
Tell Taylor...........................Author of "Down By The Old Millstream"
Danny Thomas..TV and Motion Picture Star
Lowell Thomas.......................................Radio Commentator
Eliza Jane Thompson...........................Mother of W.C.T.U. Movement
James Thurber..Novelist
Morrison R. Waite.................Former Chief Justice, U. S. Supreme Court
Mooney Warther...................................Called "World's Master Carver"
"Mad" Anthony Wayne....................Revolutionary General and Patriot
Archibald Willard.................................Painter of "Spirit of '76"
Jonathan Winters..Comedian

NEWSPAPERS IN OHIO - DAILY

NEWSPAPER	CITY & ZIP	COUNTY	D=DAILY S=SUN.	CIRC IN 1000s
Akron Beacon Journal	Akron 44328	Summit	D/S	158/227
Alliance Review	Alliance 44601	Stark	D	12
Ashland Times Gazette	Ashland 44805	Ashland	D	12
Ashtabula Star Beacon	Ashtabula 44004	Ashtabula	D/S	19/30
Athens The Messenger	Athens 45701	Athens	D/S	13/16
Beavercreek Daily News	Beavercreek 45432	Greene	D	4
Bellevontaine Examiner	Bellefontaine 43311	Logan	D	11
Bellevue Gazette	Bellevue 44811	Huron & Sandusky	D	3.5
Bowling Green Sentinel Trubune	Bowling Green 43401	Wood	D	14
Bryan Times	Bryan 43506	Williams	D	11
Bucyrus Telegraph Forum	Bucyrus 44820	Crawford	D	7
Cambridge Daily Jefferson	Cambridge 43725	Guernsey	D	13
Canton Repository	Canton 44702	Stark	D/S	61/80
Celina Daily Standard	Celina 45822	Mercer	D	10
Chillicothe Gazette	Chillicothe 45601	Rosa	D	15
Cincinnati Enquirer	Cincinnati 45202	Hamilton	D/S	199,107/ 350
Cincinnati Post	Cincinnati 45202	Hamilton	D	99
Circleville Herald	Circleville 43113	Pickaway	D	8
Cleveland Plain Dealer	Cleveland 44114	Cuyahoga	D/S	410/546
Columbus Daily Reporter	Columbus 43215	Franklin	D	4
Columbus Dispatch	Columbus 43216	Franklin	D/S	265/400
Conneaut News Herald	Conneaut 44030		D/S	4/30
Coshocton Tribune	Coshocton 43812	Coshocton	D/S	8/9
Dayton Daily News	Dayton 45402	Montgomery & Greene	D/S	179/230
Defiance Crescent News	Defiance 43512	Defiance	D/S	16
Delaware Gazette	Delaware 43015	Delaware.	D	8
Delphos Daily Herald	Delphos 45833	Delphos & Van Wert	D	3
Dover-New Philadelphia Times Reporter	New Philadelphia 44663	Tuscarawas	D/S	27/30
East Liverpool Evening Review	East Liverpool 43920	Columbiana	D	12
Elyria Chronicle Telegram	Elyria 44035	Lorain	D/S	36/39
Fairborn Herald	Fairborn 45324	Greene	D	5
Findlay Courier	Findlay 45840	Hancock	D	26
Fostoria Review Times	Fostoria 44830	Senaca & Wood	D	7.5
Fremont New Messenger	Fremont 43420	Sandusky	D	13.5
Galion Inquirer	Galion 44833	Crawford	D	5

Continued on next page

Continued from preceeding page

Gallipolis Daily Tribune	Gallipolis 45631	Gallia	D/S	6
Gallipolis Sunday Times Herald	Gallipolis 45631	Gallia	S	12
Geauga Times Leader	Chardon 44024		D/S	8/30
Greenfield Daily Times	Greenfield 45123	Highland	D	4.3
Greenville Advocate	Greenville 45331	Darke	D	8.7
Hamilton Journal News	Hamilton 45012	Butler	D/S	26/27
Ironton Tribune	Ironton 45638	Lawrence	D/S	8/9
Kent Ravenna Record Courier	Ravenna 44266	Portage	D/S	21/22
Kenton Times	Kenton 43326	Hardin	D	7.8
Lake County News Herald	Willoughby 44094	Lake	D/S	56/67
Lancaster Eagle Gazette	Lancaster 43130	Fairfield	D/S	17/17
Lima News	Lima 45802	Allen	D/S	38/49
Lisbon Morning Journal	Lisbon 44432	Columbiana	D/S	16/14
Logan News	Logan 43138	Hocking	D	5.3
London Madison Press	London 43140	Madison	D	5.5
Lorain Morning Journal	Lorain 44052	Lorain	D/S	43/47
Mansfield News Journal	Mansfield 44901		D/S	39/53
Marietta Times	Marietta 45750	Washington	D	13.2
Marion Star	Marion 43302	Marion	D/S	19/19
Martins Ferry-Bellaire Times-Leader	Martins Ferry 43947	Belmont	D/S	21/23
Marysville Journal Tribune	Marysville 43040	Union	D	6.1
Massillon Independent	Massillon 44648	Stark	D	16
Medina County Gazette	Medina 44256	Medina	D	17
Middletown Journal	Middletown 45044	Butler	D/S	23/24
Mt. Vernon News	Mt. Vernon 43050	Knox	D	10.1
Napoleon Northwest Signal	Napoleon 43545	Henry	D	5.8
Newark Advocate	Newark 43055	Licking	D/S	23/23
Norwalk Reflector	Norwalk 44857	Huron	D	9
Piqua Daily Call	Piqua 45356	Miami	D	9
Pomeroy Middleport Daily Sentinel	Pomeroy	Meiga	D/S	5/12
Pt. Clinton-Oak Harbor News Herold	Pt. Clinton 43452	Ottawa	D	6.4
Portsmouth Daily Times	Portsmouth 45662	Scioto	D/S	17/16
St. Marys Evening Leader	St. Marys 45885	Auglaize	D	6.2
Salem News	Salem	Columbiana	D	9
Sandusky Register	Sandusky 44870	Erie	D/S	24/27
Shelby Daily Globe	Shelby 44875	Richland	D	4.1
Sidney Daily News	Sidney 45365	Shelby	D	13.4
Springfield News-Sun	Springfield 45501	Clark	D/S	39/46
Steubenville Herald-Star	Steubenville 43952	Jefferson	D/S	22/22
Tiffin Advertiser Tribune	Tiffin 44883	Seneca	D/S	11/11
Toledo-The Blade	Toledo 43660	Lucus	D/S	146/207
Troy Daily News	Troy 45373	Miami	D	11/13
Upper Sandusky Daily Chief Union	Upper Sandusky 43351	Wyandot	D	4.2

Continued on next page

Urbana Daily Citizen	Urbana 43078	Champaign	D	7.3
Van Wert Times Bulletin	Van Wert 45891	Van Wert	D	7.7
Wapakoneta Daily News	Wapakoneta 45895	Auglaize	D	4.8
Warren Tribune Chronicle	Warren 44482	Trumbull	D/S	42/47
Washington Courthouse Record Herald	Washington Courthouse 43160	Fayette	D	7
Wilmington News Journal	Wilmington 45177	Clinton	D	7
Wooster Daily Record	Wooster 44691	Wayne	D	25
Xenia Gazette	Xenia 45385	Greene	D	10.4
Youngstown- The Vindicator	Youngstown 44501	Mahoning	D/S	90/137
Zanesville Times Recorder	Zanesville 43701	Muskingum	D/S	24/24

Trivia

QUESTION   How many natural inland lakes does Ohio have?

ANSWER   None. (The many lakes in Ohio are all manmade.)

QUESTION   Which Ohio restaurant has won the 5-star rating of the Mobile Travel Guide more consecutive times than any restaurant in the U.S.?

ANSWER   Maisonette Restaurant. (Cincinnati, more than a quarter of a century.)

QUESTION   Which is the longest river in Ohio?

ANSWER   Sciota River. (230 miles long, it begins in Sciota County and flows into the Ohio River, draining 6,509 square miles.)

QUESTION   What was the population of Ohio in 1800 and 10 years later?

ANSWER   45,000 and 231,000, an increase of 513%.

QUESTION   Who was the first and last Miss America winners from Ohio?

ANSWER   Mary Campbell, 1922, Columbus, and Susan Perkins, 1978, Columbus.

NEWSPAPERS IN OHIO - WEEKLY

NEWSPAPER	OFFICE & ZIP	COUNTY	CIRC (PAID) IN 1000s
Ada Herald	Ada 45180	Hardin	2.8
Amherst News Times	Amherst 44001	Loraine	2.0
Andover Pymatuning Area News	Amherst 44001	Ashtabula	2.0
Antwerp Bee Argus	Antwerp 45813	Paulding	2.0
Archbold Buckeye	Archbold 43502	Fulton	3.2
Archbold Farmland News	Archbold 43502	Fulton	7.8
Ashtabula Sentinel	Ashtabula 44047	Ashtabula	2.5
Attica Hub	Attica 44807	Seneca	2.0
Aurora Advocate	Stow 44224	Portage	4.6
Austintown Leader	Niles 44446	Mahoning	0.2
Avon Lake Press	Avon Lake 44012	Lorain	5.4
Barberton Herald	Barberton 44203	Summit	6.2
Barnesville Enterprise	Barnesville 43713	Belmont	4.9
Bedford Sun Banner	Cleveland 44124	Cuyahoga	4.8
Bedford Times-Register	Bedford 46059	Cuyahoga	4.8
Beechwood/Clintonville Booster	Columbus 43229	Franklin	3.7
Bellville Star & Tri-Forks Press	Bellville 44813	Richland	2.2
Berea News Sun	Cleveland 44125	Cuyahoga	16.0
Bethel Journal-Press	Bethel 45106	Clemont	1.3
Bexley News	Columbus 43229	Franklin	1.1
Bloomville Gazette	Attica 44807	Seneca	0.4
Blue Ash/Montgomery N.E. Suburban Life Press	Cincinnati 45249	Hamilton	9.1
Bluffton News	Bluffton 45812	Allen	3.0
Brecksville/Independence Sun Courier	Cleveland 44125	Cuyahoga	6.6
Brooklyn Sun Journal	Cleveland 44125	Cuyahoga	9.7
Brookville Star	Brookville 45309	Cuyahoga	0.3
Brunswick Sun Times	Cleveland 44125	Cuyahoga	6.1
Cadiz Harrison News Herald	Cadiz 43907	Harrison	5.8
Canal Winchester Times	Columbus 43229	Cuyahoga	2.0
Canfield Courier	Salen 44460	Mahoning	0.5
Carey Progressor-Times	Carey 43316	Wyandot	4.5
Carrollton Free Press Standart	Carrollton 44615	Carroll	7.7
Chagrin Falls-Chagrin Valley Times/Solon Times	Chagrin Falls 44022	Cuyahoga	10.2
Chagrin Herald Sun	Cleveland 44125	Cuyahoga	2.6
Cincinnati Delhi Price Hill Press	Cincinnati 45227	Hamilton	8.5
Cincinnati Hilltop News	Cincinnati 45227	Hamilton	5.7
Cincinnati Northwest Press	Cincinnati 45227	Hamilton	7.8
Cincinnati Tri-County Press	Cincinnati 45227	Hamilton	1.4
Clermont County Community Journal Press N.	Cincinnati 45225	Clermont	0.9
Clermont County Community Journal Press S.	Cincinnati 45225	Clermont	6.6
Clermont County Review	Cincinnati 45230	Clermont	1.5
Clermont County Sun	Batavia 45103	Clermont	3.1
Cleveland Hts. Sun Press	Cleveland 44125	Cuyahoga	19.3
Cleveland Sun Scoop Journal E.	Cleveland 44125	Cuyahoga	4.8
Cleveland Sun Scoop Journal W.	Cleveland 44125	Cuyahoga	16.6

Continued on next page

Continued from preceeding page

NEWSPAPERS IN OHIO - WEEKLY

NEWSPAPER	OFFICE & ZIP	COUNTY	CIRC (PAID) IN 1000s
Clyde Enterprise	Clyde 43410	Sandusky	2.5
Coldwater Mercer County Chronicle	Coldwater 45828	Mercer	3.1
Columbiana Heritage	Columbiana 44408	Columbiana	0.6
Columbus News East	Columbus 43229	Franklin	N/A
Columbus News Northwest	Columbus 43229	Franklin	1.4
Conneaut Courier	Conneaut 44030	Ashtabula	1.5
Connecticut Lake Breeze Herald	Andover 44003	Ashtabula	0.9
Continental News-Review	Continental 45831	Putman	1.3
Crestline Advocate	Crestline 44827	Crawford	2.3
Cridersville Shawnee Press	Wapakoneta 45895	Allen	1.4
Dalton Gazette & Kidron News	Dalton 44618	Wayne	1.1
Delta Atlas	Delta 43515	Fulton	1.7
Deshler Flag	Deshler 43516	Henry	1.5
Dresden Village News	Dresden 43821	Muskingum	3.5
Dublin News	Columbus 43229	Franklin	5.4
Eaton Register-Herald	Eaton 45320	Preble	6.2
Edgerton Earth	Edgerton 43517	Williams	1.3
Edon Commercial	Edon 43518	Williams	0.7
Euclid Sun Journal	Cleveland 44125	Cuyahoga	12.2
Fayette Review	Fayette 42521	Fulton	1.1
Franklin Chronicle	Franklin 45005	Warren	2.6
Fredericktown Knox County Citizen	Fredericktown 43019	Knox	1.4
Fulton Co. Expositor	Wausheon 43567	Fulton	4.3
Gahanna Rocky Fork Enterprise	Gahanna 43299	Franklin	5.4
Garfield-Maple Hts. Sun	Cleveland 44125	Cuyahoga	9.6
Georgewotn News Democrat	Georgetown 45121	Brown	5.8
Germantown Press	Germantown 45327	Montgomery	2.5
Grandview Hts. Tri-Village News	Columbus 43229	Franklin	1.8
Grove City Record	Grove City 43123	Franklin	5.4
Harrison Press	Harrison 45030	Hamilton	5.3
Hartville News	Hartville 44632	Stark	3.0
Heath Ace News	Heath 43056	Licking	4.5
Hilliard N.W.News	Columbus 43229	Franklin	2.5
Hillsboro Press Gazette	Hillsboro 45133	Highland	5.1
Huber Hts. Courier	Huber Hts. 45424	Montgomery	7.0
Huron Erie County Reporter	Huron 44839	Erie	2.3
Jackson Journal Herald	Jackson 45640	Jackson	5.6
Jefferson Co. Tri-County News	Steubenville 43952	Jefferson	0.9
Jefferson Gazette	Jefferson 44047	Ashtabula	2.2
Johnstown Independent	Johnstown 43031	Licking	2.8
Kettering-Oakwood Times	Kettering 45240	Montgomery	0.3
Lakewood Sun Post	Cleveland 44125	Cuyahoga	12.4
Lebanon Western Star	Lebanon 45036	Warren	8.5
Leesburg Citizen	Greenfield 45123	Highland	1.6
Lewisburg Leader	Lewisburg 45338	Preble	1.0
Liberty Center Press	Liberty Center 43532	Henry	1.3
Lodi Review Chronicle	Lodi 44254	Medina	2.2
Lorain County Times	Lorain 44052	Lorain	0.8
Loudonville Times	Loudonville 44842	Ashland	2.2
Louisville Herald	Louisville 44641	Stark	3.2

Continued on next page

NEWSPAPERS IN OHIO - WEEKLY

NEWSPAPER	OFFICE & ZIP	COUNTY	CIRC (PAID) IN 1000s
Lynchburg News	Greenfield 45123	Highland	0.8
Malvern Community News	Malvern 44644	Carroll	1.0
Manchester Signal	Manchester 45144	Adams	5.2
Maple Hts. Press	Bedford 44146	Cuyahoga	3.1
Mayfield Hts. Sun Messenger	Cleveland 44125	Cuyahoga	14.5
McArthur Vinton County Courier	McArthur 45651	Vinton	3.3
McConnelsville Morgan County Herald	McConnelsville 43756	Morgan	5.0
Mechanicsburg Telegram	London 43130	Champaign	0.6
Miamisburg News	Miamisburg 45342	Montgomery	7.2
Millersburg-Holmes County Hub	Millersburg 44654	Holmes	4.1
Minerva Leader	Minerva 44601	Stark	3.9
Monroe Co. Spirit of Democracy	Woodsfield 43793	Monroe	1.0
Montgomery Sycamore Messenger	Cincinnati 45242	Montgomery	4.5
Montgomery/Green Cos. Amos Suburban News	Dayton 45240	Montgomery	23.2
Montpelier Leader Enterprise	Montpelier 43543	Williams	1.5
Mt Gilead-Morrow County	Mt Gilead 43338	Morrow	4.8
Mt. Washington Press	Cincinnati 45230	Hamilton	4.7
N. Ridgeville Press & Light	N. Ridgeview 48039		6.0
New Carlisle Sun	New Carlisle 45344	Clark	4.0
New Lexington Perry County Tribune	New Lexington 43764	Perry	3.8
New London Record	New London 44851	Huron	2.9
New Washington Herald	New Washington 44854	Crawford	1.4
Newark Licking Countian	Newark 43058	Licking	3.1
Newcomerstown News	Newcomerstown 43832	Tuscarawas	3.3
Newton Falls Herald	Niles 44446	Trumbull	3.0
North Baltimore News	North Baltimore 45872	Wood	1.0
North Canton Stark County Sun	North Canton 44720	Stark	5.2
North Olmstead/Westlake Sun Herald	Cleveland 44125	Cuyahoga	18.1
Northland News	Columbus 43229	Franklin	7.9
Norton Sun Banner Pride	Wadsworth 44281	Medina	2.8
Oak Harbor Exponent	Oak Harbor 43449	Ottawa	4.0
Oberlin News-Tribune	Oberlin 44074	Lorain	2.6
Ontario Madison Tribune-Courier	Ontario 44862	Richland	1.7
Orrville Courier-Crescent	Orrville 44667	Wayne	2.4
Orwell Valley News	Orwell 44076	Ashtabula	1.3
Oxford Press	Oxford 45056	Butler	4.1
Pandora Times	Pandora 45877	Putman	0.4
Parma Sun Post	Cleveland 44125	Cuyahoga	27.8
Pataskala Standard	Pataskala 43062	Licking	4.5
Paulding Progress	Paulding 45879	Paulding	3.9
Perrysburg Messenger-Journal	Perrysburg 43552	Wood	5.2
Pickerington This Week	Columbus 43229	Fairfield	2.3
Pickerington Times Sun	Columbus 43229	Fairfield	2.3
Plain City Advocate	London 43140	Madison	1.7
Powell Olentany Valley News	Columbus 43229	Franklin	0.8

Continued on next page

NEWSPAPERS IN OHIO - WEEKLY

NEWSPAPER	OFFICE & ZIP	COUNTY	CIRC (PAID) IN 1000s
Preble County News	Oxford 45311	Preble	1.0
Putman County Sentinel	Ottawa 45875	Putman	8.6
Randolph/Englewood Independent	Englewood 45322	Montgomery	7.0
Richwood Gazette	Richwood 43344	Union	2.9
Ripley Bee	Ripley 45167	Brown	2.5
Rossford Record Jounal	Perrysburg 43552	Wood	1.7
S. Cleveland Leader	Garfield Hts. 44125	Cuyahoga	6.5
Sebring Times	Sebring 44672	Mahoning	0.7
Sharonville Suburban Press	Sharonville 45262	Hamilton	6.9
Solon Herald Sun	Cleveland 44125	Cuyahoga	3.7
Solon Times	Chagrin Falls 44022	Cuyahoga	2.8
Spencerville Journal News	Spencerville 45887	Allen	2.1
Springboro/Franklin Star Press	Springboro 45006	Warren	0.9
Stark County S.E. Press News	E. Canton 44730	Stark	2.3
Stow Sentry	Stow 44224	Summit	1.5
Streetboro/Mantua Record News	Streetboro 44214	Portage	1.0
Strongville Sun Star	Berea 44017	Cuyahoga	9.2
Strongville-The Sun Star	Cleveland 44124	Cuyahoga	10.7
Struthers Journal	Struthers 44471	Mahoning	5.0
Stryker/West Unity Advance Reporter	West Unity 43570	Williams	2.1
Sugarcreek Budget	Sugarcreek 44681	Tuscarawas	19.4
Sunbury News	Sunbury 43074	Delaware	3.2
Swanton Enterprise	Swanton 43558	Fulton	2.0
Sycamore Mohawk Leader	Sycamore 44882	Wyandot	4.5
Sylvania Herald	Toledo 43623	Lucas	4.6
Tipp City Herald	Tipp City 45371	Miami	3.2
Toledo West Herald	Toledo 43623	Lucas	32.0
Toronto Tribune	Toronto 43964	Jefferson	2.6
Twinsburg Bulletin	Bedford 44146	Summit	0.5
Upper Arlington News	Columbus 43229	Franklin	7.9
Utica Herald	Utica 43080	Licking	2.2
Vermilion Photojournal	Vermilion 44089	Erie	4.4
Versailles Policy	Versailles 45380	Darke	2.5
W.Alexandria Twin Valley News	W. Alexandria 45381	Preble	0.9
Wadsworth News Banner Prde	Wadsworth 44281	Medina	6.1
Waterville Anthony Wayne Herald	Toledo 43623	Lucas	5.0
Waverly News Watchman	Waverly 45690	Pike	3.6
Wellington Enterprise	Wellington 44090	Lorain	2.8
Wellston Sentry	Wellston 45692	Jackson	1.7
WellstonTelegram	Wellston 45692	Jackson	5.0
West Milton Record	West Milton 45383	Miami	1.8
Western Hills Press	Cincinnati 45227	Hamilton	7.7
Westerville News	Columbus 43229	Franklin	6.9
Westerville Public Opinion	Westerville 43081	Franklin	5.0
Westlake West Life	Westlake 44145	Cuyahoga	15.2
Westlake/Bay Village Times	Bay Village	Cuyahoga	1.6
Wheelersburg Scioto Voice	Wheelersburg 45694	Scioto	4.5
Willard Times Junction	Willard 44890	Huron	3.7
Woodsfield Monroe County Beacon	Woodsfield 43793	Monroe	5.4
Worthington Suburban News	Columbus 43229	Franklin	7.2
Yellow Springs News	Yellow Springs 45387	Greene	1.8
Youngstown Boardman News	Youngstown 44512	Mahoning	4.7

TELEVISION STATIONS IN OHIO

*Public Television

City / Station	Channel	Network
AKRON		
WAKC-TV Akron, 44320	CH 23	ABC
WEAO-TV Kent, 44240	CH 49*	PBS
ALLIANCE		
WNEO-TV Kent, 44240	CH 45*	PBS
ATHENS		
WOUB-TV Athens, 45701	CH 20*	PBS
WOUC-TV Athens, 45701	CH 44*	PBS
BOWLING GREEN		
WBGU-TV Bowling Green, 43402	CH 27*	PBS
CAMBRIDGE		
WOUC-TV Athens, 45701	CH 44*	PBS
CANTON		
WOAC-TV Canton, 44718	CH 67	
WDLI-TV Canton, 44718	CH 17	
CHILLICOTHE		
WWAT-TV Columbus	CH 53	
CINCINNATI		
WCET-TV Cincinnati, 45214	CH 48*	PBS
WOUC-TV Cambridge, 45701	CH 44*	PBS
WCPO-TV Cincinnati, 45202	CH 9	CBS
WKRC-TV Cincinnati, 45219	CH 12	ABC
WLWT-TV Cincinnati, 45202	CH 5	NBC
WSTR-TV Cincinnati	CH 64	
WXIX-TV Cincinnati, 45215	CH 19	FOX
CLEVELAND		
WEWS-TV Cleveland, 44115	CH 5	ABC
WJW-TV Cleveland, 44103	CH 8	CBS
WKYC-TV Cleveland, 44114	CH 3	NBC
WNBS-TV Cleveland, 44101	CH 55	
WOIO-TV Cleveland, 44120	CH 19	
WQHS-TV Cleveland, 44134	CH 61	
WUAB-TV Cleveland	CH 43	
WVIZ-TV Cleveland, 44134	CH 25*	PBS
COLUMBUS		
WBNS-TV Columbus, 43215	CH 10	CBS
WCMH-TV Columbus, 43202	CH 4	NBC
WOSU-TV Columbus, 43210	CH 34*	PBS
WPBO-TV Columbus, 43210	CH 42	
WTTE-TV Columbus, 43216	CH 28	FOX
WSYX-TV Columbus, 43216	CH 6	ABC
DAYTON		
WDTN-TV Dayton, 45401	CH 2	ABC
WHIO-TV Dayton, 45401	CH 6	CBS
WKEF-TV Dayton, 45418	CH 22	NBC
WPTD-TV Dayton, 45402	CH 16*	PBS
WRGT-TV Dayton, 45408	CH 45	FOX

Continued on next page

Continued from preceeding page

KENT
WNEO-TV
Kent, 44240

LIMA
WLIO-TV CH 35 NBC
Lima, 45802

WTLW-TV CH 44
Lima

LOUISVILLE
WDLI-TV
Louisville, 44641

MANSFIELD
WMFD-TV CH 68
Mansfield, 44906

NEWARK
WJFJ-TV CH 5
Newark

SPRINGFIELD
WTJC-TV CH 26
Springfield

STEUBENVILLE
WTOV-TV CH 9 NBC
Steubenville,
43952

TOLEDO
WGTE-TV CH 30* PBS
Toledo, 43692

WNWO-TV CH 24 ABC
Toledo, 43615

WTOL-TV CH 11 CBS
Toledo, 43615

WTVG-TV CH 13 NBC
Toledo, 43607

WUPW-TV CH 36 FOX
Toledo, 43604

WXAE-TV CH 40
Toledo

YOUNGSTOWN
WFMJ-TV CH 21 NBC
Youngstown,
44503

WKBN-TV CH 27 CBS
Youngstown,
44501

WYTV-TV CH 33 ABC
Youngstown,
44502

ZANESVILLE
WHIZ-TV CH 18 NBC
Zanesville, 43701

Trivia

QUESTION What is Ohio's top farm crop?

ANSWER Corn (22% of Ohio farm cash receipts)

QUESTION Where was world champion sharp shooter Annie Oakley born?

ANSWER Darke County. (1860)

QUESTION Where does the Ohio State Fair rank in the US?

ANSWER The largest in the Nation.

RADIO STATIONS IN OHIO
Dial Location, Format, Telephone

Abbreviations:

Btfl. - Beautiful	AB - Agricultural Broadcasting
C&W - Country & Western	AN -Agricultural Network
Cont. - Contemporary	IB - Independent Broadcasting
Cl. - Classical	M - Moody
Edu. - Educational	OEB - Ohio Education Broadcasting
MOR - Middle of Road	U - Unistar
Nost. - Nostalgia	W - Westwood One
PA - Public Affairs	

CITY STATION	DIAL LOCATION	FORMAT	NTWK.	CITY, ZIP	TELEPHONE
ADA					
WONB-FM	94.9	New Age		Ada, 45810	(419) 772-1194
AKRON					
WAKR-AM	1590	Adult Cont.		Akron, 44320	(216) 869-9800
WONE-FM	97.5	Classic Rock		Akron, 44320	(216) 869-9800
WAPS-FM	89.1	Modern Rock		Akron, 44301	(216) 434-1661
WHLO-AM	640	Cont. Christian	ABC	Akron, 44333	(216) 668-4774
WQMX-FM	94.9	Adult Cont.		Akron, 44333	(216) 434-6499
WSLR-AM	1350	C&W	ABC	Akron, 44313	(216) 836-4700
WKDD-FM	96.5	Cont.Hits	ABC	Akron, 44313	(216) 836-4700
WZIP-FM	88.1	Urban Cont. Rock	ABC	Akron, 44325	(216) 972-7105
ALLIANCE					
WDPM-AM	1310	Lite Hits	ABC	Alliance, 44325	(216) 972-7105
WZKL-FM	92.5	Adult Cont.	ABC	Alliance, 44325	(216) 972-7105
WRMU-FM	91.1	Jazz, Cl., Talk		Alliance, 44601	(216) 823-2414
ARCHBOLD					
WBCY-FM	89.5	Religious		Ft. Wayne, IN 46807	(219) 745-0576
WMTR-FM	96.1	Oldies	U, W	Archbold, 43502	(419) 445-9050
ASHLAND					
WNCO-AM	1340	MOR, Big Band	SMN	Ashland, 44805	(419) 289-2605
WNCO-FM	101.3	Country	MBS	Ashland, 44805	
WRDL-FM	88.9	Rock, Edu.	MBS	Ashland, 44805	(419) 289-5678
ASHTABULA					
WFUN-AM	970	Adult Cont. Oldies		Ashtabula, 44004	(216) 993-2126
WREO-FM	97.1	Adult Cont.		Ashtabula, 44004	(216) 993-2126

Continued on next page

CITY STATION	DIAL LOCATION	FORMAT	NTWK.	CITY, ZIP	TELEPHONE
ATHENS					
WATH-AM	970	Variety, MOR	NBC	Athens, 45701	(614) 593-6651
WXTQ-FM	105.5	Cont. Hits	MBS	Athens, 45701	
WOUB-AM	1340	News, Talk, Music	ABC	Athens, 45701	(614) 593-4554
WOUB-FM	91.3	Cl., Jazz	ABC	Athens, 45701	(614) 593-4554
BAINBRIDGE					
WKHR-FM	88.3	Big Band, Jazz		Chagrin Falls, 44023	(216) 543-9646
BARNESVILLE					
WBVN-FM	93.5	Oldies		Barnesville 43713	(614) 425-5777
BATAVIA					
WCNE-FM	88.7	Edu.		Batavia, 45103	(513) 732-3232
WOBO-FM	88.7	Variety		Owensville 45160	(513) 732-3232
BEAVERCREEK					
WYMJ-FM	103.9	Oldies	AP	Beaver-creek, 45385	(513) 429-9080
BELLAIRE					
WBHR-FM	88.7	Variety		Bellaire 43906	(614) 676-1826
WOMP-AM	1290	Cont. Hits	AP, ABC, U	Bellaire 43906	(614) 676-5661
WOMP-FM	100.5	N/A	U	Bellaire 43906	(614) 676-5661
BELLEFONTAINE					
WBLL-AM	1390	Country		Belle-fontaine, 43311	(513) 592-1045
WPKO-FM	98.3	Adult. Cont.		Belle-fontaine, 43311	(513) 592-1045
BELLEVUE					
WNRR-FM	92.1	Cont. Top 40	Sun, USA	Bellevue, 44811	(419) 483-2511
BELPRE					
WCVV-FM	89.5	Christian, News		Belpre, 45714	(614) 423-5895
WMBP-FM	91.7	N/A		Belpre, 45714	(614) 423-5673
WNUS-FM	107.1	Country	CNN	Belpre, 45714	(614) 423-8213
BEREA					
WBWC-FM	88.3	Classic Rock	UPI	Berea, 44017	(216) 826-2145

Continued on next page

CITY STATION	DIAL LOCATION	FORMAT	NTWK.	CITY, ZIP	TELEPHONE
BOWLING GREEN					
WBGU-FM	88.1	Variety, Jazz, Black		Bowling Green, 43403	(419) 372-8800
WJYM-AM	730	Religious	USA	Perrys-burg, 43551	(419) 352-4649
WRQN-FM	93.5	Oldies	U	Maumee, 43537	(419) 891-1551
BRYAN					
WQCT-AM	1520	Adult Cont.	ABC	Bryan 43503	(419) 636-3175
WBNO-FM	100.9	News		Bryan 43503	(419) 636-3175
BUCHTEL					
WAIS-AM	770	Country	ABC	Nelsonville 45764	(614) 753-2154
BUCYRUS					
WBCO-AM	1540	Adult Cont.	CBS	Bucyrus 44820	(419) 468-2326
WQEL-FM	92.7	Classic Rock	CBS	Bucyrus 44820	(419) 562-2222
CADIZ					
WWYS-FM	106.3	Adult Cont.	SMN	Winters-ville 43952	(614) 266-2700
CALDWELL					
WWKC-FM	104.9	Country	MBS	Caldwell, 43724	(614) 732-5777
CAMBRIDGE					
WILE-AM	1270	MOR	MBS	Cambridge 43725	(614) 432-5605
WCMJ-FM	96.7	Adult Cont.	MBS	Cambridge 43725	(614) 432-5605
WOUC-FM	89.1	Cl. Jazz, News	APR, NPR	Athens, 45701	(614) 593-4554
CAMPBELL					
WZKC-AM	1330	Country, Sport	NBC, BRN	Youngs-town, 44505	(216) 746-1330
CANTON					
WCER-AM	900	Religious	UPI, USA	Canton, 44708	(216) 478-6666
WHBC-AM	1480	MOR	ABC	Canton, 44711	(216) 456-7166
WHBC-FM	94.1	Adult Cont.	ABC	Canton, 44711	(216) 456-7166
WINW-AM	1520	MOR		Canton, 44705	(216) 492-5630
WRQK-FM	106.9	Rock		Canton, 44705	(216) 492-5630
WRCW-AM	1060	Adult Cont.		Canton, 44708	(216) 477-8585
WTOF-FM	98.1	Religious	USA	Canton, 44702	(216) 452-4009

Continued on next page

CITY STATION	DIAL LOCATION	FORMAT	NTWK.	CITY, ZIP	TELEPHONE
CASTALIA					
WGGN-FM	97.7	Religious	USA, CBN	Castalia, 44824	(419) 684-5311
CEDARVILLE					
WCDR-FM	90.3	Religious	CNN	Cedarville, 45314	(513) 766-7815
CELINA					
WCSM-AM	1350	Adult Cont.	ABC	Celina, 45822	(419) 586-5134
WCSM-FM	96.7	N/A	ABC	Celina, 45822	(419) 586-5134
WKKI-FM	94.3	Adult Cont.	U	Celina, 45822	(419) 586-7715
CENTERVILLE					
WCWT-FM	101.5	Adult Cont.		Centerville 45459	(513) 439-3557
CHARDON					
WATJ-AM	1560	News, Talk		Geneva, 44041	(216) 286-1560
CHILLICOTHE					
WBEX-AM	1490	Oldies	MBS	Chillicothe, 45601	(614) 773-2244
WKKJ-FM	93.3	Country	MBS	Chillicothe, 45601	(614) 773-2244
WCHI-AM	1350	MOR	U	Chillicothe, 45601	(614) 775-1350
WFCB-FM	94.3	Top 40	W	Chillicothe, 45601	(614) 775-1350
WOHC-FM	90.1	Religious		Cedarville, 45314	(513) 766-7815
WOUH-FM	91.9	Variety		Athens, 45701	(614) 594-4949
WVXC-FM	89.3	Variety, Edu.	APR, NPR, OEB	Cincinnati, 45207	(513) 745-3738
CINCINNATI					
WAIF-FM	88.3	Variety, Edu.		Cincinnati, 45206	(513) 961-8900
WAKW-FM	93.3	Religious	AP, CBN	Cincinnati, 45224	(513) 542-3442
WCIN-AM	1480	Cl., Oldies	U	Cincinnati, 45217	(513) 281-7180
WCKY-AM	1530	News, Talk	CBS, NBC	Cincinnati, 45202	(513) 241-6565
WIMJ-FM	92.5	Adult Cont.	CBS, NBC	Cincinnati, 45202	(513) 241-6565
WGUC-FM	90.9	Cl.	NPR, APR, OEB	Cincinnati, 45214	(513) 556-4444
WJVS-FM	88.3	Adult Cont.		Cincinnati, 45241	(513) 771-8810
WKRC-AM	550	Adult Cont.	ABC	Cincinnati, 45219	(513) 763-5500
WKRQ-FM	101.9	Cont. Hits	ABC	Cincinnati, 45219	(513) 763-5500

Continued on next page

CITY STATION	DIAL LOCATION	FORMAT	NTWK.	CITY, ZIP	TELEPHONE
WLW-AM	700	Adult Cont.	ABC	Cincinnati, 45202	(513) 241-9597
WEBN-FM	102.7	Classic Rock	ABC	Cincinnati, 45202	(513) 241-9597
WRRM-FM	98.5	Adult Cont.		Cincinnati, 45202	(513) 241-9898
WSAI-AM	1360	Oldies	AP	Cincinnati, 45204	(513) 471-9465
WWNK-FM	94.1	Adult Cont.	AP	Cincinnati, 45204	(513) 471-9465
WTSJ-AM	1050	Christian Cont.	USA	Cincinnati, 45231	(513) 931-8080
WUBE-AM	1230	Country	CBS	Cincinnati, 45202	(513) 721-1050
WUBE-FM	105.1	Country	CBS	Cincinnati, 45202	(513) 721-1050
WVXU-FM	91.7	Jazz, Rock	APR, NPR, AP, CNN, OEB.	Cincinnati, 45207	(513) 745-3738

CIRCLEVILLE

CITY STATION	DIAL LOCATION	FORMAT	NTWK.	CITY, ZIP	TELEPHONE
WNRJ-AM	1540	Adult Cont.	AB.	Columbus, 43229	(614) 474-3344
WTLT-FM	107.1	Christian Cont.	AB.	Columbus, 43229	(614) 474-3344

CLEVELAND

CITY STATION	DIAL LOCATION	FORMAT	NTWK.	CITY, ZIP	TELEPHONE
WABQ-AM	1540	Religious		Cleveland, 44128	(216) 231-8005
WCLV-FM	95.5	Cl.		Cleveland, 44128	(216) 464-0900
WCPN-FM	90.3	News, Jazz	APR, NPR, AP	Cleveland, 44114	(216) 432-3700
WCRF-FM	103.3	Reiligious	M, USA	Cleveland, 44141	(216) 526-1111
WCSB-FM	89.3	Variety		Cleveland, 44115	(216) 687-3523
WENZ-FM	107.9	Modern Rock	U, NBC	Cleveland, 44115	(216) 348-0108
WERE-AM	1300	News, Talk, Sports	MBS, CNN	Cleveland, 44115	(216)696-1300
WNCX-FM	98.5	Classic Rock	ABC	Cleveland, 44115	(216)696-1300
WGAR-FM	99.5	Cont. Country	ABC	Independence, 44131	(216) 328-9950
WHK-AM	1420	Business news	NBC	Cleveland, 44113	(216) 781-1420
WMMS-FM	100.7	Classic Rock	NBC	Cleveland, 44113	(216) 781-1420
WKNR-AM	1220	Sports, Talk	ABC	Cleveland, 44147	(216) 838-1220
WMJI-FM	105.7	Oldies	NBC. AP	Cleveland, 44113	(216) 623-1105
WQAL-FM	104.1	Adult Cont.		Cleveland, 44115	(216) 696-6666

Continued on next page

CITY STATION	DIAL LOCATION	FORMAT	NTWK.	CITY, ZIP	TELEPHONE
WRDZ-AM	1260	Cont. Christian	USA	Cleveland, 44141	(216) 526-8989
WRMR-AM	850	Nostalgia Music	CNN	Cleveland, 44114	(216) 696-0123
WDOK-FM	102.1	Adult Cont.	CNN	Cleveland, 44114	(216) 696-0123
WRUW-FM	91.1	Variety		Cleveland, 44106	(216) 368-2208
WWWE-AM	1100	News,Talk, Sports	ABC	Cleveland, 44113	(216) 696-4444
WLTF-FM	106.5	Adult Cont.	ABC	Cleveland, 44113	(216) 696-4444
WZAK-FM	93.1	Urban Cont.		Cleveland, 44114	(216) 621-9300
CLEVELAND HTS					
WJMO-AM	1490	Solid Gold Soul		Cleveland, 44106	(216) 795-1212
WJMO-FM	92.3	Dance Cont.		Cleveland Hts, 44118	(216) 371-3534
CLYDE					
WHVT-FM	90.5	Edu. Religious		Clyde, 43410	(419) 547-8251
WNCG-FM	100.9	Classic Hits	ABC	Clyde, 43410	(419) 547-8792
COAL GROVE					
WXVK-FM	97.1	Adult Cont.		Coal Grove, 43215	(614) 533-1500
COLUMBUS					
WBNS-AM	1460	Adult Cont.	CBS	Columbus, 43215	(614) 460-3850
WBNS-FM	97.1	Adult Cont.	CBS	Columbus, 43215	(614) 460-3850
WCOL-FM	92.3	Oldies	U	Columbus, 43215	(614) 221-7811
WCOL-AM	1230	Oldies	U	Columbus, 43215	(614) 221-7811
WMNI-AM	920	C&W	MBS, NBC	Columbus, 43215	(614) 481-7800
WBZX-FM	99.7	Rock	MBS, NBC	Columbus, 43215	(614) 481-7800
WNCI-FM	97.9	Adult Cont.		Columbus, 43215	(614) 224-9624
WOSU-AM	820	News, Public Affairs	NPR, AP, APR	Columbus, 43210	(614) 292-9678
WOSU-FM	89.7	Classical	APR, NPR	Columbus, 43210	(614) 292-9678
WRFD-AM		Religious, Farm	USA	Columbus Worthington,43085	(614) 885-5342
WRZR-FM	103.1	Rock		Columbus, 43229	(614) 846-1031
WTVN-AM	610	Adult Cont.		Columbus, 43215	(614) 486-6101

Continued on next page

CITY STATION	DIAL LOCATION	FORMAT	NTWK.	CITY, ZIP	TELEPHONE
WLVQ-FM	96.3	Rock		Columbus, 43215	(614) 486-6101
WVKO-AM	1580	Urban Cont.		Columbus, 43220	(614) 451-2191
WSNY-FM	94.7	Adult Cont.		Columbus, 43220	(614) 451-2191
CONNEAUT					
WGOJ-FM	105.5	Christian		Conneaut, 44030	(216) 599-7252
WWOW-AM	1360	Country	UPI	Conneaut, 44030	(216) 593-2233
CORTLAND					
WKTX-AM	930	Greek Nostalgia, Oldies	AP	Mecca, 44410	(216) 638-2425
COSHOCTON					
WTNS-AM	1560	Country	AP	Coshocton 43812	(614) 622-1560
WTNS-FM	99.3	Adult Cont.	AP	Coshocton 43812	(614) 622-1560
CROOKSVILLE					
WYBZ-FM	107.3	Oldies	CNN, U	Zanesville, 43702	(614) 453-6004
CUYAHOGA FALLS					
WCUE-AM	1150	Religious	UPI	Peninsula, 44264	(216) 920-1150
DAYTON					
WDAO-AM	1210	Urban Cont.		Dayton, 45417	(513) 263-9326
WDPR-FM	89.5	Cl., Jazz		Dayton, 45409	(513) 299-3297
WDPS-FM	89.5	Edu., Jazz		Dayton, 45402	(513) 223-5999
WGXMFM	97.3	C&W		Dayton, 45414	(513) 275-8434
WHIO-AM	1290	Variety, News, TAlk		Dayton, 45420	(513) 259-2111
WHKO-FM	99.1	Country		Dayton, 45420	(513) 259-2111
WING-AM	1410	Oldies	NBC, SMN	Dayton, 45429	(513) 294-5858
WONE-AM	980	Country	ABC	Dayton, 45402	(513) 224-1501
WTUE-FM	104.7	Cont. & Cl. Rock	ABC	Dayton, 45402	(513) 224-1501
WWSN-FM	107.7	Adult Cont.		Dayton, 45402	(513) 224-1137
WWSU-FM	106.9	Cont. Jazz, & Rock		Dayton, 454353	(513) 873-2000
DE GRAFF					
WDEQ-FM	103.3	Edu.		De Graff, 43318	(513) 585-5981
DEFIANCE					
WDFM-FM	98.1	Adult Cont.	ABC	Defiance, 43512	(419) 782-9336
WONW-AM	1280	C&W		Defiance, 43512	(419) 782-8126
WZOM-FM	105.9	Rock 40		Defiance, 43512	(419) 784-1059

CITY STATION	DIAL LOCATION	FORMAT	NTWK.	CITY, ZIP	TELEPHONE
DELAWARE					
WCEZ-FM	107.9	Easy Listening		Columbus, 43235	(614) 848-3108
WDLR-AM	1550	News	CNN, AB	Delaware, 43015	(614) 363-1107
WSLN-FM	98.7	Cont. Rock	ABC	Delaware, 43015	(614) 369-4431
DELPHOS					
WDOH-FM	107.1	Country	CBS	Delphos, 45833	(419) 642-3501
DOVER-NEW PHILADELPHIA					
WJER-FM	101.7	Adult Cont.		Dover, 44622	(216) 343-7755
WJER-AM	1450	Top 40	AP	Dover, 44622	(216) 343-7755
EAST LIVERPOOL					
WOHI-AM	1490	Oldies, Talk, Sports	ABC, SMN	East Liverpool, 43920	(216) 385-1490
WELA-FM	104.3	Country	ABC, SMN	East Liverpool, 43920	(216) 385-1490
EATON					
WCTM-AM	1130	Big Band, Farm	USA, IB, Sun, AB	West Alexandria 45381	(513) 456-3200
WGTZ-FM	92.9	Cont. Hits		Dayton, 45429	(513) 294-5858
EDGEWOOD					
WZOO-FM	102.5	Cont. Hits, Adult		Ashtabula, 44004	(216) 997-1025
ELYRIA					
WEOL-AM	930	MOR		Elyria,	(216) 322-3761
WNWV-FM	107.3	Smooth Jazz, Hits		Elyria, 44036	(216) 322-3761
FAIRBORN					
WMMX-AM	1110	Religious	USA	Fairborn, 45324	(513) 878-9000
FAIRFIELD					
WCNW-AM	1560	Religious		Fairfield, 45014	(513) 829-7700
WOFX-FM	94.9	Classic Rock		Dallas, TX, 75340	(513) 241-9500
FINDLAY					
WFIN-AM	1330	Adult Cont.	ABC	Findlay, 45840	(419) 422-4545
WKXA-FM	100.5	Cont. Hits	ABC	Findlay, 45840	(419) 422-4545
WLFC-FM	88.3	Cont. & Cl. Rock	UPI	Findlay, 45840	(419) 424-4571
FORT SHAWNEE					
WBUK-FM	107.5	N/A		Lima, 45802	
FOSTORIA					
WFOB-AM	1430	Adult Cont.	CBS	Fostoria, 44830	(419) 435-5666
WBVI-AM	96.7	Adult Cont.	U	Fostoria, 44840	(419) 435-5666

Continued from preceeding page

STATION	DIAL LOCATION	FORMAT	NTWK.	CITY, ZIP	TELEPHONE
FREDERICKTOWN					
WWBK-FM	98.3	Country	SMN	Frederick-town, 43019	(614) 694-1577
FREMONT					
WFRO-AM	900	Adult Cont.		Fremont, 43420	(419) 332-8218
WFRO-FM	99.1	Adult Cont.		Fremont, 43420	(419) 332-8218
GAHANNA					
WCVO-FM	104.9	Religious, Talk	CBN, USA	New Albany, 43054	(614) 855-9171
GALION					
WGLX-AM	1570	C&W	ABC	Galion, 44833	(419) 468-4664
WQLX-FM	102.3	Adult Cont.	ABC	Galion, 44833	(419) 468-4664
GALLIPOLIS					
WJEH-AM	990	Country		Gallipolis, 45631	(614) 446-3543
WGTR-FM	101.5	Classic Rock		Gallipolis, 45631	(614) 446-3543
GAMBIER					
WKCO-FM	91.9	Variety		Gambier, 43022	(614) 427-5412
GENEVA					
WKKY-FM	104.9	Adult Cont.		Geneva, 44041	(216) 466-1049
GEORGETOWN					
WAXZ-FM	97.7	Modern Country	ABC, AB.	George-town, 45121	(513) 378-6151
GIBSONBURG					
WRED-FM	95.7	Country	U	Perrysburg 43552	
GRANVILLE					
WDUB-FM	91.9	Classsic Rock		Granville, 43023	(614) 587-3008
GROVE CITY					
WWCD-FM	101.1	Variety		Columbus, 43207	(614) 444-9923
HAMILTON					
WGRR-FM	103.5	Oldies		Cincinnati, 45208	(513) 321-8900
WHSS-FM	89.5	Rock, Edu.		Hamilton, 45013	(513) 887-4832
WMOH-AM	1450	News, Talk	MBS	Hamilton, 45011	(513) 863-1111
WZRZ-FM	96.5	90's & Classic. Rock		Hamilton, 45013	(513) 868-3696
HEATH					
WHTH-AM	790	Country	UPI, CNN	Newar, 43055	(614) 522-8171
HILLSBORO					
WSRW-AM	1590	Country, Gospel,		Hillsboro, 45133	(513) 393-1590
WSRW-FM	106.7	Country		Hillsboro, 45133	(513) 393-1590

CITY STATION	DIAL LOCATION	FORMAT	NTWK.	CITY, ZIP	TELEPHONE
HOLLAND					
WPOS-FM	102.3	Religious	AP	Holland, 43528	(419) 865-5551
IRONTON					
WIRO-FM	1230	Oldies		Ironton, 45638	(614) 532-1922
WMLV-FM	107.1	Easy Listen		Ironton, 45638	(614) 532-1922
WOUL-FM	89.1	Cl., Jazz, News		Athens, 45701	
JACKSON					
WLMJ-AM	1280	C&W		Jackson, 45640	(614) 286-2141
WCJO-FM	97.7	C&W		Jackson, 45640	(614) 286-2141
JEFFERSON					
WCVJ-FM	90.9	Christian, Edu.		Jefferson, 44047	(216) 294-3854
KENT					
WJMP-AM	1520	Oldies		Akron, 44309	(216) 673-2323
WNIR-FM	100.1	Talk	CBS	Akron, 44309	(216) 673-2323
WKSU-FM	89.7	Cl.al		Kent, 44242	(216) 672-3114
KENTON					
WKTN-FM	95.3	Adult Cont.	AP, AB	Kenton, 53326	(419) 675-2355
KETTERING					
WKET-FM	98.3	Edu., Cl. Rock		Kettering, 45429	(513) 296-7669
WLQT-FM	99.9	Adult Cont.	CBS	Dayton, 45202	(513) 229-2041
LANCASTER					
WFCO-FM	90.9	Religious		Lancaster, 43130	(614) 654-8556
WLOH-AM	1320	Talk, Local & CNN	AP	Lancaster, 43130	(614) 653-4373
WHOK-FM	95.5	Country	AP	Lancaster, 43130	(614) 837-9536
WSWZ-FM	103.5	Oldies	CBS	Lancaster, 43130	(614) 687-4949
LIMA					
WCIT-AM	940	News, TAlk	CBS, MSB	Lima, 45802	(419) 228-9248
WLSR-FM	104.9	Cont. & Cl. Rock	NBC	Lima, 45802	(419) 228-9248
WGLE-FM	90.7	Cl., Public Affrs.	APR, NPR,	Toledo, 43692	(419) 243-3091
WIMA-AM	1150	Adult Cont.	ABC	Lima, 45802	(419) 223-2060
WIMT-FM	102.1	Country	ABC	Lima, 45802	(419) 223-2060
WTGN-FM	97.7	Religious	AP	Lima, 45805	(419) 227-2525
LOGAN					
WLGN-AM	1510	Adult Cont.		Logan, 43148	(614) 385-2151
WLGN-FM	98.3	Country		Logan, 43148	(614) 385-2151

CITY STATION	DIAL LOCATION	FORMAT	NTWK.	CITY, ZIP	TELEPHONE
LONDON					
WCKX-FM	106.3	Urban Cont., Bladk		Columbus, 43215	(614) 464-0020
LORAIN					
WRKG-AM	1380	Country, Gospel		Lorain, 44052	(216) 244-1380
WZLE-FM	104.9	Religious	ABC	Lorain, 44052	(216) 244-1380
MANCHESTER					
WAGX-FM	101.3	N/A		Cincinnati, 45202	(606) 635-3611
MANSFIELD					
WAPQ-FM	98.7	Adult Cont., Rock		Mansfield, 44906	(419) 747-9870
WMAN-AM	1400	Talk, News, Info.	ABC, NBC, MBS, CBS, W	Mansfield, 44901	(419) 529-2211
WYHT-FM	105.3	Top 40	ABC, NBC, MBS, CBS, W	Mansfield, 44901	(419) 529-2211
WOSV-FM	91.7	Classical	APR	Columbus, 43210	(614) 292-9678
WVMC-FM	90.7	Reliogious	APR	Mansfield, 44907	(419) 756-5651
WVNO-FM	106.1	Adult Cont.		Mansfield, 44906	(419) 529-5900
MARIETTA					
WBRJ-AM	910	News, Talk	AP, AB	Marietta, 45750	(614) 373-0910
WEYQ-FM	102.1	Cont. Hits	CBS	Marietta, 45750	(614) 373-0910
WMOA-AM	1490	Easy Listen	ABC	Marietta, 45750	(614) 373-1490
WMRT-FM	88.3	Cl., News, Talk, Jazz	ABC	Marietta, 45750	(614) 374-4800
WCMO-FM	98.5	Classic & Current Rock		Marietta, 45750	(614) 374-4802
MARION					
WDIF-FM	94.3	Adult Cont.		Marion, 43302	(614) 387-9343
WMRN-AM	1490	Adult Cont.	M	Marion, 43302	(614) 383-1131
WMRN-FM	106.9	Cont. Country	M	Marion, 43302	(614) 383-1131
MARYSVILLE					
WUCO-AM	1270	Oldies	U, AN	Marysville, 43040	(513) 644-1160
WWHT-FM	105.7	Dance		Dublin, 43017	(614) 846-9858
MASSILLON					
WTIG-AM	990	Adult Talk		Massillon, 44646	(216) 837-9900
MIAMISBURG					
WFCJ-FM	93.7	Religious, News	M	Dayton, 45449	(513) 866-2471

CITY STATION	DIAL LOCATION	FORMAT	NTWK.	CITY, ZIP	TELEPHONE
MIDDLEPORT-POMEROY					
WMPO-AM	1390	Country	ABC	Middleport 45760	(614) 992-6485
WMPO-FM	92.1	Adult Cont.	ABC	Middleport 45760	(614) 992-6485
MIDDLETOWN					
WPFB-AM	910	Music of your Life		Middle-town, 45044	(513) 422-3625
WPFB-FM	105.9	Country	SMN, MBS	Middle-town, 45044	(513) 422-3625
MILFORD					
WAQZ-FM	107.1	Rock		Hamilton, 45013	(513) 248-1072
MILLERSBURG					
WKLM-FM	95.3	Adult Cont.	ABC	Millersburg 44654	(216) 674-1953
MONTPELIER					
WLZZ-FM	89.1	N/A		Angola, IN 46703	
MORROW					
WLMH-FM	89.1	Edu.		Morrow, 45152	(513) 899-3884
MT. VERNON					
WMVO-AM	1300	MOR, News, Talk	ABC, CNN	Mt. Vernon, 43050	(614) 397-1000
WQIO-FM	93.7	Cont. Hits	CNN	Mt. Vernon, 43050	(614) 397-1000
WNZR-FM	90.9	Religious		Mt. Vernon, 43050	(614) 397-1244
NAPOLEON					
WNDH-FM	103.1	Adult Cont.	CBS, AB.	Napoleon, 43545	(419) 592-8060
NELSONVILLE					
WSEO-FM	107.7	Cont. Hits	SMN	Nelsonville 45764	(614) 753-2154
WYNO-AM	1120	Country	U	Nelsonville 45701	(614) 592-2684
NEW BOSTON					
WIOI-AM	1010	Adult Cont.	NBC, MBS	New Boston, 45662	(614) 574-6255
NEW CONCORD					
WMCO-FM	90.7	Variety, Edu.		New Concord, 43762	(614) 826-8375
NEW LEXINGTON					
WWJM-FM	106.3	Cont. Hits	AP, W	New Lexington, 43764	(614) 342-1988
NEW PHILADELPHIA					
WNPQ-FM	95.9	N/A		Urichsville, 43058	

Continued on next page

CITY STATION	DIAL LOCATION	FORMAT	NTWK.	CITY, ZIP	TELEPHONE
NEWARK					
WCLT-AM	1430	Oldies, News, Talk	MBS, ABN	Newark, 43058	(614) 345-4004
WCLT-FM	100.3	Country	MBS, ABN	Newark, 43058	(614) 345-4004
WNKO-FM	101.7	Adult Cont. Hits	UPI, CNN	Newark, 43055	(614) 522-8171
NILES					
WNRB-AM	1540	Urban		Niles, 44446	(216) 652-4443
WNCD-FM	106.1	Classic Rock		Niles, 44446	(216) 652-4443
NORTH BALTIMORE					
WHMQ-FM	107.7	Cont. Country		Findlay, 45839	(419)425-1077
NORTH RIDGEVILLE					
WJTB-AM	1040	Urban Cont.	UPI	Elyria, 44035	(216) 327-1844
NORWALK					
WVAC-AM	1510	Adult 40s-60s	CNN	Norwalk, 44857	(419) 668-8151
WLKR-FM	95.3	MOR, Adult Cont.	ABC	Norwalk, 44857	(419) 668-8151
OBERLIN					
WOBC-FM	91.5	Variety, Edu.	AP	Oberlin, 44074	(216) 775-8107
WOBL-AM	1320	Cont. C&W	AP	Oberlin, 44074	(216) 774-1320
ONTARIO					
WRGM-AM	1140	MOR	ABC	Mansfield, 44906	(419) 529-5900
OTTAWA					
WQTL-FM	106.3	Classic Rock	W, AB	Ottawa, 45875	(419) 523-4020
OXFORD					
WMUB-FM	88.5	Big Band, Jazz, News	NPR, AP, APR	Oxford, 45056	(513) 529-5885
WOXY-FM	97.7	Mod. Rock		Oxford, 45056	(513) 523-4114
PAINESVILLE					
WBKC-AM	1460	News, Talk, Adult Cont.	AP	Painesville 44077	(216) 352-1460
PARMA					
WCCD-AM	1000	Religious	USA	Cleveland, 44133	(216) 237-3300
PAULDING					
WERT-FM	99.7	Adult Cont.	SMN	Haviland, 45851	(419) 399-2053
PIQUA					
WPTW-AM	1570	Adult Stds.	U, ABN	Piqua, 45356	(513) 773-3513
WCLR-FM	95.7	Easy Cont.	U, ABN	Piqua, 45356	(513) 773-3513
PORT CLINTON					
WXKR-FM	94.5	Classic Rock	ABC	Northwood 43619	(419) 693-9957

Continued on next page

CITY STATION	DIAL LOCATION	FORMAT	NTWK.	CITY, ZIP	TELEPHONE
PORTSMOUTH					
WNXT-AM	1260	Country, Talk	ABC	Ports-mouth, 45662	(614) 353-1161
WNXT-FM	99.3	Classic Rock	ABC	Ports-mouth, 45662	(614) 353-1161
WOHP-FM	88.3	Religious, Talk	CNN	Cedarville, 45314	(513) 766-7815
WPAY-AM	1400	Soldid Gold	CBS	Ports-mouth, 45662	(614) 353-5176
WPAY-FM	104.1	Country	CBS, U	Ports-mouth, 45662	(614) 353-5176
PROCTORVILLE					
WMEJ-FM	91.9	Easy Listen		Huntington WV, 25777	(614) 867-5333
SALEM					
WSOM-AM	600	Nost.		Salem, 44460	(216) 337-9544
WQXK-FM	105.1	Country	U	Salem, 44460	(216) 337-9544
SANDUSKY					
WLEC-AM	1450	MOR	MBS, CBS, NBC	Sandusky, 44870	(419) 626-2000
WCPZ-FM	102.7	Cont. Hits	MBS, CBS, NBC	Sandusky, 44870	(419) 626-2000
SHADYSIDE					
WEEL-FM	95.7	Rock	SMN	Wheeling, WV, 26003	(314) 233-9335
SHELBY					
WSWR-FM	100.1	Oldies	AP	Shelby, 44875	(419) 347-9797
SIDNEY					
WMVR-AM	1080	Adult Cont.	MBS, ABC	Sidney, 45365	(513) 498-1055
WMVR-FM	105.5	Adult Cont.	MBS, ABC	Sidney, 45365	(513) 498-1055
SPRINGFIELD					
WAZU-FM	102.9	Cont.& Cl. Rock		Dayton, 45202	(513) 223-9445
WBLY-AM	1600	Hits of 50s-70s		Springfield 45502	(513) 399-4955
WEEC-FM	100.7	Religious	USA, AP, M	Springfield 45504	(513) 399-7837
WIZE-AM	1340	Adult Cont.		Springfield 45503	(513) 399-4955
WUSO-FM	89.1	Jazz, Cl., Blues		Springfield 45501	(513) 327-7026

Continued on next page

CITY STATION	DIAL LOCATION	FORMAT	NTWK.	CITY, ZIP	TELEPHONE
STEUBENVILLE					
WDIG-AM	950	Oldies		Steuben-ville, 43952	(614) 264-7771
WSTV-AM	1340	News, Talk	NBC, MBS	Steuben-ville, 43952	(614) 283-4747
WRKY-FM	103.5	Cont. Hits	NBC, MBS	Steuben-ville, 43952	(614) 283-4747
STREETBORO					
WSTB-FM	91.5	Heavy Rock, Metal	MBS	Streets-boro, 44471	(216) 626-4906
STRUTHERS					
WKTL-FM	90.7	Variety		Struthers, 44471	(216) 755-1435
SYLVANIA					
WWWM-FM	105.5	Adult Cont.		Oregon, 43616	(419) 691-1470
TIFFIN					
WHEI-FM	93.3	Variety		Tiffin, 44883	(419) 448-2282
WTTF-AM	1600	Adult Cont.	ABC, AB	Tiffin, 44883	(419) 447-2212
WTTF-FM	103.7	Adult Cont.	ABC, AB	Tiffin, 44883	(419) 447-2212
TOLEDO					
WCWA-AM	1230	Oldies		Toledo, 43604	(419) 248-2627
WIOT-FM	104.7	Cont.& Cl. Rock	NBC	Toledo, 43604	(419) 248-2627
WGTE-FM	91.3	Cl., Pub. Affrs.	APR, NPR	Toledo, 43692	(419) 243-3091
WOTL-FM	90.3	Religious		Toledo, 43607	(419) 537-1505
WSPD-AM	1370	News, RAlk	NBC	Toledo, 43602	(419) 244-8321
WLQR-FM	101.5	Adult Cont.	NBC	Toledo, 43602	(419) 244-8321
WTOD-AM	1560	Cl.& Cont. Country	ABC	Toledo, 43614	(419) 385-2507
WVKS-FM	92.5	Cont. Hlts		Toledo, 43615	(419) 531-1681
WVOI-AM	1520	Black		Toledo, 43613	(419) 243-7052
WWWM-AM	1470	Adult Cont.	U, SMN	Oregon, 43616	(419) 691-1470
WXTS-FM	88.3	Jazz		Toledo, 43620	(419) 244-6875
WXUT-FM	88.3	Variety. Edu.		Toledo, 43606	(419) 537-4172
TROY					
WTRJ-FM	96.9	News, Adult Cont.	SMN	Troy, 45373	(513) 339-2505

Continued on next page

CITY STATION	DIAL LOCATION	FORMAT	NTWK.	CITY, ZIP	TELEPHONE
URICHSVILLE					
WBTC-AM	1540	News, Talk, Oldies	CBS	Urichsville, 44683	(614) 922-2700
WTUZ-FM	99.9	Country	U, CNN	Urichsville, 44683	(216) 339-2222
UNIVERSITY HTS					
WUJC-FM	88.7	Variety	CNN	Cleveland, 44118	(216) 397-4437
UPPER ARLINGTON					
WRVF-FM	98.9	Adult Cont.	CNN	Columbus, 43215	(614) 488-4321
UPPER SANDUSKY					
WYNT-FM	95.9	Adult Cont.	NBC	Upper Sandusky, 43351	(513) 399-5300
URBANA					
WUHS-FM	91.7	Adult Cont., Rock		Urbana, 43078	(513) 653-3517
VAN WERT					
WBYR-FM	98.9	Cl. Rock	ABC, U	Ft. Wayne, IN 46856	(219) 4209890
WERT-AM	1220	Oldies	AB	Van Wert, 45891	(419) 238-1220
WAPAKONETA					
WZOQ-FM	92.1	Cont. Hits	ABC	Lima, 45804	(419) 222-9292
WARREN					
WANR-AM	1570	News, Talk, Urban	ABC	Warren, 44481	(216) 373-1570
WRRO-AM	1440	Oldies	ABC	Warren, 44481	(216) 373-1440
WASHINGTON COURT HOUSE					
WOFR-AM	1250	C&W, Farm	AB	Washington Court House, 43160	(614) 335-0941
WCHO-FM	105.5	C&W	AB	Washington Court House, 43160	(614) 335-0941
WAVERLY					
WXIC-AM	660	S. Gospel	ABC	Waverly, 45690	(614) 947-2166
WXIZ-FM	100.9	Country	ABC	Waverly, 45690	(614) 947-2166
WELLSTON					
WYPC-AM	1330	Country	CBS	Jackson, 45640	(614) 286-3023
WKOV-FM		Adult Cont.	CBS	Jackson, 45640	(614) 286-3023
WEST CARROLLTON					
WQRP-FM	88.1	Religious	USA	Dayton, 45409	(513) 298-4044
WEST CHESTER					
WLHS-FM	89.9	Edu.		West Chester, 45069	(513) 874-4699

Continued on next page

CITY STATION	DIAL LOCATION	FORMAT	NTWK.	CITY, ZIP	TELEPHONE
WEST UNION					
WRAC-FM	103.1	Adult. Cont.	U	West Union, 45693	(513) 544-9722
WVXM-FM	89.5	Jazz, News, Info.	NPR, OEB	Cincinnati, 45207	(513) 745-3738
WESTERVILLE					
WBBY-FM	103.9	N/A		Westerville ,43081	
WOBN-FM	101.5	Cl. & Cont. Rock		Westerville 43081	(614) 898-1557
WILBERFORCE					
WCSU-FM	88.9	Urban Cont., Jazz		Wilber- force, 45384	(513) 376-6371
WILLOUGHBY-EASTLAKE					
WELW-AM	1330	Btfl. Music, Oldies		Willoughby 44094	(216) 946-1330
WILMINGTON					
WKFI-AM	1090	Farm, Talk	ABC, MBS, NBC, APR	Wilming- ton, 45177	(513) 382-1608
WSWO-FM	102.3	Adult Cont.	ABC	Wilming- ton, 45177	(513) 382-1608
WOOSTER					
WBZW-FM	107.7	New Adult Cont.	AP	Wooster, 44691	(216) 262-0503
WCWS-FM	90.9	Variety	AP	Wooster, 44691	(216) 287-2240
WKVX-AM	960	Oldies	AP, SMN	Wooster, 44691	(216) 264-5122
WQKT-FM	104.5	C&W	AP, SMN	Wooster, 44691	(216) 264-5122
XENIA					
WBZI-AM	1500	Adult Cont.	AP, SMN	Xenia, 45385	(513) 372-3531
WDJK-FM	95.3	C&W	SMN, U	Xenia, 45385	(513) 372-3531
YELLOW SPRINGS					
WYSO-FM	91.3	News, Eclectic	APR, NPR, OEB	Yellow Springs, 45387	(513) 767-6420
YOUNGSTOWN					
WBBW-AM	1240	News, TAlk	CNN	Youngs- town, 44502	(216) 744-4421
WBBG-FM	93.3	Oldies	CNN	Youngs- town, 44502	(216) 744-4421
WGFT-AM	1500	Religious		Youngs- town, 44503	(216) 744-5115

Continued on next page

CITY STATION	DIAL LOCATION	FORMAT	NTWK.	CITY, ZIP	TELEPHONE
WHOT-AM	1390	Music of your Life		Youngstown, 44512	(216) 783-1000
WHOT-FM	101.1	Cont. Hits	AP	Youngstown, 44512	(216) 783-1000
WKBN-AM	570	News, Sports, Talk	NBC, MBS, NBC	Youngstown, 44501	(216) 782-1144
WBKN-FM	98.9	Soft Cont.	CBS	Youngstown, 44501	(216) 782-1144
WRQQ-AM	1470	Oldies		Youngstown, 44505	(216) 746-1330
WHTX-FM	95.9	Country, Rock		Youngstown, 44505	(216) 746-1330
WYSU-FM	88.5	Cl., Jazz, News	APR, NPR	Youngstown, 44555	(216) 742-3363
WYTN-FM	91.7	Religious	UPI	Youngstown, 44502	(216) 783-9986
ZANESVILLE					
WCVZ-FM	92.7	Religious, Talk	USA	Zanesville, 43701	(614) 455-3181
WHIZ-AM	1240	Adult Cont., News, Talk	NBC	Zanesville, 43701	(614) 452-5431
WHIZ-FM	102.5	Easy Listen, Talk	NBC	Zanesville, 43701	(614) 452-5431

QUESTION   What is the official name of the Ohio Turnpike ?

ANSWER   James W Shocknessy Ohio Turnpike,

QUESTION   Who invented the radar detector "fuzz buster"?

ANSWER   Dale Smith (Tipp City)

QUESTION   How many covered bridges remain in Ohio?

ANSWER   One hundred and thirty seven, (in 40 counties including Fairfield County with 16, the most.)

BOOKS ABOUT OHIO

TITLE, AUTHOR (PUBLISHER) $ PRICE

All About Ohio Almanac, by Harry Shay (Instant Info) $14.95
American Traveler: Ohio, by Irene S Korn (Smithmark) $7.98
Beauty of Ohio (LTA Pub) $9.95/$19.95
Cincinnati Today, by J Miles Wolf (A & M) $22.50
Columbus Today, by Edward Kremincki (A & M), $12.50

Images of Ohio, (LTA Pub) $6.95
Ohio: A Photo Celebration by Richard Celeste (Am Geo) $13.95
Ohio: Images of Wilderness, by Jerry Sieve (Westcliff) $12.98
Photo Album: Ohio's Canal Era, by Jack Giec (KSU) $35.00
Cleveland Architecture, (Arch Instiute Am) $14.95

Quilts: Ohio's Traditions, by Ricky Clark (Rutledge) $29.95
Cleveland: History 1796-1990, by Carol Miller (IU Press) $10.95
Encyclopedia Cleveland History, by D D VanTassel (IU) $42.95
Ohio & Its People, Geo Knepper (KST Press) $17.50
Amazing Ohio, by Damaine Vonada (Orange Frazer) $9.95

Cleveland in Picture Postcards, by R B Thompson (Vestal) $11.95
Haunted Ohio, by Chris Woodyard (Kestrel) $9.95
Haunted Ohio II, by Chris Woodyard (Kestrel) $9.95
Lake County Ohio, by Bari Smith (Smithmark) $4.98
Ohio Matters of Fact, by Damaine Vonada (Orange Frazer) $9.95

Ohio Pride: Roadside History, by Jeff Traylor(Backroads) $9.95
Ohio Trivia, by Ernie Couch (Rutledge) $5.95
Raising Kids Cheap Greater Cleveland,by L S Richardson, $7.95
Birder's Guide to the Cinci Tristate, by Folzenlogen, $ 8.95
Birds of Ohio, by Bruce Peterjohn (Indiana Univ Press) $49.95.

Greater Cleveland Garden Guide, by S McClure (Gray & Co) $14.95
Canoeing & Kayaking Ohio, by S Gillen (Countryman Press) $15.00
Dive Charts to Lake Erie, Midwest Explorer's League $6.00
Chartbook & Cruising Guides: Lake Erie, (Richardsons' Pub)$63.95
Great Fishing in Lake Erie, by Will Elliott (Stackpole Book)$14.

Cleveland's Public Golf Courses, by J Tidyman(Gray & Co) $12.95
25 Bicycle Tours in Ohio, by S Walters (Countryman Press)$11.95
50 Hikes in Ohio, by R Ramey (Backcountry Publications) $12.95
Backpack Loops & Long Day Trail Hikes, by R Ruchhoft $11.95
Hiking Ohio: Scenic Trails, by R Folzenlogen (Willow) $12.95

Cleveland Sports Legacy 1900-1945, by M Hodermarsky $15.00
Cleveland Stadium: Sixty Yrs, by J Toman (Cleveland)$19.95
Ohio Sports Almanac, by J Borgman (Orange Frazer Press) $10.95
Sports in Cleveland: An Illus. History, by J Grabowski $14.95
Bargain Hunting in Columbus, by D Keri-Brown (Lotus Press)$12.95

Fishing Guide:Western Ohio, by J MacCracken (RecGuide) $2.95
Fishing Guide:Eastern Ohio, by J MacCracken (Rec Guide)$3.95
Fishing Guide:Northwest Ohio, by MacCracken (Rec Guide)$3.95
Fishing Guide:Northern Ohio, by JMacCracken (Rec Guide)$2.95
Fishing Guide:N Central Ohio, by MacCracken (Rec Guide)$2.95

Fishing Guide:Northeast Ohio, by MacCracken (Rec Guide)$2.95
Fishing Guide:NE Central Ohio,by MacCracken (Rec Guide)$2.95
Fishing Guide:Lake Erie,by J MacCracken (Rec Guide) $4.95
Ohio Off the Beaten Path, by George Zimmerman (Globe)$9.95
Cleveland's Finest Restaurants, by Turizianni (Rest Int $7.95

Cincinnati Recipe Treasury, by M DuSablon, (OSU) $8.95
Cincinnati's Finest Restaurants, by Turizianni (Rest) $6.95
Kids and the Law, Ohio, by J Gilchrist (ProSe Pub)$8.95
Ohio Dissolution of Marriage, by LawPak, (LawPak) $23.95
Writing in Ohio, by LaVern Hall, (Writer's World Pres) $11.95

Continued on next page

Camper's Guide to Indiana & Ohio Parks, by M Little(Gulf) $15
Life in the Slow Lane: 50 Backroad Tours, by J Taylor $14.95
Ohio: Off the Beaten Path, by G Zimmerman (Globe Pequot)$9.95
Ohio State Parks,by Art Weber (Glovebox Guidebooks) $14.95
Other Peoples Business: Ohio's Best Factory Tours by J Wave

Particular Places: Traveler's Guide, by Orange Fazer Press $14
Visits to Ohio Mounds, by Vimach Assoc (Vimach Assoc) $5.95
City Maps of Ohio: Complete, (Pub Dist Service) $16.95
Ohio Atlas & Gazetteer, (DeLorne Mapping Company) $14.95
Best Recipes of Inns & Restaurants: Ohio, (Amherst) $11.95

How to Form Your Own Corp, by P Williams (Gains) $24.95
Ohio Landlord/Tenant Lawpak, LawPak, Inc $9.95
Ohio Name Change LawPak, LawPak, Inc $15.95
Starting and Operating a Business in Ohio, Ernst & Young $21.95
Cleveland for Kids, Cleveland Arts Consortium $4.95

Color Me Cleveland, by T Hudson (Gray & Co Publishers) $4.95
First Hunters: Ohio's Paleo-Indian Artifacts, by L Hothem $13.95
Indian Flints of Ohio, by Lar Hothem (Hothem House Pub) $11.95
Indian Mounds in the Middle Ohio Valley, by S Woodward $9.95
Visits to Ohio Mounds, by M Lutz (Vimach Assoc) $5.95

Hudson:A Survey of Historic Buildings, by L Newkirk, Editor $35.
Showplace of America: Cleveland's Euclid Ave, by J Cigliano$45.
Cleveland:The Making of a City, by W Rose (KSU) $75.00
Cinci Observed: Architecture & History by J Clubbe (OSU) $19.95
Haunted Ohio II, by Chris Woodyard (Kestrel Pub) $9.95

Hudson's Heritage(Ohio) by G Izant, (KSU) $32.50
An Ohio State Profile: A Year in the Life, by J Ware(OSU)$10.95
Ohio's Western Reserve: A Regional Reader,byLupold $14.00
Benchmark Ohio, 1991, by W Shkurti, Editor (OSU) $16.95
Ohio County Profiles, by Ohio Public Expenditure Council $10.95

Rebuilding Cleveland: The Cleveland Foundation, by D Title$30.50
Fishes of Ohio, by M Trautman (OSU) $63.00
Idle Weeds: The Life of an Ohio Sandstone Ridge, (OSU) $13.75
Inland Island, by J Johnson (OSU) $11.95
Woody Plants of Ohio: Trees, by E Braum (OSU) $19.50

Fishing Guide:Northern Ohio, by J MacCracken (Rec. Guide) $18.95
Fishing Guide:Southern Ohio, by J MacCracken (Rec Guide)$17.95
Fishing Guide:SouthwestOhio, by J MacCracken (Rec Guide) $3.95
Fishing Guide:Southern Ohio, by J MacCracken (Rec Guide) $2.95
Fishing Guide:Central Ohio, by J MacCracken (Rec Guide) $2.95

Eastern Great Lakes(Ohio, Indy), by Aylesworth $ 6.95
Ohio Puzzle Map,(Globe Pequot) $7.95
Ohio, by Terry Allen (WSU Art Gallery) $5.00
Ohio, by Dottie Brown (Lerner) $12.95
Ohio, by Allen Carpenter (New Enhancement) $19.93

Ohio & Other State Greats, Carole Marsh (Ohio Bks) $19.95
Ohio Automotive Directory, by T L Spelman (Auto) $24.95
Ohio Bandits, Bushwackers, by Carole Marsh (Gallopade)$14.95
Ohio Bookstore Book: A Guide, by Carole Marsh (Ohio Bk)$19.95
Ohio Business Directory, by Am Bus Dir (Am Busn) $ N/A

Ohio Canal Era: A Case Study, by Scheiber (Ohio U Pr) $15.95
Ohio Cemeteries Addendum, by Klaiber (Genealogical) $25.00
Ohio Cemetery Records, by NW Geneology Qrtly $30.00
Ohio Constitution Handbook, by T Swisher (Banks) $45.00
Ohio Consumer Law Handbook, by P Herdbeg (Banks) $40.00

Ohio Country between the Years, by C Slocum (Heritage) $22.50
Ohio "Crinkum-Crankum", A Funny Wordbook, by C Marsh $29.95
Ohio Dingbats:A Fun Book, by C Marsh (Ohio Bks) $19.95
Ohio Family Farm Heritage, by R Burton (Ferguson) $39.00
Ohio Festival Fun, by C Marsh (Gallopade) $29.95

Continued on next page

Continued from preceeding page

Ohio Fishing Maps by C J Puetz (Cnty Maps) $17.95
Ohio:From Territory to Statehood, by League of Women $10.00
Ohio:From Wilderness to Territory, by League of Women $10.00
Ohio Golfers Guide, by R Rasmussen (RSG) $6.95
Ohio Governments Perform Standards, by Greg Michels $ N/A

Ohio Guide, by Fed Writer's Proj (Somerset) $95.00
Ohio Hot Air Balloon Mystery, by C Marsh (Gallope) $14.95
Ohio in Century Three:OWL,by R Pearson (Ohio Hist Soc) $2.00
Ohio in Perspective, by K Morgan (Morgan Quinto) $16.00
Ohio in Words and Pictures, by D Fradin (Young) $17.27

Ohio Jeopardy! Ans & Quest, by C Marsh (Marsh) $19.95
Ohio Jography A Fun Run Throu Our State, by C Marsh $29.95
Ohio Kids' Cookbook, by C Marsh (Ohio Bks) $14.95
Ohio Law for Everyone, by S Wells (Law for Lay Serv) $17.95
Ohio Lib Book:Guide to Unusual Collect, C Marsh $19.95

Ohio Living Will, by W Jenkins, (Banks) $35.00
Ohio Media Book, by C Marsh (Ohio Bks) $29.95
Ohio Media Directory, (Brackemyre) $29.95
Ohio Mystery Van, by C Marsh (Gallope) $14.95
Ohio Off the Beaten Path, by G Zimmerman (Globe) $9.95

Ohio: Our State, by R Howe (Roblen) $7.95
Ohio: The Ohio Guide, by Fed Writer Proj (Am Guide) $89.00
Ohio Timeline: A Chronology of Ohio Hist, by C Maesh $14.95
Ohio Town, by H Santmyer (HarpC) $14.45
Ohio University, Then and Now, by D Dry (Harmony) $39.95

Ohio Valley German Biogr Ind, by D Tolzman (Heritage) $17.00
Ohio Women, P O'Connor (Bottom Dog) $8.00
Ohio Women:Earthbound, by I Bolls (Ohio Writers) $8.00
Ohio Zen Poems, by D Conkle (Bottom Dog Pr) $8.00
Ohio's Ghostly Greats, by D Gerrick (Dayton Labs) $4.95

Ohio's Heritage, by J Burke (Gibbs Smith) $19.95
Ohio's Most Devastating! Disaster, by C Marsh (Ohio Bks)$19.95
Ohio's Top Twenty Wrestlers, (Prof Reports) $4.95
Ohio's Unsolved Mysteries, by C Marsh (Ohio Bks) $19.95
Ohio's Western Reserve, by Harry Lupold (KSU) $14.00

Ohio, by Mary Fox, (Watts) $10.40
Ohio, by Deborah Kent (PLB) $26.60
Ohio, by Kathleen Thompson, (Raintree) $17.35
Ohio, Collected Works of Writers, (Rptr Serv) $98.00
Ohio, Collected Works of Writers-Cincinnati, (Reptr) $98.00

The State Library of Ohio

65 South Front Street, Columbus, Ohio 43266-0334
614/644-7061

PURPOSE

The State Library of Ohio serves as a research library for Ohio's government, a specialized resource for the Ohio public, and as a catalyst for the development of library and information services to Ohio's libraries and citizens.

Founded in 1817 with a collection of 509 books, the State Library of Ohio was established to provide research and information services to state government and agencies. In 1895 the State Library opened its collection to the citizens of Ohio.

Since its establishment, the State Library has grown to a collection of more than 2 million books, journals, newspapers, and government documents. Through participation in various on-line networks and through the interlibrary loan network, the State Library provides materials to other libraries across the state and the nation.

In addition, the State Library acts as the liaison between state government and the libraries of Ohio. The State Library is responsible for administering the Federal Library Services and Construction Act (LSCA) funds, helping Ohio libraries to apply for grants, develop programs, and evaluate the results. The State Library also works to bring Ohio's library and information needs to the attention of state government.

The role of libraries has changed dramatically in recent years. As libraries and library services grow and develop, the role of the State Library continues to grow to meet the new needs and challenges.

AREAS OF SERVICE

Ohio citizens can take advantage of a range of specialized services at the State Library.

GOVERNMENT DOCUMENTS

The Documents Department, Ohio's only full federal Regional Depository library, contains more than 1.5 million state and federal documents, ensuring their permanent availability and access to Ohio citizens. The State Library regularly sends copies of state documents to other libraries throughout the state to provide local access.

GENEALOGY

The Genealogy Department houses more than 14,000 volumes and 5,000 microform records, focusing on materials for Ohio, the colonial states, and states surrounding Ohio. The Genealogy Department also assists patrons by compiling publications, such as *County by County in Ohio Genealogy*, which list various resources for researching a family genealogy and through computer access to important CD-ROM databases. In addition, the Department is a depository for the materials of the Daughters of the American Revolution.

SERVICE TO THE BLIND & PHYSICALLY HANDICAPPED

The Talking Book Department contracts with the Cincinnati and Cleveland regional libraries to serve the blind and physically handicapped citizens of Ohio. The Talking Book program loans books and magazines in braille, and in recorded form on disks and cassettes. The program, through the State Library, also loans cassette and record players.

Continued on next page

Continued from preceeding page

FIELD SERVICES

By contracting with the **Field Services Department**, Ohio libraries are able to provide their local residents with bookmobile service. Field Services also organizes the National Bookmobile Conference, the only national forum for bookmobile librarians and administrators.

OTHER SERVICES

CIRCULATION

Since 1895 the State Library of Ohio has provided public access to its specialized collections of books, periodicals, and journals. The State Library also serves the information needs of Ohio citizens by assisting local libraries with back-up reference services and by filling requests for materials through the interlibrary loan network.

REFERENCE & INFORMATION

Since 1817, meeting the information needs of state government has been a major responsibility of the State Library. Any member of the Ohio Legislature or state agency employee may use the full services of the State Library. Database searches, interlibrary loan, and research assistance are all available for any work-related request.

SPECIAL SERVICES

The **Technical Services Catalog Center** offers Ohio libraries cost-effective cataloging services, as well as the opportunity to acquire machine-readable records of library holdings. The Catalog Center also coordinates the CD-ROM based Ohio Shared Catalog, which enables its members to increase their resources by sharing and combining their current catalogs of materials.

The **Conservation/Preservation Section** consults with Ohio libraries on conservation/preservation issues and disaster preparedness.

State Library Consultants work with public and institutional libraries to plan the expansion or the development of new services, resource sharing and library development. Consultants also assist libraries in applying for Library Services and Construction Act (LSCA) grants and in interpreting and complying with federal legislation, such as the Americans with Disabilities Act.

The Planning, Evaluation and Research Department annually collects and compiles information from libraries across the state to produce the *Directory of Ohio Libraries* and the *Statistics of Ohio Libraries.*

AIRPORTS & AIRLINES - OHIO

TOLL-FREE TELEPHONES
TEL.
1-800

AKRON/CANTON

American	433-7300
Continental	525-0280
Delta	221-1212
Northwest	225-2525
United	241-6522
USAir	428-4322

CINCINNATI

American	433-7300
Continental	525-0280
Continental Express	525-0280
Delta	221-1212
Delta Connection	345-3400
Northwest	225-2525
Northwest Express	525-0280
TWA	221-6522
USAir	428-4322
USAir Express	428-4322
United	241-6522
United Express	241-6522

CLEVELAND

American	433-7300
Air Canada	776-3000
Continental	525-0280
Continental Express	525-0280
Delta	221-1212
Delta Connection	345-3400
Northwest	225-2525
Northwest Express	525-0280
Southwest	531-5601
TWA	221-2000
USAir	428-4322
USAir Express	428-4322
United	241-6522
United Express	241-6522

COLUMBUS

American	433-7300
American West	247-5692
Canadian Partner	426-7000
Chrisman	535-9542
Comair	354-9822
Continental	525-0280
Delta	221-1212
Northwest	225-2525
Skyway	452-2022
Southwest	531-5601
TWA	221-2000
United	241-6522
USAir	428-4322

DAYTON

American	433-7300
Continental	525-0280
Canadian Airline Intl.	426-7000
Delta	221-1212
Northwest	225-2525
TWA	221-6522
United	241-6522
USAir	428-4322

Toledo

American	433-7300
Continental	525-0280
Delta	221-1212
Northwest	225-2525
United	241-6522
USAir	428-4322

OHIO CONVENTION & VISITORS BUREAUS AND TOURISM BOARDS

Akron/Summit Convention and
Visitors Bureau
Cascade Plaza Sublevel
Akron, OH 44308
(216) 376-4254
1-800-245-4254
Fax (216) 376-4253

Ashtabula County Convention and
Visitors Bureau
36 W. Walnut St.
Jefferson, OH 44047
(216) 576-4707

Athens County Convention and
Visitors Bureau
667 E. State St.
P.O. Box 1019
Athens, OH 45701
(614) 592-1819
1-800-878-9767 (U.S.)
Fax (614) 593-7365

Auglaize and Mercer Counties
Convention and Visitors Bureau
112 S. Front St., Suite 2
St. Marys, OH 45885
(419) 394-1294
1-800-860-4726

Bellevue Area Tourism and
Visitors Bureau
Box 63
Bellevue, OH 44811
(419) 483-5359
1-800-562-6978

Belmont County Tourism Council
Ohio Valley Mall
Unit #485
St. Clairsville, OH 43950
(614) 695-4359

Berlin Visitors Bureau
P.O. Box 177
Berlin, OH 44610
(216) 893-3467

Bowling Green Convention and
Visitors Bureau
163 N. Main St.
P.O. Box 31
Bowling Green, OH 43402
(419) 353-7945
Fax (419) 353-3693

Buckeye Lake Tourism Bureau
5192 Walnut Rd.
P.O. Box 27
Buckeye Lake, OH 43008
(614) 928-8843

Cambridge/Guernsey County Visitors
and Convention Bureau
2250 Southgate Parkway
P.O. Box 427
Cambridge, OH 43725
(614) 432-2022
1-800-933-5480
Fax (614) 432-5976

Canton/Stark County Convention and
Visitors' Bureau
229 Wells Ave. N.W.
Canton, OH 44703-2642
(216) 454-1439
1-800-533-4302 (U.S.)
Fax (216) 452-7786

Greater Cincinnati Convention and
Visitors Bureau
300 W. Sixth St.
Cincinnati, OH 45202
1-800-344-3445 (U.S. & Canada)
Fax (513) 621-2156

Clermont County Convention and
Visitors Bureau
4440 Glen-Este Withamsville Rd.
Cincinnati, OH 45245
(513) 753-7211
Fax (513) 753-7146

Convention and Visitors Bureau of
Greater Cleveland
3100 Terminal Tower
Tower City Center
Cleveland, OH 44113
(216) 621-8860
1-800-321-1004 (U.S. & Canada)
Fax (216) 621-5967

Columbiana County Visitors Bureau
130 W. Maple St.
Lisbon, OH 44432
(216) 424-9078
Fax (216) 424-9267

Greater Columbus Convention and
Visitors Bureau
10 W. Broad St., Suite 1300
Columbus, OH 43215
(614) 221-6623
1-800-354-COLS (2657)
Fax (614) 221-5618

CALL 1-800-BUCKEYE FOR OHIO TOURISM INFORMATION   Continued on next page

Continued from preceeding page

Coshocton County Convention and Visitors Bureau
P.O. Box 905
Coshocton, OH 43812
(614) 622-9315
1-800-338-4724 (U.S. & Canada)

Crawford County Visitors Bureau
P.O. Box 622
Bucyrus, OH 44820
(419) 562-4205

Dayton/Montgomery County Convention and Visitors Bureau
Chamber Plaza
5th & Main Sts.
Dayton, OH 45402-2400
(513) 226-8211
1-800-221-8234 (in OH)
1-800-221-8235 (outside OH)
Fax (513) 226-8294

Greater Defiance Area Tourism and Visitors Bureau, Inc.
P.O. Box 7010
Defiance, OH 43512
(419) 782-0864
1-800-686-GDTB (4382)
Fax (419) 782-4212

Dublin Convention and Visitors Bureau
129 S. High St.
Dublin, OH 43017
(614) 792-7666
1-800-245-8387 (U.S. & Canada)
Fax (614) 889-2888

Erie County Visitors and Convention Bureau
231 W. Washington Row
Sandusky, OH 44870
(419) 625-2984
1-800-255-ERIE (U.S. & Canada)
Fax (419) 625-5009

Fairfield County Visitors and Convention Bureau
One North Broad
P.O. Box 2450
Lancaster, OH 43130
(614) 653-8251
1-800-626-1296

Fremont/Sandusky County Convention and Visitors Bureau
1510 E. State St.
P.O. Box 643
Fremont, OH 43420
(419) 332-4470
1-800-255-8070 (U.S. & Canada)
Fax (419) 332-4359

Gallia County/Ohio Valley Visitors Center
45 State St.
Gallipolis, OH 45631
(614) 446-6882
1-800-765-6482 (U.S. & Canada)

Geauga County Tourism Council, Inc.
P.O. Box 62
Chardon, OH 44024
(216) 564-7625

Geneva-on-the-Lake Convention and Visitors Bureau and Chamber of Commerce
5536 Lake Rd.
Geneva-on-the-Lake, OH 44041
(216) 466-8600

Greene County Convention and Visitors Bureau
3335 E. Patterson Rd.
Beavercreek, OH 45430
(513) 429-9100 or (513) 372-7655
Fax (513) 429-7726

Grove City Area Visitors and Convention Bureau
P.O. Box 261
Grove City, OH 43123
(614) 875-9762 (Chamber of Commerce)
Fax (614) 875-1510 (call ahead before faxing)

Hancock County Convention and Visitors Bureau
123 E. Main Cross St.
Findlay, OH 45840
(419) 422-3315
1-800-424-3315 (U.S.)
Fax (419) 422-9508

Harrison County Tourism Council
c/o Courthouse
Cadiz, OH 43907
(614) 942-3350
Fax (614) 942-3034

Hocking County Tourism Association
P.O. Box 350
Logan, OH 43138
(614) 385-6836
1-800-589-7503
Fax (614) 385-7259

Jackson Area Tourist & Convention Bureau, Inc.
210 Main St.
Jackson, OH 45640
(614) 286-2722

Knox County Visitors Bureau
236 S. Main St.
Mount Vernon, OH 43050
(614) 392-6102
1-800-837-KCVB (5282)
Fax (614) 393-1590

Lake County Visitors Bureau, Inc.
34835 Ridge Rd.
Willoughby, OH 44094
(216) 951-5700
1-800-368-LAKE (5253)
Fax (216) 951-4545

Greater Lawrence County Area Convention and Visitors Bureau
101 Sand & Solida Rd.
P.O. Box 488
South Point, OH 45680
(614) 894-3838 or (614) 532-9991
Fax (614) 894-3836

Continued on next page

Continued from preceeding page

Licking County Convention and
Visitors Bureau
50 W. Locust St.
P.O. Box 702
Newark, OH 43058-0702
(614) 345-8224
1-800-589-8224
Fax (614) 345-5141

Lima/Allen County Convention and
Visitors Bureau
147 N. Main St.
Lima, OH 45801
(419) 222-6045
Fax (419) 229-0266

Greater Logan County Area
Convention and Tourist Bureau
100 S. Main St.
Bellefontaine, OH 43311
(513) 599-5121
Fax (513) 599-2411

Lorain County Visitors Bureau
611 Broadway Ave.
Lorain, OH 44052
(216) 245-5282
1-800-334-1673
Fax (216) 245-5342

Mansfield/Richland County Convention
and Visitors Bureau
52 Park Ave. W.
Mansfield, OH 44902
(419) 525-1300
1-800-642-8282 (U.S. & Canada)
Fax (419) 524-7722

Marietta Tourist and Convention Bureau
316 Third St.
Marietta, OH 45750
(614) 373-5178
1-800-288-2577 (U.S. & Canada)
Fax (614) 373-7808

Marion Area Convention and
Visitors Bureau
206 S. Prospect St.
Marion, OH 43302
(614) 382-2181
Fax (614) 387-7722

Medina County Convention and
Visitors Bureau
124 W. Lafayette Rd.
Suite 100
Medina, OH 44256
(216) 722-5502
Fax (216) 723-4713

Meigs County Chamber of Commerce
200 E. Second St.
Pomeroy, OH 45769
(614) 992-5005
Fax (614) 992-7942

Mercer County
(see Auglaize & Mercer Counties CVB)

Miami County Visitors and
Convention Bureau
3147 North Co. Rd. 25-A
P.O. Box 159
Troy, OH 45373
(513) 339-1044
1-800-348-8993 (U.S. & Ontario, Canada)
Fax (513) 339-4541

Monroe County Tourism Council
P.O. Box 643
Woodsfield, OH 43793
(614) 472-5499
Fax (614) 472-0745

North Ridgeville Visitors Bureau
7307 Avon Belden Road
North Ridgeville, OH 44039
(216) 327-3737
Fax (216) 327-3737 (call before faxing)

Ottawa County Visitors Bureau
109 Madison St.
Port Clinton, OH 43452
(419) 734-4386
1-800-441-1271 (U.S.)
Fax (419) 734-9798

Oxford Visitors and Convention Bureau
118 W. High St.
Oxford, OH 45056
(513) 523-8687

Perry County Convention and
Visitors Bureau
116 S. Main St.
New Lexington, OH 43764
(614) 342-3547
Fax (614) 342-5305

Pickaway County Visitors Bureau
135 W. Main St.
P.O. Box 462
Circleville, OH 43113
(614) 474-4923

Portage County Convention &
Visitor's Bureau
173 S. Chillicothe Rd.
Aurora, OH 44202
(216) 562-3355
1-800-648-6342

Portsmouth Convention and Visitors
Bureau
P.O. Box 509
Portsmouth, OH 45662
(614) 353-1116
Fax (614) 353-5824

Reynoldsburg Visitors Bureau
7374 E. Main St., Suite 1
Reynoldsburg, OH 43068
(614) 866-4888
Fax (614) 860-0002

Ross/Chillicothe Convention and
Visitors Bureau
5 W. Water St.
P.O. Box 353
Chillicothe, OH 45601
(614) 775-0900

Continued on next page

Continued from preceeding page

Seneca County Convention and Visitors Bureau
37 S. Washington St.
Tiffin, OH 44883
(419) 447-5866

Springfield Area Convention and Visitors Bureau
333 N. Limestone St., Suite 201
Springfield, OH 45501
(513) 325-7621
Fax (513) 325-8765

Greater Steubenville Convention and Visitors Bureau
P.O. Box 278
Steubenville, OH 43952
(614) 282-6226
Fax (614) 282-6285

Sugarcreek Tourist Bureau and Information Center
106 W. Main St.
P.O. Box 158
Sugarcreek, OH 44681
(216) 852-4113 or 852-2223

Greater Toledo Convention and Visitors Bureau
401 Jefferson Ave.
Toledo, OH 43604
(419) 321-6404
1-800-243-4667 (U.S.)
Fax (419) 255-7731

Trumbull County Convention and Visitors Bureau Inc.
650 Youngstown-Warren Rd.
Niles, OH 44446
(216) 544-3468
1-800-672-9555 (U.S. & Canada)
Fax (216) 544-5615

Tuscarawas County Convention and Visitors Bureau
P.O. Box 926
New Philadelphia, OH 44663
(216) 364-5453
1-800-527-3387 (U.S.)

Van Wert Area Convention and Visitors Bureau
118 W. Main St.
Van Wert, OH 45891
(419) 238-4390

Warren County Convention and Visitors Bureau
777 Columbus Ave.
Lebanon, OH 45036
(513) 933-1138
1-800-433-1072 (U.S. & Canada)
Fax (513) 933-2912

Wayne County Visitor and Convention Bureau
P.O. Box 77
237 S. Walnut St.
Wooster, OH 44691
(216) 264-1800
1-800-36-AMISH (362-6474)
(outside area code 216)

Westerville Visitors and Convention Bureau
5 W. College Ave.
Westerville, OH 43081
(614) 794-0401
1-800-824-8461 (U.S. & Canada)
Fax (614) 882-2085

Williams County Visitors Bureau
Bryan Area Chamber of Commerce
138 S. Lynn St.
Bryan, OH 43506
(419) 636-2247

Wyandot County Visitors & Convention Bureau
P.O. Box 357
Upper Sandusky, OH 43351
(419) 294-3349

Youngstown/Mahoning County Convention and Visitors Bureau
101 City Centre One
Youngstown, OH 44503-1810
(216) 747-8200
1-800-447-8201 (U.S.)
Fax (216) 747-2331

Zanesville/Muskingum Convention and Visitors Bureau
P.O. Box 3396
114 N. 6th St.
Zanesville, OH 43702-3396
(614) 453-5004
1-800-743-2303 (U.S.)

OHIO TRAVEL INFORMATION CENTERS

Eighteen travel information centers located off major routes throughout Ohio are available to the traveler, with 14 of the centers open year-round. The centers are staffed by trained personnel who will answer questions, provide assistance and literature on travel attractions for every region of the state.

Most of the following centers are open daily year-round. All mileage approximate.

Ashtabula County (I-90 Westbound). One mile from the Pennsylvania line, near Conneaut. (216) 593-6298.

Belmont County (I-70 Westbound). Rest area five miles west of St. Clairsville. (614) 782-1644.

Butler County (I-75 Northbound and I-75 Southbound). Rest area two miles south of the S.R. 63 interchange with I-75, near Monroe. Northbound (513) 779-4607; Southbound (513) 779-4701.

Montgomery County (Dayton). At U.S. Air Force Museum, Wright-Patterson A.F.B. off Springfield St. Accessible from I-75, I-675, S.R. 4 or I-70 (exit 41 off I-70, take S.R. 4 South to Harshman Rd. South, turn east on Springfield St.). Hrs. 9-5. Closed New Year's, Thanksgiving & Christmas. (513) 256-4445.

Preble County (I-70 Eastbound). Rest area three miles from the Indiana line, near Gettysburg. (513) 437-0978.

Stark County (Canton). For northbound/southbound traffic: Just off I-77 & Fulton Rd. (exit 107-A), next to Pro Football Hall of Fame. Hrs. 9-5. Closed New Year's, Thanksgiving & Christmas. (216) 452-0243.

Trumbull County (I-80 Westbound). Rest area one mile from the Pennsylvania line near Hubbard. (216) 534-9144.

Tuscarawas County (I-77 Southbound). Rest area two miles north of Dover on I-77. Open daily Apr.-Oct., hrs. 8:30-4:30. (216) 364-6404.

Warren County (I-71 Northbound & I-71 Southbound). Rest area five miles north of Lebanon on I-71. Northbound (513) 932-9293; Southbound (513) 932-3538.

Washington County (I-77 Northbound). Rest area is located approximately six miles north of Marietta. (614) 373-8806.

Wood County (I-75 Northbound & I-75 Southbound). Rest area one mile south of U.S. 6 interchange with I-75, near Bowling Green. Northbound (419) 686-3191; Southbound (419) 686-5001.

SEASONAL

Erie County, intersection of U.S. 250 & S.R. 2, Sandusky. Open May 29-Sept. 6. Hrs. 8-6.

Licking County, Buckeye Lake. Located at the S.R. 79 exit off I-70 (truck stop). Open May 15-Oct. 3, hrs. 10-6. Contact: Theresa Faryman (614) 928-8843.

Miami County, at I-75 & S.R. 36, Piqua. Open Memorial Day to Labor Day, Tues.-Sun., hrs. 10-7. Contact: Miami Co. V.C.B. 1-800-348-8993.

Portage County at Portage Service Plaza, adjacent to west lanes of I-80 Turnpike. Located 12.2 miles west of Warren (Gate 14) interchange. Open through Labor Day. (216) 296-5834.

Richland County, Mansfield. Hanley Rd. at L-K Motel, just off S.R. 13 & I-71. Open May 29-Sept. 30, hrs. 9-5. Contact: Mansfield/Richland County CVB at 1-800-642-8282 or (419) 525-1300.

Williams County at Tiffin River Service Plaza, adjacent to east lanes of I-80 & I-90 Turnpike. Located 7.4 miles east of the Bryan-Montpelier (Gate 2) interchange. Open through Labor Day. (419) 924-2418.

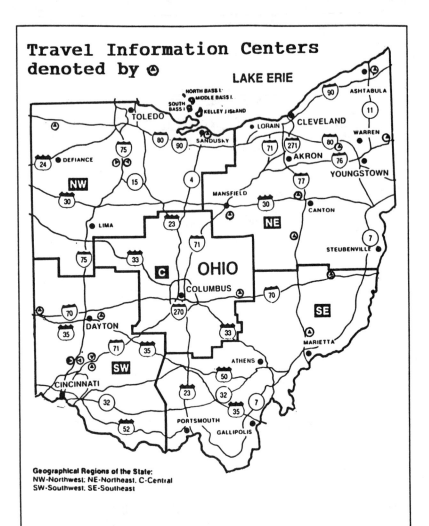

Travel Information Centers denoted by ⊙

LAKE ERIE

Geographical Regions of the State:
NW-Northwest; NE-Northeast; C-Central
SW-Southwest; SE-Southeast

OHIO
the heart of it all!

CALL 1-800-BUCKEYE FOR OHIO TOURISM INFORMATION

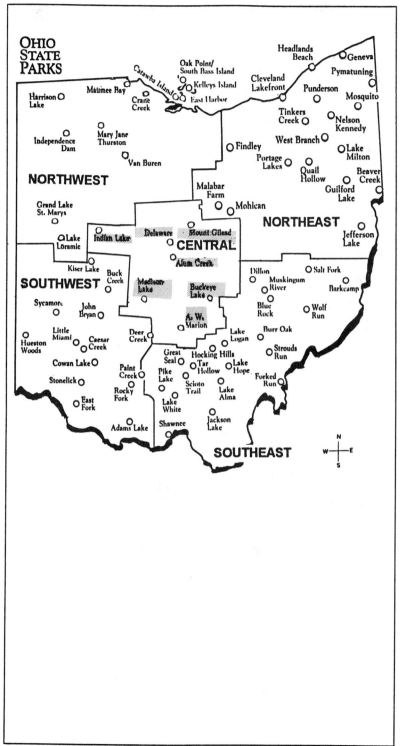

OHIO STATE PARKS

Harrison Lake

Independence Dam

Mary Jane Thurston

NORTHWEST

Maumee Bay

Crane Creek

Van Buren

Catawba Island

Oak Point/ South Bass Island

Kelleys Island

East Harbor

Findley

Portage Lakes

Grand Lake St. Marys

Lake Loramie

Indian Lake

Kiser Lake

SOUTHWEST

Buck Creek

Sycamore

Little Miami

Hueston Woods

Cowan Lake

Stonelick

East Fork

John Bryan

Caesar Creek

Paint Creek

Rocky Fork

Adams Lake

Malabar Farm

Mohican

Delaware

Mount Gilead

CENTRAL

Alum Creek

Madison Lake

Buckeye Lake

A. W. Marion

Deer Creek

Great Seal

Pike Lake

Hocking Hills

Tar Hollow

Scioto Trail

Lake White

Shawnee

Jackson Lake

Lake Logan

Lake Hope

Lake Alma

Headlands Beach

Cleveland Lakefront

Tinkers Creek

West Branch

Quail Hollow

Geneva

Pymatuning

Punderson

Mosquito

Nelson Kennedy

Lake Milton

Beaver Creek

Guilford Lake

NORTHEAST

Jefferson Lake

Dillon

Muskingum River

Blue Rock

Burr Oak

Strouds Run

Forked Run

Salt Fork

Barkcamp

Wolf Run

SOUTHEAST

N W—E S

Source - Dept. Of Natural Resources

Ohio State Parks

	COUNTY	PARK SETTING	LAND IN ACRES	WATER IN ACRES	FISHING	SWIMMING	HIKING TRAILS	PICNIC SHELTERS	RESTAURANT	BRIDLE TRAILS	HUNTING
NORTHWEST											
Catawba Island	Ottawa	■	18	L Erie	●			●			
Crane Creek	Ottawa, Lucas	■	79	L Erie	●	●	.5	●			●▲
East Harbor	Ottawa	■	1152	L Erie	●	●	7	●			●
Grand Lake St. Marys	Auglaize, Mercer	➤	500	13,500	●	●		●			●
Harrison Lake	Fulton	✳	142	107	●	●	3	●			
Independence Dam	Defiance, Henry	➤	604	River	●		3	●			
Kelleys Island	Erie	■	661	L Erie	●	●	5	●			●
Lake Loramie	Shelby, Auglaize	➤	400	1655	●	●	10	●			●
Mary Jane Thurston	Henry, Wood	➤	555	River	●		1	●			●
Maumee Bay	Lucas	↔	1845	57	●	●	10		●	8	●
Oak Point	Ottawa	■	1	L Erie	●						
South Bass Island	Ottawa	■	35	L Erie	●	●		●			
Van Buren	Hancock	✳	236	60	●		5	●		2	●
NORTHEAST											
Beaver Creek	Columbiana	❋	3038	River	●		16			23	●
Cleveland Lakefront	Cuyahoga	■	463	L Erie	●	●		●			
Findley	Lorain	✳	838	93	●	●	10	●			●▲
Geneva	Ashtabula	■	698	L Erie	●	●	3	●			●
Guilford Lake	Columbiana	✳	92	396	●	●		●			
Headlands Beach	Lake	■	125	L Erie	●	●	3	●			
Jefferson Lake	Jefferson	◆	906	27	●	●	10	●			●
Lake Milton	Mahoning	✳	1000	1685	●	●		●			●
Malabar Farm	Richland	✳	914	3	●		4		●	12	
Mohican	Ashland, Richland	↔	1294	River	●	●	9	●	●	▲	▲
Mosquito Lake	Trumbull	●	3961	7850	●	●	2			10	●
Nelson Kennedy	Portage	✳	167	0			1.5				
Portage Lakes	Summit	➤	2443	2520	●	●	5	●			●
Punderson	Geauga	↔	846	150	●	●	8.5	●			
Pymatuning	Ashtabula	●	3500	14,000	●	●	3	●			●
Quail Hollow	Stark	✳	698	2			12			4	
Tinkers Creek	Portage, Summit	✳	740	20	●	●	3.5	●			
West Branch	Portage	●	5352	2650	●	●	3.4	●		20	●
CENTRAL											
Alum Creek	Delaware	●	5213	3387	●	●	9.5			50	●▲
A. W. Marion	Pickaway	✳	308	146	●		6				●
Buckeye Lake	Fairfield, Licking	➤	175	3382	●	●		●			●
Deer Creek	Pickaway, Fayette	↔	6348	1277	●	●	5		●	14	●▲
Delaware	Delaware	●	1815	1330	●	●	6				●▲
Indian Lake	Logan	➤	648	5800	●	●	2	●			●

▲ - On adjacent or nearby state forest or wildlife lands
◆ - With pet camping available
* For Lodge and Cabin reservations, call 1-800-282-7275
** For Mohican Lodge reservations, call 1-800-472-6700

Travel Tip: "Phone First" when you need additional state park information.

	SPEED LIMITS	FUEL	RAMPS	BOAT RENTAL	LODGES	CABINS	CAMPGROUND	TOTAL SITES	ELECTRIC SITES	SHOWERS	FLUSH TOILETS	RENT-A-CAMP	GROUP CAMP	HORSEMEN'S CAMP	PARK OFFICE TELEPHONE
NORTHWEST															
Catawba Island	UNL	•													(419) 797-4530
Crane Creek	UNL														(419) 898-2495
East Harbor	UNL	•	•	•			•	570	•	•			•		(419) 734-4424
Grand Lake St. Marys	UNL	•	•	•			•	206	•	•	•		•		(419) 394-3611
Harrison Lake	EMO	•					✦	178	•	•	•	•	•		(419) 237-2593
Independence Dam	UNL	•					✦	40							(419) 784-3263
Kelleys Island	UNL	•					✦	129	•	•			•		(419) 797-4530
Lake Loramie	UNL	•					•	184	•	•	•	•	•		(513) 295-2011
Mary Jane Thurston	UNL	•					•	15							(419) 832-7662
Maumee Bay	NMP		•	•	•		✦	256	•	•	•				*(419) 836-7758
Oak Point	UNL														(419) 797-4530
South Bass Island	UNL	•					•	135					•		(419) 797-4530
Van Buren	EMO						✦	48					•		(419) 299-3461
NORTHEAST															
Beaver Creek							✦	55					•	•	(216) 385-3091
Cleveland Lakefront	UNL	•	•	•											(216) 881-8141
Findley	EMO	•	•				✦	283	•	•	•	•	•		(216) 647-4490
Geneva	UNL	•	•			•	✦	91	•	•	•	•			(216) 466-8400
Guilford Lake	10 hp	•					•	42							(216) 222-1712
Headlands Beach	UNL														(216) 257-1330
Jefferson Lake	EMO	•					✦	100					•		(614) 765-4459
Lake Milton	UNL	•	•												(216) 654-4969
Malabar Farm							✦	15						•	(419) 892-2782
Mohican		•	•	•	•		✦	177	•	•	•		•		**(419) 994-4290
Mosquito Lake	UNL	•	•				•	234							(216) 637-2856
Nelson Kennedy															(216) 564-2279
Portage Lakes	UNL	•					✦	104							(216) 644-2220
Punderson	EMO	•	•	•	•		✦	201	•	•	•	•			*(216) 564-2279
Pymatuning	10 hp	•	•			•	•	373	•	•	•		•		(216) 293-6329
Quail Hollow													•		(216) 877-6652
Tinkers Creek															(216) 296-3239
West Branch	UNL	•	•				•	103				•	•		(216) 296-3239
CENTRAL															
Alum Creek	UNL	•	•				✦	297	•	•	•	•			(614) 548-4631
A. W. Marion	EMO	•	•				✦	60					•		(614) 474-3386
Buckeye Lake	UNL	•													(614) 467-2690
Deer Creek	UNL	•	•	•	•	•	✦	232	•	•	•	•	•	•	*(614) 869-3124
Delaware	UNL	•	•	•			✦	214	•	•	•		•		(614) 369-2761
Indian Lake	UNL	•					✦	443	•	•	•	•	•		(513) 843-2717

LEGEND FOR BOATING LIMITS
EMO - Electric Motors Only
NMP - No Motors Permitted
UNL - Unlimited Horsepower

LEGEND FOR PARK SETTING
■ Lake Erie
➤ Canal
✳ Quiet Retreat
↔ Resort
❀ River
✦ Hill Country
● Great Lake

Continued on next page

Ohio State Parks

OHIO STATE PARKS	COUNTY	PARK SETTING	LAND IN ACRES	WATER IN ACRES	FISHING	SWIMMING	HIKING TRAILS	PICNIC SHELTERS	RESTAURANT	BRIDLE TRAILS	HUNTING
Madison Lake	Madison	*	80	106	●			●			●
Mount Gilead	Morrow	*	140	32	●		3	●			
SOUTHWEST											
Adams Lake	Adams	*	48	47	●		1	●			
Buck Creek	Clark	●	1910	2120	●	●	5.5	●			●
Caesar Creek	Warren, Clinton	●	7941	2830	●	●	32	●		25	●▲
Cowan Lake	Clinton	●	1075	700	●	●	4.5	●			●
East Fork	Clermont	●	8420	2160	●	●	21	●		57	●▲
Hueston Woods	Preble, Butler	↔	2971	625	●	●	15	●	●	6	
John Bryan	Greene	❀	750	River	●		10	●			
Kiser Lake	Champaign	*	474	396	●	●	4.5	●			●
Little Miami	Greene, Warren	❀	452	River	●		45			45	
Paint Creek	Highland, Ross	●	9000	1200	●	●	8	●		25	▲
Rocky Fork	Highland	●	1384	2080	●	●	4	●	●		●
Stonelick	Clermont	*	1058	200	●	●	7				●
Sycamore	Montgomery	*	2295	5	●		5.5	●		6.5	●
SOUTHEAST											
Barkcamp	Belmont	*	1115	117	●	●	4	●		9	●
Blue Rock	Muskingum	✦	335	15	●	●	3	●		▲	▲
Burr Oak	Athens, Morgan	↔	2592	664	●	●	10	●	●	8	●
Dillon	Muskingum	●	6030	1660	●	●	10	●			●▲
Forked Run	Meigs	✦	715	102	●	●	4				●▲
Great Seal	Ross	✦	1864	0			21	●		17	●
Hocking Hills	Hocking	✦	2331	17	●	●	22	●	●	▲	▲
Jackson Lake	Jackson	*	93	242	●	●	4	●			
Lake Alma	Vinton	*	219	60	●	●	4	●			
Lake Hope	Vinton	✦	3103	120	●	●	13	●		▲	●▲
Lake Logan	Hocking	*	300	417	●	●	1				●
Lake White	Pike	*	21	337	●	●		●			
Muskingum River	Wash., Morg., Musk.	❀	120	River	●		1				
Pike Lake	Pike	✦	600	13	●	●	6			▲	▲
Salt Fork	Guernsey	↔	17,229	2952	●	●	14.3	●	●	25	●▲
Scioto Trail	Ross	✦	218	30	●		12			▲	●
Shawnee	Scioto	↔	1100	68	●	●	5	●	●	▲	●
Strouds Run	Athens	✦	2606	161	●	●	13	●			●
Tar Hollow	Ross, Hocking	✦	619	15	●	●	4	●		▲	●
Wolf Run	Noble	✦	1143	220	●	●		●			●

▲ - On adjacent or nearby state forest or wildlife lands
✦ - With pet camping available
* For Lodge and Cabin reservations, call 1-800-282-7275
** For Mohican Lodge reservations, call 1-800-472-6700

OHIO STATE PARKS	SPEED LIMITS	FUEL	RAMPS	BOAT RENTAL	LODGES	CABINS	CAMPGROUND	TOTAL SITES	ELECTRIC SITES	SHOWERS	FLUSH TOILETS	RENT-A-CAMP	GROUP CAMP	HORSEMAN'S CAMP	PARK OFFICE TELEPHONE
Madison Lake	EMO		•												(614) 852-2919
Mount Gilead	EMO		•				•	60					•	•	(419) 946-1961
SOUTHWEST															
Adams Lake	EMO		•												(614) 858-6652
Buck Creek	UNL	•	•	•			•	◆ 101	•	•	•				(513) 322-5284
Caesar Creek	UNL		•					◆ 287	•	•	•	•		•	(513) 897-3055
Cowan Lake	10 hp	•	•	•			•	◆ 237	•	•	•				(513) 289-2105
East Fork	UNL		•					◆ 416	•	•	•	•		•	(513) 734-4323
Hueston Woods	10 hp	•	•	•	•	•	•	◆ 490	•	•	•		•		*(513) 523-6347
John Bryan							•	100					•		(513) 767-1274
Kiser Lake	NMP		•	•				◆ 140					•	•	(513) 362-3822
Little Miami															(513) 897-3055
Paint Creek	UNL	•	•	•			•	◆ 199	•	•	•				(513) 365-1401
Rocky Fork	UNL	•	•	•			•	◆ 220	•	•	•				(513) 393-4284
Stonelick	EMO		•					◆ 153	•	•	•	•			(513) 625-7544
Sycamore													•		(513) 854-4452
SOUTHEAST															
Barkcamp	EMO		•	•				◆ 151	•				•	•	(614) 484-4064
Blue Rock	EMO		•					◆ 101	•				•	•	(614) 674-4794
Burr Oak	10 hp	•	•	•	•	•	•	◆ 100	•	•	•				*(614) 767-3570
Dillon	UNL	•	•	•			•	◆ 195	•	•	•				(614) 453-4377
Forked Run	10 hp		•	•				◆ 198	•				•	•	(614) 378-6206
Great Seal								◆ 15						•	(614) 773-2726
Hocking Hills	EMO						•	◆ 170	•	•			•	▲	(614) 385-6841
Jackson Lake	10 hp							◆ 36							(614) 682-6197
Lake Alma	EMO							◆ 60	•						(614) 384-4474
Lake Hope	EMO		•	•				◆ 223	•	•			•	▲	(614) 596-5253
Lake Logan	10 hp		•	•											(614) 385-3444
Lake White	UNL		•				•	38							(614) 947-4059
Muskingum River	UNL		•					◆ 20							(614) 452-3820
Pike Lake	EMO		•			•	•	112	•				•		(614) 493-2212
Salt Fork	UNL	•	•	•	•	•	•	◆ 212	•	•	•		•	•	*(614) 439-3521
Scioto Trail	EMO		•					◆ 58	•				•		(614) 663-2125
Shawnee	EMO	•	•	•	•	•	•	◆ 107	•	•	•			▲	*(614) 858-6652
Strouds Run	10 hp		•	•				◆ 80					•	•	(614) 592-2302
Tar Hollow	EMO		•					◆ 96	•				•	▲	(614) 887-4818
Wolf Run	10 hp		•					◆ 140	•				•		(614) 732-5035

LEGEND FOR BOATING LIMITS
EMO - Electric Motors Only
NMP - No Motors Permitted
UNL - Unlimited Horsepower

LEGEND FOR PARK SETTING
■ Lake Erie ❀ River
➤ Canal ◆ Hill Country
❋ Quiet Retreat ● Great Lake
↔ Resort

SELECT OHIO ATTRACTIONS

Of the state's diversifed attractions, AAA placed its star of recognition on the following:

ATTRACTION	LOCATION	TELEPHONE
Quaker Square	Akron	(216) 253-5970
Stan Hywet Hall and Gardens	Akron	(216) 836-5533
Sauder Farm & Craft Village	Archbold	(419) 446-2541
Sea World	Aurora	(216) 562-7131
Hale Farm & Village	Bath	(216) 575-9137
Adena	Chillicothe	(614) 773-2111
Cincinnati Art Musuem	Cincinnati	(513) 721-5204
Cincinnati Zoo & Botanical Gardens	Cincinnati	(513) 281-4700
Taft Museum	Cincinnati	(513) 241-0343
Cleveland Health Education Museum	Cleveland	(216) 231-5010
Cleveland Museum of Art	Cleveland	(216) 421-7340
Cleveland Museum of Natural History	Cleveland	(216) 231-4600
Western Reserve Historical Society	Cleveland	(216) 721-5722
Columbus Zoo	Columbus	(614) 645-3400
Cosi, Ohio's Center of Science & Industry	Columbus	(614) 228-6362
Franklin Park Conservatory	Columbus	(614) 221-6623
Ohio Historical Center	Columbus	(614) 297-2300
Ohio Village	Columbus	N/A
Roscoe Village	Coshocton	(614) 622-8710
Cuyahoga Valley National Recreation Area	Brecksville	(216) 526-5256
U.S. Air Force Museum	Dayton (Fairborn)	(513) 255-3284
Warther Musuem	Dayton	(513) 343-7513
Museum of Ceramics	East Liverpool	(216) 386-6001
Hayes Presidential Center	Fremont	(419) 332-2081
Kings Island	Kings Mills	(513) 398-5600
Serpent Mound	Locust Grove	(513) 587-2796
Kingwood Center	Mansfield	(419) 522-0211
The Living Bible Museum	Mansfield	(419) 524-0139
Campus Martius: Museum of the Northwest Territory	Marietta	(614) 373-3750
President Harding Home & Museum	Marion	(614) 387-9630
Lawnfield	Mentor	(216) 255-8722
Schoenbrunn Village State Memorial	New Philadelphia	(216) 339-3636
Perry's Victory & International Peace Memorial	Perrysburg	(419) 874-4121
Cedar Point	Sandusky	(419) 626-0830
Toledo Museum of Art	Toledo	(419) 255-8000
Neil Armstrong Air & Space Museum	Wapakoneta	(800) 282-5393
Ohio Caverns	West Liberty	(513) 465-4017
Mill Creek Park	Youngstown	(614) 740-7108
National Road-Zane Grey Museum	Youngstown	(614) 872-3143
Zoar Village	Zoar	(216) 874-3211

For Ohio Travel Information Call

1-800-BUCKEYE

OHIO
the heart of it all!®

OHIO COUNTY FAIRS

Source - Ohio Fair Managers Assn.,
Ohio Dept. of Agriculture, &
U.S. Trotters Assn.

STATE FAIR	DATE	HARNESS RACING	TELEPHONE
Columbus	MID-AUG	◉	(614) 644-4000

COUNTY (CITY)	DATE	HARNESS RACING	TELEPHONE
ADAMS (West Union)	LATE JUL		(513) 544-3290
ALLEN (Lima)	LATE AUG	◉	(419) 228-7141
ASHLAND (Ashland)	LATE SEP	◉	(419) 289-0466
ASHTABULA (Jefferson)	MID AUG	◉	(216) 576-7626
ATHENS (Athens)	MID AUG	◉	(614) 593-8421
AUGLAIZE (Wapakoneta)	MID AUG	◉	(419) 753-2144
BELMONT (St. Clairsville)	MID SEP		(614) 425-2263
BROWN (Georgetown)	LATE SEP		(513) 378-3558
BUTLER (Hamilton)	LATE JUL	◉	(513) 892-1423
CARROLL (Carrollton)	LATE JUL	◉	(216) 739-3524
CHAMPAIGN (Urbana)	MID AUG	◉	(513) 653-5340
CLARK (Springfield)	LATE JUL	◉	(513) 323-3090
CLERMONT (Owensville)	LATE JUL	◉	(513) 724-7834
CLINTON (Wilmington)	MID AUG	◉	(513) 584-2904
COLUMBIANA (Lisbon)	LATE AUG	◉	(216) 223-1946

Continued on next page

COUNTY (CITY)	DATE	HARNESS RACING	TELEPHONE
COSHOCTON (Coshocton)	EARLY OCT	⊙	(614) 622-2385
CRAWFORD (Bucyrus)	LATE JUL	⊙	(419) 683-2711
CUYAHOGA (Berea)	MID AUG	⊙	(216) 243-0090
DARKE (Greenville)	LATE AUG	⊙	(513) 548-5044
DEFIANCE (Hicksville)	LATE AUG	⊙	(419) 658-2520
DELAWARE (Delaware)	LATE SEP	⊙	(614) 362-3851
ERIE (Sandusky)	MID AUG		(419) 359-1602
FAIRFIELD (Lancaster)	MID OCT	⊙	(614) 653-3041
FAYETTE (Washington C.H.)	LATE JUL	⊙	(614) 335-5856
FRANKLIN (Hilliard)	LATE JUL	⊙	(614) 876-7235
FULTON (Wauseon)	EARLY SEP	⊙	(419) 335-6006
GALLIA (Gallipolis)	EARLY AUG		(614) 379-2785
GEAUGA (Burton)	EARLY SEP	⊙	(216) 834-1846
GREENE (Xenia)	EARLY AUG	⊙	(513) 767-1571
GUERNSEY (Old Washington)	MID SEP	⊙	(614) 489-5888
HAMILTON (Carthage)	EARLY AUG	⊙	(513) 761-4224
HANCOCK (Findlay)	EARLY SEP		(419) 423-9273
HARDIN (Kenton)	MID SEP	⊙	(419) 673-9289
HARRISON (Cadiz)	MID JUL	⊙	(614) 942-2603
HENRY (Napoleon)	MID AUG	⊙	(419) 599-1320
HIGHLAND (Hillsboro)	MID SEP		(513) 393-1681
HOCKING (Logan)	MID SEP	⊙	(614) 385-6704
HOLMES (Millersburg)	MID AUG		(216) 893-2967
HURON (Norwalk)	MID AUG	⊙	(419) 668-9762
JACKSON (Wellston)	MID JUL	⊙	(614) 988-2631
JEFFERSON (Smithfield)	MID AUG		(614) 765-5156
KNOX (Mt. Vernon)	LATE JUL	⊙	(614) 397-5216
LAKE (Painesville)	LATE AUG	⊙	(216) 354-3339
LAWRENCE (Proctorsville)	MID JUL		(614) 533-0106
LOGAN (Bellefontaine)	LATE JUL	⊙	(513) 599-4178
LORAIN (Wellington)	LATE AUG	⊙	(216) 647-2781
LUCAS (Maumee)	LATE JUL		(419) 893-2127
MADISON (London)	MID JUL	⊙	(614) 852-3023

Continued on next page

COUNTY (CITY)	DATE	HARNESS RACING	TELEPHONE
MAHONING (Canfield)	EARLY SEP	◉	(216) 533-4107
MARION (Marion)	LATE JUN	◉	(614) 382-2558
MEDINA (Medina)	EARLY AUG	◉	(216) 723-9634
MEIGS (Pomeroy)	MID AUG		(614) 992-5182
MERCER (Celina)	MID AUG		(419) 586-3635
MIAMI (Troy)	MID AUG		(513) 335-7492
MONROE (Woodsfield)	LATE AUG	◉	(614) 472-0555
MONTGOMERY (Dayton)	EARLY SEP	◉	(513) 224-1619
MORGAN (McConnelsville)	MID SEP	◉	(614) 962-2709
MORROW (Mt. Gilead)	LATE AUG	◉	(419) 947-1611
MUSKINGUM (Zanesville)	MID AUG	◉	(614) 872-3912
NOBLE (Caldwell)	LATE AUG	◉	(614) 732-2104
OTTAWA (Oak Harbor)	LATE JUL	◉	(419) 898-1971
PAULDING (Paulding)	MID JUL		(419) 399-5302
PERRY (New Lexington)	LATE JUL		(614) 342-3047
PICKAWAY (Circleville)	LATE JUN	◉	(614) 474-2085
PIKE (Piketon)	EARLY AUG	◉	(614) 947-5253
PORTAGE (Randolph)	LATE AUG		(216) 325-7476
PREBLE (Eaton)	LATE JUL	◉	(513) 456-3748
PUTNAM (Ottawa)	LATE JUN	◉	(419) 523-4628
RICHLAND (Mansfield)	MID AUG	◉	(419) 747-3717
ROSS (Chillicothe)	MID AUG	◉	(614) 634-2921
SANDUSKY (Fremont)	LATE AUG		(419) 665-2500
SCIOTO (Lucasville)	MID AUG		(614) 259-2726
SENECA (Tiffin)	LATE JUL	◉	(419) 447-7888
SHELBY (Sidney)	LATE JUL	◉	(513) 492-7385
STARK (Canton)	LATE AUG	◉	(216) 452-0621
SUMMIT (Tallmadge)	LATE JUL	◉	(216) 688-9906
TRUMBULL (Cortland)	MID JUL	◉	(216) 637-6010
TUSCARAWAS (Dover)	LATE SEP	◉	(216) 343-0524
UNION (Marysville)	LATE JUL	◉	(513) 642-9918
VAN WERT (Van Wert)	EARLY SEP	◉	(419) 238-9270
VINTON (McArthur)	EARLY AUG		(614) 596-4995

Continued on next page

Continued from preceeding page

COUNTY (CITY)	DATE	HARNESS RACING	TELEPHONE
WARREN (Lebanon)	LATE JUL	⊙	(513) 932-2636
WASHINGTON (Marietta)	EARLY SEP	⊙	(614) 373-1347
WAYNE (Wooster)	MID SEP	⊙	(216) 264-7498
WILLIAMS (Montpelier)	MID SEP	⊙	(419) 485-5130
WOOD (Bowling Green)	EARLY AUG	⊙	(419) 352-0441
WYANDOT (Upper Sandusky)	MID SEP	⊙	(419) 294-4320

INDEPENDENT AGRICULTURAL FAIRS

COUNTY (CITY)	DATE	HARNESS RACING	TELEPHONE
ALBANY (Athens Co.)	MID SEP		(614) 698-5843
ATTICA (Seneca Co.)	MID AUG	⊙	(419) 426-1081
BARLOW (Washington Co.)	LATE SEP		(614) 678-2138
BELLVILLE (Richland Co.)	LATE SEP		(419) 886-2687
HARTFORD (Licking Co.)	MID AUG	⊙	(614) 893-4881
LOUDONVILLE (Ashland Co.)	EARLY OCT		(419) 994-4391
RICHWOOD (Union Co.)	EARLY SEP	⊙	(513) 642-2134

Trivia

QUESTION How much of Lake Erie is within the Ohio boundary?

ANSWER Two and a quarter million acres.

QUESTION What is the fishing nickname for Lake Erie?

ANSWER "Walleye Capital of the World." (more than 3 million are caught annually.)

QUESTION How many people in the US could visit Ohio in a one day drive?

ANSWER 140,000,000

OHIO STATE PARKS

● COUNTY FAIR
+ INDEPENDENT FAIR
** STATE FAIR

LEGEND:

The map indicates the location of the 87 County Agricultural Fairs, the 7 Independent Agricultural Fairs and the Ohio State Fair.

OHIO *festivals* & EVENTS

FESTIVAL	DATE	TELEPHONE
Geauga County Maple Festival, Chardon .... Early	Apr.	216-286-3007
Wild Turkey Festival, McArthur .... Early	May	614-596-5033
Dennison Railroad Festival, Dennison .... Late	May	614-922-8768
Moonshine Festival, New Straitsville .... Late	May	614-394-2838
Feast of the Flowering Moon, Chillicothe .... Late	May	614-775-0900
Port Clinton Walleye Fest., Port Clinton .... Late	May	419-732-2864
Old Fashioned Ice Cream Festival, Utica .... Late	May	614-892-3728
Deercreek Dam Days, Williamsport .... Early	June	614-986-5863
Old Car Club Spring Festival, Lancaster .... Early	June	n/a
National Clay Week Fest., Uhrichsville .... Mid	June	614-922-3028
Lorain International Festival, Lorain .... Late	June	n/a
4th of July Celebration, Ashville .... Early	July	n/a
First Town Days, New Philadelphia .... Early	July	216-339-1599
Ohio Hills Folk Festival, Quaker City .... Early	July	614-679-2470
Pottery Festival, Crooksville/Roseville .... Mid	July	n/a
Salem Jubilee, Salem .... Mid	July	216-337-3473
Carnation City Festival, Alliance .... Early	Aug.	n/a
No. Ridgeville Corn Fest., No. Ridgeville .... Mid	Aug.	n/a
Parade of the Hills, Nelsonville .... Mid	Aug.	n/a
Pemberville Free Fair, Pemberville .... Mid	Aug.	n/a
Bratwurst Festival, Bucyrus .... Mid	Aug.	419-562-BRAT
London Marigold Festival, London .... Late	Aug.	614-852-1582
Obetz Zucchinifest, Obetz .... Late	Aug.	614-491-1080
Ohio Tobacco Festival, Ripley .... Late	Aug.	n/a
Sweet Corn Festival, Millersport .... Early	Sept	614-467-3943
Portsmouth River Days, Portsmouth .... Early	Sept	n/a
Milan Melon Festival, Milan .... Early	Sept	n/a
Ohillco Days, Wellston .... Early	Sept	419-499-2766
Reynoldsburg Tomato Fest., Reynoldsburg ... Early	Sept	614-384-6942
Marion Popcorn Festival, Marion .... Early	Sept	614-866-2861
Mantua Potato Festival, Mantua .... Mid	Sept	216-274-8093
American Soya Festival, Amanda .... Mid	Sept	n/a
Crestline Harvest Festival .... Mid	Sept	n/a
International Mining & Mfg. Fest., Cadiz .... Mid	Sept	n/a
Johnny Appleseed Festival, Lisbon .... Mid	Sept	216-424-9184
Tiffin-Seneca Heritage Festival, Tiffin .... Mid	Sept	419-447-2303
Jackson County Apple Festival, Jackson .... Mid	Sept	n/a
Ohio Honey Festival, Hamilton .... Late	Sept	513-683-2220
Geneva Area Grape JAMboree, Geneva .... Late	Sept.	216-466-JAMB
Holmes County Antique Fest., Millersburg .... Late	Sept.	216-674-3975
Ohio Swiss Festival, Sugarcreek .... Early	Oct.	216-852-4113
Galion Octoberfest, Galion .... Early	Oct.	419-468-6692
Ohio Gourd Show, Mt. Gilead .... Early	Oct.	419-946-3302
Autumn in the Hills, New Lexington .... Early	Oct.	n/a
Bob Evans Farm Festival, Rio Grande .... Early	Oct.	614-245-5305
Apple Butter Festival, Burton .... Early	Oct.	216-834-4012
Fall Fest. of Léaves, Bainbridge .... Mid	Oct.	n/a
Circleville Pumpkin Show, Circleville .... Late	Oct.	614-474-4224
Holidays Festival, Dalton .... Early	Dec.	216-682-1327